SCOTTISH SOCIETY, 1500–1800

SCOTTISH SOCIETY
1500–1800

EDITED BY

R. A. HOUSTON

Lecturer in Modern History, University of St Andrews

AND

I. D. WHYTE

Lecturer in Geography, University of Lancaster

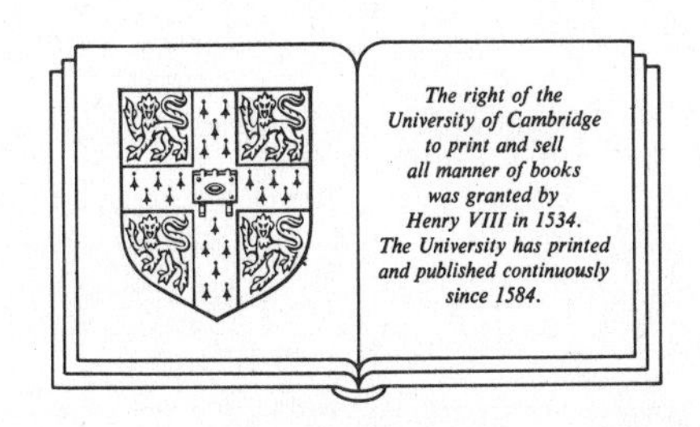

CAMBRIDGE UNIVERSITY PRESS

CAMBRIDGE

NEW YORK NEW ROCHELLE MELBOURNE SYDNEY

Published by the Press Syndicate of the University of Cambridge
The Pitt Building, Trumpington Street, Cambridge, CB2 1RP
32 East 57th Street, New York, NY 10022, USA
10 Stamford Road, Oakleigh, Melbourne 3166, Australia

First Published 1989

Printed in Great Britain
at the University Press, Cambridge

British Library cataloguing in publication data

Scottish society, 1500–1800.
1. Scotland. Social conditions, 1500–1800.
I. Houston R. A. (Robert Allen), 1954–
II. Whyte, I. D. (Ian D.).
941.1

Library of Congress cataloguing in publication data

Scottish society, 1500–1800 / edited by R. A. Houston and I. D. Whyte.
Bibliography: p.
Includes index.
Contents: Population mobility in early modern Scotland / I. D. Whyte – Scottish food and Scottish history, 1500–1700 / A. Gibson and T. C. Snout – Continuity and change in urban society, 1500–1700 / M. Lynch – Women in the economy and society of Scotland, 1500–1800 / R. A. Houston – (Social response to agrarian "improvement" / T. M. Devine – "Pretense of blude" and "place" of their dwelling" / R. A. Dogshon – North and south / R. Mitchison – Scotland and Ireland, 1600–1800 / L. M. Cullen – Kindred adjoining kingdoms / K. E. Wrightson.
1. Scotland – Social life and customs. 2. Scotland – History – 16th century.
3. Scotland – History – 17th century. 4. Scotland – History – 18th century.
5. Scotland – Social conditions.
I. Houston, E. A. (Robert Allan). 1954–
II. Whyte, Ian (Ian D.)
DA772.S32 1988
941.1–dc19 88-5004

ISBN 0 521 32522 6

CE

For my mother and to the
memory of my father. R.A.H.

To the memory of my parents. I.D.W.

CONTENTS

TABLES

NOTES ON CONTRIBUTORS

LEWIS CULLEN is Professor of Modern History at Trinity College, University of Dublin.

TOM DEVINE is Personal Professor in History at the University of Strathclyde.

ROBERT DODGSHON is Professor of Geography at University College of Wales, Aberystwyth.

ALEX GIBSON is a Research Fellow in the Department of Modern History at the University of St Andrews.

RAB HOUSTON is a Lecturer in Modern History at the University of St Andrews.

MICHAEL LYNCH is a Lecturer in Scottish History at the University of Edinburgh.

ROSALIND MITCHISON is Emeritus Professor of Social History at the University of Edinburgh.

CHRISTOPHER SMOUT is Professor of Scottish History at the University of St Andrews.

IAN WHYTE is a Lecturer in Geography at the University of Lancaster.

KEITH WRIGHTSON is a Lecturer in History at the University of Cambridge.

ABBREVIATIONS

APS	*Acts of the Parliament of Scotland*
CSP	*Calendar of state papers*
Edin. Recs.	*Extracts from the records of the burgh of Edinburgh*
GRO	General Register Office
NLS	National Library of Scotland
NSA	*New statistical account of Scotland*
OSA	*Old statistical account of Scotland*
PP	*Parliamentary papers*
RPC	*Register of the privy council of Scotland*
SRO	Scottish Record Office
SBRS	*Scottish burgh record society miscellany*

INTRODUCTION: SCOTTISH SOCIETY IN PERSPECTIVE

R.A. HOUSTON AND I.D. WHYTE

Scotland before 1750 was a small and rather poor country whose significance for European political, economic and, to a lesser extent, intellectual life was at best peripheral. Her economy and society were transformed in the century after 1750 by agrarian and industrial changes which catapulted Scotland to prominence in world affairs, a standing that the early modern period had barely presaged. Until the advent of a largely urbanised and industrialised society in the nineteenth century, historians have tended to assume that the social structure of Scotland retained archaic forms which had long disappeared from more 'developed' countries such as England. Scotland's economy and level of wealth in the pre-industrial period have often seemed closest to those of Scandinavian countries or Ireland. Not only was Scotland peripheral to mainstream European history, but her society was so distinctive as to be of little relevance to an understanding of social organisation and change in a wider context. This introductory chapter sets out to question these preconceptions by analysing Scottish society between the Renaissance and the Industrial Revolution in a European context and, by presenting a brief and accessible outline of social structures and trends, to assess the typicality or distinctiveness of Scotland.

In this task, the social historian is constrained by the comparative lack of academic research on pre-nineteenth-century Scottish society. Some aspects of Scottish social history have always been attractive to the Scots themselves, but the society of Scotland in the past has received remarkably little attention from scholars. While the Scots love their history, their conception of it is generally based on vague, romantic myths about clans and tartans, poets and Pretenders.[1] Partly due to the centralisation of archives in Edinburgh and the lack, until recently, of regional record offices, Scotland has failed to develop a strong tradition of local amateur historical study of the kind which has flourished in England. One result of

[1] B.P. Lenman, 'Reinterpreting Scotland's last two centuries of independence' (1982):217–19. We should like to thank the contributors for their comments on this introduction.

this is that the popular image of Scottish society in the past is probably further removed from the scholarly 'reality' than in any other European country. Coupled with this are the preconceptions of academic historians, both within and without Scotland. The Scottish historical 'establishment' has always been small and, until recently, intensely conservative in its approaches, and has tended to concentrate its attention on institutions like the church, or on the high and mighty, ignoring the mass of the population in the past as well as the concerns of social historians in England and Europe.[3]

For its part, the outside academic community has treated Scotland as a geographically peripheral nation about which little is known and whose relevance to wider European trends is limited. Described by early modern English travellers in a universally hostile manner, and only slightly more charitably by continental commentators,[4] the Scottish people appear in English historiography as nuisances, villains or curiosities. This attitude is partly a reflection of the lack of interest of a south-east English power base for its Celtic periphery, heightened in the case of Scotland by its late incorporation into Britain. Behind the smokescreens of Scotland's distinctive social structure and institutions, which supposedly 'require special treatment',[5] and the oft-repeated claim that the sources for proper social history do not exist, English and European historians have tended to ignore the Scottish dimension.[6]

Scotland did indeed have certain distinctive institutions. Roman law, extensively adopted in Scotland from the late fifteenth century, placed much greater emphasis on written codes than did English common law which treated custom as a powerful consideration.[7] Scotland had a separate monarchy until 1603; her own Parliament until 1707; a vigorously Calvinist church after 1560; an education system funded and constituted in a different way from England; a different currency whose pound was worth about 8 per cent of English sterling during the seventeenth century and

2 For example see G. Donaldson, *Scotland, James V to James VII* (1965).

3 Some nineteenth-century scholars and antiquarians did investigate curiosities such as witchcraft and other 'superstitions': e.g. A. Grant, *Essays on the superstitions of the Highlanders* (1811). Modern scholars have also produced work of European significance on the subject: e.g. C. Larner, *Enemies of God* (1981).

4 P.H. Brown (ed.), *Early travellers in Scotland* (1891); J.K. Cameron, 'Some continental visitors to Scotland' (1986).

5 J.F.C. Harrison, *The common people of Great Britain* (1985): 19. See also L.A. Clarkson, 'The writing of Irish economic and social history' (1980) and on sources I.D. Whyte & K.A. Whyte, 'Sources for Scottish historical geography' (1981).

6 R.A. Houston, 'British society in the eighteenth century' (1986): 464–6; D. Cannadine, 'British history: past, present – and future?' (1987) treats British and English history as synonymous.

7 J.H. Langbein, *Prosecuting crime in the Renaissance* (1974); *An introduction to Scottish legal history* (1958).

different weights and measures.[8] There were also features of Scottish society which marked it out from that of England: a less prominent middling group in rural society until the later eighteenth century, composed of tacksmen (see below) in the Highlands and tenant farmers in the Lowlands rather than owner-occupiers, more extensive poverty and a lower standard of living, higher levels of emigration, a more obviously martial society, pronounced regional differences in social organisation and language between Highland and Lowland,[9] a demographic regime in which famine featured until well into the eighteenth century.[10] There are, as yet, no clear indications of distinctive farming regions with related patterns of settlement, and society in Scotland in the pre-industrial period in the same way as in Lowland England or France: in terms of its field systems, crops and livestock management Scotland appears to have been more homogeneous than many European countries during early modern times.[11] Despite these contrasts with neighbouring countries, in many respects social structures and social changes in Scotland did not follow unique paths between the Renaissance and the Industrial Revolution when viewed in a wider European context.

POPULATION AND ECONOMY

Scotland was a small country with a small population. Although estimates of population totals before Webster's census of 1755 are based on little more than educated guesswork, it is probable that from perhaps 500,000 inhabitants in 1500, numbers rose to 7–800,000 in the later sixteenth century, a million in 1700 and 1.6 million at the time of the first official census in 1801.[12] There are signs that growth came fastest in the later sixteenth and early seventeenth centuries, numbers stagnating thereafter until a renewed and sustained period of increase began in the second half of the eighteenth century. The chronology resembles that of England, though the mechanisms probably differed and the Scottish rates of increase never matched the increase of at least 1 per cent per annum of English population at its most buoyant, possibly due in part to higher levels of emigration.

8 S.G.E. Lythe & J. Butt, *An economic history of Scotland* (1975):81–4; T.C. Smout, *A history of the Scottish people, 1560–1830* (1972) is easily the best introduction to the social history of Scotland though a rapidly growing body of new research is beginning to date some of the interpretations.

9 C.W.J. Withers, *Gaelic in Scotland* (1984):*passim*; M. Gray, *The Highland economy, 1750–1850* (1957).

10 M.W. Flinn, *Scottish population history* (1977):233–7.

11 J. Thirsk, *The agrarian history of England and Wales, vol. 5, part 1, 1640–1750* (1985); I.D. Whyte, *Agriculture and society in seventeenth-century Scotland* (1979):19–22. The tone of this introduction is often tentative, reflecting the patchy nature of research in certain areas.

12 J.G. Kyd, *Scottish population statistics* (1952); Lythe & Butt (1975):3; N.L. Tranter, *Population and society, 1750–1940* (1985).

Household size was similar to other north-west European countries, at about five persons, and its composition changed very little over the period 1500–1800. Scotland provides no support for an evolutionist view of shifts from large and complex family units to small and simple ones with industrialisation, though it is possible that larger, extended families may have been commoner in the Highlands.[13]

Key issues such as trends in nuptiality and fertility remain uncertain because of the patchy survival and poor quality of essential sources such as parish registers of baptisms, marriages and burials, but it is argued that Scotland possessed a 'high pressure' demographic regime similar to France or perhaps Ireland, where high birth rates were matched by swingeing mortality, and where crises of subsistence remained a central fact of life until the end of the seventeenth century in the Lowlands and well into the eighteenth century in the Highlands.[14] Gibson and Smout imply in chapter 2 that the homeostatic regime which adjusted population and resources in England (through changes in the age of women at first marriage responding to the standard of living) was not matched in Scotland. Population trends were instead dominated by mortality caused by famine and disease to a later date than in England, and the accelerating population growth of the late eighteenth century appears, as it did in Sweden, to have been attributable mainly to improvements in life expectancy. The average life span certainly seems to have been lower in Scotland than in England: 30 years or less rather than 35 during the mid-eighteenth century. This pattern only changed in Scotland, like France, after the middle of the eighteenth century when mortality fell dramatically.[15] Reasons for this included innoculation against smallpox, autonomous changes in the virulence of disease, and a decline in famine deaths thanks to more efficient agricultural techniques, the advent of the potato, improved transport, and more effective poor relief. Scotland appears to have resembled England in having a late age at first marriage for women – 23 to 26 on average, though female celibacy was more extensive. Illegitimacy was higher than in France (and in England until c.1750) and levels increased in the late eighteenth century as they did all over Europe. The level of bastardy rose steadily from about 1 per cent in the 1650s to around 5 per cent by 1800. Between 1660 and 1760 the illegitimacy ratio for Scotland as a whole was around 4 per cent. For the Central Lowlands the figure was lower, 2–3 per cent but for the Highlands 3–6 per cent and Caithness 7–9 per cent.[16]

There are some suggestions that the Highlands may have been more like

[13] E.A. Wrigley & R.S. Schofield, *The population history of England, 1541–1871* (1981):213–15, 246–8; Flinn (1977):107–297.

[14] Flinn (1977):164–86.

[15] Tranter (1985):34–63; R.A. Houston, 'The demographic regime, c.1750–c.1830' (1988).

[16] Tranter (1985):53–4; Flinn (1977):279–82; L. Leneman & R. Mitchison, 'Scottish illegitimacy ratios' (1987).

Ireland in experiencing almost continuous population growth throughout the period, despite the fact that the region was worse hit than the Lowlands by the famines of the 1690s.[17] A growing imbalance between population and resources during the eighteenth century forced many Highlanders into seasonal or permanent migration out of the area and condemned those who remained to live on increasingly marginal landholdings.[18] A similar rise in the volume of temporary and permanent migration can be found in many upland areas of Europe.[19] People whose lives had been disrupted by subsistence crises and, in the second half of the eighteenth century, displaced Highlanders and the victims of agricultural change in the Lowlands moved overseas in large numbers and from the sixteenth century onwards emigration was probably a more significant element in Scottish society than any other country in Europe except Ireland.[20]

Another option was to migrate within Scotland, usually to the Lowlands and often to a town, for population mobility was extensive, as Whyte shows in chapter 1. The royal burgh of Edinburgh, excluding satellites like the Canongate and Leith, grew from a community of 12,000 in 1560 to 20,000–25,000 in 1635, 30,000,–50,000 by 1700 and to 82,000 at the time of the 1801 census. Scottish urban growth was, along with England's, the fastest in Europe during the eighteenth century, most of this growth being fuelled by immigrants from the countryside.[21] Urban growth occurred throughout much of the early modern period, but particularly in the later sixteenth and early seventeenth centuries and again after 1750, the two periods of most rapid growth for the Scottish population as a whole. Recovery from the economic dislocations of the 1640s and 1650s was slow for towns like Dundee,[22] but smaller centres and the great towns of Glasgow and Edinburgh flourished. Although Edinburgh was the largest Scottish town until the late eighteenth century, only then being overtaken by Glasgow, the capital never held such a large proportion of the urban population of Scotland, or indeed of the total population, as London did for England. Major regional centres like Glasgow, Dundee, Aberdeen, Perth and some lower-rank centres like Inverness and Dumfries in less highly urbanised areas were probably of greater relative significance as centres of wealth and trade than the larger provincial towns of England, a situation

[17] R.E. Tyson, 'Famine in Aberdeenshire, 1695–99' (1986): 32.

[18] T.M. Devine, 'Temporary migration and the Scottish Highlands in the nineteenth century' (1979c).

[19] R.A. Dodgshon, *Land and society in early Scotland* (1981): 289–92; O. Hufton. *The poor of eighteenth-century France* (1974): 69–106; M.W. Flinn, *The European demographic system* (1981): 65–75; F. Braudel, *The Mediterranean and the Mediterranean world in the age of Philip II* (1972): 41–5.

[20] Tranter (1985): 126–46.

[21] J. de Vries, *European urbanization 1500–1800* (1984): 39, 199–231. The very approximate population figures are the result of poor documentation.

[22] T.M. Devine, 'The Cromwellian Union and the Scottish burghs' (1976).

more comparable with France. Unlike England, sixteenth- and seventeenth-century Scotland witnessed the creation of many new burghs, though comparatively few became substantial urban centres.[23]

Table 1 *Percentages of the population of England and Scotland living in towns with 10,000 or more inhabitants, 1500–1800*[24]

	England	Scotland
1500	3	2
1600	6	3
1700	13	5
1750	16	9
1800	20	17

Although based on the amalgamation of population estimates of varying quality for individual towns the above table illustrates three important points. First, virtually all the urban growth took place in the Central Lowlands of Scotland which contained approximately half of the nation's people. The image of Scotland before the later eighteenth century has often been of a country where urbanisation had made limited progress yet the Lowlands at least were quite highly urbanised by the seventeenth century even if many of the towns were small. Urbanisation was highly regionalised since the Highlands had no towns of any size. Second, Scotland's urban population grew at the same rate as that of England between 1500 and 1600, at a much faster rate after 1700, albeit from low initial levels, and nearly doubled in the second half of the eighteenth century. This rapid increase was unique in contemporary Europe. Paisley, for instance, quadrupled in size between 1755 and 1801.[25] Third, these figures are a useful indicator of the rapid pace of economic change after 1750. Until the eighteenth century, demand for the services which large towns could offer and the agricultural surplus to feed them were limited. Agricultural productivity was still low in 1700 since the proportion of the population who were net consumers of food (town-dwellers and rural artisans) cannot have exceeded 25 per cent – probably less than French levels and half those obtaining in England.[26]

Despite her position on the periphery of Europe, Scotland's overseas trade links generated contacts with most parts of north-western Europe

[23] G.S. Pryde, *The burghs of Scotland* (1965); I.H. Adams, *The making of urban Scotland* (1978): 11–47.

[24] de Vries (1984): 39. The urban hierarchy of England was more exceptional in a European context than that of Scotland.

[25] A. Dickson & W. Speirs, 'Changes in class structure in Paisley, 1750–1845' (1980): 60–1.

[26] E.A. Wrigley, 'Urban growth and agricultural change' (1985): 700, 718–20.

and occasionally with places further afield in the Mediterranean, Russia and, from the later seventeenth century, across the Atlantic. This was true even of the sixteenth century, and brought new ideas and products back to Scotland's people. Intellectual exchange took place with European universities such as Paris before the Reformation, Heidelberg and Huguenot academies like Saumur after it, and an increasingly special relationship developed with Dutch universities from the 1620s. The legal and medical schools at Leiden were particularly significant between 1675 and 1725, judging from the number of Scots who matriculated.[27] Scotland was part of the intellectual mainstream in early modern Europe and during the eighteenth-century Enlightenment became a leader.

Trade with Europe was the jewel in Scotland's economic crown before the eighteenth century, since the domestic economy laboured under many constraints. These included a shortage of skilled labour, poor transport and communications, lack of ready cash, limited investment in industry, circumscribed domestic markets, poor agricultural techniques and an unfavourable climate. Yet the pattern of overseas trade – exports dominated by unprocessed or partly processed primary products, imports by manufactures, luxuries and some essential raw materials such as timber and, in years of famine, emergency supplies of grain from the Baltic – underlines the poor and undeveloped nature of her economy before the eighteenth century when compared with England (but not with Ireland or Scandinavia).[28] Moreover, as Lynch discusses in chapter 3, the distinctive pattern of Scottish overseas trade constrained the development of craft skills and the range of occupational structures in Scottish towns until well into the seventeenth century. Edinburgh had about twenty different craft occupations in the early sixteenth century, roughly a quarter of the number in contemporary Norwich, a town of approximately the same size. In the lower reaches of urban society it was the norm to have more than one occupation.[29]

Economic change can be summarised as follows. The sixteenth to early seventeenth century was a period of population growth when agriculture changed relatively little, but overseas trade expanded. Inflation was not a serious problem until the later sixteenth century and Scotland was less affected by wars than many continental nations in the early modern period.[30] However, these developments were halted in the 1630s, 1640s and 1650s by political and military dislocations from which Scotland's

27 R. Feenstra, 'Scottish-Dutch legal relations in the seventeenth and eighteenth centuries' (1986): 130, 132, 136; Cameron (1986): 55–6.

28 T.C. Smout (ed.), *Scotland and Europe, 1200–1800* (1986); *Scottish trade on the eve of the Union* (1963); S.G.E. Lythe, *The economy of Scotland in its European setting, 1550–1625* (1960).

29 M. Lynch, 'The social and economic structure of the larger towns' (forthcoming); *Calendar of State Papers Relating to Scotland* (CSP) vol. XIII, part 2 (1969): 1119.

30 J. Wormald, *Court, kirk and community* (1981): 45–6.

economy recovered only slowly in the later seventeenth century. Subsistence agriculture was overwhelmingly practised in the Highlands. The surplus of livestock which was creamed off to supply the cattle trade to the Lowlands and England, which became prominent from the later seventeenth century, was largely extracted by landowners as rent and brought little benefit to the farmers themselves. In the more advanced Lowlands the commercial element in agriculture was greater – Dodgshon has estimated that perhaps a quarter of the farmers in those areas closest to the coast and the major towns were producing wholeheartedly for the market in the later seventeenth and early eighteenth centuries.[31] Elsewhere most farmers had some involvement with the market, however modest, and this element was to increase gradually from the seventeenth into the eighteenth century. The 1690s were disastrous for agriculture and the 1700s for some sectors of finance because of the failure of the Darien scheme, but the remainder of the eighteenth century witnessed slow recovery, then accelerating industrial and agricultural productivity coupled with rapid industrialistion, rising real wages and a healthy overseas trade based primarily on Glasgow.[32]

STRUCTURE AND CHANGE IN SCOTTISH SOCIETY

It is commonly assumed that Scotland's economic backwardness went hand in hand with, or was indeed partly caused by, primitive social structures such as the Highland clans. There are few contemporary analyses of the nature of Scottish society of the sort which have proved so helpful to historians of early modern England.[33] Scottish sermons are almost invariably dry and theological, with few remarks about obedience, deference and order of the kind found so frequently in England, though the Scottish clergy were not averse to making political judgements from the pulpit.[34] The clergy talked about man and God but not about man and man. Formal tables of ranks of the kind which existed in seventeenth-century France or eighteenth-century Prussia were unknown in Scotland.[35] Descriptions tended to focus on political or legal standing and generally do

[31] Dodgshon (1981): 265.

[32] Smout (1963): 244–53; T.M. Devine, *The tobacco lords* (1975); 'The Union of 1707 and Scottish development' (1985).

[33] K.E. Wrightson, *English society, 1580–1680* (1982): 17–38.

[34] R.M. Mitchison, *Life in Scotland* (1978): 41.

[35] Y-M. Bercé, 'La mobilité sociale, argument de révolte' (1979); J-M. Constant, 'La mobilité sociale dans une province de gentilshommes et de paysannes: la Beauce' (1979): 12–14; P. Goubert, *The ancien régime* (1973): 168–92; A. Wyczański, 'La stratification sociale au XVIe siècle vue par les gens de l'époque' (1979); D. Saalfeld, 'Die ständische Gliederung der Gesellschaft Deutschlands im Zeitalter der Absolitismus' (1980): 478, 481. The term 'noble' in eighteenth-century Germany could have 1 of 9 recognised definitive adjectives associated with it such as 'old', 'imperial', 'court'.

not go beyond the simplest classification. Bishop Leslie split the society into churchmen, noblemen and commons (by which he meant burgesses): a conception of 'Estates' which had little importance for everyday life.[36] Adam Smith remarked on social structure, differentiation and change in his *Wealth of Nations* (1776) as did John Millar in *The origin of the distinction of ranks* (1771), both writers reflecting the Enlightenment's drive to develop general theories of the development of societies. More particular was Peter Williamson's *Edinburgh directory* of 1773–4 listing citizens in order of rank starting with Court of Session judges, advocates, writers to the signet and so on.

Social gradations were more subtle, stratification more complex in practice. At the parish level, one kirk session saw its parishioners ranked between 'masters, free holders, feuers, proprietors and servitors of the ground'.[37] Urban elites were anxious to maintain the distinction between those with burgess privileges and the rest, though this was in decline in the late seventeenth century.[38] We must therefore study the distribution of wealth, status and occupations in Scottish society, and analyse the relations of power and authority between the different groups. Using tax documents, inventories and estate records, we can establish a ranking of occupations by wealth in both urban and rural society, and can emphasise both the unequal distribution of wealth between elites and the rest of the population and also the gradations within groups such as tenant farmers which, by the later seventeenth century, had become increasingly visible in differences in housing and material possessions.[39] Taxation schedules reveal the extent to which wealth was polarised in the Lowlands during the 1690s. Assuming that the number of hearths in a house is an approximate indicator of the wealth and social standing of the family living in it, we can see that in West Lothian 69 per cent of all those who paid the hearth tax (the exempt poor must have lived in single hearth dwellings) did so on one hearth only, 14 per cent on two hearths and only 10 per cent on four or more. For Dumfries-shire the figures are 63 per cent, 21 per cent and 7 per cent respectively. This profile is more reminiscent of eighteenth-century Ireland than Lowland arable England.[40] Scottish society was, nevertheless, differentiated by wealth and status at an early date.

Access to land determined the wealth and well-being of the vast majority of Scotland's people, as it did throughout early modern Europe. Great

36 P.H. Brown, *Scotland before 1700* (1893): 173–83; Larner (1981): 45.
37 SRO CH2/471/1 f.1.
38 T.M. Devine, 'The merchant class of the larger Scottish towns in the seventeenth and eighteenth centuries' (1983a): 93–104.
39 Whyte (1979): 162–8; I.D. Whyte & K.A. Whyte, 'Poverty and prosperity in a seventeenth-century Scottish farming community' (1988); Dodgshon (1981): 226–9.
40 D. Adamson (ed.), *West Lothian hearth tax, 1691* (1981); R.B. McDowell, 'Ireland in 1800' (1986): 670–1.

proprietors dominated land ownership,[41] their economic power protected and reinforced by their hold on political life, the judicial system and social values. In this respect Scotland resembled Denmark, where farmers and labourers were exploited by the great lords and where in 1789 1 per cent of the population owned 56 per cent of the national wealth, or Norway where a substantial independent peasantry did not exist.[42] There was no active land market among the peasantry despite the existence of feuing and wadsetting (see below), and an acceleration of buying and selling of heritable property in the later eighteenth century, principally by the merchants and professionals of the larger towns.[43] The dominance of the great nobles remained. Crown, burghs and owner-occupiers held a small proportion of the land in Scotland, the only regions with any substantial numbers of peasant proprietors being the west-central Lowlands and the south west.[44] The Western Isles represent one of the most extreme examples of the general pattern, land being held in large blocks and changes of ownership by sale (as opposed to inheritance) rare.[45] In between were areas like East Lothian and Fife where average estate size was smaller and the land market comparatively more developed.

Scotland had no real equivalent of the celebrated English yeoman freeholder, except perhaps a handful of small lairds and portioners (heirs to part of a heritable estate) numbering perhaps 8,000 in the later seventeenth century.[46] English copyholders were paralleled in sixteenth-century Scotland by a few 'kindly tenants' and by the only slightly more numerous 'rentallers', but most of these tenures were converted to ordinary leasehold in the late sixteenth and early seventeenth centuries.[47] Small owner-occupiers holding land by heritable 'feu ferme' tenure became more numerous from the middle of the sixteenth century with the break up of ecclesiastical estates in the years before and immediately following the Reformation of 1560 (see below) but their importance in rural society was purely local and many of them were bought out by larger lairds during the seventeenth century. An observer summarised this distinctive feature of Scottish society compared with England when he wrote, probably in the 1580s, of the 'defect in proportion among the commonality, viz. that there

[41] L. Timperley, 'The pattern of landholding in eighteenth-century Scotland' (1980): 142–7.
[42] S. Dyrvik, 'The social structure of Norway and Denmark' (1979b): 66–9; J. Oldervoll, 'The rural society of Norway' (1979): 72–8; L. Soltow, 'Wealth distribution in Denmark in 1789' (1979): 138.
[43] Timperley (1980): 148–52; Devine (1983a): 104–7; R. Callander, 'The pattern of landholding in Aberdeenshire in the seventeenth and eighteenth centuries' (1986): 7.
[44] Timperley (1980): 144.
[45] F.J. Shaw, *The northern and western islands of Scotland* (1981): 16.
[46] R.M. Mitchison, *From lordship to patronage* (1983): 80. In his contribution to this volume Wrightson notes that certain areas of England also lacked this substantial, independent middling group.
[47] M.H.B. Sanderson, *Scottish rural society in the sixteenth century* (1982): 58–63.

are so few of the middle rank of subjects among them that are able to live competently and honestly of their own and by that means are as a band to tie together the two extremes' of society, 'viz. the higher sort and the rascality'.[48]

In addition to the medieval feudal tenures an individual could hold land by one or all of the following: tack (lease), feu (heritable) or wadset (redeemable mortgage). For most Scottish peasants, access to the land was by leasehold: in seventeenth-century Shetland only 1 will in 20 mentions feu duty payment (indicating proprietorship), but 76 per cent had land rent owing.[49] The short leases which prevailed in the later sixteenth and seventeenth centuries, smallholdings, inefficient agricultural methods and high rent levels weakened any incentive which tenants might have had to invest labour or capital in improvements, although paternalistic attitudes by proprietors usually ensured security of tenure in practice from one generation to another provided that the tenants were suitably productive and deferential.[50] The Hally family held the same farms at Tullibardine on the Atholl estates throughout the years 1688–1783 and average lease duration rose from 9 or 11 years in 1725 to 15 or 19 in 1760.[51] Longer, written leases became generally more frequent in the second half of the seventeenth century and indicated the development of more commercial attitudes in landlord–tenant relations but these were not a complete novelty.[52] Long leases and substantial security of tenure had also been more common in the fifteenth and early sixteenth centuries when tenants were in short supply.[53]

Rural society was headed by the landowners. Next came the tenant farmers who worked the land through their own labour, that of their families and by employing cottars and servants. Tenant farmers were far from being a homogeneous group although the gradations within tenant society are far from clear.[54] The sizes of the holdings which they worked, their wealth, and their influence in local affairs probably varied considerably within and between communities. In upland Aberdeenshire tenants accounted for 50 per cent or more of the male pollable population of some parishes in the poll tax returns of the 1690s while in the Lothians they might account for less than 20 per cent.[55] In the upper reaches of the Aberdeenshire Dee and Don, where many farms were divided between 8 or more small tenants, tenant society was comparatively undifferentiated and

[48] CSP Scotland vol. XIII, pt 2 (1969): 1119. [49] Shaw (1981): 77.
[50] Whyte (1979): 137–62; I.D. Whyte & K.A. Whyte, 'Continuity and change in a seventeenth-century Scottish farming community' (1984a).
[51] L. Leneman, *Living in Atholl: a social history of the estates, 1685–1785* (1986): 16, 40.
[52] Whyte (1979): 152–61.
[53] Wormald (1981): 51–4.
[54] I.D. Whyte & K.A. Whyte, 'Some aspects of the social structure of rural society in seventeenth-century Lowland Scotland' (1983).
[55] Whyte (1979): 141–5.

there was probably little distinction between tenant and cottar. In the Lothians, by contrast, there was a marked difference between the larger tenants and the cottars. In such areas the distinction between the wealthy capitalist farmer and his labourers that was so characteristic of the nineteenth century was already beginning to emerge in the seventeenth.[56]

An important difference between the rural societies of Scotland and England lay in the comparative lack of landless people in the former. As in Ireland, many people in Scotland had access to at least some land, though the size of their plots was often tiny. Cottar families formed the bulk of the rural population in many Lowland parishes and a high proportion of farm servants were probably also drawn from this group. However, cottars, and indeed many tenants, were very definitely land-poor.[57] In essence, cottars rented small plots of land from tenant farmers in exchange for their labour and that of their families if they were married. They were effectively farm labourers, removable at will.[58] Again, there were regional variations in the extent of this social group. In Renfrewshire, cottars and sub-tenants were less numerous than in Midlothian or Lowland Aberdeenshire because small, tenanted holdings were more available and more people could achieve the status of tenant.[59] Subletting was more frequent in Scotland and Ireland than in England, and its distribution around Scotland was determined by population pressure and by the need of landlords for certain types of labour: during the fifteenth century some monastic estates created whole cottar communities to fulfil these requirements.[60]

Cottars lived close to the margins of subsistence on very small plots of land. In the Highlands in the later eighteenth century there was a great increase in the number of people with very small holdings, tied to the development of kelp burning, fishing and illicit whisky distilling. This development is particularly noticeable in the Western Isles after c.1770: Hebridean cottars were called 'scallags'.[61] In the Lowlands many cottars took up industrial by-employments to supplement their incomes. This was so common in the Lothians that the poll tax schedules of the 1690s pick out for special mention those cottars without a craft employment. In south-east Scotland weavers, smiths and wrights usually worked to meet local demand but in rural Angus the putting-out system of yarn and cloth production for regional and national markets was more extensive.[62] The economically marginal position of the cottars as a group is highlighted by

56 Dodgshon (1981): 206–17.
57 Dodgshon (1981): 214–17; W. Doyle, *The old European order, 1660–1800* (1978): 115; Leneman (1986): 58–62.
58 See S. Sogner, 'Freeholder and cottar. Property relationships in the peasant community' (1976): 185–6 for a Norwegian comparison.
59 Dodgshon (1981): 206–14; Whyte (1979): 141–5.
60 Sanderson (1982): 43.
61 J.M. Bumsted, *The people's clearance* (1982): 36.
62 I.D. Whyte, 'Proto-industrialisation in early-modern Scotland' (1988); Tyson (1986): 35.

the frequency with which they appear in poor relief records. A list of household heads exists for the parish of Dairsie in Fife (1747). This gives occupations and can be compared with accounts of the sums disbursed to the poor by the kirk session, which administered relief. All those in receipt of relief were cottars: men, women and children afflicted by poverty and chronic seasonal unemployment.[63] In subsistence crises, such as the Highland famine of 1782–3, mortality and migration were greatest among this group.

The urban poor were a more diverse occupational group, comprising servants, casual labourers, journeymen artisans, beggars, vagrants and orphans in some numbers alongside the core of widows and the infirm. Three-quarters of all those receiving relief in Aberdeen 1695–1705 were women of whom two-thirds were widows.[64] Poor relief was more abundant in towns than in rural areas, especially in Edinburgh which attracted large numbers of starving countryfolk in periods such as the later sixteenth century and the 1690s.[65] Edinburgh between 1570 and 1620 was the London of the north, albeit a tenth of the size.[66] In years of bad harvest, the poverty net could catch even tenants, artisans and burgess families. A church survey of Perth in 1584 revealed that a quarter of the town's population of about 4,500 were poor.[67] During the 1690s, when adverse climatic conditions produced a string of disastrous harvests, a contemporary claimed that a fifth of Scotland's million inhabitants were reduced to the status of vagrants.[68] This is almost certainly an exaggeration, but Scotland was a much poorer country than England and vagrancy remained a serious problem into the nineteenth century, long after it had ceased to be so in England.[69]

The foregoing discussion relates primarily to Lowland Scotland. One distinctive feature of Scottish society compared with that of England was the pronounced regional variation similar to that of France, Spain or Italy: remarkable in so small a country. Galloway had strongly particularist tendencies, even in the later seventeenth century, but the principal divide was between the Highlands and Islands on the one hand and the Lowlands on the other. While a great deal of ink has been spilled on the subject of Highland clans, the origins, development and social functioning of the clans is still poorly understood. Some writers have suggested that the clan

63 R. Mitchison, 'Who were the poor in Scotland, 1690–1820?' (1988): 141.
64 Tyson (1986): 39.
65 Flinn (1977): 169–70.
66 A.L. Beier, *Masterless men: the vagrancy problem in England, 1560–1640* (1985): *passim* on vagrancy and the English metropolis.
67 We are grateful to Michael Lynch for this information.
68 Flinn (1977): 170.
69 R.A. Cage, *The Scottish poor law, 1745–1845* (1981); Beier (1985). For France see Hufton (1974): 219–44.

system had an early origin and remained static thereafter, becoming increasingly anachronistic by the seventeenth and early eighteenth centuries so that a clash with the increasingly commercialised world of the Lowlands and England was inevitable. Others have claimed that clan society was more flexible and responsive to change so that social conditions in the Highlands had changed substantially by the early eighteenth century from late medieval times. These themes are taken up by Dodgshon in chapter 6. Highland society was less markedly stratified than Lowland in terms of wealth, at least below the level of tacksmen and chiefs, and its organisation was more militarised. A tacksman held land directly from a chief, acting as military middleman and farmer of rents from his area; he was the social and economic delegate of the landowner who mediated relations between lord and peasant.[70] After the Reformation the Calvinist church was slow to penetrate the Highlands, and Catholicism (or, more precisely, a syncretic form of Christianity) survived extensively there. While Catholicism was proscribed by central government and the Calvinist church, the Highlanders were not politically disadvantaged in the same way as Irish Catholics, and social divisions between lord and peasant were not hardened by religious differences as happened in Ireland.[71]

Social differences were, however, reinforced by linguistic separation. The Northern Isles had a Norse legal system and traces of the language (Norn or Danska) until the seventeenth century.[72] Especially obvious was the Gaelic/Scots-English split, marking cultural, educational, linguistic, religious and social differences. Scotland had been a Gaelic-speaking nation in the early Middle Ages, but by the start of the sixteenth century this tongue was confined to the Highlands and parts of the south west.[73] The rest of the population spoke Scots, originally a distinct language in the view of some but in early modern times increasingly converging with English. A social dimension was added to the linguistic divide as the Highland gentry and aristocracy came during the eighteenth century increasingly to favour the culture and tongue of the Lowlands to that of their Gaelic roots.

The decay of Gaelic was also partly due to temporary migration to and economic contacts with the towns of the Lowlands. Indeed towns were an increasingly important influence on economy and society over the early modern period. In the early sixteenth century even the major burghs were still comparatively small and the medieval concept of a town as a free and democratic community of burgesses was not entirely inappropriate. Elec-

[70] I. Donnachie, 'Economy and society in the seventeenth century in the Highlands' (1986): 54–5.

[71] J.C. Beckett, 'Introduction: eighteenth-century Ireland' (1986): lvii; R.E. Ommer, 'Primitive accumulation and the Scottish *clann*' (1986).

[72] J. Bukdahl, *Scandinavia past and present* (1959): 136.

[73] Withers (1984): 1–41; V.E. Durkacz, *The decline of the Celtic languages* (1983): 1–95.

tions to burgh offices were still being held by open ballot of all the burgesses in some burghs.[74] Urban society was differentiated by variations in wealth and status, the most notable gulf being that between the 'free' burgesses and the 'unfree' inhabitants. By the later sixteenth century, when source material becomes more abundant, it is clear that urban society contained many gradations of wealth and status. A tax schedule for Edinburgh in 1565 shows that the wealth of merchants varied from less than £20 Scots to £29,000 Scots with a quarter of the merchant community (about 100 men) paying 70 per cent of the assessment of that occupational group.[75] Average wealth was much lower than for contemporary English merchants. Wealth was unequally distributed among craftsmen too. Of 496 on an Edinburgh tax list of 1583, half paid a sixth of the total assessment while the top 15 per cent paid 56 per cent.[76]

During the sixteenth and early seventeenth centuries the nature of burgh society changed markedly under the impact of a variety of influences. Among the most important of these were the rapid rise of urban populations (especially in the larger burghs), the effects of inflation, the growing interference of central government in urban politics and a rapidly increasing burden of taxation. Many burghs had close ties with their immediate localities and it was not uncommon for nobility and gentry to exercise considerable influence, sometimes benign, sometimes despotic, in the affairs of their local burghs. The doubling of the populations of many burghs in the later sixteenth and early seventeenth centuries led to a more marked division within the ranks of the burgesses. As had occurred in late medieval England, town government became more elitist and oligarchical in character.[77] In the past, tensions within the burgess community have been presented in terms of conflict between the merchant and craft guilds, the latter struggling to gain a foothold on burgh councils which were dominated by the former. Recent research has, however, shown that the real split which was opening up was not between merchants and craftsmen but between a rising elite of merchant and craftsmen entrepreneurs who were increasingly differentiated in wealth, status and power from the ordinary merchant burgess and master craftsman.[78]

Change in Scottish urban society from an essentially medieval structure towards something more recognisably modern has usually been ascribed to the period from the later seventeenth century onwards. Certainly the removal of the restrictive trading monopolies of the royal burghs in 1672 must have had some impact on the towns but these had already been in decay for some time. More important was the rapid erosion of burgess controls, the beginnings of the development of the Atlantic economy, the

[74] *Ibid.*, 214–26; M. Lynch, *Edinburgh and the Reformation* (1981): 3. [75] *Ibid.*, 16.
[76] *Ibid.*, 35–6.
[77] Lynch (1984): 8–10. [78] Lynch (forthcoming).

proliferation of new market centres indicating an expansion of internal trading, and the introduction of new credit structures like bills of exchange.[79] Nevertheless, many of the social and economic changes which have been identified in the later seventeenth century appear to be ones of degree rather than kind, as Lynch discusses in chapter 3. More recent research has shown that Scottish urban society was characterised by greater change during the sixteenth and early seventeenth centuries than has been previously appreciated. While the structure of merchant and craft guilds continued to dominate urban life these became more flexible in terms of whom they admitted and in their operation. The later seventeenth century did witness some changes in burgh society. The development of a variety of manufactories including textiles, paper, glass, and soap production probably increased the proportion of urban workers who were not burgesses and who operated outside the traditional guild framework and also at times outside the town walls.[80] However, as with many areas of Scottish social history, generalisations must remain tentative because of the patchy nature of research.[81]

Important social changes took place during this period in rural as well as urban society, the cumulative effect of which was to accentuate the existing polarisation of wealth and status. Two principal developments account for these changes. The first took place mainly in the sixteenth century and arose from a large-scale transfer of church lands to the laity. Carried out through the medium of 'feuing', the granting of land in perpetuity in exchange for a cash sum and a yearly payment of feu-duty, this transfer worked partly to the benefit of sitting tenants, about a third of whom were able to buy their land and thus become independent freeholders with security of tenure. Their feu duties, initially quite high, were fixed and their value fell rapidly with the sixteenth-century inflation of prices. However, for every sitting tenant who was able to buy his holding, there was at least another whose land was sold out from under them to the nobility or lairds.[82] There was continuity in landholding but also dispossession. Feuing was not the only social change in the sixteenth century. Customary tenures of a kind similar to English copyhold were also being eroded as landlords tried to keep up with price inflation by converting such tenures to ordinary leasehold and increasing rents as often as possible. Associated with this development was the general rise in population during the sixteenth century, a European phenomenon, which meant that there was growing pressure on the available land.[83] Subsistence crises in the 1590s and 1620s drove people off the land for good in areas such as Aber-

[79] Devine (1983a); Whyte (1979): 178–92. [80] Smout (1963): 236–7.
[81] For example, see T. Donnelly, 'The economic activities of the Aberdeen merchant guild, 1750–99' (1981).
[82] Sanderson (1982): 64–7, 108–17, 125–37. [83] Lythe & Butt (1975): 3.

deenshire.[84] Of course, not everyone suffered. Feuars tied in to fixed and low rents were able to benefit from price inflation and even in Aberdeenshire there was probably an overall increase in the number of landowners until the 1630s.[85]

Developments during the sixteenth century were fundamental in shaping social structure and social relations during the following two centuries, notably by strengthening even further the economic and social power of the landowners. The most fundamental gulf in early modern Scottish society was the one separating those who worked the land from those who owned it. In England a family could, with hard work and good fortune, rise from the ranks of the husbandmen through the yeomanry to achieve gentry status over a couple of generations.[86] In Scotland this was probably always more difficult and is likely to have become harder still over time. Proprietors might borrow money from their wealthier tenants but their hold on the land market ensured that land was rarely disposed of in small enough parcels to give such tenants an entry to proprietorship.[87] Scottish society had been more fluid and open during the fourteenth and fifteenth centuries than in the seventeenth and eighteenth centuries and social distinctions between the gentry and the rest of society less marked thanks to the existence of a core of substantial peasants.[88] By contrast with the sixteenth century, the seventeenth saw change operating at a lower level in society in many areas as holding amalgamation by proprietors began to create a more prosperous and commercially oriented group of tenants who were slowly beginning to accumulate capital. This group became increasingly differentiated from the growing proportion of the population made up by the cottars and the poor.[89] In some parts of Scotland, landownership became increasingly difficult even for lairds and prosperous bourgeois. In 1667 there were 621 landed proprietors in Aberdeenshire but by 1771 the buying up of small estates had reduced this to just 250.[90] Only in the Highlands did the seventeenth century see an increase in small proprietors and there was certainly a growth in bourgeois landownership around Glasgow after c.1740 and around Aberdeen and Edinburgh in the second half of the eighteenth century.[91] The trend in the Highlands was reversed in the second half of the eighteenth century as

[84] Flinn (1977): 124. [85] Callander (1986): 1.
[86] Wrightson (1982): 26–32, though, as Wrightson points out in his contribution to this volume, we still know very little about the extent of and mechanisms behind social mobility in England.
[87] Whyte & Whyte (1988): 76–7. [88] Wormald (1981): 51–3.
[89] Whyte (1979): 137–62.
[90] Callander (1986): 2, 4–5.
[91] *Ibid.*; A. MacInnes, 'Political disruption and social change within Scottish gaeldom' (1987); Mitchison (1983): 170; Devine (1983a): 104–7.

rising land values and falling interest rates made it attractive and possible to redeem mortgages.[92]

Social mobility for the bulk of the population was checked by the problems of a limited land market and polarisation of landholdings over time. At the top of the hierarchy, social mobility from the burgeoning professional and commercial classes into the landowning class proper was probably rarer than in England except through intermarriage or the acquisition of estates through mortgage defaults. However, the professions were a major refuge for younger sons of landed families. Between 1707 and 1751 fully 96 per cent of entrants to the Faculty of Advocates of Edinburgh came from landed backgrounds but only a third of boys apprenticed to Edinburgh merchants, reminiscent of Stone's argument that the English gentry and professions saw themselves as equal but trade was somehow beneath most of them.[93]

The second major development in rural society began at the end of the seventeenth century and became increasingly important in the eighteenth. This was the decrease in number and increase in size of farm holdings. Commercialisation of farming and urban growth encouraged the spread of new crops and rotations, enclosure and improved agricultural techniques.[94] In the Lammermuirs, a mainly pastoral area in southern Scotland, there were about 1,000 farms during the seventeenth century but only 840 in 1800 and 720 in 1850. Some upland farms were abandoned but most were rationalised into larger holdings.[95] This trend characterised much of Lowland Scotland, even if change was slower to occur in areas such as Aberdeenshire.[96] Not only were the number of tenancies reduced, but also many smaller feuars or 'bonnet-lairds' sold out to the great estates which proved more resilient to the economic fluctuations of the later seventeenth and early eighteenth centuries.[97] This is the closest Scottish society came to the contemporary 'decline of the English yeoman'. Because peasant proprietorship had never been important in Scotland it did not decline in the same way as it did across much of Europe after c.1650.[98]

Changes also took place below the tenant class. Sub-tenancy was being phased out on some estates in the first half of the eighteenth century, but declined most rapidly between 1770 and 1815. A buoyant agricultural labour market meant that these developments did not necessarily cause unemployment or depopulation, something the apologists of 'Improve-

[92] Bumsted (1982): 34.

[93] L. Stone & J.C.F. Stone, *An open elite? England, 1540–1880* (1984); N.T. Phillipson, 'The social structure of the faculty of advocates in Scotland, 1661–1840' (1980).

[94] Whyte (1979): 113–33, 192–218.

[95] M.L. Parry, 'Changes in the extent of improved farmland' (1980): 185–90.

[96] Whyte (1979): 137–62; I.D. Whyte & K.A. Whyte, 'Patterns of migration of apprentices to Aberdeen' (1986): 81–91.

[97] M.H.B. Sanderson, 'The feuing of Strathisla' (1974): 1–11.

[98] Doyle (1978): 103.

ment' were keen to stress. There were jobs for farm labourers and industrial expansion created niches for displaced cottars in the hand-loom weaving of woollen, linen and, by the end of the eighteenth century, cotton textiles.[99] But agricultural change did alter the social structure by widening the gulf between farmers and their labourers since it became increasingly difficult for a man from a cottar background to work his way up to the tenancy of a large farm, though mobility in both directions between the ranks of the cottars and the smaller tenants remained frequent. In some regions, notably the north east, reclamation of waste land created a class of crofters which formed an intermediate stratum in rural society.[100] The trend was accelerated by the population increase of the later eighteenth century which took place, as in England and Norway, mostly among the lower classes.[101] Important though they were, these social changes took place only slowly. There was no equivalent of the nineteenth-century Highland clearances, except perhaps on a small scale in the south west where in the early eighteenth century shifts to a commercial land exploitation policy (cattle raising rather than the traditional mixed agriculture) by new owners made change more rapid and painful than elsewhere in the Lowlands.[102]

Before the eighteenth century, social change in the Highlands was gradual although the impact of commercialisation was starting to be felt with the development of the cattle trade and the beginning of estate reorganisation along more efficient lines: in Argyllshire for example.[103] When more rapid change did come it was much more painful than in the Lowlands. To finance their participation in Lowland culture, Highland landowners had to espouse alien, commercial values which broke the traditional bonds of society.[104] Always polarised in terms of wealth, Highland society became culturally differentiated. The gulf between Highland and Lowland society had grown over time as the Lowlands became more urbanised, anglicised, law-abiding, Protestant and commercially oriented.[105] From the end of the sixteenth century both church and state mounted a campaign to reduce the independence of the Highlands, to suppress Catholicism there, and to curb the perceived threat to order and stability which the region presented. After 1750 the north-west Highlands

[99] A.J. Durie, *The Scottish linen industry in the eighteenth century* (1979):38–9, 59–60, 74–7, 124–7; T.M. Devine, 'The demand for agricultural labour in East Lothian' (1979d); Devine (ed.), *Farm servants and labour in Scotland, 1770–1914* (1984b):*passim.*

[100] M. Gray, 'North-east agriculture and the labour force, 1790–1875' (1976):87–93.

[101] D. Levine, *Family formation in an age of nascent capitalism* (1977):58–87, 146–52; Dyrvik (1979b):68.

[102] Smout (1972):290; J. Leopold, 'The Levellers' revolt in Galloway in 1724' (1980).

[103] E. Cregeen, 'Tradition and change in the West Highlands of Scotland' (1979):113.

[104] *Ibid.*, 108–10; Ommer (1986):138; Withers (1984):100–15.

[105] Smout (1972):39–46.

and Islands of Scotland came more closely to resemble Ireland than the adjacent Lowlands.

Change in urban society took place more steadily over the period. Stratification by wealth increased through time and towns began to fill up from below. Poverty was a serious and chronic problem for major burghs from the later sixteenth century onwards. Apprentices who had served their time found it increasingly difficult to set up as independent masters and had to remain as journeymen. A small nucleus of masters came to exist alongside a growing number of journeymen, hardening the division between employer and employee. As in many rural areas, social mobility became harder during the eighteenth century.[106] The beneficiaries of urban growth were the merchants, specialist craftsmen and, above all, the professional classes: lawyers, doctors, clergy and teachers. Edinburgh lawyers and writers were developing as a wealthy, powerful and self-conscious group during the reign of James VI, proliferating after the Restoration and again after the Union of 1707. Their wealth and status among the 'quasi-gentry' were consolidated after the middle of the century by the development of distinctive suburban residential areas of which Edinburgh's New Town and the early extension of Glasgow west of the medieval High Street are the best known.[107] Most obvious in the large centres such as Edinburgh, Glasgow, Aberdeen and Dundee, urban growth produced increasing occupational specialisation even in smaller centres. This was already well developed in the textile and shoemaking towns of the west-central Lowlands; Kilmarnock and Paisley for example, and the labour force became increasingly proletarianised in the course of the eighteenth century. Poverty, disease, low educational standards and crime became increasingly prevalent in the mushrooming towns.[108] As towns grew from the sixteenth century onwards, their administration became more oligarchic, dominated by a wealthy elite. The traditional concept of an urban 'community' which had been easily sustained in compact towns of a few thousand people was all but lost in the rapidly growing urban centres of the eighteenth century.[109] Even in the sixteenth century it was under threat. Civic ceremony only appeared in its mature form in the late fifteenth and early sixteenth centuries as a way of coping with increasing social differentiation but it died out towards the end of the sixteenth century.[110]

[106] Smout (1972):339; Durie (1979):78–9. R.A. Houston's own research on Edinburgh between 1660 and 1760 confirms this: e.g. the 1734 wages dispute between journeymen tailors and their masters. SRO CS230/E/1/15.

[107] A.J. Youngson, *The making of classical Edinburgh* (1966); A. Gibb, *Glasgow, the making of a city* (1982).

[108] Dickson & Speirs (1980); R.A. Houston, 'Marriage formation and domestic industry' (1983c):217–19.

[109] Lynch (1984).

[110] We are grateful to Michael Lynch for this information.

SOCIAL RELATIONSHIPS

Describing social structures and change is comparatively straightforward but analysing the quality of social relationships is less so. The basis of society was created by the family and by kinship links. Research on the family in Scotland is still in its infancy although it is usual to assume that there was strong patriarchal control: husband, father and master lorded it over wife, children and servants, the male position consolidated by the law and by the prevailing assumptions of the society. Children were regarded by writers of the time as morally vulnerable and in need of discipline but there is no evidence of particularly hard attitudes towards them nor of any major shift in the conception of childhood as a phase of life.[111]

Women were closely involved in many areas of economic life but occupied a largely subordinate role in society as Houston shows in chapter 4. Kin use and recognition were far from extensive even in the sixteenth century, and the importance of kin beyond the nuclear family was on the wane even among the upper classes over the period. Scots kinship was agnatic in contrast with the cognatic system in England, descent being counted from a male ancestor and kin bonds generally reckoned between males, identification being helped by the use of a kin 'name'. Women were added to, or subtracted from, male kin groups.[112] In the Lowlands at least, kinship was as unimportant as an organising principle for economic, social and cultural relationships as it was in sixteenth- and seventeenth-century England, though until well into the seventeenth century the law continued to stress the central importance of an injured party in any criminal case, including living relatives in the case of murder.[113]

Recent work on English society has argued that the nature of social organisation and personal relationships was distinguished from all other early modern peoples by a fundamental 'individualism'.[114] Property was owned by individuals rather than groups, kinship was unimportant as an organising principle in economic and social relations, and aspirations for personal advancement were identifiably 'modern'. Because of the organisation of some Scottish agricultural tenures, it has sometimes been assumed that farming was a communal affair with shared responsibilities and the division of gains and losses. Farms could be rented to more than one tenant in two ways. Joint tenancy arrangements granted the land to a group of people under one lease for a single payment. This system was

[111] C. Beveridge, 'Childhood and society in eighteenth-century Scotland' (1982); C. Camic, *Experience and enlightenment* (1985): 126–40; H. & K. Kelsall, *Scottish lifestyle 300 years ago. New light on Edinburgh and Border families* (1986): 64–79, 84–5; R.K. Marshall, 'Wetnursing in Scotland, 1500–1800' (1984); R. Wall (ed.), *Family forms in historic Europe* (1983) for European comparisons.

[112] Wormald (1981): 30. [113] *Ibid.*, 69–70; Wrightson (1982): 44–51.

[114] A. Macfarlane, *The origins of English individualism* (1978).

already uncommon by the early seventeenth century. Multiple tenancy meant that a person rented a specific share of a farm for his sole use. In neither case was co-operation beyond herding, stocking and possibly ploughing any more extensive than in the common fields of England. At the same time, single-tenancy units formed a growing proportion of farms, and it is likely that economic individualism was the prevailing ethos even on those in multiple tenancy. Even where a farm was held in joint or multiple tenancy, shares of land were not necessarily equal.

Historians conventionally speak of the close personal structure of past Scottish society. Institutions and relationships from military recruitment in the Highlands to the legal system codified during the sixteenth and seventeenth centuries were very personal and family-oriented in concept.[115] Some have gone so far as to argue that the mutual dependence of different groups in society established a social consensus, and that equality of opportunity in education from the seventeenth century helped to create a level of social harmony and an absence of class distinctions unparalleled elsewhere in early modern Europe.[116] Direct evidence of harmony and co-operation are difficult to come by in documents which, with the possible exception of baron court books,[117] tend to focus on friction. Certainly, by the fifteenth century serfdom had disappeared from Scotland, and from then on, in the Lowlands at least, with the exception of coal and salt workers who were personally bound to the owner of the land they worked on until 1799,[118] relationships between superior and inferior were mainly on a contractual, economic basis. Some feudal structures did survive, notably carriage and labour services levied on tenant farmers, the obligation to grind corn at the lord's mill (thirlage) and even military service in some areas,[119] but feudal relationships were much weaker than in seventeenth- and eighteenth-century Burgundy, Italy or eastern Europe.[120] After the Restoration, the power of the lords over the peasantry began to fade as direct social, legal, cultural and economic contacts came increasingly to be mediated by the state and by middlemen. This was most obvious in the Highlands but even there blind loyalty to the clan chief was not (and had never been) universal.

Rural life was not wholly dominated by the landlords. The middling

[115] J. Wormald, 'Bloodfeud, kindred and government in early modern Scotland' (1980): 88–96.

[116] G. Donaldson, *Scotland: the shaping of a nation* (1974): 237.

[117] A baron court was one where the landowner had seigneurial jurisdiction over those living on his lands. Its operation is discussed in Whyte (1979): 44–7, and Smout (1972): 115–18.

[118] R.A. Houston, 'Coal, class and culture: labour relations in a Scottish mining community, 1650–1750' (1983a): 3–4; C. Whatley, 'A saltwork and the community: the case of Winton, 1716–19' (1984).

[119] Whyte (1979): 35–6.

[120] Doyle (1978): 104; Goubert (1973): 82–7, 126–8; H. Kamen, *European society, 1500–1700* (1984): 150–6.

ranks played an intermediary role in economic regulation and social control which in some cases mediated the power of the lairds and in others supplemented it. The most important local institution was the kirk session, the agent of the Protestant Reformation in the localities. Headed by the parish minister, this body comprised the church precentor, who acted as clerk, and twelve or so elders and deacons. These were godly laymen drawn principally from the tenants, craftsmen and tradesmen of the parish. Take the case of the parish of Stow in the uplands south-east of Edinburgh. Between 1626 and 1652 a quarter of appointments to the kirk session were heritable proprietors, a tenth comprised millers and craftsmen, and the remainder were tenant farmers. In the urban parish of the Canongate (1630–52), three-quarters were master craftsmen.[121] Members of the kirk session were charged with detecting and reporting offences against the moral and religious precepts of the church – mostly sexual misdemeanours, drunkenness, blasphemy, verbal abuse and breaches of the sabbath – and with the administration of poor relief within their own section of the parish.[122] At a secular level there were 'birlay courts' made up of local tenants who acted like English petty constables and manorial officials in ensuring good neighbourhood, cropping and stock control.[123] All these posts were, to a varying degree, held in rotation, and as a result perhaps one adult male in every four or five would have had experience of some form of office-holding, however humble, during his life. In the towns, which had more administrative layers, the proportion was probably higher. The city of Aberdeen recruited 466 separate individuals as constables between 1657 and 1700 from a population of at most 10,000 people.[124] Among the middling ranks of urban and rural society a majority of adult males would have served in secular or ecclesiastical office.

Of course, this is not to say that there was no awareness of social distinctions. Consciousness of rank was manifest in all circumstances. Witnesses to a baptism were usually drawn from the same social and geographical group as the parents. At the other end of life, James Johnston, cooper in Liberton, who died in 1727, made no mention of his soul in his will, but specified 'my body to be decently interred in Liberton church yard according to my rank and degree'.[125] Deponents before civil and criminal courts often drew the distinction between a man with the dress and demeanour of a 'gentleman' and others, a division fixed in print in the introduction to Forbes' almanac of 1685 which distinguished its readers –

[121] W. Makey, 'The elders of Stow, Liberton, Canongate and St Cuthbert's in the mid-seventeenth century' (1970).

[122] Kirk sessions were approximately the same as English select vestry cum church courts.

[123] Whyte (1979): 47–9.

[124] G. Desbrisay, '"Menacing their persons and exacting on their purses": the Aberdeen justice court, 1657–1700' (1986): 76–7.

[125] SRO CC8/8/91.

'noblemen, gentlemen, merchants and others' – from the 'Vulgar'.[126] Indeed, as early as the fifteenth century, Wormald speaks of an 'obsession with status' expressed in repeated sumptuary legislation.[127]

In terms of social relationships, judgements about the common people of Scotland were often pessimistic. One commentator, James Harrington, believed they were 'little better than the cattle of the nobility'.[128] Indeed, some landowners had a far from fatherly attitude to their subordinates, and apparently friendly relationships in the lord's court were belied by private remarks. A seventeenth-century Earl of Strathmore condemned his tenants at Castle Lyon for being 'a race of evill doers, desolate fellowes and mislabourers of the ground'.[129] Opportunities to misuse the tenantry were numerous because of the power of the lords: they controlled the land market, borrowed money from their tenants, extracted a high level of surplus in rents and grassums (occasional payments), rack-rented by allowing tenants to bid for holdings, and made evictions with ease.[130] Despite similarities of wealth between well-off tenants and some lesser lairds there is little evidence of socialising between them suggesting that the status and self-perception of the groups were different.[131] There are many small but telling examples of the pervasive role of social structure in influencing day to day life. Well-off burgesses convicted of an offence at Aberdeen's Justice Court in the second half of the seventeenth century paid heavier fines than their social inferiors but were never subjected to the pain and humiliation of corporal punishment which was meted out to the young, females and the poor.[132]

Harsh social relationships were increasingly apparent in the Highlands and Islands during the eighteenth century because of the contrast with the earlier organic, reciprocal nature of social relations, but comments are numerous about the limited altruism of sixteenth-century Lowland lords when faced with the erosion of their incomes by inflation. The short leases which most tenants held in the sixteenth century made it easy to pass on to them the burden of inflation, and, as in southern Spain or parts of France and Italy, landlords were able to extract a high proportion of the available surplus, a feature of Scottish society which reinforced poverty among the lower ranks and which helped to perpetuate the gulf between landowner and tenant.[133]

Relations between tenants and lords were not exclusively those of exploitation and oppression of the former by the latter. It is likely that in the later sixteenth and early seventeenth century population pressure and

[126] W.R. MacDonald, 'Scottish seventeenth-century almanacs' (1966): 262.
[127] Wormald (1981): 32.
[128] J.G.A. Pocock (ed.), *The political works of James Harrington* (1977): 240.
[129] Dodgshon (1981): 130.
[130] Whyte & Whyte (1988): 73–6; Whyte (1979): 158.
[131] Kelsall (1986): 85–6.
[132] Desbrisay (1986): 86.
[133] Whyte & Whyte (1988): 76.

inflation soured relations but that when tenants were in short supply and rents hard to collect, as in the later seventeenth and early eighteenth centuries, paternalism's kinder face was shown. Landlords were, for example, prepared to grant remissions from rent to hard-pressed tenants in bad years such as the 1690s and they were the main providers of poor relief to their dependents throughout our period. Gaelic poetry from the Atholl estates 1760–90 almost always portrays the Duke and his factors in a good light.[134] The memoirs of an eighteenth-century footman, John MacDonald, refer to the upper classes in a favourable way, mentioning acts of generosity, the local reputation of a laird, an owner's great wealth, in a way which shows implicit acceptance of aristocratic values. He concludes humbly: 'Gentlemen know the world better than we'.[135] There was probably widespread acceptance of the ideology of domination and its everyday economic and social manifestations but the popular image of a closely-knit society based on mutual respect and need is a serious distortion of reality.

Access to the land and the social relationships it created in rural areas had fundamental implications for relations of power and authority. Scottish rural society was marked by a comparative absence of popular unrest.[136] There were sporadic outbursts of protest such as the 'great convocations made in the realm to resist the lords of the ground' in 1457 or the Levellers of south-west Scotland in the 1720s, a body of tenants and cottars opposed to enclosure for cattle farming, but in general rural riot was very rare. Urban populations were more vocal about grain shortages (such as in the burghs of south Fife in 1720), political and religious changes (anti-Protestant riots at Glasgow in the later sixteenth century, anti-Catholic at Edinburgh in the 1670s) or taxation, and there was an appreciable rise in the level of unrest towards the end of the eighteenth century with meal riots, militia riots and anti-clearance disturbances affecting both town and country.[137] Even so, the level of disturbance was much lower than in most European countries: there is no Scottish equivalent of the 'peasant furies' of seventeenth-century France, nor of the grain and enclosure riots of sixteenth- and early seventeenth-century England. Popular protest was sporadic, spontaneous, ephemeral and was not a regular means by which Scotland's rural population expressed its views and orchestrated its relations with authority. Sixteenth-century urban craftsmen tended to take to the courts rather than the streets for redress of grievances.[138]

[134] Leneman (1986): 64–8; Bumsted (1982): 31.

[135] J. Macdonald, *Travels in various parts of Europe, Asia and Africa* (1927 edn): 50.

[136] Wormald (1981): 50–1.

[137] K. Logue, *Popular disturbances in Scotland, 1780–1815* (1979); 'Eighteenth-century popular protest: aspects of the people's past' (1980); T.M. Devine, 'Stability and unrest in rural Scotland and Ireland, 1760–1840' (1987) and his chapter in this volume.

[138] Lynch (forthcoming). Plays and ballads as well as acts of arson could be used to attack class injustice and unpopular individuals, though this was probably less common than in

Absence of protest cannot be attributed wholly to coercion by military force – powers of repression were less than in Ireland – though this was used against the Levellers in 1724, in suppression of the Jacobites and the control of the various types of late eighteenth-century riot. Central government played comparatively little part in the lives of ordinary people during the sixteenth and seventeenth centuries, fiscally, legally or administratively. Regular royal taxation was a sixteenth-century development and any form of taxation was feared and resented. In the localities, the power of landlords was buttressed by a network of courts which could deal with most civil and criminal cases. Courts of barony and regality, among others, meant that pre-eighteenth-century justice was private, local and amateur rather than central and professional. As a result most people, even in the Lowlands, had little to do with central authority. Patronage and personal links remained significant from the humblest interactions of the village level to high politics with local independence jealously guarded. For example, attempts to introduce Justices of the Peace on the English model in the early seventeenth century were unpopular and largely unsuccessful. Efforts to integrate the Highlands and Islands into a national polity were even less successful, perhaps because of the naked hostility to Gaelic values shown in, say, the 1609 Statutes of Iona. This apparent 'weakness' of the crown in fact helped to produce beneficial results, notably a comparative absence of friction between central and local authority shown in the relations between crown and towns which were 'peaceful to a degree rare in Europe', though the demands of the crown on the towns were undoubtedly increasing in the later part of the reign of James VI.[139]

Yet central government was beginning to penetrate localities, especially after the end of the sixteenth century and again from the late seventeenth century. There were five main reasons for this. First the growing power of centralised justice. Civil courts were reformed in the 1530s (based on the Edinburgh Court of Session) and criminal ones in the 1590s. Edinburgh lawyers strove to extend their sway over all of Scotland, a signal example being the replacement of Norse by Roman law following the expulsion of Earl Patrick Stewart from Shetland 1611–12. After 1672 the reconstituted High Court of Justiciary and its circuit courts from 1708 helped to extend central criminal justice over all of Scotland even before the abolition of heritable jurisdictions in 1747. Second, the growth of internal trade and marketing brought more people into contact with towns and with officials. Extensive credit networks, operated notably by Edinburgh lawyers and merchants, were usually secured by wadset or personal bond. Third, the reformed church after 1560, with its hierarchy of courts, its schools and its

late eighteenth-century Ireland. E.J. Cowan, 'Calvinism and the survival of folk' (1980); McDowell (1986): 676.

[139] Wormald (1981): 14–17, 46, 162–3 and *passim*.

efforts to convert the Catholic Highlands, acted as a force for integration. Fourth, a general growth of taxation and bureaucracy. Fifth, and particularly significant in the Highlands, military service outside the local area and military campaigns against it.[140]

Other, indirect, sources of discipline were similarly unhelpful to the authorities. The poor laws encompassed comparatively few people and could not be used as a means of social control over the whole of society. More important was the judicial system, since Scots criminal law was weighted against the accused to a greater degree than English and the whim of the judge was more important – as the radicals found to their cost in the 1790s.[141] The dispersed nature of Scottish rural settlement may also have militated against group action. Social change occurred gradually for the most part, removing the sharp goad which could have provoked riot. In addition there was no long-established tradition of independent action by the ordinary rural people.

The nature of protest also differed from that in England or Europe. Unlike England, rural protests were almost never led by the gentry and clergy, hardly surprising in the latter case since the men of God often came from gentry backgrounds and were usually paid by the substantial landowners in the parish. The Scottish Kirk was very much the mouthpiece of the lairds, the Duke of Argyll thinking it not amiss to use the church on Tiree to announce changes in his leasing policy in 1756.[142] Those worth more than 40 shillings of freehold had the vote in English counties but the qualification in Scotland was more than £30 sterling and it is therefore hardly surprising that political participation was restricted to a mere handful: there were only 2,662 names on the freeholders' list in 1788 out of some one and a half million people, and only half of the names on the roll belonged to real individuals.[143] Before 1660 the vote was limited to a handful of feudal landowners, and the extension of the franchise after this date was part of their effort to increase their hold on society rather than an expression of democratic ideals. It is perhaps not surprising that the Scots had a reputation for being less politically militant at parliamentary elections than the English or Irish, especially before 1660.

An absence of riot did not preclude other expressions of discontent or the existence of violent means of solving disputes between individuals or groups. The strong grip maintained by the lairds over the rural masses in

140 B.P. Lenman & G. Parker, 'The state, the community and the criminal law in early modern Europe' (1980); S.J. Davies, 'The courts and the Scottish legal system, 1600–1747: the case of Stirlingshire' (1980); Withers (1984).

141 T. Johnston, *History of the working classes in Scotland* (1920): 223; Smout (1972): 417.

142 *Ibid.*, 322. However, the kirk sessions were not completely in the pockets of the lairds as they sometimes pursued even the rich and powerful when they offended against moral prescriptions.

143 Bumsted (1982): 16; W. Ferguson, 'The electoral system in the Scottish counties before 1832' (1984): 264–6.

the Lowlands produced a relatively orderly, authoritarian society. The solution of disputes by force died out over most of the Lowlands in the later seventeenth century. This was a major change from earlier conditions and was marked in the landscape by the abandonment of fortified houses and their conversion or replacement by undefended mansions.[144] The lords' domination in the Highlands and the North could be used as a weapon against each other, as in the struggle between the houses of Huntly and Moray in the North East in the late 1580s and early 1590s, or against the political establishment, as became clear in 1715 and 1745. A century before, the crown determined to spread law and order to the 'Hielands, where nane officer of the law may goe for fear of their lives' but success was slow to come.[145] Cattle raiding continued in the Highlands until the middle of the eighteenth century, the Lochaber district being one of the worst areas for freelance cattle reiving.[146] The Highland margin was described in 1694 as 'a perfect nurserie of thieves' and in 1721 the Duke of Atholl talked of a way of life when he described 'the abominable trade of thieving'.[147]

The other troublesome region, the Borders, had effectively ceased to be a problem by the end of James VI and I's reign: feuds and large-scale group theft had disappeared there by the 1620s. Violence and a tradition of independent action among the lairds was slower to end north of the Border than south for two reasons. First, the Scottish gentry were less closely tied to the central government politically or socially than were their counterparts in Cumberland or Northumberland. Remoteness from central authority and the laissez-faire nature of royal control before the later sixteenth century allowed family feuding to survive to a later date than in England. The 'feud' was much less violent than is often assumed: it could describe any dispute and the concept of groups in opposition helped to contain civil and criminal actions.[148] Second, the existence of separate governments and legal systems in Scotland and England until 1603 made escape across the Border simple. The creation of a Border Commission which could operate in both countries solved the interstitial problems which allowed bandits to continue operating in other parts of Europe such as the boundaries between the Low Countries, Germany and France or areas of Spain.[149] Scotland was always a very disciplined, if not necessarily very orderly, society, but probably not any more intrinsically violent than England. The legal system stressed compensation rather than retribution as the end of

[144] Smout (1972): 180–3. [145] Cregeen (1979): 100.
[146] B.P. Lenman, *The Jacobite clans of the Great Glen* (1984b).
[147] Leneman (1986): 148–50; F.J. Shaw, 'Sources for the history of the seventeenth-century Highlands' (1986): 13–14.
[148] Wormald (1980): 55–6.
[149] C.M.F. Ferguson, 'Law and order on the Anglo-Scottish Border, 1603–1707' (1981); T.I. Rae, *The administration of the Scottish frontier 1513–1603* (1966); A. Blok, 'The peasant and the brigand: social banditry reconsidered' (1972); H. Kamen, 'Public authority and popular crime: banditry in Valencia, 1660–1714' (1974).

justice for most of the early modern period. Depersonalised justice was not the norm and local, informal settlement of disputes by lairds, clergy and neighbours was extensive.[150]

RELIGION, EDUCATION AND POPULAR CULTURE

To some extent at least, the lack of religious divisions in Scottish society may help to account for the low level of riot, especially when contrasted with sixteenth- and seventeenth-century France or Germany. There was no 'German Peasants War' in Scotland and none of the fierce iconoclasm and bloody massacres of sixteenth-century France. Scotland is often portrayed as an archetypal Protestant country on Dutch or German lines. The conventional image of the Protestant Reformation in Scotland is of mass support for Calvinism; in fact recent research has shown that popular support for the Protestant cause was very slight before the (mainly political) Reformation of 1560 and there is little evidence to suggest that the Scottish church in the 1550s was in a particularly bad state. Even in the 1560s and 1570s Calvinism drew its support principally from urban merchants and professionals and from the gentry as it did in France.[151] Some dioceses such as Dunblane took a very conservative stance at the Reformation, other areas such as Fife or Angus were more receptive to the reformed faith.

The Scottish church tried to make the population godly and obedient, and seems to have been fairly successful, at least in the seventeenth century. Unlike Dutch Calvinists, the Scots were able to impose godly discipline on all members of the parish community, and not simply on the minority who chose to join the congregations and to submit voluntarily.[152] The kirk session used the testimonial system and religious sanctions such as excommunication and withholding baptism to enforce its viewpoint.[153] For troublesome cases it could work with the secular magistrate in the best Genevan tradition. This desire for order and conformity was common to all religious and political elites in early modern Europe. The heyday of church discipline took place in the seventeenth century, but even then there were problems in ensuring conformity and some parts of Scotland remained staunchly Catholic or traditional. Indeed, the drive for religious conformity was conspicuously less successful than in contemporary Sweden. Growing religious diversity from the time of the Restoration destroyed the hold of Calvinist discipline as both lairds and people began to find

[150] Wormald (1981):38.
[151] Lynch (1981):214–22; I.B. Cowan, *Regional aspects of the Scottish Reformation* (1978).
[152] B.P. Lenman, 'The limits of godly discipline in the early modern period with particular reference to England and Scotland' (1984a):135; M. Lynch, 'Scottish Calvinism, 1559–1638' (1985).
[153] R.A. Houston, 'Geographical mobility in Scotland, 1652–1811' (1985b):380–1.

alternatives to the (post-1690) Presbyterian Kirk. The Secession of 1733, the creation of a 'Relief Church' in 1761 and finally the great Disruption of 1843 mark out the eighteenth and early nineteenth centuries in Scotland (as in England) as the golden age of religious pluralism.[154] Eighteenth-century social and intellectual life were increasingly secular in their emphasis but this development stemmed from the religious discipline and aspirations of the seventeenth century.[155]

Determining the quality and quantity of religious belief among the population at large is notoriously difficult. Scotland was regarded by observers such as Daniel Defoe as a particularly godly nation but he probably exaggerated.[156] This was certainly a religious age, but as in other European countries the extent of mass commitment was very variable. An interest in religion is obvious at the grass roots level from concern over the choice of a new minister to the dramatic enthusiasm shown at the famous evangelical revival meetings at Cambuslang in the 1740s.[157] Yet, in the eighteenth century, church attendance was far from universal and the 5 acts of the Scottish parliament (not to mention the 15 of the General Assembly of the Church of Scotland between 1690 and 1726) to enforce observance of the sabbath suggest that efforts were less than totally successful. Thomas Boston, an eighteenth-century preacher, was saddened by poor attendance at church.[158] Sober piety rather than vehement emotional commitment characterised popular religion. Nor was Scotland solidly Presbyterian after the Reformation: the first model presbyteries were not set up until 1581, episcopacy prevailed to 1638 and from 1662 to 1690, and there were always areas such as the north east which favoured this form of organisation throughout. Recusancy flourished in the south west in the late sixteenth century and Jesuit missions operated in the north and west of Scotland between the 1670s and 1770s. The reformed kirk was represented in most Highland parishes by 1574 but popular support seems to have been very slight.[159]

The kirk sessions of post-Reformation Scotland were not simply instruments of moral and religious control. They also carried the administrative burden of the parochial responsibility for poor relief. Scottish poor relief

[154] A.D. Gilbert, *Religion and society in industrial England* (1976); A.J. Hayes, *Edinburgh Methodism, 1761–1975* (1976).
[155] A.C. Chitnis, *The Scottish enlightenment: a social history* (1976).
[156] R.A. Houston, *Scottish literacy and the Scottish identity* (1985a): 259.
[157] Mitchison (1983): 171–3.
[158] R.D. Brackenridge, 'The enforcement of Sunday observance in post-Revolution Scotland, 1689–1733' (1969): 44; D.J. Withrington, 'Non-church going, c.1750–c.1850: a preliminary study' (1971).
[159] M.H.B. Sanderson, 'Catholic recusancy in Scotland in the sixteenth century' (1970); J. Kirk, 'The kirk and the Highlands at the Reformation' (1986); A.C. MacWilliam 'A Highland mission: Strathglass, 1671–1777' (1973); W. Ferguson, 'Problems of the established church' (1972); Withers (1984): 31–7, 160–81.

was more personal, informal and flexible than the English system and until the eighteenth century was probably less effective. Similar laws were in force but they operated differently in practice. Voluntary collections were organised by the kirk, the funds administered and disbursed by kirk session members. In times of crisis, parish poor relief was probably a small proportion of total income for the indigent who were aided by multiple inputs from formal and informal charity, including friends, neighbours, landlords, relatives, begging and private charities. Few stayed on poor relief for very long since in Scotland it was regarded as a temporary measure rather than permanent support as it became increasingly in England during the seventeenth century.[160] Compulsory rating was unusual and unpopular, an expedient to be adopted only in desperation and, unlike in England, casual begging was still tolerated. Overall, the system resembled that of France or Prussia more than of England or Denmark.[161]

Elements of social and cultural continuity and change are encapsulated in the Scottish witchcraze. The Scottish witch-hunt was bloodier than that in England, with approximately ten times the number of executions per head of population. A higher proportion of Scottish witches were men: a fifth compared with a tenth in England. The executions took place later than in England, and the timing of the most severe episodes was slightly different: in England the peaks came in the middle and late sixteenth century, in Scotland between the 1620s and 1660s. Where English witchcraft was extensive, hardly an Essex parish escaping some contact with witchcraft prosecutions, Scottish witchcraft was localised in certain communities such as Paisley in 1697, and concentrated in the east-central Lowlands; it was almost unknown in the Highlands and Islands where Catholic and pagan survivals made some of the proscribed activities of the witches much more widely acceptable. Some of these differences can be attributed to the distinctive social characteristics of the two countries, others to the Roman legal system which allowed the use of torture in Scotland and which emphasised covens and the pact with the devil much more than in England. The nature of confessions therefore differed and there were more multiple cases of necromancy in Scotland.[162]

Continuity was also evident in education and culture. With education as with poor relief, the 'reformers inherited and retained attitudes and beliefs from their predecessors'.[163] The Protestant reformers of 1560 had advocated widespread education as the best way of protecting and nourishing

160 R. Mitchison 'The making of the old Scottish poor law' (1974); Tyson (1986):36; Leneman (1986):111.

161 Mitchison (1974); McDowell (1986):676–8 for an Irish comparison; Doyle (1978):132–3 and C. Lis & H. Soly, *Poverty and capitalism* (1979):88, 95 for a European comparison.

162 Larner (1981); C. Larner, *Witchcraft and religion: the politics of popular belief* (1984):69–78.

163 Wormald (1981):76; J. Durkan, 'Education in the century of Reformation' (1959).

the new faith, and of providing trained officials for church and state. However, it was not until the seventeenth century that Acts of the Scottish Parliament (1616, 1633, 1646 and 1696) set up a network of parish and burgh schools funded partly by the landowners and partly by fees; a few gifted poor might receive free education. By the end of the seventeenth century most parishes in the Lowlands had an official school and teacher, though in the Highlands educational provision was poor throughout the period and in the eighteenth century the most significant improvements were brought about by an independent, Edinburgh-based charitable body called the SSPCK (Society in Scotland for Propagating Christian Knowledge). The parochial system was supplemented by adventure or private schools which relied solely on fees and which usually taught only elementary subjects such as reading, writing and religious knowledge. This arrangement was very different from England where schools were mostly funded by fees or by charitable endowments.[164]

Differences in institutions and the dynamic role of Calvinism in encouraging literacy are said to have created one of the most literate populations in the seventeenth- and eighteenth-century world, on a par with major success stories such as Sweden, New England and Prussia. Scotland did enjoy high literacy but it was very far from being exceptional in a European context. Despite differences in the structure and funding of education between the two countries, literacy levels were similar in Scotland and England, and almost identical in Lowland Scotland and the four northern counties of England: 75 per cent male illiteracy c.1640 and 35 per cent c.1760. Scotland never managed to equal the near-total literacy of New England men during the eighteenth century and there is no firm evidence of a particularly pervasive reading tradition on the Swedish model. Demand for serious religious, historical and literary works does seem to have been more broadly based in Scottish society than it was in England.[165] Achievements were confined to the Lowlands since education, and indeed the habit of keeping formal documentation and using written forms for social and cultural purposes, were poorly developed in the Highlands, which remained steeped in illiteracy until well into the nineteenth century.[166]

Scotland had three universities in 1500 and a fourth when Edinburgh was established in 1583. Glasgow's flagging fortunes were revived in the 1570s by Andrew Melville, whose influence spread in some measure to the other centres and enabled Scotland to participate in the European 'edu-

[164] J. Scotland, *The history of Scottish education*, vol. 1 (1969):3–177; Houston (1985a):111–30.
[165] *Ibid.*, 20–109; P. Laslett, 'Scottish weavers, cobblers and miners who bought books in the 1750s' (1969); T.C. Smout, 'Born again at Cambuslang' (1982).
[166] J. Bannerman, 'Literacy in the Highlands' (1983); Withers (1984):116–60; Shaw (1986):11; Houston (1985a):70–83.

cational revolution' of the period.[167] These institutions were small, cheap to attend and accessible. Some Scots went abroad while foreigners came to Scotland for higher education. The social spectrum of students was much broader than at Oxford and Cambridge and the proportion of eligibles among the highest in Europe. Furthermore, and with the notable exception of St Andrews, Scotland's universities flourished in the eighteenth century when institutions of higher learning elsewhere in Europe were generally experiencing stagnation or contraction. Improvements in curricula and teaching methods put Scottish universities in the forefront of European intellectual advances, and the proportion of the population attending rose steadily during the eighteenth and nineteenth centuries.[168]

Universities were vital to the flowering of the Enlightenment in the major cities of an otherwise poor and backward country. The Scottish Enlightenment was an elite phenomenon which had its origins in the nation's educational system, political history, close-knit society, economic development and international ties, and in the declining role of religion in social and intellectual life. Scotland's contribution to this European movement lay notably in the fields of medicine, law, philosophy, 'economics', geology and history, its particular emphases being on 'civic humanism' (obligation, personal morality and social coherence), natural jurisprudence and the concept of 'improvement' in economy and society; the ultimate goal was an improved understanding of, and ability to shape, human society.[169]

The world of Hume, Smith, Robertson and Carlyle, of learned societies and elite clubs has been extensively studied. By contrast, research into Scottish mass culture is poorly developed beyond work on Burns, Hogg and other popular poets.[170] It is, nevertheless, possible to make some tentative generalisations. The culture of the printed word was gaining in strength throughout our period. The first printing press was set up at Edinburgh c.1507–8 and low production costs made the capital a centre of printing for England and Europe during the eighteenth century. Yet print did not wholly replace the traditional oral culture. Among the common people of the Lowlands and throughout the Highlands, recreations, and indeed much of the process of socialisation, were grounded in face-to-face interactions. Oral culture in the Highlands was rich and densely textured. Featuring ballads and tales about heroes, lords, wars and love, it resem-

167 Scotland (1969): 24–37; L. Stone, 'The educational revolution in England, 1540–1640' (1964).

168 Scotland (1969): 134–73; Camic (1985): 165–79; R.N. Smart, 'Provinces of the Scottish universities, 1560–1850' (1974); W.M. Mathew, 'Origins of Glasgow students, 1740–1839' (1966); R.L. Kagan, *Students and society in early modern Spain* (1974).

169 D. Daiches, P. Jones & J. Jones (eds.), *A hotbed of genius. The Scottish enlightenment, 1730–1790* (1986); Camic (1985); Chitnis (1976).

170 A. Mitchell & C.G. Cash, *A contribution to the bibliography of Scottish topography* (1917): 514–33 for printed sources.

bled Ireland and north-western France more than England. In the Inverness and Dingwall area during the later seventeenth and early eighteenth centuries frequent efforts were made by kirk sessions to stamp out activities such as well-dressing, bonfires, guising, penny weddings and dancing, suggesting that elements of traditional popular culture were strong.[171]

By comparison, the popular culture of the central Lowlands and south east was ritually impoverished. Recreations included golf, archery, tavern-haunting, fencing, hunting and riding for the upper classes while football, drinking, walking, dancing, the abuse of animals by humans and other animals and miscellaneous fireside sociabilities formed the staple of working-class leisure. Group sociability focused around baptisms, weddings and burials with drink playing a central role.[172] The Scots appear to have been less musical than the French, English or Welsh though there was a flourishing ballad tradition, notably in the Northern Isles and north-east Lowlands. Music at both a popular and elite level had flourished before the Reformation and the post-Reformation church did not immediately proscribe it: some towns retained minstrels long after the Reformation and it is possible to argue that (the largely monodic) folk music flourished throughout the seventeenth century.[173] By the 1630s, however, church music was mostly in the form of plain metrical psalms. Much popular culture went underground in the seventeenth century but re-emerged and flourished in the eighteenth despite rearguard actions by the kirk and Societies for the Reformation of Manners; a 'dancing boom', the replacement of the pipes by the fiddle and the writing of new songs are examples.[174]

There were three reasons for the relatively impoverished nature of Lowland Scotland's popular culture in the seventeenth and eighteenth centuries. First, the Calvinist proscription of many traditional festivities such as Yule, condemnation of 'promiscuous dancing' and excessive drinking, and insistence on the profitable (godly) use of spare time helped to curb many communal recreations. The worst 'killjoy' period was the middle of the seventeenth century, but it would be wrong to regard the reformed kirk as a necessarily philistine or depressing institution since it clearly fostered education and other cultural forms. Prolonged campaigns against certain types of wedding festivities produced no long-term decline of these forms of sociability. However, many of the pre-Reformation urban

[171] M. Martin, *A description of the western isles of Scotland* (1703); S. Maclean, 'Obscure and anonymous Gaelic poetry' (1986). We are grateful to Bob Dodgshon for the information about Inverness and Dingwall.

[172] Kelsall (1986):89–92. [173] Cowan (1980).

[174] D. Johnson, *Music and society in Lowland Scotland in the eighteenth century* (1972); J.L. Campbell, *Highland songs of the Forty-Five* (1984); Wormald (1981):56–72, 187–9; D. Buchan *The ballad and the folk* (1972); T.J. Byres, 'Scottish peasants and their song' (1976).

rituals such as Hammermen's plays in Perth and Edinburgh, deemed to smack of popery, did suffer during the 1570s and 1580s.[175] The censorious attitude of the reformed church was based not only on religious precepts but also on a concern for order shared with secular authorities which made church and magistrates nervous of large gatherings. Second, rural settlement outside the south-east of Scotland was dispersed and nucleated villages of the kind found in Lowland England or many parts of France and Spain did not exist. This militated against activities which involved the participation of large numbers of people. Finally, developing cultural polarisation followed social and economic differentiation in the eighteenth century ensuring that the traditional recreations became restricted increasingly to the lower orders while the richer and better educated middling ranks took up new activities which would remove them physically and culturally from association with those recreations.[176] There was something of a cultural revival after the end of the seventeenth century. Royal patronage of music and the theatre declined when the court left Edinburgh in 1603 and despite a brief revival in the 1670s it was not till the early eighteenth century that they began to develop once more, particularly in the towns. Professional theatre and music flourished in Edinburgh from the 1720s and this, along with the social 'season', intellectual clubs and the widespread drinking of hot beverages in tea and coffee houses, spread to the lesser urban centres during the eighteenth century.[177]

This volume presents a series of studies of major themes in Scottish social history. These are designed to serve as overviews of their respective fields, but at the same time they incorporate the findings of recent research. Throughout the book, emphasis has been placed on setting the Scottish experience within the context of other contemporary European societies. Taken individually and collectively the chapters on towns, women, the standard of living, population mobility, the Highlands and socio-economic change emphasise the recent nature of much work on Scottish social history, stressing new perspectives, new questions about the nature of Scottish society in the past, and new directions for future research.

This book is not designed to be comprehensive, but in order to place the specifically Scottish material within a broader context we have invited an English and an Irish social historian to provide perspectives from the outside. Its aim is to tell those not raised in the sometimes narrow

175 A.J. Mill, 'The Perth hammermen's play' (1970a); 'The Edinburgh hammermen's Corpus Christi Herod pageant' (1970b).

176 P. Burke, *Popular culture in early modern Europe* (1978).

177 D.F. Harris, *Saint Cecilia's Hall* (1899); J.H. Jamieson, 'Social assemblies of the eighteenth century' (1933).

traditions of Scottish history about her society in the early modern period and to illustrate its relevance to a broader and fuller understanding of the nature of European societies and the ways in which they changed before the Industrial Revolution.

1

POPULATION MOBILITY IN EARLY MODERN SCOTLAND

I.D. WHYTE

INTRODUCTION

Population mobility has attracted the attention of social and economic historians and historical geographers seeking to understand past societies. Levels and patterns of geographical mobility reflect many aspects of social conditions and are in turn an important influence on society. Geographical mobility is closely linked to social mobility, together demonstrating the degree to which past societies were fixed and rigid or fluid and permeable. Population mobility is also closely linked as both a dependent and an independent variable to family and household structures, regional contrasts in agricultural systems, holding structures and patterns of rural industry, and levels of urbanisation and is therefore an important social indicator and determinant.

Recent research has altered the image of geographical mobility in pre-industrial European societies, overturning past preconceptions which regarded them as being static and immobile.[1] Studies of rural mobility and migration to the towns have shown that movement was normal, particularly among younger people, though often over limited distances.[2] For early modern England, population mobility has been linked to the development of the economy and society in the prelude to the Industrial Revolution.[3] Given that Scotland underwent major social and economic changes between the sixteenth and later eighteenth centuries, the question arises as to whether the scale and pattern of mobility in Scotland was comparable with England or, more generally, with the patterns which have been identified more widely in Western Europe. The Scots were highly mobile both at home and overseas in the nineteenth century; was this a recent development or was it also a feature of Scottish society in earlier times? The remarkable mobility of the Scots within Europe during the sixteenth and seventeenth centuries has often been commented on.[4] As

[1] M. Flinn, *European demographic system 1500–1820* (1981):65–75. [2] *Ibid.*
[3] P. Clark, 'Migration in England' (1979):57–8.
[4] T.A. Fischer, *The Scots in Germany* (1902); T.A. Fischer, *The Scots in Sweden* (1907); J. Harrison, *The Scot in Ulster* (1888).

emigration is often an extension of internal population movements this implies high levels of mobility at home; but can this be demonstrated?

Little attention has been paid to internal migration in Scotland before the nineteenth century. Even Flinn's major study of Scottish population considered mobility only as an incidental demographic factor.[5] Within the last few years, however, two things have become clear. First, there are a number of untapped or under-exploited sources capable of shedding light on population mobility in pre-industrial Scotland. Second; preliminary analysis indicates that high levels of mobility did exist and that in many respects Scotland's experience was similar to that of the rest of North-Western Europe. The present chapter considers patterns of population mobility in early modern Scotland and assesses their implications for Scottish society. The main features of geographical mobility in Scotland are compared with those of other contemporary European societies. The limitations of current knowledge will rapidly become apparent and some future lines of enquiry will be suggested. Attention is focused on mobility within Scotland. Emigration, which has received much more attention in the past, is not considered.

CONTROLS ON MOBILITY: GEOGRAPHICAL AND ECONOMIC

Population mobility in early modern Scotland was influenced by a range of geographical, economic, demographic, social, legal and institutional factors. The ruggedness of Scotland's topography has often been stressed as a barrier to communications but this should be seen as channelling mobility in particular directions rather than necessarily inhibiting it. The importance of coastal and freshwater transport should not be forgotten.[6] Travel by water was easier than journeying overland, even for the poorest migrants. Efforts by Edinburgh's burgh council to stop beggars from arriving by sea at Leith from Fife and other destinations show that an early modern equivalent of hitch-hiking was available even to vagrants.[7] Nevertheless, one might look for signs that mobility increased over time in terms of levels of movement and the distances travelled as communications improved and the penetration of commercialisation into once-remote rural areas generated more contact with the outside world.

In cultural terms the strongest barrier to mobility was the divide between Highland and Lowland, a distinction based on differences in language as well as society which existed by the fourteenth century and sharpened thereafter.[8] This gulf was only an extreme example of the settled

[5] M. Flinn (ed.), *Scottish population history* (1977).
[6] T.C. Smout, *Scottish trade* (1963): 12–15.
[7] M. Wood, *The burgh of Edinburgh 1665–80* (1950): 255.
[8] T.C. Smout, *A history of the Scottish people* (1972): 39–43.

Lowlander's distrust of the more footloose Highlander, instances of which can be found throughout Europe in early modern times.[9] Contact between Highland and Lowland did occur though. There was a two-way traffic in agricultural produce across the Highland line, Highlanders bringing livestock, timber and other upland commodities to Lowland markets in exchange for grain.[10] In the seventeenth century, the taking of Lowland cattle to the hill grazings or 'shielings' and the droving of Highland livestock to the Lowlands was also becoming commonplace.[11] However, Highland society was largely closed to Lowlanders until as late as the first half of the eighteenth century, although some groups of people, such as merchants, the clergy and the military did travel there, while Highlanders who ventured into the Lowlands tended to be regarded with suspicion and mistrust.[12] Perhaps the most important change in general patterns of mobility in Scotland during the eighteenth century was the increasing permeability of the Highland/Lowland boundary with the development of seasonal and permanent migration from the Highlands.

In early modern England, Ireland, France and elsewhere in Europe there were often marked contrasts between the economic and social structures of adjacent regions leading to migratory movements between them.[13] Much emphasis has been laid on the contrast between arable and wood pasture areas in early modern England. Surplus population tended to move from champion areas to wood pasture or upland regions in search of opportunities though this might be reversed in years of dearth when starvation forced the inhabitants of these more marginal areas on to the roads towards the cereal-growing Lowlands.

In Scotland there does not appear to have been any counterpart of England's wood-pasture regions as areas of in-migration and squatter settlement. Some medieval hunting forests were opened up for colonisation as late as the sixteenth century; but these internal frontiers were few in number and limited in extent.[14] Although there were variations in agriculture with an emphasis on cereal production in the more fertile Lowland areas and a greater concentration on livestock rearing in the uplands there was probably less regional variation in Scottish agriculture than in many European countries.[15] The tenurial status of much rough pasture in Scotland effectively prevented the development of fringes of squatter

[9] F. Braudel, *The Mediterranean and the Mediterranean world*, vol. 1 (1972): 44–7.

[10] Smout (1963): 3.

[11] I.D. Whyte, *Agriculture and society* (1979): 85–6, 234–42.

[12] A.J. Youngson, *After the Forty-Five* (1973): 11–12.

[13] J. Thirsk, *Agrarian history of England and Wales* (1967): 1–112; O. Hufton, *The poor of eighteenth-century France* (1974): 69–88; L.M. Cullen, *The emergence of modern Ireland* (1981): 91–2, 111.

[14] R.A. Dodgshon, *Land and society* (1981): 178–80; J.M. Gilbert, *Hunting reserves in medieval Scotland* (1979).

[15] Whyte (1979): 19–22.

settlement which could absorb surplus manpower from the more populous Lowlands. A good deal of rough pasture was held as commonty, in shared ownership between two or more proprietors.[16] Under this system the rights of proprietors could only be maintained with the land in stinted pasture. Encroachment for cultivation by squatters infringed the heritors' collective rights and was vigorously resisted. This helps to explain why upland regions with concentrations of rural industry never developed in Scotland as they did in the Pennines or Switzerland. Dodgshon has shown that there were broad regional differences in average holding sizes in seventeenth-century Scotland; holdings were smaller in the North East, increasing in size southwards towards the Lothians and the Merse. They were smaller again in the western Lowlands.[17] This must have produced differences in the social structures of communities; in the proportion of tenants, cottars, farm servants and landless labourers and also in the hierarchy of tenant farmers. It is unlikely, however, that such contrasts led to marked patterns of mobility due to movements those in search of land as did the contrasts between champion and wood pasture areas in England. In Scotland, holding structure was a matter of landlord policy, and excessive subdivision due to population pressure does not appear to have been countenanced before the advent of crofting in the north-west Highlands at the end of the eighteenth century in the way in which it sometimes occurred in Ireland.[18] On the other hand the maintenance until the later eighteenth century of the cottar system, whereby much of the extra-family labour on tenanted farms was provided not by landless labourers but by cottars who sublet small shares of the arable and grazing in return for providing regular or seasonal assistance, meant that access to land, albeit in a modest way, was fairly general.

CONTROLS ON MOBILITY: DEMOGRAPHIC, SOCIAL AND INSTITUTIONAL

Population levels and their relation to resources were an important influence on mobility in pre-industrial Europe though the link between demographic growth and mobility could operate in different ways. In England population growth in the sixteenth and early seventeenth centuries caused poverty and increasing vagrancy.[19] In Ireland, however, it has been suggested that population growth in the seventeenth and eighteenth centuries decreased internal mobility by making it harder for families to move and take up new land in other areas.[20] Unfortunately, we

[16] I.H. Adams, 'Division of commonty' (1967). [17] Dodgshon (1981):214–17.
[18] Cullen (1981):89–91.
[19] J. Pound, *Poverty and vagrancy* (1971). [20] Cullen (1981):89–91.

know little about demographic trends in Scotland in the sixteenth and seventeenth centuries. There are certainly indications of a substantial rise in population;[21] Edinburgh doubled in size during the century after 1540, particularly after the plague of 1584.[22] Much of this growth is likely to have been generated by migration from the countryside, suggesting a build-up of rural population. The same period witnessed the large-scale emigration of Scots to the continent as traders and mercenaries,[23] and to Ulster.[24] It also saw increasing stress on problems of poverty and vagrancy at home.

These indications suggest a growing population pressing on limited resources with growing involuntary mobility among the poorer elements of society. To a greater extent than in England the effects of secular population growth in Scotland seem to have been checked by periodic subsistence crises and, particularly in the seventeenth century, by emigration.[25] There are some indications that the Highlands may have had a separate demographic regime from the Lowlands, with a relatively steady build-up of population from the early seventeenth to the later eighteenth century. In the Lowlands, population growth may have levelled off in the mid-seventeenth century due partly to the famine of 1623, the epidemics of the 1640s, and continued emigration,[26] but there may have been some renewed build-up before the onset of the famine of the late 1690s as vagrancy appears to have been on the increase once more.[27] Mortality and emigration due to this crisis checked population growth abruptly; recovery was so slow that the population enumerated by Webster in 1755 may not have been much greater than that of the early 1690s.[28] The continuation of major subsistence crises down to the end of the seventeenth century in the Lowlands and later in the Highlands suggests that the kind of mobility termed by Clark 'subsistence migration' persisted longer than in England.[29] Clark has shown that in England the operation of the Poor Laws, and restrictions on settlement culminating in the Settlement Act of 1662, which may merely have institutionalised changes already occurring in society, helped to reduce long-distance migration from the late sixteenth to the late seventeenth century.[30] On the other hand landlord control over population movement and settlement in England could be patchy as the distinction between open and closed rural parishes emphasises.[31] In Scotland the power of landlords to control population on their estates through tenancy and the operation of baron courts, and at a parish level as

[21] M.P. Maxwell, *Scottish migration to Ulster* (1973): 26–7.
[22] M. Lynch, *Edinburgh and the Reformation* (1981): 3.
[23] G. Donaldson, *The Scots overseas* (1966): 30–3.
[24] Maxwell (1973).
[25] Flinn (1977): 4–8.
[26] *Ibid.*, 116–49.
[27] This is suggested by the growing vagrancy problem in Edinburgh during the 1670s and 1680s. Wood, (1950): 250, 268, 381; H. Armet, *The burgh of Edinburgh 1681–89* (1954): xlviii.
[28] Flinn (1977): 13.
[29] P. Clark, 'The migrant in Kentish towns' (1972): 117–63.
[30] Clark (1979).
[31] B.A. Holderness, *Pre-industrial England* (1976): 49.

kirk session elders, was considerable. As Mitchison has shown, the original Scottish Poor Law was modelled on that of England but developed differently, particularly in its failure to provide relief for the able-bodied but unemployed poor.[32] Poor relief was undertaken by individual kirk sessions and the lack of effective central control meant that considerable differences could exist in the ways in which parishes organised relief and the scale of charity provided, even at the end of the seventeenth century. Whether this produced local drifting of vagrants from stricter towards more generous parishes remains to be demonstrated. Between the sixteenth and the early eighteenth century, and in some measure even later, Scotland was characterised by a fluid group of begging poor, always substantial but liable to increase dramatically during crisis years such as 1623 and the later 1690s. In Scotland, population mobility is likely to have been encouraged by the inability of central authorities to make legislation against vagrancy stick and by the fact that many kirk sessions provided some charity to non-resident paupers. The lack of strictly-enforced settlement laws also encouraged mobility.

The most effective controls on population movement were local rather than national. Kirk sessions issued testimonials certifying the good conduct of individuals, without which they might not have been permitted to settle in another parish.[33] However, the variability of survival of testimonials among kirk session records may indicate that the operation of the system was patchy and that movements without certificates was possible. Some landowners passed acts in their baron courts prohibiting the settling of new cottars or the sheltering of strangers without permission.[34] This might suggest draconian local control over population movements but some instances clearly relate to crises, such as the later 1690s, when there were unusual numbers of people on the roads and parish poor relief was stretched trying to meet the needs of resident poor.

Some groups such as coal and salt workers had their mobility restricted legally by a form of serfdom. Burgh councils sometimes tried to control the movement of labour, particularly at harvest time. In 1680, for example, the burgh authorities of Peebles were concerned at the potential shortage of labour for harvesting on the burgh's own lands due to inhabitants going as far as the Lothians to help with the harvest.[35] The legislation against vagrants was probably more strictly applied in the towns, particularly Edinburgh where the authorities were under the eye of the Privy Council, though they could lodge in suburbs outside the burgh limits.[36] Neverthe-

[32] R. Mitchison, 'The old Scottish poor law' (1974):58–93.

[33] R.A. Houston, 'Geographical mobility in Scotland' (1985b):379–94.

[34] E.g. Scottish Record Office (SRO) Clerk of Penicuik muniments GD 18/695 Lasswade court book, 1696.

[35] *The burgh of Peebles 1652–1714* (1910):98–9.

[36] H. Armet, *The burgh of Edinburgh 1689–1701* (1962):85, 100, 106, 133, 154.

less, the frequency with which Edinburgh's burgh council issued proclamations requiring non-resident beggars to remove from the city on pain of whipping or imprisonment suggests that these measures had little effect. Overall official attempts to control population movements, and in particular vagrancy, whether at a national or more local scale, appear to have had limited success and there were probably fewer effective institutional constraints to geographical mobility than in England.

RURAL–URBAN MIGRATION

Rural–urban migration was an important element in population mobility in early modern Western Europe. As average death rates in capital cities and larger provincial towns were higher than in rural areas, a constant influx from the countryside was required to maintain urban populations and allow for growth. Two broad categories of migrant to pre-industrial towns have been defined by Clark: betterment migrants who were generally young, single and upwardly mobile, and subsistence migrants, motivated by influences driving them out of the countryside as much as the positive attractions of the towns.[37] These groups can be distinguished in pre-industrial Scottish towns though not always with clarity. Together they produced a pattern in which, against a background of steady in-migration, the larger towns experienced surges of incomers motivated by both push and pull factors. Down to the 1640s, epidemic diseases, particularly bubonic plague, could kill a substantial proportion of a town's population in a single season. In Edinburgh the outbreaks of plague in 1644–5 are estimated to have taken 9,000–12,000 lives, some 25–33 per cent of the population.[38] Such disasters were commonly followed by waves of migrants seeking opportunities. Apprenticeship migration to Edinburgh in the aftermath of the 1644–5 epidemics was almost three times the level for the previous few years.[39] On the other hand, dearth in the countryside could cause rural dwellers to flood into the towns in search of food and charity. This section will focus on the 'betterment' type of migrant, 'subsistence' migrants being considered below, see pp. 54–7.

It has been suggested that Scotland was lightly urbanised in the sixteenth and seventeenth centuries, and compared with many parts of Europe this was true.[40] De Vries has shown, however, that by 1600 the proportion of Scotland's population living in the larger towns exceeded that of Scandinavia, Switzerland and most of Eastern Europe.[41] By 1700 Scotland was more highly urbanised than Germany and by 1750, France.

37 Clark (1972). 38 Flinn (1977): 147.
39 F.J. Grant, *Register of apprentices of the city of Edinburgh* (1906).
40 G. Gordon & B. Dicks, *Scottish urban history* (1983): 1.
41 J. de Vries, *European urbanisation* (1984): 39; E.A. Wrigley, 'Urban growth and agricultural change' (1985): 683–728.

The proportion of Scotland's population living in the larger towns nearly doubled from a very low level between 1500 and 1600, and doubled again between 1600 and 1700, a rate which was twice that of England. By the end of the eighteenth century Scotland was one of the most urbanised societies in Europe. Much of this growth must have been generated by sustained migration, surely one of the most important influences on economic development and social change in Scotland in the seventeenth and eighteenth centuries. Scotland's urban hierarchy contrasted with that of England. At the end of the seventeenth century Edinburgh held less than 5.0 per cent of Scotland's population while London had 10.6 per cent of England's, but Scotland had a higher proportion of her population living in other towns with over 10,000 inhabitants,[42] a situation more comparable with France where provincial cities were larger and more independent than in England. In some respects Scotland's urban hierarchy resembled that of England minus London. One might thus expect there to have been marked regional patterns of movement into Scotland's main provincial centres with Edinburgh playing less of a national role than London.

Migration into Scotland's major towns can be studied using various sources. Apprenticeship records are available for many Scottish burghs. Apprenticeship migration was not a surrogate for all urban in-migration but it may have been representative of the movement of young, single people who formed the most dynamic component of the migration stream.[43] Analysis of apprenticeship migration to Edinburgh in the seventeenth and eighteenth centuries has shown that the capital did have a national apprenticeship migration field, drawing recruits from every part of Scotland.[44] There was a marked distance decay effect with a high proportion of migrants originating from areas close to the city. Numbers of migrant apprentices were greatest from source areas with high population levels but dropped with increasing distance from Edinburgh. Additional factors distorted the migration field so that when the effects of population and distance are allowed for, certain areas sent more or fewer migrants than predicted. In the late seventeenth century most of south-east and central Scotland sent more apprentices to Edinburgh than predicted, as did Aberdeenshire, while Fife, Perthshire, Angus and Kincardineshire sent fewer. Fife and the Tayside lowlands contained many burghs offering local opportunities to prospective apprentices, but the pull of Glasgow was not yet strong enough to check the flow of apprentices to Edinburgh from west-central Scotland. High levels of migration from the south-east probably relate to the lack of other large urban centres in this area while those

[42] de Vries (1984):39.

[43] J. Patten, 'Movement of labour to three pre-industrial East Anglian towns' (1976):114.

[44] A.A. Lovett, I.D. Whyte & K.A. Whyte, 'Poisson regression analysis and migration fields' (1985):317–32.

from Aberdeenshire may be explained by contacts generated through coastal trade.

During the eighteenth century, Edinburgh's apprenticeship migration field contracted in an irregular fashion. There was a fall in the proportion of apprentices drawn from south-west and west-central Scotland, Argyll and Bute and the Borders. Migration from Fife, Angus and Kincardineshire remained low. On the other hand migration from Highland Perthshire, Inverness, Ross, the Moray Firth, Caithness and Shetland was higher than expected. The reduced flow of apprentices from west-central Scotland and the south-west Highlands was probably due to the rise of Glasgow and other urban centres in the western Lowlands. The drop in migrants from the Borders may reflect increasing contact with England after 1707 and the growing attractiveness of Tyneside for Scottish workers.[45] On the other hand, as the Highlands became more integrated with the rest of Scotland, migration from this region to Edinburgh grew. Edinburgh's role as the centre of east-coast trade and the business contacts which this generated may help explain the high levels of migration from the Moray Firth and beyond. The differential contraction of Edinburgh's migration field due to the growing importance of other urban centres parallels that of London at an earlier date.[46]

The changing pattern of apprenticeship migration to Glasgow complements that of Edinburgh.[47] In the seventeenth century, Glasgow drew apprentices from a limited area. Lanark, Renfrew and Dumbartonshire accounted for 77 per cent of migrant apprentices between 1625 and 1649. Few apprentices came from Ayrshire, Galloway or the Highlands. From about the 1730s there was a widening of the recruitment area largely due to an increase in apprentices from the Highlands. By the mid-eighteenth century Argyll was supplying 22 per cent of Glasgow's migrant apprentice tailors compared with under 3 per cent at the start of the century. At the same time the city's pull increased eastwards, drawing more apprentices from Stirlingshire and Perthshire. By the end of the century, apprentice tailors were also being recruited from more distant counties like Inverness, Ross, Sutherland and Caithness. By contrast apprenticeship migration into Aberdeen and Inverness remained remarkably stable.[48] These two burghs dominated lightly urbanised regions with no real competing centres. Seventy-five 75 per cent of migrants to each town were drawn from

[45] R.A. Houston, 'Aspects of society in Scotland and north-eastern England c.1550–c.1750' (1981):93.

[46] J. Wareing, 'Recruitment of apprentices to the London companies, 1486–1750' (1980):241–9.

[47] The information on migration to Glasgow is based on an analysis of 2,000 records from various trades incorporations in the Strathclyde Regional Archives. I am extremely grateful to Mr R. Dell, the chief archivist, for making available a set of transcripts of seventeenth-century apprenticeship origins.

[48] I.D. Whyte & K.A. Whyte, 'Migration of apprentices to Aberdeen and Inverness' (1986).

with a 40 kilometre radius. Aberdeen's migration field did, however, become increasingly curtailed to the south, probably due to the growing pull of Dundee.

It would be a mistake to consider apprenticeship migration fields as completely homogeneous. As Houston has shown, apprentices to Edinburgh merchants mostly came from landed backgrounds as did those of goldsmiths and surgeons.[49] Apprentices to lower-status trades were more likely to be drawn from craft or tenant backgrounds. There were close links between guild status, the social origins of apprentices, and the average distance migrated. Recruits to higher-status guilds were drawn from a wider area than those coming into lower-status ones.

Marriage registers are useful for examining female migration to Scottish towns. The format of some Scottish urban registers allows analysis of the movement of women before as well as at marriage. Where a woman lived in a town when the banns of marriage were proclaimed but her father was recorded as living elsewhere, then a migratory move had probably been made before, rather than at, marriage. With irregular marriages, the period of residence in the town prior to marriage may have been brief. In most instances, however, the move is likely to have been made some time before marriage for the purposes of employment. As with virtually all sources only one move is recorded. One cannot assume that a single move between home and town had always been made or that the father's parish of residence was invariably that of his daughter's birth, but in a high proportion of cases this was probably so. Where the residence of a woman was given as being with her father in a parish outside the town then presumably migration took place at rather than before marriage. In such cases the contact leading to marriage may have arisen in various ways. The groom may originally have come from the bride's place of residence, and maintained contact after migrating to the town. Alternatively, the bride may have lived in the town, met her marriage partner there, and then returned home. A third possibility is that contact was made during regular trips into or out of the town by one of the partners; to attend markets for instance. This last form of contact would involve a more local field of activity corresponding to the 'marriage distances' of previous studies, and would tend to reduce the average distance migrated by women in this class compared with those migrating before marriage.

The scope of such detailed marriage registers for migration studies can be illustrated by the case of eighteenth-century Edinburgh.[50] For all categories of women there was a widening of the migration field during the eighteenth century, in contrast with the contraction for apprenticeship migration, and with the trend for English towns at this period. Women

[49] Houston (1981): 277–9.
[50] Scottish Record Society, *Register of marriages of the city of Edinburgh* (1926).

moving to Edinburgh before marriage, many of them probably as domestic servants, tended to come from further afield than apprentices. There was a clear difference in the migration fields of women moving to Edinburgh before and at marriage, the latter migrating over shorter distances on average. Many marriages in the latter group were probably generated by everyday contacts between the inhabitants of the city and its immediate hinterland.

There were marked changes in the pattern of female migration to Edinburgh during the eighteenth century. There was a steady increase in the numbers of women from England who moved to Edinburgh. In the first decade of the eighteenth century women migrating before marriage from English origins accounted for only 0.4 per cent of the total whose origins were recorded. By 1780–9 the figure had risen to 4.6 per cent. The most important origins were Northumberland (1.6 per cent) and London (1.2 per cent); the remainder of the origins were dispersed throughout England. This shows that growing contact with England after 1707 was generating population flows in both directions, many of the girls moving to Edinburgh probably being the daughters of Scottish expatriates. Within Scotland the proportion of women migrating from the Lothians and Fife remained stable while migration from the Borders did not fall as drastically as for apprentices. This may have been due to the continuing high demand in Edinburgh for female domestic servants, while the industries of Tyneside would have attracted men rather than women. There was a fall in the proportion of female migrants from west-central Scotland. In relation to the growing population of this area this probably represents a significant relative decline. On the other hand the contribution of the Highlands increased dramatically. In 1700–9 only 1.2 per cent of girls migrating to Edinburgh before marriage came from the Highlands but this rose to 11.6 per cent by the 1780s. Edinburgh was a focal point for the hiring of Highland workers for the Lothian harvest,[51] and it is likely that a proportion of Highland girls on temporary visits would have met and married partners in the capital. The Highlands may also have been a good source of cheap female servants. A similar, if scaled down, pattern is discernible for the small manufacturing centre of Kilmarnock in the mid eighteenth century. Sixty-three per cent of female migrants before marriage came from within twenty-two kilometres of the burgh but fifteen per cent had travelled more than eighty kilometres including one or two individuals who had come from as far afield as Aberdeen, East Lothian and Ross-shire.[52] Further work of this kind may reveal the pattern of movements into other Scottish towns, identifying local migration fields and their evolution through time.

[51] W. Howatson, 'The Scottish hairst' (1982): 17.

[52] GRO OPR 597.

Even where urban marriage registers do not record pre-marriage migration, patterns of marriage distances, the distances between parishes of residence of brides and grooms at the time of marriage, are useful general indicators of mobility.[53] They have the advantage of including people at all social levels and, as Scottish registers usually record the proclamation of banns rather than the marriage itself, they list brides moving out of a parish at marriage as well as those moving in. A study of marriage distances for the three East Lothian burghs of Haddington, Musselburgh and Prestonpans show a distinct tendency for the mean marriage distance to increase between the seventeenth and late eighteenth centuries.[54] In the case of Prestonpans the average distance migrated at marriage almost trebled between the early seventeenth and late eighteenth centuries, probably as a result of the emancipation of the coal and salt workers who formed a substantial proportion of the population.[55] Although mean distances migrated at marriage increased significantly for all three towns, median distances did not change greatly indicating that patterns of marriage mobility for the bulk of the population did not change greatly while there was a significant increase in long-distance marriage contacts among a limited social group; generally speaking, the professional and middle classes. A study of levels of marriage endogamy in Kilmarnock, whose marriage register consistently gives occupational data for much of the eighteenth century, emphasises the contrasts which existed between different social groups. Among higher-status groups, like merchants and maltmen, with a smaller pool of potential partners available locally, around a third of marriages involved brides from outside the parish. By contrast the figure for a low-status occupation like a collier was only five per cent.[56]

Overall the pattern of migration into Scottish towns during the seventeenth and eighteenth centuries matches that for contemporary England.[57] There was a good deal of long-distance migration to Edinburgh which tended to increase during the later eighteenth century with a growing influx of Highlanders though, as with English towns during the seventeenth and eighteenth centuries, there was a contraction in the migration fields of some groups such as apprentices due to the rise of competing centres. Other Scottish towns tended to have more markedly regional patterns of recruitment.[58]

[53] J. Millard, 'Marriage horizons' (1982): 10–31; P.E. Ogden, 'The collapse of traditional peasant society in France' (1980): 152–79.

[54] GRO OPR 705, 709, 718. [55] Smout (1972): 168–70. [56] GRO OPR 597.

[57] J. Patten, *English towns 1500–1700* (1978): 125–45.

[58] Continuity into the nineteenth century is shown by C.W.J. Withers, 'Highland migration' (1985): 295–318.

POPULATION MOBILITY WITHIN THE COUNTRYSIDE

While migration to the towns was increasingly important in Scotland during early modern times, movements within the countryside were far more significant in total. The basic features of rural population mobility have been considered by Houston in a study based on testimonials, certificates of good moral conduct issued by kirk sessions.[59] He showed that levels of rural population mobility were high, and that much of the movement was over short distances, a characteristic also identified in Lockhart's study of movement into planned villages.[60] Much of the turnover was due to the frequent movement of farm servants, producing peaks of migration around the hiring times of Whitsunday and Martinmas. Tradesmen (many of whom may have been cottars) were also a mobile group with tenants being less migratory. Women were more mobile than men overall. Around three-quarters of the migrants travelled less than ten kilometres. There were indications of an increase in the average distances travelled from the seventeenth to the later eighteenth centuries, particularly into parishes containing or adjacent to towns, but the testimonials did not allow rates of mobility to be estimated. The parallels with patterns which have been demonstrated for contemporary England are striking. It is not clear though whether the turnover rates in Scottish communities were as high as in England or lower like in parts of France or Germany. More research at a local level is necessary to establish this. This section explores the background to the patterns established by Houston and others, highlighting some influences on the mobility of different social groups.

In the past, emphasis has been laid on the insecurity of Scottish tenants under systems of short leases or year-to-year agreements.[61] If this did cause insecurity one might expect the tenantry to have been fairly mobile. This relationship has been suggested for Ireland though Cullen also stresses the importance of poverty and lack of resources in encouraging tenant mobility.[62] Yet if any group in Scottish rural society should have been stable it should have been the one which actually farmed the land and, as in Ireland, one would expect the larger farmers to have been less mobile than the smaller ones.[63]

Despite the prevalence of short leases in Scotland there is evidence that during the seventeenth century proprietors often had paternalistic attitudes towards tenancy, allowing families to continue in occupation from one generation to another. Tenants who could not meet their full

59 Houston (1985b). 60 D.G. Lockhart, 'Migration to estate villages' (1980): 35–43.
61 J.E. Handley, *Scottish farming in the eighteenth century* (1953): 120.
62 Cullen (1981): 90–1.
63 *Ibid.*

rents were often given considerable latitude. Eviction for non-payment of rent did occur but does not seem to have been particularly common. There is no case for assuming that short leases in themselves necessarily caused high levels of turnover among tenants.[64]

Tenants are the best recorded group in Scottish rural society in the seventeenth and eighteenth centuries as they figure prominently in estate papers. There is plenty of scope for detailed community studies using leases, accounts and rentals in conjunction with other sources such as testaments, kirk session records and parish registers.[65] Tenant mobility on the estates of the Earls of Panmure in Angus has been studied in depth in this way.[66] There were two distinct groups of tenants, stayers and movers. Nearly a fifth of the tenants occupied the same holdings for twenty years or more; holdings often passed from father to son, or from a tenant to his widow and then to a son. On the other hand 37 per cent of the tenants appear in the estate records for five years or less. Some may have left the estate, some must have died. Others may have moved downwards to the ranks of the cottars.

Movements of tenants from farm to farm within the estate can also be detected from the rentals. Between 1660 and 1710 only 16 per cent moved in this way. Most moves were over very short distances, usually to a neighbouring farm: 76 per cent were under 5 km, 54 per cent under 3 km. The farm structures at Panmure and on many other Lowland estates often allowed tenants to alter the amount of land which they worked without migrating. On multiple-tenant farms a tenant could increase or decrease the size of his share. Another option was multiple leasing, taking two holdings on neighbouring farms. Such non-migratory adjustments formed the majority of changes in holding size. This may indicate a desire to minimise risk. Such changes involved expanding from a base of land whose qualities were known and working with familiar neighbours. A move to another farm might increase the risk of failure by requiring the tenant to work unfamiliar land in co-operation with new neighbours.

Further aspects of tenant mobility can be examined by comparing estate records with other sources. For the Panmure barony of Downie only 28 per cent of tenants entering holdings between 1670 and 1714 appeared in the baptism register at an earlier date. However, 40 per cent of tenants taking on larger holdings had been baptised in the parish against only 21 per cent of smallholders and 20 per cent of cottars. This

[64] Whyte (1979): 152–62; I.D. Whyte & K.A. Whyte, 'Continuity and change in a seventeenth-century Scottish farming community' (1984a): 159–69.

[65] I.D. Whyte & K.A. Whyte, 'Mobility in a seventeenth-century Scottish rural community' (1984b): 45–53.

[66] Whyte & Whyte, 'Continuity and change' (1984a).

suggests that tenants of larger holdings formed a more stable group on these estates, and that smaller tenants and cottars were more mobile.

Another aspect of tenant mobility is the turnover rates of holdings through time. One might expect that during major subsistence crises starving tenants would abandon their farms and take to the roads. This did occur under extreme conditions; in the interior of the North East during the later 1690s and perhaps more generally in 1623. If a crisis was less severe, however, it could slow down turnover. At Panmure there was a lower turnover of holdings during the later 1690s than in the years before. Under such circumstances there may have been nowhere else for the tenants to go. Proprietors and estate officers would have been unlikely to evict tenants who could not pay their rents when there was little chance of finding suitable replacements, or of recovering the arrears of the evicted farmers.

An interesting set of relationships which has yet to be explored concerns the links between mobility and inheritance strategies among the farming population. Given that tenants were effectively excluded from the land market, what strategies did they adopt for setting up their children and how did this affect mobility? At Panmure it was not uncommon for son to follow father in the same holding but another option was for a tenant to set up his son elsewhere on the estate. In one important respect this differed from the strategies practised by English yeomen. Without a peasant land market tenants had no control over the availability of land for setting up their children. The farm structure of an estate was determined by the proprietor and his administration and while there was some flexibility, excessive subdivision to accommodate the sons of tenants with limited resources does not appear to have been practised. Indeed, in the later seventeenth and early eighteenth centuries the trend was towards holding amalgamation, creating fewer large units.[67] Wills suggest that while efforts were made to provide small portions for younger sons and daughters most of the value of the farm stock and often the holding itself went to one son, presumably the eldest in most cases.[68] While some younger sons may have stayed at home and helped to work the family holding there is little evidence of this in the poll tax lists of the 1690s.[69] Many tenants' sons must have been unable to become established locally on a holding. Some may have stayed as cottars and tradesmen, others may have left to form part of the flow of migrants to the towns. The mobility of cottars may often have been

67 Whyte (1979): 137–45.

68 I.D. Whyte & K.A. Whyte, 'Poverty and prosperity in a seventeenth-century Scottish farming community' (1988).

69 The poll tax returns for Aberdeenshire and Renfrewshire have been published: J. Stuart (ed.), *List of pollable persons within the shire of Aberdeen* (1844); D. Semple (ed.), *Renfrewshire poll tax returns* (Paisley, 1864).

linked with that of tenants. Leases frequently stipulated that when a tenant left his holding his cottars and subtenants should move with him.[70] On the other hand cottars were also free agents; the large number of cottarages, the limited possessions and livestock of most cottars, and the flexibility provided by the trades which many of them practised, may have made mobility easier than for many tenants. Cottars are less well documented than tenants. At Panmure, however, the register of Monikie parish allows some Panmure cottars to be identified, and aspects of their mobility to be studied.[71] From 1703 to 1714 the proportion of cottars moving within the barony (24 per cent) was higher than that of tenants (15 per cent). The cottars were not uniformly mobile though; there seem to have been two groups of mobile and stable men as with the tenants.

Lowland Scotland was similar to England in that a high proportion of young, single men and women in rural areas left home in their teens to work as farm and domestic servants in other households. Until more detailed local studies are undertaken it is unclear whether Scottish servants left home at similar ages to their English counterparts or were younger. The origins of this system in England go back to late medieval times at least.[72] In Scotland farm servants were too numerous in the sixteenth century for this group not to have existed at an earlier date. Farm servants are also poorly documented; they do not appear in estate records or parish registers and, aside from cases of fornication in kirk session registers, they are more often referred to in general terms in the records of Justices of the Peace. Farm servants were common in Orkney, Shetland and the Hebrides in the seventeenth century[73] and presumably must have existed in other parts of the Highlands but it is not clear whether systems of hiring and mobility in these areas were comparable with the Lowlands. They were more frequent in lowland arable areas than in the pastoral uplands of southern Scotland. In Lowland Scotland, farm servants normally hired themselves out for a year, as in England and, as Houston has shown, they commonly moved from one master to another, though usually over limited distances.[74] This is directly comparable with Kussmaul's findings for English farm servants.[75]

It is important to note, however, that by the later eighteenth century farm service was in decline over much of southern England, giving way to the use of day labourers, while the system was maintained in slightly modified forms in Scotland and northern England.[76] The persistence of long-hire systems of labour in Scotland, with a change of employment

[70] For a published example see C.S. Romanes, *Melrose regality records*, vol. 1 (1914): 133.
[71] Whyte & Whyte (1984b).
[72] A. Kussmaul, *Servants in husbandry* (1981).
[73] F.J. Shaw, *The northern and western islands of Scotland* (1981): 191–2.
[74] Houston (1985b): 384–5. [75] Kussmaul (1981): 49–68.
[76] T.M. Devine (ed.), *Farm servants and labour in Lowland Scotland* (1984b).

normally occurring at the end of the contract, may have maintained rural population mobility at higher levels than in many parts of rural England remote from the attractions of the growing industrial centres.

Much less information is available concerning mobility within the Highlands. Emphasis has been placed on the marked cultural differences which existed between the Highlands and the Lowlands into the eighteenth century, and on the conservative and reactionary character of Highland society.[77] The much discussed but little researched structure of clan society with its stress on kinship and inter-clan hostility does not appear conducive to geographical mobility, and might lead one to suppose that levels of mobility were low until the sometimes traumatic changes which followed the 1745 rebellion.[78] On this basis the rise of large-scale temporary and permanent migration from the area (see below) can be interpreted as a late eighteenth-century phenomenon caused by the belated integration of this region into the capitalist economy of the rest of Britain.

For the Highlands, the poor quality or total lack of many of the sources which shed light on population mobility in the Lowlands prior to the later eighteenth century makes the testing of these assumptions difficult. It has not, however, been demonstrated convincingly that levels of mobility were significantly lower in the Highlands than the Lowlands between the sixteenth and mid-eighteenth centuries and there are certainly pointers which suggest that mobility there was greater than has sometimes been supposed. Regular contacts between the West Highlands and Ulster, and trade with the Lowlands are important features of the seventeenth century.[79] Moreover, Lenman has pointed out that inter-clan violence diminished markedly during the later seventeenth and early eighteenth centuries and that there was less homogeneity of surnames among the lower levels of clan society than has often been supposed, suggesting that Highland society was not as tightly compartmentalised as has sometimes been portrayed and that a good deal of mobility did occur.[80] Macpherson's study of marriage patterns in the parish of Laggan from late-medieval times indicated that persistent directional patterns of marriage contact existed.[81] There was relatively little contact southwards with Perthshire, or the south-west Highlands, to the east or north of the Great Glen, and none into the Lowlands. Instead, contacts were channelled down the Spey valley. This pattern remained stable until the early nineteenth century and Macpherson suggested that the directional focus may have been tied to economic linkages with the Moray Firth lowlands such as the taking in of

[77] Smout (1972): 39–46.
[78] R.E. Ommer, 'Primitive accumulation and the Scottish *clann*' (1986).
[79] B.P. Lenman, *The Jacobite clans* (1984b): 17–27. [80] *Ibid.*, 7, 26.
[81] A.G. Macpherson, 'Migration fields in a traditional Highland community' (1984): 1–14.

lowland cattle to the summer shielings and the purchase of grain from coastal arable areas.

Studies of population mobility in England have indicated that the marriage horizons of lower status groups such as farm labourers were more limited than those of wealthier farmers. Such contrasts existed in Scotland too. In Monikie parish in Angus, tenants were far more likely to choose partners from outside their parish of residence than were cottars.[82] With tenants, the local pool of prospective brides of similar status would have been more limited while the importance of a girl's dowry in allowing the married couple to set up on a holding of their own may also have made the choice of partner a matter requiring more care.

POVERTY, VAGRANCY AND SUBSISTENCE MIGRATION

Most visitors to Scotland in the sixteenth and seventeenth centuries who recorded their impression commented on the country's poverty.[83] A notable feature is the persistence of major subsistence crises. Southern England was free of such crises from the end of the sixteenth century, and the north from the 1620s. Scotland experienced a national crisis in the later 1690s and the Highlands continued to suffer periodic, albeit attenuated, famine throughout the eighteenth century, notably in 1782.[84] It is probable that as in France a combination of small holdings, inefficient farming systems and the lack of integrated national markets in basic foodstuffs combined in Scotland with more marginal climatic conditions for cereal cultivation, helped to put the population at risk. The reserves of many farmers were comparatively slender, suggesting that smaller tenants must have lived their lives on the verge of poverty, terribly vulnerable to the effects of even a single poor harvest.[85]

If poor relief had been as generous as in England poverty and potential starvation might have been reduced but the relief provided to resident poor by most kirk sessions was designed as a supplement rather than a full support.[86] Mitchison's study of East Lothian parishes during the 1690s shows that while some kirk sessions distributed their resources to maximum effect others restricted expenditure at the expense of letting their resident poor starve.[87] In such circumstances it is not surprising that during major subsistence crises people took to the roads in large numbers. One commentator estimated that the numbers of begging poor doubled to 200,000 during the later 1690s.[88] The figures are dubious but the scale of

[82] Whyte & Whyte (1984b). [83] P.H. Brown (ed.), *Early travellers in Scotland* (1891).
[84] Flinn (1977): 234–5. [85] Whyte & Whyte (1988): 74–7.
[86] R.A. Cage, *The Scottish poor law, 1745–1845* (1981): chap. 1.
[87] Mitchison (1974): 76–80. [88] Flinn (1977): 170.

increase may be realistic. A severe crisis could set even substantial tenants on the roads. The result was dislocation in the countryside and an influx of poor into the towns. There are hints of this for Edinburgh in 1623, and more evidence from the 1690s when the burgh council set up a relief camp for vagrants in the Greyfriars churchyard.[89] Smaller towns experienced similar problems.[90] Superimposed on this was a general drift of the poor and unemployed to the towns which was probably most evident during periods of population pressure – the late sixteenth and early seventeenth century for instance – although foreign wars in the later seventeenth century may also have caused trade slumps forcing industrial workers on to the streets.[91] There are fewer indications of large-scale population movements of this kind in the Lowlands during the eighteenth century. Improvements in agricultural productivity, more effective administration of poor relief, and measures by landlords during years of shortage may have helped. Vagrants from the Highlands still filtered into the Lowlands though after years of dearth like 1740 and 1782.[92]

There was also a more perennial problem of vagrancy during the sixteenth and seventeenth centuries. As in Tudor England the authorities seemed obsessed with the problems of vagrancy and poverty, the former being viewed rather more seriously.[93] The Scottish legislation echoes that of England in considering the able-bodied poor who were capable of work as potential or actual vagabonds, a threat to social order, while reserving charity for the old and infirm. It is unlikely that as in England a rise of population, accompanied in the later sixteenth century by substantial inflation, lay behind the problem of vagrancy. Some of the underlying causes of poverty and vagrancy in England, such as depopulation due to engrossing and enclosure, may not have applied to Scotland. Others, such as the effects of industrial slumps may well have occurred in Scotland but have yet to be pinpointed. In England poverty diminished as agricultural productivity rose and population growth slackened in the later seventeenth century while more effective poor relief and controls on settlement helped to reduce vagrancy. It is not clear to what extent emigration and demographic checks such as the famine of 1623 and the epidemics of the 1640s improved the balance of population to resources in Scotland but vagrancy appears to have been growing again in the 1680s and early 1690s,[94] and despite the fall in population at the end of the century it continued to be a problem.

Beier has shown that in England there was a considerable difference between the official view of vagrants as a major threat to the state and

[89] *Ibid.*, 119–20; Armet (1962): 208–10, 213, 228. [90] *Peebles burgh records* (1910): 162.
[91] Flinn (1977)): 165–6. [92] *Ibid.*, 235.
[93] The legislation relating to poverty and vagrancy is reviewed in Cage (1981).
[94] Flinn (1977): 165–6.

reality.[95] The same was probably true in Scotland but there may have been more reason for the authorities there, and the population in general, to fear vagrants. In a country where the rural population was dispersed in small clusters and single dwellings, sorning – begging with menaces – could threaten small outlying communities. With so much sparsely settled upland and moorland, beggars could easily move around and congregate. Despite the popular image, it was unusual for vagrants in England to travel in large groups. In Scotland this may have been more common. During subsistence crises whole families were on the road but at other times bands of beggars are recorded.[96] Sometimes they could terrorise a whole district but such celebrated examples as the gipsy leader James Macpherson who was hanged in Banff in 1700 were probably rare.[97]

A detailed study of kirk session records would provide a clearer picture of vagrancy in Scotland. Those for Monikie parish show that 20 per cent of all payments between 1660 and 1710 were to groups of vagrants.[98] Of payments to individuals, 73 per cent were to men and 27 per cent to women, proportions which are comparable with the sex ratios of English vagrants. The kirk session register sometimes suggests why people were on the road. The most common reason was blindness or physical deformity, accounting for 40 per cent of payments to individuals where details were given, with sickness accounting for another 5 per cent. The next largest group (11 per cent) was those whose homes or possessions had been destroyed by fire. Some payments were made to people whose distress was clearly only temporary; shipwrecked sailors, discharged soldiers and victims of robbery. Such people may only have required assistance to return home. Despite the claims which have sometimes been made against rack renting, there were few bankrupt tenants. The remaining payments went to people whose designations indicate that they had formerly had some social status. Men designated as 'Mr', or 'gentleman', and women styled 'gentlewoman' made up 19 per cent of individual payments; former schoolmasters, ministers, doctors, merchants and burgesses another 9 per cent. Perhaps the decline in the fortunes of such people prompted particular generosity so that they are over-represented: perhaps there were some plausible rogues on the roads too, but a testament would normally have been required as proof of such status.

Beier has shown that the broad patterns of movement of vagrants in England were not random, but consisted of distinct directional flows from upland to lowland and from west to east.[99] The lack of data on origins of Scottish vagrants makes direct comparison difficult but there was certainly

[95] L. Beier, 'Vagrants and the social order in Elizabethan England' (1974):3–29.
[96] Flinn (1977):123–6.
[97] Smout (1972):206. [98] Whyte & Whyte (1984b).
[99] A.L. Beier, *Masterless men: the vagrancy problem in England 1560–1640* (1985):32–47.

a drift of vagrants from the Highlands to the Lowlands in the eighteenth century and probably earlier.[100] Beier noted, however, that many vagrants operated within a much more limited radius of their parish of origin.[101] In a similar way some of the vagrant poor recorded in Monikie were moving around a restricted area, possibly through a regular circuit of parishes.[102] For example, William Bouack, sometime schoolmaster at Forfar, appeared for several consecutive years, always at the same season, payments made to him being grouped between September and early October. William Lyell, variously described as 'poor man', and 'stranger' appeared once every summer for several years, generally in July. It is possible that in Scotland at this time movements of vagrants were more tied to the countryside where food of various kinds could have been more easily obtained than in the towns. The patterns described in Monikie parish may have been linked to seasonal rhythms in the market for casual labour. Where kirk session records are well kept for groups of contiguous parishes it may be possible to examine these suggestions in more detail.

THE RISE OF TEMPORARY MIGRATION

A feature of population mobility in Scotland during the eighteenth century was the rise of large-scale seasonal migration.[103] This has direct parallels with the development of movements of labour from upland to lowland areas in England and Ireland, as well as on the continent.[104] The seasonal migration of labour to help with the lowland harvest can be detected in the seventeenth century although the evidence is scanty.[105] The movement of workers from Tweeddale and other upland areas of the eastern Borders to the harvest in the Merse and the Lothians is recorded while there was also a movement of workers from the burghs to the surrounding countryside at harvest time.[106] During the eighteenth century, however, temporary migration from the Highlands became prominent. There are indications that some Highlanders were migrating to the Lowlands for the harvest in the late seventeenth century; some who sought temporary work in the Lowlands during the later 1690s refused to return home because conditions there were so bad.[107] Large-scale seasonal migration was, however, a phenomenon of the later eighteenth century.

The growing use of migrant labour in the Lowlands may have been linked to agricultural reorganisation with a gradual removal of cottars and

[100] Flinn (1977): 169. [101] Beier (1985): 70–2. [102] Whyte & Whyte (1984b).

[103] T.M. Devine, 'Highland migration to Lowland Scotland 1760–1860' (1983b): 137–49; Howatson (1982).

[104] E.J.T. Collins, 'Migrant labour in British agriculture' (1976): 38–59; Cullen, (1981): 91–2; Hufton, (1974): 69–115.

[105] Howatson (1982): 15–17. [106] *Peebles burgh records* (1910): 87, 98.

[107] Flinn (1977).

greater emphasis on trimming the full-time labour force on farms. By the end of the century seasonal migration was characteristic not so much of those parts of the Highlands which were adjacent to the Lowlands, where permanent out-migration was more common, but of the far north and west. In these areas steady population growth, a need for cash to meet rising rents, and the lack of alternative sources of employment at home provided the incentives which drove many Highland girls south to work in the harvest fields.[108]

CONCLUSION

Population mobility is a recurrent theme in the parish descriptions of the Old Statistical Account which were written during the 1790s. Superficially, much of the movement recorded there seems linked to recent changes in the economy; farm amalgamation and the reduction of cottar holdings were causing movement out of some rural parishes, while the creation of planned estate villages, often with concentrations of textile manufacture, were attracting people to others. The major manufacturing districts were drawing people from purely agricultural areas. However, this chapter has shown that there was comparatively little that was new in these patterns, except perhaps their scale. Some types of population mobility – subsistence migration and vagrancy – declined from the sixteenth century to the eighteenth, some such as seasonal migration increased. Others, such as urban in-migration and movement within the countryside were a constant theme; if they increased in the later eighteenth century there had nevertheless been considerable mobility in earlier times. The patterns which have been identified emphasise how closely Scotland's experience corresponded with England's and the rest of Western Europe's. Although quantitative data from the analysis of particular communities will be required to confirm it the picture so far suggests that population turnover in Scotland was probably closer to the high levels recorded in some English communities than the lower levels which have been found in France and Germany.

There is a need, however, for further work to establish some of the differences between Scotland's patterns of population mobility and those of her neighbours. The scale and nature of vagrancy and the characteristics of mobility in Highland society before the later eighteenth century would be especially worthy of further investigation, in particular whether the structure and operation of the clan system acted as a check to population mobility. Much of this chapter has considered mobility at a generalised level. There is considerable scope for further detailed work particularly local studies utilising a range of complementary sources. It is only through such local studies that the general patterns will be substantiated and regional and smaller-scale variations detected.

[108] Devine (1983b).

2

SCOTTISH FOOD AND SCOTTISH HISTORY, 1500–1800

A. GIBSON AND T.C. SMOUT

The purpose of this chapter is, firstly, to discuss a change in the nature of Scottish diet between the late Middle Ages and the mid-eighteenth century, a change which decreased the total consumption of animal-based foods per head and increased that of grain-based food. It is not our intention to present a detailed history of Scottish diet for the period in all its complexity nor to measure its nutritional adequacy: the latter task is one to which we shall return elsewhere.[1] Nor is it our intention to compare fully Scottish dietary experience with that of other countries and regions: that interesting work must be left to a time when there is wider agreement on methodology in analysing diets, more research on change in the long term and, above all, a stronger revival of interest in early modern dietary history in Scandinavia and England on the part of economic historians.[2]

The sources we have used for this part of the paper are as imperfect as time has left them. Before the seventeenth century they are almost entirely qualitative. For the seventeenth and eighteenth centuries they improve slightly, in so far as certain detailed diets have survived enabling a few quantitative analyses to be made of the food provided in selected institu-

[1] This is part of an investigation into prices, wages and the standard of living in Scotland 1580–1780, supported by the ESRC: we hope to present our main conclusions in a book. This chapter owes a great deal to the helpful criticisms and observations of many people. In particular we would like to thank the two editors of this collection of essays, and also Robert Dodgshon, Norman Macdougall, Sylvia Price, Gavin Sprott, David Stevenson and Lorna Weatherill.

[2] For recent studies of European diet, see e.g. *Annales: économies, sociétés, civilisations*, 30 (1975): a special number of 'Histoire de la consommation'; *Pour une histoire de l'alimentation*, receuil de travaux présentés par J.J. Hermardinquier, *Cahiers des Annales* no. 28, (1970); A. Wyczański, *La Consommation alimentaire en Pologne aux XVIe et XVIIe siècles* (1985); A. Fenton (ed.), *Food in perspective: proceedings of the Third International Conference on Ethnological Food Research* (1977); C. Shammas, 'Eighteenth-century English diet and economic change' (1984); C. Shammas, 'Food expenditures and economic well-being in early modern England' (1983). Shammas' work is the closest parallel in English history at the moment to the work of the *Annales* school, but papers presented at the regular seminar in food history at Kings College London have also dealt with various aspects of the early modern nutritional problem. For Scandinavia, see in particular M. Morell, 'Eli. F. Heckscher. The "Food Budgets" and Swedish food consumption from the sixteenth to the nineteenth century' (1987), which revises the pioneering estimates of E.F. Heckscher, *Sveriges Ekonomiska Historia från Gustav Vasa* (1935–49).

tions. We have disregarded, for these immediate purposes, the food set before the upper classes at court, on the top tables of noble households and at universities, since our focus is rather upon the experience of the commonality. Most of the evidence, therefore, for all periods, is necessarily treated by the traditional methodology of piling example upon example, of considering the evidence of travellers, the observations of contemporaries and gleanings from other primary sources. Our conclusions, however, are fully borne out by our quantitative examples, wherever quantification has been possible.

The second purpose of the paper is to speculate on the underlying causes of these changes and to relate them to changes in the Scottish economy, particularly in the history of internal trade. Our argument, then, will first attempt to demonstrate that there was a change from a situation in which a large number of the Scottish population ate quantities of meat, cheese, butter and milk in their diet, to one in which most people tasted animal-derived foodstuffs relatively seldom apart from broths and perhaps milk. Oatmeal became overwhelmingly dominant in diet, ultimately supplemented by potatoes. Such an alteration can only be seen as a deterioration in the quality of life, for European peoples have always shown a marked preference for meat over farinaceous food when given the option, and rises or falls in the consumption of meat are always regarded as significant evidence of alterations in the standard of living in the controversies over nineteenth-century welfare.[3] Moreover, food has comprised much of the standard of living until very recent times. Even as late as 1957 the average British household spent a third of its annual income on food.[4] Scottish data for the mid-nineteenth century would suggest that 50 per cent of income spent on food was then nearer the working-class norm. French evidence for the seventeenth century suggests that 80 per cent (after rent and taxes are subtracted) was spent on food and the famous 'basket of consumables' constructed by Phelps Brown and Hopkins to measure long-term trends in England was similarly four-fifths food, one fifth fuel and clotning.[5] A change involving a decline in the consumption of animal-derived foods would, therefore, represent a clear deterioration in average welfare.

That such a deterioration took place in Scotland is a conclusion which goes so much against the grain of the historical optimist that it demands proof. As we have already indicated, the evidence is patchy, impressionistic and not without ambiguity, but considered in its entirety it does add up to a probability so strong that it has to be taken seriously. This would not have

[3] E.L. Jones, *The European miracle: environments, economies and geopolitics in the history of Europe and Asia* (1981): 56; E.J. Hobsbawm, 'The British standard of living 1790–1805' (1964): 94–104.

[4] *Family expenditure survey; report for 1984 giving the results for the United Kingdom* (1986): 25.

[5] I. Levitt & T.C. Smout, *The state of the Scottish working class in 1843* (1979): 274; H. Phelps Brown and S.V. Hopkins, *A perspective of wages and prices* (1981): 14.

disturbed Scotland's first notable economic historian, I.F. Grant, who in 1930 could write that 'it is quite surprising to remember that until the seventeenth century the people were probably largely meat-eaters';[6] nor would it have surprised Fernand Braudel, who summarised much evidence of the carnivorous habits of the inhabitants of Northern Europe between the fourteenth and the sixteenth centuries, before a general reversion to a more exclusively farinaceous diet after about 1550.[7] Drummond and Wilbraham considered that in England 'the poor countryman's food' contained much more meat in the fifteenth and early sixteenth centuries than subsequently and Shammas considers that there is 'clear cut evidence of a decline in milk and cheese consumption' among the English poor, comparing the seventeenth and the eighteenth centuries. Swedish evidence similarly points to a halving of animal-based calories in the diets of agricultural labourers between the sixteenth century and the seventeenth and eighteenth.[8] Cullen stresses that in Gaelic Ireland diet before 1600 was neither grain-based nor meat-based, though it was based on animal products: 'mainly on milk, both liquid and in its many solid and semi-solid forms': there were, he says 'two dietary changes in the seventeenth century, greater consumption of grain and increased use of the potato'.[9] But dietary change and its implications do not seem at the moment to be part of the mainstream of Scottish historical thinking.

What is the evidence in Scotland for the early period? Let us start with the military. The earliest account of the diet of the Scots is that of Jean Froissart writing in the third quarter of the fourteenth century and describing the particular circumstances of raiding parties over the English border:

> When they make their invasions into England, they march from twenty to four-and-twenty leagues without halting, as well by night as by day ... their habits of sobriety are such, in time of war, that they will live for a long time on flesh half sodden, without bread, and drink the river water without wine ... Under the flaps of his saddle, each man carries a broad plate of metal; behind the saddle, a little bag of oatmeal: when they have eaten too much of the sodden flesh, and their stomach appears weak and empty, they place this plate over the fire, mix with water their oatmeal, and when the plate is heated, they put a little of the paste upon it, and make a thin cake, like a cracknel or biscuit, which they eat to warm their stomachs; it is therefore no wonder, that they perform a longer day's march than other soldiers.[10]

6 I.F. Grant, *Social and economic development of Scotland before 1603* (1930): 555–6.

7 F. Braudel, *Capitalism and material life, 1400–1800* (1973): 127–33. See also the evidence summarised by I. Blanchard, 'The continental European cattle trade, 1400–1600' (1986): 453–5.

8 J.C. Drummond & A. Wilbraham, *The Englishman's food: a history of five centuries of English diet* (1939): 52; Shammas (1984): 262; Morell (1987): 103.

9 L.M. Cullen, *The emergence of modern Ireland* (1981): 140–2.

10 P.H. Brown (ed.), *Early travellers in Scotland* (1891): 8–9.

Military rations, at least, appear as a mixed diet of meat and oatcakes with the meat predominating. A similar impression is given, two centuries later, by a Scottish recruiting officer visiting Denmark in 1564 who declared that the men he offered to bring over from Scotland to fight the Swedes would need but few provisions – water and milk for drink, fresh flesh and a little bread.[11]

The provisioning of the *James*, one of James IV's great ships, lying in harbour at Newhaven for twenty-four days in 1513 provides a partial corrective to this picture of an almost completely carnivorous soldiery: the ship was provisioned almost daily, having 40 men on board, so there was no question of naval stores being put aboard for their special keeping qualities. Everyone received daily what probably amounted to some 14 ounces of bread, 15 ounces of beef, 3 ounces of mutton, 12 ounces of herring and a good deal of ale. This would have provided almost exactly 3,500 calories a day (a reasonable requirement for an active man); about a quarter of this came from the meat and another fifth from the fish.[12] This, of course, means that meat accounted for fewer calories than in the two earlier examples, but still provided a generous proportion of the daily requirement. The difference could be due to the first two references applying to Borderers (as Froissart's probably does) or to Highlanders, and the latter to Lowlanders. A greater degree of meat-eating is to be expected at this stage in upland, pastoral populations. Alternatively, it could be accounted for by the first two applying to soldiers and the last to seamen, for whom fish was an obvious practical alternative to meat.

It may be objected, however, that the military are never typical and are often spoiled, compared with the civilian population, by an employer who needs to keep them fighting fit. Nevertheless, late medieval peasants and craftsmen in the Lowlands appear also to have had high expectations of a meaty diet. I.F. Grant describes the arrangements at Cupar Abbey where craftsmen were given meat or fish daily as part of their wage in kind, and cites the specific example of a mason and his son who engaged themselves for life in exchange for 'a 2 and a half acre croft, 6 merks wages yearly and daily allowance of food consisting of meat or fish, five short white cakes, and half a gallon of convent ale'.[13] Travellers convey the impression that this sort of thing was not unusual. Thus John of Fordoun remarked in the mid-1380s that the Scots were a people 'rarely indulging in food before sunset and contenting themselves, moreover, with meat, and food prepared

[11] I am indebted to Thomas Riis for this reference, from Rigsarkivet, Copenhagen, TKIA.A.95 III, fasc. 'Skotske høvedsmaend'.

[12] *Accounts of the Lord High Treasurer of Scotland*, vol. 4 (1905): 464–8. Details of the conversions used here and later in the paper to translate contemporary quantities of food and drink into modern equivalents and to calculate their calorie content, are available from the authors, who intend to publish them in due course elsewhere.

[13] Grant (1930): 299–300.

from milk', and Aeneas Sylvius who visited Scotland in the early fifteenth century said that 'the common people are poor, and destitute of all refinement. They eat flesh and fish to repletion, and bread only as a dainty.'[14]

Any single comment of this kind can perhaps be disregarded as exaggeration or sensation-mongering: it is the cumulative effect which is impressive. Thus in 1498 Don Pedro de Ayala noted that 'they have more meat in great and small animals than they want'. Nicander Nucius in 1545 said that the Scots had 'so many oxen, and so many flocks of sheep that wonder arises in the beholders on account of the multitude of them', adding 'they abound in butter, cheese and milk'. Estienne Perlin writing in 1551–2 found plentiful and cheap provisions, not least meat: 'They have plenty of cows and calves, on which account their flesh is cheap; and in my time bread was tolerably cheap'.[15]

If meat and its products were indeed of great importance in supplying the general needs of society, as well as those of the elite, one would expect to find special care taken over animal supplies in times of famine and scarcity. Down to the start of the seventeenth century, but very seldom thereafter, Parliament and Privy Council were constantly worrying about animals as well as about grains during dearths. Thus, in February 1551 the Privy Council, 'havand respect to the greit and exhorbitant derth' forbade the export of 'ony fische, flesche, nolt or scheipe, cherse, butter or ony uther kynd of victuallis or viveris quhatsumever furth of this realme to ony part of Ingland'.[16] A similar problem and regulation arose the following year. In 1562, the Privy Council forbade the eating of meat in Lent, partly on health grounds (they were careful not to refer to any possible religious grounds) but mainly because the severe winter had killed so much livestock, sheep in particular, that unless conservation measures were taken there would be an extreme dearth 'to the greit hurt of the commone weill'.[17] Food shortages of 1565 and 1567, on the other hand, were related to bad harvests of grain, but in March 1568 the eating of meat in Lent was again banned to conserve supplies: 'for the commoun weill.'[18] There were similar regulations in the 1570s and 1580s.[19] In 1592 Parliament again prohibited the export of sheep and cattle because of national scarcity, and in the famine of 1598, when Dumfries was hard pressed for food, the local magistrates purchased cattle in the surrounding countryside and had them brought into the burgh.[20]

Relatively early in the following century the authorities ceased to concern themselves with meat supplies in time of famine: the last occasion on which the government banned the export of beasts and the slaughter of

[14] Brown (1891): 27; P.H. Brown, *Scotland before 1700* (1893): 12.
[15] Brown, (1891): 43, 60–1, 74.
[16] RPC I: 14. [17] RPC I: 127, 200. [18] RPC I: 402, 571, 611.
[19] RPC II: 680; III: 74, 84; APS III: 104, 452.
[20] APS III: 577; I.F. Grant (1930): 400.

lambs, and enjoined three meatless days a week, was in 1615, and then not because of general dearth but specifically because the price of livestock had risen unduly following a severe winter.[21] The terrible famine of 1622–4 occupied much of its attention, but the Privy Council never, during that crisis, attempted to regulate flesh supplies: nor did it do so again in later crises.

Another indication of change is the shifting balance between exports of hides and live cattle. In the fifteenth and sixteenth centuries the exports of hides from Scottish ports recorded in the exchequer rolls ran to many thousands a year: they peaked at about 48,000 in 1556, having increased from about 15,000 in the 1460s to about 30,000 in the 1540s. In the seventeenth century, by contrast, the export trade in cattle hides fell very steeply: 11,000 a year was the reported quantity around 1614 and this had probably declined to even lower levels, perhaps only a few hundred in most years by the last quarter of the century.[22] On the other hand, the trade in live cattle increased. Despite the anxiety of the Privy Council it was not, apparently, on a very large scale in the sixteenth century, though droving was already an identifiable feature of inter-regional trade. Exports certainly grew after the Union of Crowns and up to 48,000 beasts were crossing the Border in the 1660s, up to 60,000 by the 1690s.[23] It must be presumed in the earlier period that the Scots ate the original contents of the hides, but that in the later one the animals were digested in English stomachs while the Scots ate something else.

We should not, however, necessarily conclude that it was the price of meat that normally made the difference between life and death in a famine even before 1600. There is a fairly general impression that it was the price of grain that mattered *in extremis*, and this even from the fifteenth century. Thus the Auchinleck chronicler described the year 1439: 'The samyn tyme thar was in Scotland a gret derth for the boll of quheit was at xls. and the boll of ete mele xxxs. and werraly the derth was so gret that thair deit a passinge peple for hungere.'[24]

At least in the Central Lowlands, as we shall see, many more calories could always have been procured in the sixteenth century (it is hard to say if this could happen earlier) by spending a merk on oatmeal than a merk on mutton or beef and, for the very poor, oatmeal may always have been the only staff of life. The question which cannot be clearly answered is how

[21] RPC X: 312–13. However, under mysterious circumstances (and not in relation to general dearth) cattle exports were again forbidden for a time in 1625. See RPC 2nd series, vol. I: 121, 138–9.

[22] I. Guy, 'The Scottish export trade, 1460–1599' (1986): 74; Historical Manuscripts Commission, *Report on the manuscripts of the Earl of Mar and Kellie preserved at Alloa House* (1904): 70–4; T.C. Smout, *Scottish trade on the eve of Union, 1660–1707* (1963): 217–19.

[23] D. Woodward, 'A comparative study of the Irish and Scottish livestock trades in the seventeenth century' (1977): 147–64.

[24] W.A. Craigie (ed.), *The Asloan manuscript*, vol. 1: 216.

many other people also fell into that category. An impression survives that until the end of the sixteenth century they were relatively few.

Regional variations in diet, which must always have existed, began to be described from the final part of the sixteenth century. Bishop Leslie in 1568 described the Highlanders as accustomed to a mixed diet in which some ate rye, wheat, pease, beans and especially oats, but 'grettest delyte' they had in beef. Of the Borderers he says that they lived mainly on flesh, milk, cheese and 'sodden' beir [barley, presumably in broths], adding that they made little use of bread.[25] They sound like the shepherds of an earlier generation, in Lyndsay's *Complaynt of Scotland*, who made 'greit cheir of euyrie sort of mylk', that is, butter, cheese, curds and so on, but who had no bread 'bot ry caikes and fustean skonnis maid of flour'.[26] However, Leslie's description in these terms seems to imply a perceived distinction, by then, between the dietary habits of the uplands and the other areas.

This appears to be correct. Lowland diet soon began to be described as based almost exclusively on grains. Fynes Morison, visiting Scotland in 1598 but not penetrating to the hills, described the population as eating 'little fresh meate' (though he did refer to consumption of salted meat) and added 'they vulgarly eate harth Cakes of Oates, but in Cities have also wheaten bread'.[27] In 1605 Sir Thomas Craig, addressing the advantages that might come to England and Scotland by a mutual union, was clear about a striking difference between the Lowlands and Highlands. His purpose was to consider the true wealth of Scotland, since 'Nowadays national plenty is a question of food and clothing; and in the matter of food we are as well off as any other people'. He went on in these terms:

> Less fertile than England she may be, but she lacks none of the necessaries of life. Fewer of her people die of starvation . . . Nowhere else is fish so plentiful . . . We have meat of every kind . . . We eat barley bread as pure and white as that of England and France.

Then he added, in respect to the commonality:

> Our servants are content with oatmeal, which makes them hardy and long-lived. The greater number of our farm hands eat bread made of peas and beans . . . should there be a bad harvest the Highlanders are able to supply us with cheese, which is often used, without any injury to health when the supply of cereals is short.

The Highlanders themselves, however, he described in terms like that of Bishop Leslie thirty years earlier, as a robust, long-lived, active people, 'in spite of their entire dependence on cheese, flesh and milk, like the Scythians', a description which would fit contemporary Gaelic Irishmen.[28]

To some extent, however, the Highland–Lowland contrast must have

[25] Brown (1893): 161, 167. [26] Grant (1930): 303. [27] Brown (1891): 88–9.

[28] C. Sanford Terry (ed.), *Sir Thomas Craig's 'De Unione Regnorum Britanniae Tractatus*, Scottish History Society, 1st series, vol. 60 (1909): 416–17, 447.

been overdrawn by Craig. We know that at Taymouth, the gateway to the Breadalbane Highlands in Perthshire, the local cleric related in his memorandum book years of scarcity to years of high grain prices in 1563 and 1572, just as a contemporary Lowland chronicler would have done.[29] We know from surviving Highland rentals, especially in the west, that meal production could often be of great significance. Thus Breadalbane in 1594 was producing as rent in kind 28 'bolls of bere', 710 stones of cheese and 50 stones of butter: a calculation suggests that only 15 per cent of the calorific value of that food was in grain. Conversely, Lewis in 1580 was already producing 5,760 bolls of meal, 1,160 cows and 640 sheep: in this case 87 per cent of the calories of the rental came from the meal.[30] The production profile was largely a function of the altitude, climate and fertility of the land, which was more varied than outsiders imagined. Nevertheless, there is no reason to believe that Craig's basic observation was not true: that Highlanders still depended, to a degree that Lowlanders no longer did, on consuming the produce of their own flocks and herds.

By 1600, therefore, we may postulate a situation in which animal-derived foods were important to the commonality only in upland areas. The story of the next two centuries or so is of the continuing dominance of oatmeal in the Lowlands, and a gradual change away from the consumption of animal-derived food in the Highlands. The importance of oatmeal in the Lowlands from the early seventeenth century onwards is unquestioned. The first unequivocal reference to porridge we have been able to find comes from the English traveller James in 1615; after emphasising the boiled meat dishes, broths and stews with which he was entertained by the gentlemen in whose houses he stayed, he gave an account of a 'pottage they make of oate meale floure boiled in water, which they eate with butter, milk or ale' as being 'eaten by the common people and school children at breakfast, and by Ladies allso'. He also referred to the 'meaner sort' in Berwickshire eating pease bread, a local peculiarity of taste noted in south-east Scotland to the nineteenth century.[31]

All subsequent accounts of Lowland diet, whether from the records of institutions or the descriptions of travellers and contemporaries, over the next 250 years emphasise the primacy of oatmeal – in a very striking contrast to the earlier period. Take, for example, seventeenth-century military diet. In 1639 the covenanting army was provisioned 'to everie souldier two pound weight of aite bread in the day and twentie eight ounce

[29] Grant (1930):302.
[30] Calculated from data provided by R.A. Dodgshon, 'Highland chiefdoms, 1500–1745: a study in redistributive exchange' (1987).
[31] E. MacGillivray 'Richard James, 1592–1638; description of Shetland, Orkney and the Highlands of Scotland' (1953):53–4. Despite the title, the description of food is general to all Scotland.

of wheat bread ane pynt of aile in the day'.[32] It is almost certain that this diet is for two men, a soldier and his 'follower': if so it would have yielded an adequate 3,300 calories, two-thirds from oatbread. A similar military calculation c.1689 'of the Provisions Necessary for 100 men for a month' again provided two-thirds of the nutrition from oatmeal, though with a quarter from butter and cheese and the rest from ale and brandy.[33] It all seems quite different from Froissart and the Danish mercenaries.

It was the same among civilians. An orphan's diet from Hutcheson's Hospital in Glasgow in 1649 shows that 82 per cent of the nutrition came from oatbread, 5 per cent from meat and 8 per cent from fish.[34] Another from the Dean Orphan Hospital in Edinburgh in 1740 shows 75 per cent from meal, 8 per cent from meat and 3 per cent from fish.[35] The servants in the pay of the Duke of Gordon at Gordon Castle in 1739 were enjoying a better diet at his table than most: they got 62 per cent of their nutrition from bread and meal but 19 per cent from ale, 11 per cent from meat and 7.6 per cent from butter.[36] A slightly more severe and less affluent employer, Lady Grisell Baillie at Mellerstain in 1743, provided 73 per cent through bread and meal, 12 per cent through ale, 11 per cent with meat and 5 per cent with fish.[37] The average of 8 known diets analysed in Scotland between 1639 and 1743 yields a daily mean per head of 19.7 ounces of meal and 2.1 imperial pints of ale. Because all these were from institutions or in other ways 'sheltered' they may be slightly more plentiful and varied than the common experience, reflecting to some degree the expectations of middle-class employers or charitable donors. Nevertheless, the figures compare closely with later estimates. Robert Hope, writing in Sinclair's *General Report of the Agricultural State of Scotland* in 1814, which summarised the data from the investigations of the 1790s as well as describing the contemporary scene, stated that at breakfast a man would consume 15.5 ounces of oatmeal: at the same time he observed that the rural labourers of Scotland used beef and mutton 'very sparingly'.[38] Such

[32] G.M. Paul (ed.), *Fragment of the diary of Sir Archibald Johnston, Lord Warriston, May 21–June 25, 1639*, Scottish History Society, 1st series, vol. 26 (1896): 55.

[33] SRO GD 26/9/525.

[34] J.D. Marwick (ed.), *Extracts from the records of the burgh of Glasgow, 1630–1662* (1881): 178–9.

[35] SRO GD 1/40/16/(1). See also J. Richardson, 'Some notes on the early history of the Dean Orphan Hospital' (1949).

[36] SRO GD 44/52/131/7–11, tabulated in B.L.H. Horn 'Domestic life of a duke. Cosmo George, 3rd Duke of Gordon' (1977).

[37] R. Scott-Moncrieff (ed.), *The household book of Lady Grisell Baillie 1692–1733*, Scottish History Society 2nd series vol. 1 (1911): 277–8. Shammas (1984) found that late eighteenth-century English families in the north obtained 50 per cent of their nutrition from cereals, 12 per cent from meat, 16 per cent from dairy produce and eggs, 8 per cent from potatoes and vegetables, 13 per cent from sugar, treacle, tea and beer etc. In the south 66 per cent was from cereals, 12 per cent from meat, 5 per cent from dairy produce, 3 per cent from potatoes and vegetables, 14 per cent from sugar, treacle, tea and beer. Plainly Scottish diet was less 'modern' than either of these.

[38] R. Hope, 'On rural economy' (1814).

quantities could not be eaten as porridge, for the meal would swell in the milk to amount to about ten bowls. But they could be eaten as brose, in about three bowls. Although these amounts seem extremely large by the standards of the present day, oatmeal was, as farinaceous foods go, highly concentrated and nutritious. In Poland and France in the early modern period the common people ate, per head per day, up to about a kilo of rye or wheat bread to get as many calories: that was almost twice as much as the Scots' oats.[39]

In travellers' accounts of the seventeenth and eighteenth centuries there are plenty of references to the Lowlander's eating oatmeal – most famously, Samuel Johnson's aphorism about a food for horses in England being the support of the people in Scotland.[40] But as for meat, a new impression was given, by visitor and native alike, of extreme scarcity either through brusque comments about the Scots, 'flesh meat they seldom or never taste', or observations about the marketing: 'For half the year, in many towns of Scotland there is no beef or mutton to be seen in the shambles and, if any, it is like carrion meat, yet dearer than ever I saw in England'.[41]

These comments, at first from a Jacobite in 1729, agree with recollections at the end of the century when meat consumption was beginning to rise again in some Lowland localities. For example, the agricultural reporter for Ayrshire in 1793 observed that: 'So small was the consumption of butcher meat in this province 50 years ago that there were not more than fifty head of cattle killed in the country town of Ayr, at that period, although it contained from 4 to 5,000 inhabitants'.[42]

Hugo Arnot attempted an estimate of the meal, flour and meat consumed within Edinburgh around 1777: calculations from his figures suggest that even then the inhabitants of the capital obtained less than 6 per cent of their nutrition from meat, compared with 70 per cent from meal.[43] There is in fact some evidence that in favoured places at the very end of the eighteenth century meat was beginning to re-enter the working-class diet on a more significant scale, but characteristically every time modern plenty was brought into account it was contrasted with former scarcity. Thus at Crieff, the scene of one of the famous 'trysts' where

[39] Wyczański (1985):203. [40] S. Johnson, *A dictionary of the English language* (1773).

[41] J. Mackintosh of Borlum, *An essay on ways and means of enclosing* (1729):131; D. Herbert (ed.), *The works of Tobias Smollett* (1887):559. The quotation is from Humphrey Clinker, first published in 1771. He gives a good description of the daily meals of 'the country people of North Britain': 'Their breakfast is a kind of hasty pudding of oatmeal, or peasemeal eaten with milk. They have commonly pottage to dinner composed of cale or cole, leeks, barley or big and butter, and this is reinforced with bread and cheese made of skimmed milk. At night they sup on sowens flummery of oatmeal'. He further comments that a pickled herring is a delicacy, but some peasants have potatoes and most parsnips in their gardens.

[42] W. Fullarton, *General view of the agriculture of the county of Ayr* (1793):11–12. He further observed that meat was only used formerly in winter for broth, 'the rest of their food consisting at that time only of porridge, oatmeal cakes and some milk or cheese'.

[43] H. Arnot, *The history of Edinburgh* (1779):345.

animals from the Highlands were sold to Lowland and English drovers, the minister wrote in the *Statistical Account* of 1791 that 'ten times' more butcher's meat was sold locally than 20 years before. At Kilbarchan, one of the most prosperous handloom-weaving villages, his colleague wrote that 'about 20 years ago tea and butcher's meat were very seldom tasted by any of the lower ranks. Now they are more or less used by people of every description'. The reporter for Cambuslang, outside Glasgow, said that in 1791 'a great deal of butcher's meat is consumed', and compared it with the scarcities of thirty years earlier when 'only gentleman farmers killed their fat cattle'. A similar impression is given for Ayr.[44] It is evident, however, that such localities were exceptional, and that there was no general return to meat-eating by most people within the eighteenth century or for a long time afterwards. When meat was consumed at all by most Scots over most of this period it was generally in the form of broth, with an occasional feast of haggis or blood pudding to utilise the offal. In the broth would go barley and kale – 'kaill' is indeed a common Fife dialect word for broth to this day: the greens from the cottars' kailyard were an important source of vitamin C.

If meat was scarce, what of butter, cheese and milk? The evidence on the first two is not encouraging in the Lowlands: apart from the soldiers' diet of 1689, butter appears in our institutional diets only at Gordon Castle and, 'when cheap' at the Dean orphanage on Saturdays and Sundays, and cheese only at the Edinburgh orphanage and Mellerstain. Arnot considered Edinburgh to be badly supplied with butter and said that hardly a piece of tolerable cheese was made for sale in Scotland. Smollett was slightly more optimistic, mentioning butter in the pottage and a cheese made of skimmed milk as part of the daily meals of the 'country people of North Britain'. Commentators in the *Statistical Account* sometimes mention it as a rarity of working-class consumption that had increased in favoured areas, like meat. It was still rare, except among better-paid workers in the Western Lowlands, at the time of the Poor Law Commissioners' Report in 1843.[45]

On milk the evidence is uncertain and historians divided; Marjorie Plant and Maisie Steven, for example, stress its abundance and accessibility and Henry Hamilton its scarcity.[46] Certainly by the nineteenth century its use was widespread in the countryside. Robert Hutchison in his classic investigation into the diet of the rural labourer found some milk in the diet of almost all of the families he surveyed.[47] The same was true of the Poor

[44] M. Steven, *The good Scots diet: what happened to it?* (1985): 14.

[45] Arnot (1979): 347; Herbert (1887): 559; Levitt & Smout (1979) chap. 2.

[46] M. Plant, *The domestic life of Scotland in the eighteenth century* (1952): 101–2; Steven (1985): 37–45; H. Hamilton, *Life and labour on an Aberdeenshire estate, 1735–50* (1946): xiii–xiv; H. Hamilton, *History of the homeland*, (1947): 65.

[47] R. Hutchison, 'Report on the dietaries of Scotch agricultural labourers' (1869): 1–29.

Law investigation of 1843, and Robert Hope in the *General Report* of 1814 shows that milk was equally common at the beginning of the nineteenth century – all the different types of labourers then had a quantity of milk with their food though the amount varied from one district to another.[48] But our institutional diets, where they mention milk at all, do so in a way that implies its unimportance. Most strikingly, the orphans in Edinburgh in 1739 were allowed a mere fifth of a pint a week compared with six pints of ale: in the Merchant Maiden Hospital (where the children were of higher social status) there was, daily, milk for breakfast and ale for supper.[49] Similar emphasis appears in Glasgow University in 1640, where a quarter of a pint a day is allowed compared with five times as much beer.[50] All these are urban diets, and there is an implication in Lady Grisell Baillie's account book that at Mellerstain, milk could, but only on occasion, be substituted for ale.[51] There are also infrequent references to milk in the *Statistical Account*: one interesting example is the entry for Hamilton where a man and his wife, both working as prosperous weavers and supporting three children under five, spent 3s. 8d. on 'three pecks of oatmeal and two pecks of barley meal', a mere 8d. on 'butter, cheese, bacon, other meat' and only 1s. on 'milk, salt, onions, potatoes'.[52]

On the whole the balance of evidence for much of the eighteenth century seems to favour Hamilton who, discussing the accounts of Monymusk between 1735 and 1750, noted that: 'Milk does not appear in the accounts, partly because it was produced locally and no market price had been placed on it, and partly because the amount consumed was very small. Dairy farming was as yet little practised, cows being valued for their powers of draught and for their meat.'[53] If this was the case, an increase of milk-drinking in the Lowland countryside in the closing decades of the eighteenth century or around the start of the nineteenth century could indeed be accounted a significant improvement in diet over the previous period.

The diet as described seems bleak and bare to modern tastes. Were there extras? The cottage gardens that held kale sometimes held other greens and roots like parsnips; hedges, then as now, yielded brambles. Most leases down to the end of the seventeenth century and some even later demanded the payment of 'kain' hens and sometimes of ducks or eggs, which suggests that tenants (though perhaps not cottars) had the chance of enlivening their diet with the occasional fowl or dish of eggs. Both the Merchant

[48] Levitt & Smout (1979): 25, 39, 48; Hope (1814): 253–8.

[49] SRO GD 1/40/16(1); E.S. Towill, 'The minutes of the Merchant Maiden Hospital' (1956).

[50] Glasgow University Archives 26732–3.

[51] Scott-Moncrieff (ed.) (1911): 277–8. The implication in Douglas concerning north-east Scotland (1782) – see footnote 66 – is, however, the reverse: milk was more general, ale the substitute.

[52] Cited in Steven (1985): 85.

[53] Hamilton (1946): xiii–xiv.

Maiden Hospital and the Dean Orphan Hospital in Edinburgh provided eggs: in the former, three per child per week, in the latter 'eggs when cheap'. Nor should the chance of catching (or poaching) rabbits be overlooked: there are farm servants still alive who recall as children eating practically no meat except snared rabbit. Fish was also available, especially herring, but also saith, haddock, cod, codling, whiting and various kinds of shellfish including (in the Firth of Forth) oysters. Celia Fiennes in 1698 found on the Solway coast that she could buy 'two pieces of Salmon halfe a one neer a yard long and a very large Trout of an amber coullour' for 9d. sterling, and noted that cheap fish meant that the population had abundant provisions. How much was eaten depended partly on distance from the sea; Edinburgh was well provided, and the students of St Andrews ate a great deal in their diet. A 'herring road' led over the Lammermuirs connecting Dunbar with the central Tweed valley. On the other hand most servants' diets, where they mention fish, refer only to small quantities: some 5 per cent of calorie intake at Mellerstain (in the Tweed valley) is typical and Smollett's remark that 'a pickled herring is a delicacy' for most Scottish country people was probably not wide of the mark.[54] Fish, like butter, cheese and meat itself, was present in the diet in small quantities: only along the coasts can it have had much nutritional importance.

What of Highland diet in the period after 1600? The evidence does not include any institutional records, but the outline of change is fairly clear. Martin Martin, writing of his native Hebrides at the end of the seventeenth century, observed already that 'the generality eat but little Flesh, and only Persons of distinction eat it every day ... and they eat more Biol'd than Roasted'. He went on to describe a diet of butter, cheese, milk, potatoes, cabbage and oatmeal – 'the latter taken with some bread is the constant Food of several Thousands of both Sexes in this [Syke] and other Isles, during the Winter and Spring'.[55] The passage is interesting both for its early references to potatoes and because of its emphasis on the continuing significance of other animal products – butter and cheese – even when meat itself was unobtainable on the common table.

That feature, however, was not destined to last, and there was a steady decline thereafter in animal produce consumed. Pococke could describe the diet of the inhabitants of Durness, Sutherland in 1760 as milk, curds, whey and oatmeal.[56] Pennant, travelling mainly in the Highlands in 1769 and 1772, only once, in many references to diet, noted the presence of meat. Of the people of Arran he observed that 'their diet is chiefly potatoes and meal, and during winter some dried mutton or goat is added to their hard fare'.

[54] Herbert (1887): 559; C. Morris (ed.), *The illustrated journeys of Celia Fiennes* (1984): 173.
[55] M. Martin, *A description of the western isles of Scotland* (2nd edn, 1716): 201.
[56] D.W. Kemp (ed.), *Bishop Pococke's tours in Scotland, 1747–1760*, Scottish History Society, 1st series vol. 1 (1886): 127.

He mentions only three groups who had milk in their diet: Highland shepherds drank 'milk, whey and sometimes, by way of indulgence, whiskey'; the married servants on Skye had as their common food, 'Brochan, a thick meal-puddin, with milk, butter or treacle' and the inhabitants of Lismore were forced to live on boiled sheep's milk throughout the spring in the absence of much else. Of milk or dairy produce consumption among the inhabitants of Arran, Jura or the Aberdeenshire Highlands and Buchan, Pennant makes no mention. Marshall, in a survey of the Central Highlands in 1794, describes the low tenantry as seldom tasting animal food and living predominantly on oatmeal which they consumed along with milk 'and its products'.[57] Certainly butter and cheese had almost disappeared by the time of the surveys carried out for the *New Statistical Account* and the Poor Law Commissioners in the 1840s, though milk was then again relatively widely reported. Some of the comments then were highly significant. At Alvie it was reported that butter and cheese 'they must sell to pay the rent', at Croy that 'poultry, butter and eggs are all for the market', and at Glenshiel that 'butter and cheese, though favourite articles, they can rarely indulge in'. Incidentally there is a very similar observation concerning late eighteenth-century Ayrshire, to the effect that the wives of small tenants, though expert at making butter and cheese, could not give their children any, or eat much themselves, as it was all produced for the market.[58]

Highland diet in the eighteenth century was, therefore, increasingly dominated by oatmeal imported from the Lowlands and from Ireland, supplemented to a significant degree by fish and shellfish on the coasts, and gradually after 1750, by potatoes. By 1794 William Marshall had no problem in describing potatoes (mainly consumed in winter) as 'the greatest blessing that modern times have bestowed on the country', having 'more than once saved it from the miseries of famine'.[59] Potatoes were then also of substantial importance to the Lowland poor, though only one of our pre-1750 institutional diets mentions them (at the Edinburgh orphanage in 1740 where they provided 5 per cent of the calories). Arnot in 1777 calls them the 'chief article' for the capital's poor.[60] The Highlanders, however, became predominantly dependent on potatoes in a way the Lowlanders never did. In 1846 the Committee on Famine Relief in the north estimated that in the Highlands 75 per cent of the daily intake of food was procured by the population from potatoes, in the Lowlands only 25 per cent.[61] There are several striking examples in the Poor Law Commission Report of 1843 of potato and meal-based diets. To cite only one, an able-bodied labourer

[57] Pennant (1776b): 200, 244, 357, 415; T. Pennant, *A tour of Scotland in 1769* (1776a): 131, 147; W. Marshall, *General view of the agriculture of the central Highlands* (1794): 21.

[58] Levitt & Smout (1979): 26; W.K. Dickson (ed.), 'Memories of Ayrshire about 1780 by the reverend John Mitchell' (1939).

[59] Marshall (1794): 21. [60] Arnot (1779): 347. [61] Levitt & Smout (1979): 24.

in full employment in the inland parish of Urquhart consumed 8 to 10 pounds of potatoes a day, along with half a pound of oatmeal and a quart of milk.[62] No doubt Highlanders were still able to poach a little venison, rabbit, and salmon and even under the regime of the new sheep runs they were allowed the privilege of devouring the occasional diseased or 'braxy' mutton. Bilberries, hips, haws, wild cherries and so forth were more plentiful in the glens than in the Lowlands. Nevertheless, here was a vast change from the 'Scythians' of 1605, with their 'entire dependence on cheese, flesh and milk', even if some allowance has to be made for earlier overstatement.

The evidence presented so far indicates that there was indeed an alteration in the character of Scottish diet between the late Middle Ages and the onset of the Industrial Revolution, which most would regard as a drop in the national standard of living. The heyday of famine and scarcity in all of Scottish history probably fell, roughly, between the middle of the sixteenth and the middle of the seventeenth century, although there were bad shortages even in the fifteenth century (and earlier), one severe national lapse later in the 1690s, and a few dearths in the eighteenth century that led to no surge of famine-induced deaths except, once or twice, in the Highlands.[63] But dearth can have many causes, from climatic deterioration to maldistribution of purchasing power and other forms of 'entitlement'.[64] Relevant among them may be the fact that although a bad year for animals may take longer to recover from as breeding stock has to be built up again, cereals are inherently more liable to be affected by yearly alterations of glut and shortfall than livestock, and increasing dependence on oats may have been riskier than at least partial dependence on meat, along with oats. That problem was solved in the course of the eighteenth century, though not quickly, by better transport facilitating the movement of food from areas of plenty to areas of scarcity, by improved and more varied cropping and by more plentiful and efficiently distributed charity.[65]

The new diet, it is worth emphasising, was at least as nutritious as the old. Oatmeal provided the basis for an uncommonly healthy diet and appears to have been available in generous quantities to the population except in the years of dearth. Numerous commentators spoke of the vigour of the Scottish people despite their almost meatless diet. Thus Francis Douglas, writing in 1782 of the food of small farmers in the North East, remarked that they lived on 'oatmeal, milk and vegetables, chiefly red cabbage in the winter season and coleworts for the summer and spring'. Flesh was never seen in their houses except at Christmas and Shrove

[62] *Ibid.*, 24–5. [63] T.C. Smout, 'Famine and famine relief in Scotland' (1977).
[64] A. Sen, *Poverty and famines: an essay on entitlement and deprivation* (1981).
[65] Smout (1977):25–8.

Tuesday, and at baptisms and weddings. Nevertheless 'they are strong and active, sleep sound and live to a good old age'.[66] Since there is no nutritional element in meat that cannot be secured equally from other commodities, properly selected, we need not be so surprised. Oatmeal is rich in vitamins and also contains calcium and various important trace elements: supplemented by kale in the soup for vitamin C, and an occasional meal of herring or offal for additional vitamin A, as well as by beer and sometimes milk, it provided excellent and healthy fare, almost certainly better in most respects than the diet of the urban Scot at the end of the nineteenth century. Where there were problems they had to do with skin troubles, usually described as 'scrofula' or 'the itch' and associated in the contemporary mind with excessive consumption of oatmeal. They occurred, for example, in the two Edinburgh children's hospitals, where there were few or no green vegetables in the diet.

The standard of living, however, has fundamentally to do with human ability to exercise choice, including the choice to live in an unhealthy way if one prefers. The deterioration which we are postulating consists in the simple fact that people would not have chosen the later diet primarily of oatmeal and potatoes if the earlier one containing more meat and animal produce had still been available to them. Even in this period the upper classes and the middling orders (for example, clergy, lawyers, merchants, the larger tenants, students) still ate substantial amounts of meat. Everything goes to suggest, then as now, that when incomes begin to rise, either generally or individually, one immediate choice was to replace a substantial proportion of grain-based food with animal-based food. The population, in the course of time, put the clock back to what they chose to regard as a higher standard of living.

Since the initial change from more or less animal food was likely to conflict with the preferences of the great majority, what brought it about? We might envisage three mechanisms, not mutually exclusive, through which it could be mediated. These are: a fall in incomes, a change in relative prices and the development of a market. The first, then, would be a fall in the average income of the population so that they could no longer afford the food they wanted. For the relatively small number who lived primarily by wage employment (especially small at the start of the period, much less so at its conclusion) we have been able to detect over the period 1600–1780

[66] F. Douglas, *A general description of the east coast of Scotland from Edinburgh to Cullen* (1782): 138–9. Here there may be a contrast with England, for Shammas (1984): 258, found evidence of inadequate calorie intake in English labouring diets in the late eighteenth century, partly, she suggests, because sugar, with its 'quick energy rush' had been substituted for older and better foods, including oatmeal-based ones. She also found poorhouses in the early modern period offering a daily diet with calorific content 'in the low to middle 2000s': *ibid.*, 262.

only one striking feature, of sharp random variation in annual real income around a level trend, determined by the vacillations in the price of bread or meal around a traditional money wage. Real wages, in other words, were largely stable in the long term, at least to 1750, a point which contrasts interestingly with English and Irish experience. There are certainly whole decades of improvement, whole decades of deterioration, but over the entire period no decisive trend.[67] This, of course, may well not apply in the late Middle Ages, for which no data have yet been systematically collected or analysed: there may be a significant deterioration from 1480 to 1600 but in 1480 even fewer would have been in paid employment.[68]

The main determinant of income and food choice at the start of our period, however, was not money wages but the size of the average landholding and the proportion of the population that could secure a holding big enough to render them secure and affluent. On that there is a general impression from the work of Dodgshon that holding size fell in the sixteenth century, and continued to fall in the Highlands in the seventeenth and eighteenth centuries: in the Lowlands the later experience was more varied, with some areas following the Highland pattern, and others, under the impact of farming for the market, polarising into a smaller number of larger holdings and a great many semi-dependent cot holdings.[69] If this outline is valid, it does appear that most people would get poorer.

A second possibility is that there was a fundamental alteration in relative prices, that the price of meat rose significantly compared with the price of grain and went beyond the purchasing power of the commonality. This could happen if, for example, land that had formerly been used only for rough grazing was taken under the plough, and the ratio of grain to meat production thereby changed. It was Pedro de Ayala's opinion in 1498 that 'corn is very good, but they do not produce as much as they might because they do not cultivate the land', and he went on to describe a process of cultivation that was labour-saving but to his eye grossly inefficient.[70] Dodgshon and Whyte have both described ways in which in the seventeenth and early eighteenth centuries Lowland farmers and landowners strove to raise productivity – through reclamation, gradual introduction of the 'faugh' break, liming, consolidating holdings in some areas, more legume cultivation and so on.[71] By the late seventeenth century there were observations by Sibbald and others that a third of the pasture land

67 This is the broad preliminary conclusion of our larger study, to be reported in book form elsewhere.

68 Dr N.J. Mayhew of the Ashmolean Museum, Oxford, is co-ordinating data collection for a survey of Scottish prices before 1550.

69 R.A. Dodgshon, *Land and society in early Scotland* (1981).

70 Brown (1891):43.

71 Dodgshon (1981); I.D. Whyte, *Agriculture and society in seventeenth-century Scotland* (1979).

had been ploughed up and there was little to be seen now between Lowland settlements save laboured land.[72]

The island of Islay appears to demonstrate a dramatic case of an increasing surplus of grain. In 1542 the tenants paid their lord 324 bolls of meal, 2,161 stones of cheese, 301 sheep, 301 cows, 301 hens and 301 geese: in 1614 the rental was identical except that the meal rents had risen sevenfold to 2,193 bolls. The calorie output of the rental consequently tripled, and the proportion provided by meal rose from 38 per cent to 73 per cent.[73] Rental figures are not, of course, output figures; they exclude at least what the tenants produced for their own consumption. Nevertheless, there must have been a very large increase in the output of oats on Islay in the second half of the sixteenth century, possibly analogous to the revolution in farming and output that was to take place in Ulster in the following century. It is quite possible that rising population (enabling more labour-intensive husbandry to take place), more land under cultivation and new methods brought from the Lowlands wrought a transformation in some of the islands as it did in Ireland.

The evidence for an alteration in relative prices is not, however, favourable to the suggestion that meat became relatively dearer in the few places for which we have evidence, and assessed burghal prices indicate that the cost of a day's calorie intake obtained from mutton was almost always between four and six times the cost of the same calories obtained from oat bread.[74]

In detail the picture is complex. In Glasgow, in the 1580s the cost of 1,000 calories drawn from mutton cost about 450 per cent of the cost of 1,000 calories drawn from meal; that fell, slowly but persistently, to about 350 per cent in the 1720s. In Edinburgh there was an increase from 400 to 600 per cent in the last two decades of the sixteenth century, followed by a drop back to 400 per cent by 1670 but a return to over 550 per cent in the next decade, perhaps reflecting the great disaster for stock in the Borders in the 'thirteen drifty days' of the winter of 1674. In Aberdeen there was a fall from 700 per cent around 1560 to 400 per cent at the end of the century, followed by an uncertain trend that culminated in a rise to 600 per cent again between 1650 and 1690. Earlier evidence is hard to find and harder to interpret, but such data as we have been able to examine lend no support at all to the notion that there was ever anything like parity between the cost of calories from meat and meal, at least in Lowland markets where both were sold.[75] The extention of arable at the expense of pasture is likely to have

[72] T.C. Smout & A. Fenton, 'Scottish agriculture before the improvers' (1965).
[73] Dodgshon (1985).
[74] Collected for our ESRC project, 'Prices, wages and the standard of living in Scotland 1580–1780' and to be published in due course.
[75] The details will be reported in our larger study.

been brought about by the pressure of demand for grain from poor people who could not afford meat anyway.

The third possibility is that while the market was under-developed most people lived off their own farms and ate what was available locally, but when trade increased they imported meal as a food, as by selling animals and dairy produce for grain they could obtain far more calories for the same price, and thus either support more numerous families or pay a higher rent to their lord. Few would doubt that inter-regional trade did expand rapidly in the early modern period in Scotland, especially Highland–Lowland trade and later also Highland–Irish trade. Even in the first decade of the sixteenth century cattle were being driven from Crown lands in Trotternish on Skye for use in the Lowlands and there are later sixteenth-century references to a cattle trade from such diverse localities as Mull, Glenmoriston and Glenshiel. In 1565 there is a reference to the regular practice of driving 'ky furth of Ergyle to be sauld in the lawland' at Perth, Stirling, Dumbarton and Renfrew. Significantly, it had been interrupted by evil men.[76] With more peaceful times in the Highlands in the seventeenth century, and with the pacification of the Borders following the Union of the Crowns, the trade manifestly grew. There are signs of its significance as an export to England within the first 30 years after 1603, and by 1664 as many as 48,000 were estimated by the English to have crossed the Border. By 1700, though some years were even higher than 1664, only about half that number were regularly paying duty at the Border. The figure of 40,000 is quoted again in 1724 and in 1740; by 1757 Postlethwayt put it at 80,000 a year, entirely possible considering that some late seventeenth-century years had already reached 60,000.[77]

We cannot easily establish what proportion were Highland animals, for a significant number came from the uplands of Dumfries and Galloway where the success of the trade caused the Leveller anti-enclosure riots of 1724. But the main droving market even in the early eighteenth century was at Crieff on the Highland line, later at Falkirk: soon after 1601 we know that animals were being driven from Skye and in 1705 John Spreull regarded it as axiomatic that 'the strongest and best of our Cattle from both the South and North *Highlands*, that are able to travel are Exported, and either the old or weaklie Cattle are kept at home'.[78]

The sale of cattle, however, was by no means the only element in the early commercialisation of the Highlands. I.F. Grant chronicles sales of

[76] Grant (1930): 545–6; S.G.E. Lythe, *The economy of Scotland in its European setting, 1550–1625* (1960): 11.

[77] Woodward (1977): 147–64; T.C. Smout, 'Where had the Scottish economy got to by the third quarter of the eighteenth century (1983): 56; J. Thirsk (ed.), *The agrarian history of England and Wales*, vol. 5, pt 2 (1985): 14.

[78] J. Spreull, *An accompt current betwixt Scotland and England* (1705): 14–15, 26–9, 31, 56, 63–4.

herring, salmon, timber, skins and hides even in the sixteenth century.[79] All these items grew in significance. John Spreull was a Glasgow merchant who knew the west Highlands from personal travel and trading experience at the opening decade of the eighteenth century. He drew attention not only to cattle and fish exports but also to the well-established trade in 'Highland Galloway' horses at Dumbarton Fair (he himself had exported 50 on a boat to Surinam and reported 'an great price by Sugars got for them'). He had observations about the sale of Highland slate and quarry stone, of wild skins and of butter ('I know in the West *Highlands* at *Mackcloud* and *Mackdonalds* Lands, there is a fine Yellow Butter and well made, as ever I saw from Ireland': but it was exported in too large and dirty barrels). He was also concerned about the exploitation of the woods: oak timber and oak bark was being sent to Ireland in large quantities. Cameron of Lochiel had improved his fir woods and was selling to Ireland and to Glasgow, Grant of Rothiemurchus to the north-east Lowlands and to England.[80]

All this commerce, apparently flourishing by 1700, made further large strides in the first half of the eighteenth century. The English ironworks at Invergarry and elsewhere consumed a good deal of oakwood: very large quantities of tan bark came to be used in the tanneries of Glasgow: Easdale and other slate was used in Inverness as well as in Edinburgh and on the Clyde.[81] There is, it will be noted, no evidence whatever that the ending of the 1745 rebellion introduced 'commercialisation' into the Highlands. It had been there long before and the failure of Jacobitism probably had a minimal effect on the economic history of the Highlands.

The exchange of all these commodities was for other food. In 1555, at a time of dearth in Scotland, the western burghs were exempted from the general prohibition on victual shipments in order to be able to send to the Isles 'bacin bread, ale and aqua vitae'.[82] Normally, however, the import was meal, either from the Lowlands or, from the end of the seventeenth century, from Ireland. *The Letter Book of Bailie John Steuart of Inverness, 1715–1721* most clearly shows the intensity of the competition between the Moray Firth and Ireland in the supply of the Highlands. Shipping meal in exchange for cash raised by the sale of animals at Crieff, or in exchange for salmon, was the backbone of Bailie Steuart's business: and he found the illegal 'porting of Eirish meall to the West cost and Inverlochie' the main hinderance to his business.[83] Laura Cochran detected in the first three decades of the eighteenth century about 4,500 quarters of oats and oatmeal being moved annually from Ireland to Scotland: but this was from entries

[79] Grant (1930): 543–50. [80] Spreull (1705).

[81] H. Hamilton, *An economic history of Scotland in the eighteenth century* (1963): 189–193, 243; W. Mackay (ed.), *The letter book of bailie John Steuart of Inverness, 1715–1752*, Scottish History Society, 2nd series, vol. 9 (1915): xxiv.

[82] Grant (1930): 545. [83] Mackay (1915): xv.

in the Irish customs books and if the importers habitually evaded the officials on the Scottish side, they may equally have avoided paying duty to the officials on the Irish side. Even so, in some years (1700, 1723) as many as 16,000 quarters of meal were reported as having crossed from Ireland. In the aftermath of the 1745 rising the Lord Lieutenant of Ireland, Lord Chesterfield, imposed a total embargo on the export of meal to Scotland in the hope of bringing the rebels to their knees, and, indeed, the loyal General Campbell found himself unable to provision his own troops: 'this country and the whole west of Scotland is threaten'd with famine' he wrote from Inveraray.[84] One way or another, it is easy to see how the market economy had made the Highlands increasingly dependent on food from outside.

Two further points about market growth might be stressed here. What happened in the Highlands, especially in the seventeenth and eighteenth centuries, is also likely to have happened in parts of the Lowlands and especially in the Borders a little earlier: that is to say, remote and upland areas would increasingly have been brought into the commercial exchange network and an opportunity would have presented itself to exchange animals and animal-derived food for grain-derived foods. Next, what happened in the Highlands under the impact of commercialisation has close parallels with what is happening in parts of Africa today: as the market takes over, with the concomitant rise of a waged labour force and the decline of subsistence farms, diet has turned away from meat and other protein-rich foods and towards an increased intake of maize and other cereals. As in the Highlands, this has been accompanied by population growth and by the decline of wild land, with a further narrowing of food supply as the opportunity to hunt game has declined.[85]

If it is accepted that a decline in real incomes (mainly through smaller average holdings), possibly (but not probably) an alteration in the grain–meat price ratio making meat too expensive, and certainly the rise of a trade exchanging Highland goods for Lowland meal lay behind the alteration in diet, what underlying forces can have lain behind these developments? Again, we suggest three possibilities: firstly, that population rose through some exogenous factor over which the Scots had no control; secondly, that it rose through an endogenous factor, over which they could, in some sense, exercise control; and thirdly that the structure of social relations, through the lairds' power over landholding, determined the direction of change. Although these are not necessarily mutually exclusive forces, it is not necessary either to envisage all three working at once.

84 L.E. Cochran, *Scottish trade with Ireland in the eighteenth century* (1985): 93–107; J. Fergusson, *Argyll in the Forty-Five* (1951):87–8.

85 We are obliged to anthropologist colleagues for these parallels.

The first possibility is that some exogenous factor created a substantial increase in population in the course of the sixteenth and early seventeenth centuries. We know next to nothing about late-medieval population levels in Scotland, but impressions from the growth of towns, from the multiplication and intensification of settlements and analogies with Scotland's closest neighbours, England, Ireland and Norway, all suggest very strongly that there was such population growth, possibly a doubling or even more between 1500 and 1650.[86] Quite possibly this was due to recovery from the late-medieval plagues, as is the accepted explanation in Norway, though for later sixteenth-century England, Wrigley and Schofield attribute near equality of importance to the factors of declining death rate and rising birth rate.[87] Whatever the reason, rising population could only lead to smaller holdings, and perhaps to squeezing some out to the towns: if the latter, the enlargement of an urban market for a rural surplus of food was likely.

It is also possible that an increased rural population made it feasible to find enough labour to improve agricultural productivity per acre and calorie output per head. Given the fact that arable cultivation is labour intensive, but that far more calories can be raised from an acre under grain than from an acre under grass, the net effect of rising population in a region suitable for corn but not growing much of it for lack of manpower, might possibly be to increase the quantity of food per head while narrowing the dietary choice. The problem of how quickly marginal returns to increasing labour inputs decline and whether rising numbers encourage sufficiently rapid technological change is much debated on the world stage between neo-Malthusians and the followers of Ester Boserup.[88] The argument that zero marginal returns were quickly reached in sixteenth-century England, and that new technology was relatively slow to arrive, though no doubt valid for England and parts of the Scottish Lowlands, may not be equally so for other parts of Scotland if population in poorly endowed and upland areas had dropped to very low levels in the fourteenth centuries and much land had simply gone over to a system of extensive pastoralism. The case of Gaelic Ireland, which probably had a population of under one million in 1600, suggests that extra labour (as well as extra capital and a new technology) was necessary before it could escape from the traditionally low productivity practices of herding and shifting cultivation. The impressions of Ayala in 1498 of the lack of effective corn production in Scotland at the

[86] E.A. Wrigley & R.S. Schofield, *The population history of England, 1541–1871* (1981): 244; L.M. Cullen, 'Population trends in seventeenth-century Ireland' (1975); S. Dyrvik *et al.*, *Norsk Økonomisk Historie 1500–1970*, Bind I (1979a): 16–31.

[87] Wrigley & Schofield (1981): 244.

[88] D.B. Grigg, *Population growth and agrarian change: an historical perspective* (1980); R.I. Rothberg & T.K. Rabb (eds.), *Hunger and history; the impact of changing food production and consumption patterns on society* (1983).

turn of the century and the findings of Dodgshon and Whyte on agrarian improvement between that point and 1780, come to mind.

However, whether output of calories per head increased or fell as a consequence of rising population, if the exogenous factor was important the Scots had no other way of accommodating population on the land except by shifting towards a more cereal-based diet than they enjoyed in the earlier period.

The second possibility is that, since a population can exercise at least a crude degree of control over its overall size through varying age of marriage and nuptiality, the Scottish population at some point grew or continued to grow, endogenously, by increasing the birth rate. This could have come about either at the close of the Middle Ages as a reaction to a favourable man–land ratio producing an easy living and giving an incentive to early marriage, or somewhat later as a reaction to an improvement in the calorie-carrying capacity of the ground, especially if an arable-oriented agriculture required a greater input of labour, which would enable more people to stay at home and marry earlier. It could also be assisted by a more favourable environment for buying additional calories through trade in Highland–Lowland exchange. In any case, if this hypothesis is accepted, in some sense the population itself made a set of choices that led it to exchange a more desirable diet and a larger holding for the alternative good of earlier marriage and more children.

It may be objected that the term 'choice' is inappropriate here, since it can scarcely be imagined that a group of peasants sat down to calculate that if they followed a particular strategy they would end up eating less meat but raising more babies. On the other hand the notion of control implies some kind of choice and different societies at different times have reacted very differently to increases in their output – sometimes, as in eighteenth-century Ireland or twentieth-century India, by increasing family size in a way that stabilises, or even diminishes, the average standard of living. The suggestion here is that substantial numbers of Scots may have gone for the second option, in effect for cultural and perhaps unconscious reasons preferring more children to any alternative good when the situation allowed any option. If they did so, they would have no option but to feed them on cereals.

That the intensification of Highland–Lowland exchange was indeed one change that would increase the population-carrying capacity of an area can be illustrated by the following calculation. Let us suppose that, around 1760, total sales of Highland cattle within and without Scotland amounted, on average, to 260 a day, or around 95,000 a year, being 80,000 sold to England and 15,000 sold for consumption within the Lowlands.[89] Our

[89] In 1777, over 10,000 black cattle a year were being slaughtered in Edinburgh, but not necessarily all Highland animals: Arnot (1779): 345. He also refers to the slaughter of

calculations suggest each animal might carry about 200 lb of meat, which would generate 47 million calories a day: but if sold for oatmeal in a situation where every 1,000 calories of beef could buy about 5,000 calories of meal at prices then ruling, the net 'calorie gain' for the Highlands would be 187 million. If each person in the Highlands on average needed 2,000 calories for subsistence, the proceeds would support about 86,000 extra souls. The total population of Scotland at Webster's census was 1,265,000 of which some 20 per cent lived in the Highlands and Hebrides proper – say about 250,000 people.[90] The cattle trade does not, however, by any means represent the entire export of the region at the middle of the eighteenth century as sales of fish, skins, bark and charcoal were also significant. It is therefore arguable that up to two-fifths of the existing Highland population could have been entirely supported by this trade, if all the proceeds from it had gone to the peasants and the peasants had chosen to use the income to support larger families.

Everyone knows, however, that all the proceeds did not go to the peasants; there was the question of rent, and as the standard of living of Highland and Lowland landlords alike increased sharply and obviously in the seventeenth and eighteenth centuries, clearly a proportion (but certainly not all) of the proceeds went to finance the ever more conspicuous consumption of an elite.[91] This raises our third possibility, arising from the facts of social structure, which we may call the exploitation factor. Perhaps a major spur to change came from landlords, who had the power to increase rents and the chance to do so when rising population increased the competition for holdings between tenants and induced the pangs of land-hunger. If simultaneous commercial possibilities arose for selling food, to the towns, inter-regionally, or outwith the country, they could then compel the tenantry to surrender more of their surplus and beat them down to living closer to subsistence and eating a higher proportion of cereals in their diet.

There is a good deal to suggest that the power of the landlords over the population was indeed increasing in the seventeenth and eighteenth centuries and that it was a good deal more extensive in all parts of Scotland than it was in many countries, like Norway, Sweden, Denmark and North Germany, where alternative tenure patterns survived to secure the peasant from the absolutism of the lord, or where the Crown pursued a policy of deliberate 'peasant protection', *Bauernschultz*, to keep an independent

120,000 sheep and lambs in a year, which gives some indication of how the borders could be similarly affected by the meat trade.

[90] J.G. Kyd (ed.), *Scottish population statistics including Webster's analysis of population 1755*. Scottish History Society, 3rd series, vol. 44 (1952).

[91] E. Richards, *A history of the Highland clearances* (1982), vol. 1; M. Gray, *The Highland economy, 1750–1850* (1957).

farming class as a counterpoise to the lords.[92] In Scotland the independent peasant class represented by the 'kindly tenants' failed in law to make their tenure a secure freehold, unlike the copyholders in England. If, in the Lowlands, many of them became small feuars in the land sales of kirk and crown in the sixteenth century, it was only to lose this independence in land sales to the local lairds in the seventeenth and early eighteenth centuries.[93] Outside the South-West not many independent peasants were left by 1750.[94] In the Highlands an additional opportunity was offered to put the screws on by the decline of clan violence, a long drawn out process that occupied all the period from 1600–1750. Macleod of Macleod, for example, enjoyed a very substantial jump in his rental following the end of his feuds with Macdonald of Sleat at the start of the seventeenth century.[95] This was not so much because of the benefits of peace to his people, as because he did not any longer have to rely on them turning out in battle; he could treat them as producers rather than fighters, and he no longer had the need to win their goodwill by favourable concessions in land or rent conditions. The animals and dairy produce he accepted in rent were quickly sold outwith the region. Much the same sort of thing must have happened to a lesser degree rather earlier in other parts of Scotland with the decline of feud. In the Borders it would certainly have had great significance after 1603.

In the Highlands at least, it is surely right to think of the landowners' avid response to the approaches of Lowland merchants as a main incentive to dietary and all other social changes. At first the chiefs found that if they removed the home-grown food as rent, they had to organise an import of meal to keep the population up or to allow it to grow.[96] Later, with the immense boon of the potato, they substantially reduced even that need: the population could live on a cheap homegrown calorie provider and almost everything else could go to swell the rent roll. As it appeared to the minister of Little Dunkeld in the 1790s: 'It has saved the tenants from the ruinous necessity of purchasing meal for their families ... by means of this root the produce of the parish is fully adequate to the maintenance of its inhabitants'.[97]

To exploitation, however, every peasant had, in the early modern world, a series of theoretical responses even if physical resistence was out of the question, as it appeared to be in Scotland. If he didn't like it, he could leave

[92] T.C. Smout, 'Landowners in Scotland, Ireland and Denmark in the age of improvement' (1987): 79–97.

[93] M.H.B. Sanderson, *Scottish rural society in the sixteenth century* (1982); M.H.B. Sanderson, 'The feuing of Strathisla: a study in sixteenth-century social history' (1974): 11–12.

[94] L. Timperley, 'The pattern of landholding in eighteenth-century Scotland' (1980): 137–52.

[95] I.F. Grant, *The Macleods: the history of a clan, 1200–1956* (1959): 247.

[96] Mackay, (1915) has many instances of lairds organising the importation of meal, for example, 69–70, 416–17.

[97] Steven (1985): 14.

and go to another area, to the towns or to the colonies. The eighteenth-century Scots, both Highland and Lowland, did all three in search of a chance to better themselves and even made conscious use of the threat of emigration to lower rents, as was very clear in the Highlands between the 1760s and 1803.[98] Nevertheless, it is possible that the Highlanders' love of their land, trust of their chiefs and ignorance of the outside world due to their geographical and linguistic isolation exposed them to exploitation to a greater degree than those in most other rural areas, so that they had become, by 1843, the poorest and the worst fed of all the Scots. The Lowlanders' more flexible response, by contrast, enabled them to market their labour power more effectively as the industrial and agricultural revolutions got underway. By the 1840s it was the Central Belt, urban and rural divisions alike, where the labouring classes had made most gains in real income and obtained a slightly wider dietary choice than their forebears in the seventeenth and eighteenth centuries.

It is not possible, on the data presently available, to come to a final conclusion as to the relative importance of the various factors discussed here. What is surely clear, however, is firstly that the changes in diet enabled far more people to survive and occupy the country than would have been possible without them, and, secondly that the need for food exchange was the major factor behind the growth of the internal market. A decline in the standard of living is not, after all, the only thing that can be deduced from the history of food in Scotland.

[98] J.M. Bumsted, *The people's clearance. Highland emigration to British North America, 1770–1815*, (1982):57–81.

3

CONTINUITY AND CHANGE IN URBAN SOCIETY, 1500–1700

M. LYNCH

INTRODUCTION

The 150 years after 1500 saw the reshaping of urban society in Scotland. There was in the last quarter of the sixteenth century a significant recovery in the level of exports after a slump which had lasted since the early fourteenth century. A series of political crises, beginning with the Reformation, brought the burghs to an unaccustomed position at the front of the political stage. That, in turn, encouraged unprecedented interference in burgh affairs by central government and a much more co-ordinated urban voice in national politics, with the emergence in the 1550s of the Convention of Royal Burghs as the regular assembly for the commissioners of the chartered towns. Those towns and their townspeople had, in common with the rest of Scottish society, experienced modest demands for revenue from Scotland's medieval kings. From the 1530s onwards they were confronted by spiralling tax bills, which brought into the tax net sectors of the urban population previously exempt; one of the most striking differences between urban society in 1500 and 1650 was the dramatic increase in its taxpaying sector.[1] There was in the same period (as in much of northern Europe), a significant if usually unquantifiable rise in the population of towns.[2] There was probably no increase in the proportion of the Scottish people living in towns. But this growth was important for its impact on urban society, as it was the first significant rise in population for fully three centuries. It is difficult to believe that the combined effect of these novel pressures, which were mostly concentrated in the second half of the sixteenth century, left the social fabric of the medieval burgh community undisturbed.

For most historians, however, the decisive period of change – from medieval burgh to pre-industrial town – has lain between 1660 and 1720. It was symbolised by the parliamentary act of 1672 which partly removed from the royal burghs the anachronistic trading monopolies which had for

[1] These items are discussed in M. Lynch (ed.), *The early modern town in Scotland* (1987): 2–4, 13–29, 55–75, 84–99. For overseas trade, A.W.K. Stevenson, 'Trade between Scotland and the Low Countries in the later Middle Ages' (1982): 271–84; I. Guy, 'The Scottish export trade, 1460–1599' (1982): 166–74.

[2] J. de Vries, *European urbanisation, 1500–1800* (1984): 255–7.

centuries insulated and protected them from the competition of burghs of barony. These private or seigneurial foundations had been comparatively slow to develop in Scotland; in England they accounted in 1400 for two-thirds of all boroughs, but in Scotland for only a half.[3] Their growth in Scotland occurred particularly in the seventeenth century. Faced with such a marked shift in the control of the economy from town to country, the royal burghs were forced to review the elaborate web of protectionism with which they had surrounded themselves. Decisive changes took place in the league table of towns, especially in the last quarter of the seventeenth century. Urban society itself could not escape the effects of the new atmosphere: by the 1680s the controls on entry to burgess-ship and merchant guilds were beginning to be relaxed; the system of formal apprenticeship was showing signs of breaking down.[4]

It may be necessary to consider two watershed periods rather than one in the development of Scottish urban society: the late sixteenth century as well as the later seventeenth and early eighteenth centuries. The question is partly one of perspective. Seventeenth-century historians have tended to underestimate the amount of movement within the pre-1660 economy. Sixteenth-century tax rolls show repeated minor fluctuations in the league table of towns. Fluctuations in exports and sharp competition for declining overseas markets, as revealed in the customs records from the 1370s onwards, produced dramatic rises and falls in the relative standing of many burghs, large and small, over the next two centuries. It needs to be recognised that monopoly and protectionism had not brought stability to the economy of the royal burghs in the medieval period. Sixteenth-century historians, by contrast, run the risk of over-emphasising the degree of change in the early modern town if they do not recognise that the conjunction of key elements which marked the close of that century did not survive throughout the next. Two of the four elements identified earlier, the level of outside political interference and rising fiscal demands, continued apace. But the two other factors were substantially modified: the pressure of population growth probably eased after 1650, except in the largest towns, and the export trade, which underpinned the traditional economy of most royal burghs, underwent a transformation after 1670 with the collapse of old overseas markets for two staple commodities, hides and rough woollen cloth. Equally important, for historians of either century, is to identify the linkages between the two periods in order to produce a balanced picture of what has elsewhere been called 'the collision of continuity and change'[5]

[3] M. Lynch, M. Spearman & G. Stell (eds.), *The Scottish medieval town* (forthcoming).

[4] Most of the seventeenth-century rolls are tabulated and analysed in T.C. Smout, *Scottish trade on the eve of Union, 1660–1707* (1963): 131–51, 282–3. See Table 5 for details of tax rolls 1535–1705.

[5] P. Clark & P. Slack (eds.), *Crisis and order in English towns, 1500–1700* (1972): 40.

which gripped towns and town life over the whole of the early modern period.

A LATE SIXTEENTH-CENTURY WATERSHED?

Part of the case for a watershed in the half-century after 1575 lies in the argument that the most dramatic aspect of a collision between continuity and change was the revision of the relationship between the burghs and the crown. The process had begun in the 1530s, although it was not until the 1580s that urban society was confronted with regular fiscal demands by the crown. Merchants were faced with the first wholesale duty on imports in 1597. In 1621 James VI's administration threatened to impose a package of novel taxes on the new growth area of the urban economy, the provision of credit, either by straightforward loan or on wadset mortgage. The threat was partly averted, but only at the price of greater conventional taxation.[6] The screw was turned further during the reign of Charles I; in the first 30 months of his reign Edinburgh paid more tax than in the last 25 years of James VI's. It was turned further still by the Covenanting and Cromwellian regimes.[7] The result was a marked increase in the tax-paying sector of urban populations; in Edinburgh in the 1580s the wealthier craftsmen were obliged to pay their taxes individually rather than on the traditional corporate basis; in the 1630s the tax net was increased by over 40 per cent, pulling within it for the first time groups like lawyers and occasional residents, such as lairds and merchants of other burghs, who were outwith the burgh community as formerly defined.[8] By the 1680s, when the basis for taxation became valued rent rather than the proceeds of trade or craft, the distinction between burgh inhabitants and burgesses, who alone had comprised the burgh community, had been all but lost.

Yet the fiscal demands of the government were only part of the rearrangement of the standing of the royal burghs within the community of the realm. From the 1530s onwards there was escalating interference by the crown in burgh government, with provosts and eventually whole town councils being planted on burghs, as unquestioning loyalty to the crown increasingly became the litmus test of their relations. These demands reached a climax in the early 1620s but were resumed, on a still greater scale, in the 1670s and 1680s, resulting in their specific rejection in the Claim of Right of 1690.

There was a drastic revision of the position of the burghs in national politics and the core of the change lay in the long majority of James VI.[9] The new royal authoritarianism which surfaced towards the end of the

6 Lynch (1987): 71–3.
7 *Ibid.*, 17; D. Stevenson, 'The burghs and the Scottish Revolution', in Lynch (1987): 179–80.
8 Lynch (1987): 17, 72–3. 9 *Ibid.*, 63–75.

sixteenth century was matched by the increasingly authoritarian nature of burgh government. There was a two-stage process taking place, the components and the timing varying from one burgh to another. With the incorporation of craft guilds there was in most burghs a limited admission of members of the leading crafts to both the town council and the merchant guild; but there also subsequently developed a clamour of various unrepresented groups in burgh society, ranging from lawyers to unincorporated crafts, for some voice in urban politics. In some burghs the two stages overlapped but in most the first stage was reached somewhere in the period 1475–1625; the second stage belongs to the late sixteenth century and virtually the whole of the seventeenth. The first stage marked the recognition of a craft aristocracy, which varied from one town to another – in Edinburgh it comprised metal workers, skinners and tailors; in Perth, metal workers and bakers. The second stage saw some of that craft aristocracy struggling to retain status and political influence as economic circumstances turned against it.[10] The effects of both stages of the process were, however, much the same. Urban society was, especially in the larger towns, gradually developing a complex middling sort, partly dependent on the old guild structure but also, particularly in the service sector, quite unrelated to it. Yet urban society, as it became more differentiated, also became more oligarchical. New emblems of authority, such as the constables of the new Justice of the Peace courts,[11] were found to involve the swelling middling sort, but power was in reality being concentrated in fewer hands. The old head courts of the burgh continued, but as symbols of an increasingly toothless body, the medieval burgh community.

The Reformation did not produce any immediate or serious challenge to urban establishments, whose authority was often enhanced by the new outlets available to them, as godly magistrates or elders of the kirk session.[12] The Reformation had not generally come to the towns on a wave of popular Protestantism, and where there was already political tension, as in Perth, it did not join forces with a programme for religious reform. As in the late city Reformation in Germany, so the rather late Reformation in Scotland took place against a background of urban decay and a certain amount of Erasmian or Catholic reform; it was usually implemented from above by urban establishments rather than forced upon them from below. The first real Protestant populism came a generation later, during the Melvillian controversies of the 1580s, when it was fuelled by a new breed of charismatic preachers and religious politics spilled for the first time out of the council chamber. From that point onward, however, burgh authorities had increasingly to cope with a new-style urban Calvinist for whom the

[10] *Ibid.*, 10, 27.
[11] G. Desbrisay, 'The Aberdeen justice court, 1657–1700' (1986): 76–8; Lynch (1987): 16.
[12] A. White, 'The impact of the Reformation on a burgh community' (1987): 92.

tradition of burgh government by 'the best and worthiest' of the town meant little.[13]

If the Reformation had little immediate impact on either the ethos or personnel of burgh government, its influence in another sphere of urban life, civic ceremony, was profound. It did not mark the final act in a long decay of the habits of medieval town life, for both the incorporation of crafts and civic ceremony were very recent developments. The medieval fabric of urban society was never so complete in Scotland as in the first half of the sixteenth century. Its diversity was reflected in the different craft altars recently established; its organic unity was located in the refurbished burgh collegiate churches, which still housed all the community; and its sense of ordered hierarchy was symbolised by the new Corpus Christi procession.[14]

The near-wholesale removal of civic ceremony and religious cult in Scottish towns was all the more serious in its impact because they were such recent developments. It is probably no coincidence that freemasonry was so widespread in seventeenth-century Scottish towns. The Reformation had created a vacuum which led to a new uncertainty both in the ethos of the craft guild and in urban politics. Crafts which had formerly been reasonably content with their status, as acknowledged by the new civic ceremonies, began by the 1580s to claim a place on burgh councils as compensation. On occasion, as in Dundee during the long dispute in the early years of the seventeenth century over the monopoly of the provostship by the landed Scrymgeour family, this new political stridency could combine with religious radicalism. The Dundee campaign was led by the outspoken minister, Robert Howie whose doctrine, the Privy Council decided, smacked of 'alteration of the government'.[15] Yet such an alliance was unusual, even during the fevered politics of the late 1630s and 1640s. Relative stability in urban politics remained the norm throughout the seventeenth century. Where urban political crises did occur, they were usually the result of outside intervention in civic government.

This overriding stability was the more remarkable because the burgh was by 1600 clearly no longer 'one society', even if the pretence was maintained that it was. In the largest burghs the single urban parish was broken up into more manageable units in the 1590s as a direct result of population growth. Edinburgh's ministers wanted eight parishes to cater for the town's 8,000 adult communicants, but had to settle, for a time, for four; Aberdeen's ministers cast lots to decide their vocations in the

[13] M. Lynch, 'Scottish Calvinism, 1559–1638' (1985): 239–41. Cf. the similar background analysed in K. von Greyerz, *The late city Reformation in Germany: the case of Colmar, 1522–1628* (1980): esp. 196–201.

[14] E. Bain, *Merchant and craft guilds* (1887): 55–61; D. McRoberts, *The Fetternear banner* (1957): 16–17. For England see M. E. James 'Ritual drama and social body' (1983).

[15] Lynch (1987): 76; *RPC*: vii.97.

burgh's two new parishes. It was the reformed church which thought hardest about the implications of the changes taking place in both urban and rural society during the long reign of James VI. Urban ministers recognised the problem, but did not agree on a solution: the single *corpus christianum* was cast aside in Edinburgh, Aberdeen and Glasgow, but retained in Dundee and Perth, where a team ministry was devised to hold on to the past.[16]

A LATE SEVENTEENTH-CENTURY WATERSHED?

The more familiar case for a watershed somewhere between 1660 and 1720, has three general facets: a decisive restructuring in the league table of Scottish towns, especially after 1670, with the rise of Glasgow as its key feature; the removal of the centuries-old monopoly of the royal burghs in trade and the erosion of various features of the privilege and restriction which their charters had permitted them to erect to deter outsiders; and the emergence of a number of new and more sophisticated business practices used by merchants. The themes are linked, in that some historians have argued a causal connection between them: that the towns which did best in this period were those which proved able to escape the restrictive habits of the medieval urban economy, pre-eminent among them being Glasgow.[17]

Was there a decisive restructuring of the urban hierarchy in the second half of the seventeenth century? By the 1690s, Perth, one of 'the four great towns of Scotland' (in the fourteenth century), had a pollable population akin to Musselburgh, one of a cluster of satellite towns around Edinburgh and still only a burgh of regality. Lanark, important enough to be represented from 1369 at the Court of the Four Burghs, the precursor of the mid-sixteenth-century Convention, had in the 1690s fewer paid hearths than Greenock, one of Glasgow's satellites, confirmed as a burgh of barony only in 1635.[18]

The rise of Glasgow in the tax rolls of the royal burghs seem dramatic. It was fifth in 1583, fourth, equal with Perth, in 1635, and second by 1670; it paid 4 per cent of all burgh taxation in 1612 and 20 per cent in 1705.[19] Yet there are not one but a series of spectacular rises to explain in the tax or customs rolls of the sixteenth and seventeenth centuries, including those of the Fife ports, which quadrupled their share of taxation between 1535 and 1600. If the seventeenth and early-eighteenth centuries saw the rise of

16 Lynch (1984): 18.

17 For the best analysis of towns after 1660, see T.M. Devine, 'The merchant class of the larger Scottish towns in the seventeenth and early eighteenth centuries' (1983a): 92–111, esp. 93–6.

18 Stevenson (1982): 141; G.S. Pryde, *The burghs of Scotland: a critical list* (1965): nos. 18, 234, 332; I.D. Whyte, 'The occupational structure of Scottish burghs in the late seventeenth century' (1987): 224–5; D. Adamson (ed.), *West Lothian Hearth Tax 1691* (1981): 103, 115.

19 T.C. Smout, 'The development and enterprise of Glasgow, 1560–1707' (1960): 194–5.

Glasgow, the fifteenth and sixteenth had seen the even more remarkable rise of Edinburgh. In the 1370s Edinburgh paid 23 per cent of all customs on exports; by 1500 this had risen to 57 per cent and by 1600 to 72 per cent.[20]

The case for seeing the later seventeenth century as a watershed neatly fits Jan de Vries' thesis on European urban development. He sees the period 1650–1750 as 'the age of the rural proletariat', with urban population growth throughout Europe being confined to large cities, and a slowing-down of demographic increase in most other towns.[21] Although the case for the rise of Glasgow has been made forcibly,[22] the converse thesis – of wholesale decay or outright decline of other, smaller Scottish towns – has not as yet been made explicit. Both aspects of the thesis need, however, to be set against the pattern, which had indelibly marked the three centuries prior to 1650, of the instability of medium and smaller-sized towns in Scotland. Was the rise of seventeenth-century Glasgow different from the rise and fall of many Scottish towns throughout the late medieval period? Was the slippage of Aberdeen, Perth and Dundee, which had with Edinburgh comprised 'the four great towns' for three centuries prior to 1650, but in 1705 paid only half of the share of the tax they had in 1535, different from previous falls of other prominent towns, like Linlithgow or Montrose in the fifteenth century or Haddington in the sixteenth?[23] The notion of a watershed occurring after 1660 needs a longer-term context to sustain it, and this is attempted later in the chapter.

Alternatively, did the seventeenth century see a decisive move in certain towns away from the body of burgh custom and law which had apparently regulated urban life since the legal foundation of royal burghs in the twelfth and thirteenth centuries? Was Glasgow, which again tends to be seen as the test case, noticeably different, either in ethos or occupational structure, from contemporary towns of a similar size? The characteristics of Glasgow, the seventeenth-century 'boom town',[24] need to be viewed as part of a wider question, of the striking variations amongst larger towns in their social and economic structure, which was already marked by 1500.

The case for a watershed in the late seventeenth century depends also on evidence regarding the emergence of new business practices and the advent of a new, freer atmosphere in town life – with Glasgow often acting as the pacesetter. Yet both themes can, in many respects, be traced over a much longer period and point to continuity in urban life rather than sudden innovation, whether in the Restoration period or earlier. Long-term

[20] Stevenson (1982): 258; Guy (1982): 170; Lynch (1987): 8.

[21] de Vries (1984): 257–8; see also E.A. Wrigley, 'Urban growth and agricultural change: England and the continent in the early modern period' (1985): 708–10, 724–5.

[22] See esp. Smout (1960): 195–6.

[23] M. Lynch, 'Towns and townspeople in fifteenth-century Scotland' (forthcoming, 1988).

[24] T.C. Smout, 'The Glasgow merchant community in the seventeenth century' (1968): 53.

business partnerships had been established amongst groups of Edinburgh's merchant princes in the 1620s and 1630s; the chartering of ships and direct investment in shipping by such merchants also belongs to the same period, as does the decisive shift of trade away from the staple port of Veere to other Dutch ports, especially Amsterdam and Rotterdam. The formulation of a credit system, based either on bills of exchange or on transferable and heritable bonds, also belongs to the 1630s rather than the 1680s. The tendency to see such developments as marking the escape from the bondage of the restricted practices of the medieval burgh is largely caused by the focus of historians on the period between 1660 and 1720.[25] Most of the apparent new departures in business practices had a longer history.

It is unlikely that merchants waited until the late seventeenth century to trade actively in other towns, establish close contacts outside their home port to make arrangements to buy produce direct from landowners.[26] The Dundee guild court was swamped, at the turn of the sixteenth century, by cases of merchants from other burghs setting up their booths in its streets.[27] The 1692 Report revealed that Edinburgh merchants owned most of the shipping based in Pittenweem, but similar Edinburgh interests in Kinghorn and Inverkeithing probably explain why they were jointly assessed for taxation until 1587.[28] Aberdeen overseas merchants by the 1590s spent much of the year based in Leith or Dundee. Edinburgh's wealthiest merchant in the 1560s, William Birnie, had contacts with many north-east lairds and exported as much salmon out of Dingwall, Wick, Inverness and Findhorn as the total amount routed through Leith. Other Edinburgh merchants in the same period exported cloth through Stirling, wool skins through Stirling, Haddington, Linlithgow and St Andrews, and fish through Aberdeen and Dundee as well as northern ports.[29] The difference between the two periods lies more in the nature of the evidence and the survival of contracts than in the closeness of town and country or town and town.

Similarly, the apparent strict monopolistic interests of members of the merchant guildry, sometimes traced to the period 1680–1720, can be detected, on a temporary or experimental basis, a century or more earlier; Dundee's guildry cut its entry fee by 80 per cent in 1696, but had before either made a short-term cut, as in 1654, or even admitted large numbers

[25] J.J. Brown, 'Merchant princes and mercantile investment in early seventeenth century Scotland', (1987): 125–6, 129–34, cf. Devine (1983a): 97, 106; Smout (1963): 81–3, 88–9, 117, which detected a use of bills of exchange after 1625. See J.J. Brown, 'The social, political and economic influences of the Edinburgh merchant elite, 1600–38' (1985): 148–72, for details of changes in shipping routes.

[26] Cf. Smout (1963): 76–7.

[27] A.J. Warden (ed.), *Burgh laws of Dundee* (1872): 147–8.

[28] SBRS Misc. (1881): 139, 141, 145.

[29] SRO Edin. Tests., 10 March 1569; SRO, E71/32/3, 8, Port Books 1563 and c.1570.

free, as in the early 1630s. It had raised its rate, in 1593, not as part of a consistent policy of keeping outsiders to a minimum but because it had previously admitted 'great numbers' in defiance of 'the auld acts'.[30] This is a cautionary example, which suggests that the history of the Scottish town needs to be looked at in a broader way than as the history of the institutions which made it up. The merchant guild was, in a sense, a monopolists' club but even the most exclusive of clubs needs from time to time to indulge in a recruitment drive in order to preserve its standing: in 1654 it did so to counter 'the great dearth of men and trade' within Dundee.[31] A variety of circumstances had forced towns to reconsider, long before the Restoration period, the apparently immutable medieval laws of monopoly and privilege, which reserved the right to engage in inland trade to the select community of burgesses and access to overseas trade to the members of the still more exclusive merchant guild. The later sixteenth century was spotted with examples, in each of the major towns, of action to bar outsiders or suburban dwellers from the merchant guild or burgess-ship, followed by a change of mind which brought about just the opposite.[32] The door to burgh privilege was not permanently closed before the Restoration; nor was it always open. The eventual adoption on a permanent basis of an open-door policy towards the end of the seventeenth century had been preceded by a long period of probation.

The size and economic makeup of towns has a fundamental impact on social structures and the dynamics of social change. The essential background to developments in urban society between 1500 and 1800 is provided by shifts in the composition of the urban hierarchy which were related to economic performance.

THE PRE-INDUSTRIAL TOWN: A NEW FRAMEWORK

Historians of seventeenth-century Scottish towns, especially those who have worked with an 'eye on eighteenth-century trends',[33] may have thought of the medieval town as more static or uniform than it actually was. They may also have underestimated the shifting circumstances of the sixteenth century which helped to produce both changes in the medieval burgh community and changes of mind in the burgh establishment as to how to react to them. Medieval historians have tended to focus on the history of the burgh as a chartered incorporation and to stress the continuity over centuries of institutions and custom.[34] Their combined effect has been to indicate a sharp break, usually in the period 1660–1720.

30 Devine (1983a): 94; Warden (1872): 134, 139, 153. 31 *Ibid.*, 139.

32 M. Lynch, 'The social and economic structure of the larger towns, 1450–1600' (forthcoming).

33 Smout (1960): 207.

34 Eg. see G.W.S. Barrow, *Kingship and unity* (1981): 84; Devine (1983a): 108.

An alternative framework is possible, stressing fluctuations rather than stagnancy in the economic circumstances of burghs in the three centuries before 1660. Although the basis of Scotland's medieval trade underwent drastic change in the late seventeenth century, the resultant pattern of urban decay and instability persisted. The same thesis would be sceptical that towns had rigidly adhered for centuries to a body of burgh law and custom which was described as 'a jumble' even when it was first drawn up, about 1250.[35]

Most late medieval towns stagnated or decayed; but a few did prosper against the background of a prolonged slump in overseas trade. They did so because, like seventeenth-century Glasgow, they proved more able to adapt to changing circumstances, partly by slipping the collar of the restricted practices laid down in the Burgh Laws. Over the fourteenth and fifteenth centuries there was a hidden transformation of many of the larger towns, as they diversified their economies out of wool and cloth into leather or metal working. By 1500 the occupational structure of the 'four great towns' (Edinburgh, Aberdeen, Dundee and Perth) had appreciably altered, with each moving in its own distinctive direction. By then the composition of the merchant guild varied markedly from one town to another, both in terms of size and the proportions of craftsmen admitted to them.[36] In many ways the term 'the medieval burgh' is only the convenience of historians of both medieval and later periods. The underlying reality was of different towns variously trying to adapt to major shifts in the patterns of trade, inland as well as overseas, with mixed success. Scotland, like other small European countries, had marked regional economic differences; this was as true of the urban sector as it was of the rural.[37]

The evidence for the study of Scottish towns is fragmentary and uneven until the sixteenth century or later. Yet there are two important sets of data which permit a broader perspective. These are the customs rolls, which record the export trade of most burghs from the 1370s onwards with reasonable regularity, and the tax tolls, which survive as a series from 1535 and are based on a range of indicators of economic performance.

Over the century after 1535 the tax rolls reveal four general patterns.[38] The most obvious is the dominant position of Edinburgh, which was being consolidated over the whole period: in 1535 it was assessed at a little less than the joint taxation on the next three largest burghs; by 1635 it paid more than the next four put together. Yet those larger towns – Dundee, Aberdeen, Perth and Glasgow – were, like towns of a similar size in England,[39]

[35] A.A.M. Duncan, *Scotland: the making of the kingdom* (1975): 482.
[36] Lynch *et al.* (forthcoming).
[37] Wrigley (1985): 722. [38] See table 5, below.
[39] N. Goose, 'English pre-industrial urban economies' (1982): 25; P. Clark (ed.), *Country Towns in Pre-industrial England* (1981): 11–12.

themselves consolidating their positions in relation to smaller towns in their own regions.

The third trend needs closer scrutiny of the table but is no less marked. A large number of towns underwent a series of fluctuations in their assessments until early in the seventeenth century. Some of the larger towns were affected – Perth's assessment rose three times and fell seven times between 1550 and 1635; Glasgow's conversely rose six times and fell three times over the same period. Yet on the whole it was middle-ranking towns which were most usually and most markedly affected. It is a pattern which suggests recurrent, short-term crises in many if not most medium-sized towns for much of the sixteenth century. In England, similar fluctuations have been described as mere undulations within a general pattern of relative stability in most towns,[40] but in Scotland, where a far larger proportion of towns were directly dependent on the vagaries of overseas trade, it seems more appropriate to see them as localised but severe urban crises. The towns which enjoyed relative immunity from both the rise of Edinburgh and the consolidation of larger regional centres were those with a highly specialised function[41] as small ports, concentrating on the export of fish, salt or coal. The tax on the fishing ports of south-east Fife increased four-fold by the end of the century, the most dramatic of the patterns in the sixteenth-century tax rolls.

Yet tax assessments provide only a rough measure of the economic performance of individual towns. Assessments reflected many things, including assets, such as burgh lands, mills and fishings which together made up the common good, as well as size; they reflected the stake in inland as well as overseas trade. The difference becomes obvious if two taxes on the burghs, levied within a month of each other in 1587, are compared (see table 2). One was a part of the normal series of taxes on the royal burghs, subjected to periodic revision. The other was, unusually, based on overseas trade and was designed to meet the shortfall in revenue to the crown since it had leased the customs to farmers in 1583, with disappointing results.

The most obvious point about the customs tax was that no royal burgh was rendered exempt, even if some, like Forfar and Tain, had their assessments cut to a nominal fraction. Every royal burgh, whether port or inland town, provincial centre or local market centre, depended to some extent on the export trade in staple commodities – raw wool, skins, hides, cloth and, to a lesser extent, fish, salt and coal. The chartered towns were dependent to a remarkable degree on the products of a primitive and largely pastoral rural economy. This made them vulnerable to fluctuations

40 A. Dyer, 'Growth and decay in English towns' (1979): 59–70; but cf. C.V. Phythian-Adams, 'Dr Dyer's urban undulations', *ibid.* (1979): 73–6.

41 Goose (1982): 27–8.

Table 2 *Percentage assessments on the burghs in the general tax and customs tax on overseas trade of 1587*[42]

	General tax	Customs tax	Variation
EDINBURGH	28.8	38.1	+9.3
Haddington	1.9	0.7	−1.2
Dunbar	0.5	0.5	—
North Berwick	0.3	0.1	−0.2
Total for E. LOTHIAN	2.7	1.3	−1.4
Crail	1.0	1.6	+0.6
Anstruther	2.0	2.4	+0.4
Pittenweem	1.2	2.0	+0.8
Dysart	2.5	3.3	+0.8
Kirkcaldy	1.3	2.5	+1.2
Kinghorn	0.7	1.0	+0.3
Burntisland	0.6	1.5	+0.9
Total for S.E. FIFE	9.3	14.3	+5.0
Dunfermline	0.8	0.3	−0.5
Linlithgow	1.0	0.5	−0.5
Stirling	2.0	1.3	−0.7
Inverkeithing	0.3	0.3	—
Total for UPPER FORTH	4.1	2.4	−1.7
Dundee	10.8	9.5	−1.3
Perth	6.0	7.5	+1.5
Cupar	1.6	0.8	−0.8
St Andrews	3.5	2.8	−0.7
Brechin	1.4	0.6	−0.8
Arbroath	1.0	0.1	−0.9
Montrose	1.9	2.0	+0.1
Forfar	0.5	0.1	−0.4
Total for TAY	26.7	23.4	−3.3
Aberdeen	9.2	7.2	−2.0
Elgin	1.4	1.6	+0.2
Inverness	1.5	1.8	+0.3
Banff	0.6	0.7	+0.1
Cullen	0.3	0.2	−0.1
Forres	0.5	0.2	−0.3
Nairn	0.3	0.0	−0.3
Tain	0.5	0.1	−0.4
Total for NORTH EAST	14.3	11.7	−2.6

[42] Burgh Convention Records: i. 246–7, 253–4.

Table 2 (*cont.*)

	General tax	Customs tax	Variation
Glasgow	3.3	2.5	−0.8
Dumbarton	1.0	0.8	−0.2
Renfrew	0.9	0.1	−0.8
Rutherglen	0.3	0.1	−0.2
Lanark	0.9	0.3	−0.6
Total for UPPER CLYDE	6.4	3.8	−2.6
Ayr	2.2	2.5	+0.3
Irvine	1.2	0.6	−0.6
Rothesay	0.4	0.3	−0.1
Total for LOWER CLYDE	3.8	3.4	−0.4
Whithorn	0.5	0.2	−0.3
Wigtown	1.0	0.2	−0.8
Kirkcudbright	1.0	0.5	−0.5
Dumfries	1.8	1.6	−0.2
Total for SOLWAY	4.3	2.5	−1.8
Peebles	0.8	0.3	−0.5
Lauder	0.3	0.1	−0.2
Jedburgh	1.2	0.5	−0.7
Selkirk	0.6	0.2	−0.4
Total for BORDERS	2.9	1.1	−1.8

in local supply and variations in demand in their overseas markets. Their dependence on staple exports was complemented by a reliance on imports of many manufactured goods. This highly distinctive two-way pattern of Scotland's overseas trade had a direct bearing on all royal burghs. It constricted, to a degree remarkable in northern Europe, the breadth of the occupational structure of many towns well into the seventeenth century. It is not until then that the technique of counting numbers of different occupations is worthwhile. English visitors were struck by the lack of handicrafts in even the large Scottish towns in the 1580s.[43] Overseas trade may have been the jewel in Scotland's economic crown, but it also acted as a straitjacket for most of its towns, rendering them liable to drastic fluctuations in their economic fortunes.

[43] *CSP*: xii. no. 906.

Table 3 *Percentage share of customs revenue of the leading exporting burghs, 1500–99*[44]

	1500–9	1510–19	1520–9	1530–9	1540–9	1550–9	1560–9	1570–9	1580–9	1590–9
Edinburgh	57.3	55.2	62.6	74.3	51.6	55.8	39.7	56.3	61.1	72.0
Aberdeen	15.1	11.7	10.3	10.7	12.7	12.6	19.1	11.2	8.4	5.1
Dundee	5.0	7.9	6.6	7.2	8.0	5.8	9.5	7.0	6.1	4.8
Perth	3.5	4.4	4.0	3.0	2.2	2.5	4.1	3.1	2.9	1.1
Haddington	2.7	3.5	3.7	2.9	1.7	0.3	0.4	0.5	0.2	0.7
Dumbarton	2.6	2.3	0.7	0.3	0.3	1.0	0.6	1.8	2.5	2.8
Ayr	2.2	2.3	1.3	1.1	1.4	1.1	1.6	1.1	0.7	0.6
Stirling	2.0	1.4	1.6	1.9	1.8	1.3	2.3	1.5	1.0	1.0
Kirkcudbright	1.8	1.7	0.7	0.4	0.5	0.3	0.1	0.1	0.1	—
Montrose	1.6	1.3	1.8	2.8	2.7	2.2	3.2	1.8	1.4	0.7
Linlithgow	0.9	1.3	0.7	0.8	1.0	0.7	0.6	0.1	—	0.0
Dysart	0.7	0.7	0.8	0.6	1.3	0.6	0.3	0.5	0.2	0.7
Pittenweem Group	0.7	1.1	1.6	2.5	7.4	8.1	11.4	8.6	7.5	3.9
Inverness	0.4	0.5	0.7	1.1	2.4	1.6	4.2	2.9	—	—

[44] These figures are wholly based on data compiled by Isabel Guy for her thesis. I am grateful to her, Angela Lamb, who compiled the material, and Professor T.C. Smout for generously allowing me access to this data. The Pittenweem group also includes Anstruther, Easter and Wester.

The degree of dependence of individual towns and even regions on overseas trade did, however, vary markedly. Here the variations between the two taxes of 1587 are revealing. All the ports of south-east Fife paid more in the customs tax – the only region where this was so. All the towns of the Borders, Solway, the Upper Clyde (including Glasgow) and the Upper Forth (except for Inverkeithing) paid less. Ayr was the only west-coast port with a large enough stake in the export trade for its tax to rise. Only Montrose and Perth of the Tay towns found themselves paying more, and in the north east a trio of Inverness, Elgin and Banff, which may have benefited from a sharp rise in salmon exports rather than a revival in their old share of the export trade in skins and hides.[45] The contrasts reflect the growing imbalances in the share of the export trade and the cut-throat competition amongst exporting burghs.

The picture which emerges from the more voluminous evidence of the customs rolls is similar (see table 3). The 'four great towns of Scotland' still headed both league tables in the early sixteenth century. Yet the tax assessments tend to understate movements, up or down, in any sector of urban performance as well as reporting them belatedly. Edinburgh's share of the export trade was consistently double or more the tax assessment on it. Similarly, the tax rolls accurately reflect the steadiness of Aberdeen's export trade throughout the first three-quarters of the sixteenth century but seriously under-represent its slump in the 1590s, when it fell by more than a half. A third of the four basic patterns revealed by the tax rolls is also amply confirmed: the increasing share of the export trade claimed by the small Fife ports was spectacular, the revenue from the group of ports around Pittenweem rising fifteen-fold by the 1560s. Their fall in the seventeenth century would be equally dramatic.[46] Yet, again, there was nothing new in this.

In the 1370s Scotland's overseas trade had been shared out much more evenly. The quartet of burghs – Linlithgow, Haddington, Montrose and Lanark – ranked highest after 'the four great towns' had accounted for no less than 20 per cent of it.[47] By 1500 only one of that quartet – Haddington – retained its position and the share of the towns ranked fifth to eighth had shrunk to 10 per cent. Haddington had been sixth amongst exporting towns in the 1370s, had crept up to fifth after the collapse of Linlithgow's overseas trade in the fifteenth century and was assessed as fifth for taxation in 1535. By 1601 it had dropped to tenth, and by 1635 to twelfth. Its slippage was as characteristic of the shifts in the fortunes of medium-sized

[45] This can only be conjectural as no customs returns are extant for Elgin in this period and those for Inverness after 1567 are unspecific. But between 30 per cent and 100 per cent of Banff's custom was paid on salmon 1574–82.

[46] Smout (1963): 136–7. [47] Stevenson (1982): 229n.

towns in the later medieval period as was the parallel rise of Glasgow from eleventh in 1535 to fourth equal in 1635.

The real difference between the sixteenth century and the two centuries which preceded it lay in the overall levels of exports. Scottish overseas trade had been in a profound slump since the early fourteenth century, which induced a scramble amongst leading towns for a greater share of diminishing exports. The continuing rise of Edinburgh had forced other towns, both great and small, to diversify their economies as it took a larger slice of different parts of the export trade. This process continued virtually unchecked through the sixteenth century, despite the general upward movement in trade which began in the 1570s.

So the decay of many medium-sized towns, which had marked Scottish urban history in the later medieval period, continued throughout the sixteenth century, despite the improvement in overseas trade. The larger towns were, by contrast, able, like a number of English provincial towns,[48] to ride out the crises of the sixteenth century with a less drastic fall in their income from overseas trade. Perth was the most badly affected of these towns, both in terms of fluctuations in trade and demographic crises. Aberdeen, with a markedly different occupational structure from Perth, was the most stable of the larger towns during the sixteenth century in terms of its tax assessments but was actually weathering a sustained fall in its income from exports; this was especially marked in the 1590s, when many of its overseas merchants deserted the town to spend at least part of the year in rival ports like Leith and Dundee, leaving Aberdeen's port, as the guild court lamented, 'a dry pond'.[49] Of the leading towns, only Edinburgh was increasing its export trade both in percentage and real terms and its continuing rise was the most important of a series of factors which constrained the performance of other major towns.

The combined evidence for the performance of the larger towns points to two conclusions. First: apart from Edinburgh, none was able to increase at the general rate of the late sixteenth-century rise in the export trade. In some cases, their income from exports was actually falling by the end of the century but their relative share of overseas trade within the regions of which they were the focal points was usually rising. Along with other, smaller ports they may have been forced more into coastal trade to complement the growing stranglehold of Leith as an exporting centre for most of the traditional staple commodities. This points to a second conclusion: that there was by the later sixteenth century, in Scotland as in England, a general gain in *inland* trade by the larger regional centres, at the expense of smaller chartered towns.[50]

The same period also saw the creation of many burghs of barony. The

48 P. Clark (ed.), *Country towns in pre-industrial England* (1981): 15.
49 Lynch (1987): 12.
50 Clark (1981): 5–7, 11–12.

dictum that the burgh of barony was the inevitable competitor of the royal burgh is uncomfortably rigid. It seems more likely that the relationship between town and country was changing in ways which accommodated the growth of burghs of barony *and* the consolidation of the greater regional centres. The losers were the older, small or medium-sized royal burghs, dependent on their chartered status as local market centres. So it may be that in the seventeenth century the distinctive Scottish phenomenon of a lack of middle-ranking inland towns was becoming more pronounced. The corollary of this shrinking of historic market towns such as Forres, Brechin or Lanark was the growth of newer satellite towns with a variety of specific or complementary functions around the major centres – such as Musselburgh and Dalkeith for Edinburgh and Paisley or Greenock for Glasgow.

The essential framework for the study of the pre-industrial town in Scotland lies in the distinctive and unbalanced character of its export trade, which remained essentially unchanged until the last quarter of the seventeenth century. The long slump in Scotland's markets overseas, which lasted from the fourteenth century until the late sixteenth, was reflected in a pattern of widespread urban decay and retrenchment, sharpened by intense competition amongst the royal burghs and recurrent crises for individual towns. The upturn in the export trade in the last quarter of the sixteenth century did not significantly alter the pattern, for much of the increased activity was absorbed either by small, specialist east-coast ports or by Edinburgh, which by 1600 accounted for almost three-quarters of the export trade. Equally, the beginnings of an upturn in inland trade in the same period did little to ameliorate the position of the smaller royal burghs, as it went either to new local rivals, in the form of licensed market centres, or to provincial centres, forced increasingly to rely on coastal and inland trade because of the slippage in their share of overseas trade.

POPULATION SIZE

A major difficulty in discussing the relative importance of Scottish towns is the absence of evidence of their size before the hearth and poll taxes of the 1690s. Yet there is an unnoticed indicator of the relative size of Scottish towns in the early seventeenth century, in the form of a tax levied by the Covenanting regime on the basis of valued rent. It has the added advantage of including six baronial burghs, which were not subject to conventional taxation. It thus allows a unique glimpse of the importance of Edinburgh's satellites, South Leith and Canongate, both of which were large enough to figure in the first dozen towns. The combined total of valued rent for greater Edinburgh was almost 38 per cent, helping to explain why the capital's assessment for normal taxation was raised to 36

Table 4 *Rank lists of 1639 tax on burgh rents and 1635 tax roll*

		1639 'Tenth' of burgh rents		1635 tax roll	
ranking		valued rent in £ Scots	% paid	% paid	ranking
1	Edinburgh	130,000	32.8	28.8	1
2	Aberdeen	54,481	13.7	8.0	3
3	Glasgow	23,643/15/0	6.0	5.5	4=
4	Dundee	20,000	5.0	9.3	2
5	South Leith	12,230	3.1	—	—
6	St Andrews	11,093/6/8	2.8	3.0	6
7	Dumfries	10,666/13/4	2.7	2.2	9
8	Perth	10,000	2.5	5.5	4=
9	Inverness	8,888/16/8	2.2	2.0	11
	Montrose	8,600	2.2	2.7	7
11	Canongate	7,533/6/8	1.9	—	—
12	Ayr	7,011	1.8	2.1	10
13	Stirling	5,640	1.4	1.8	12=
14	Haddington	5,197/13/4	1.3	1.8	12=
	Irvine	5,142	1.3	1.2	19
	Elgin	5,066/13/4	1.3	1.0	20=
	Kirkcaldy	5,000	1.3	2.3	8
18	North Leith	4,054/6/8	1.0	—	—
19	Burntisland	4,000	1.0	0.8	24
	Linlithgow	4,000	1.0	1.5	15=
21	Kirkcudbright	3,353/10/2	0.9	1.0	20=
22	Dumbarton	3,189/18/0	0.8	0.6	29=
23	Banff	2,666/13/4	0.7	0.4	39
	Cupar	2,666/13/4	0.7	1.2	17=
25	Lauder	2,433/6/8	0.6	0.3	43=
	Rothesay	2,333/6/8	0.6	0.3	43=
	Forfar	2,293/6/8	0.6	0.6	29=
	Tain	2,266/13/4	0.6	0.6	29=
	Dunbar	2,247/17/6	0.6	0.3	40=
	Brechin	2,210	0.6	1.0	20=
31	Culross	2,080	0.5	0.6	29=
	Dysart	2,030	0.5	1.5	15=
	Arbroath	2,000	0.5	0.5	34=
	Dunfermline	2,000	0.5	0.6	29=
35	Renfrew	1,666/13/4	0.4	0.5	34=
	Lanark	1,473/6/8	0.4	0.8	25
	Peebles	1,400	0.4	0.5	34=
38	Rutherglen	1,340	0.3	0.3	43=
	Anstruther E.	1,333/6/8	0.3	1.6	14
	Cullen	1,333/6/8	0.3	0.2	47=
	Jedburgh	1,333/6/8	0.3	0.9	23
	Kinghorn	1,299	0.3	0.7	28

Source: BL, ADD. MSS. 33262. Book of valuations (1639), 63–5.

Table 4 (*cont.*)

ranking		1639 'Tenth' of burgh rents		1635 tax roll	
		valued rent in £ Scots	% paid	% paid	ranking
	Crail	1,253/6/8	0.3	1.2	17=
	Inverkeithing	1,200	0.3	0.5	34=
	Forres	1,133/6/8	0.3	0.3	42
	Dingwall	1,066/13/4	0.3	—	—
	Pittenweem	1,066/13/4	0.3	0.8	26=
	Selkirk	1,000	0.3	0.5	34=
49	Stranraer	833/6/8	0.2	—	—
	Nairn	673/6/8	0.2	0.2	47=
	Anstruther W.	666/13/4	0.2	0.3	40=
52	Wigtown	400	0.1	0.8	26=
53	Kilrenny	266/13/4	0.1	0.2	50=
54	Dornoch	200/13/4	0.1	—	—
55	Annan	no returns	—	0.2	50=
	Lochmaben		—	0.2	50=
	New Galloway		—	0.1	54
	North Berwick		—	0.2	47=
	Sanquhar		—	0.2	50
	Whithorn		—	0.3	43=

per cent in 1649. The league table which the 1639 tax produces is worth considering in detail for it revises the conventional list in a number of ways (see Table 4).

A certain amount of caution is necessary in treating the spectacular figure for Edinburgh itself. A previous tax based on valued rent of 1635 is extant, revealing some 3,900 households and 900 business premises; the total rent for domestic households was the same as in 1639: £130,000. But in the capital, rents averaged £33 *per annum*, ranging from £6 in the poorest section of the town, on the south side of the Grassmarket, to £360 in the most fashionable parts of the High Street, the preserves of Edinburgh's lawyers and merchant princes.[51] It is unlikely, apart from in the Canongate and perhaps also in Aberdeen, where there is more evidence of local nobles and gentry keeping a town residence than in other provincial centres, that there would elsewhere be either such high levels of rent or such a sustained disparity.

Rents elsewhere were more even and much more modest. So although it is unsafe to use the 1639 returns from Edinburgh or Aberdeen for an analysis of comparative size, they may be used as an indicator of the relative sizes of most other Scottish towns. The returns may also, with

[51] W.H. Makey, 'Edinburgh in mid-seventeenth century' (1987): 205–15.

caution, be used to give an approximate notion of actual population, although they are better at indicating groups of towns of similar size than the precise populations of individual towns. Various small and medium-sized burghs, in making their reports to a royal commission in 1692, indicated a range of rents of £2 to £20 but for most the range was narrower at between £4 and £8. Dunfermline, which had 220 houses and 287 families in 1624, was given a total for valued rent of £2,000 in 1639, which indicates an average rent of £7 *per annum*.[52] If this figure was assumed to be typical of most towns, it would show that a town like Dunfermline, with a population of some 1,200, paid £2,000 in valued rent. On the same basis, the 1639 list reveals the distinct lack of medium-sized towns of between 2,000 and 4,000 people, which would be expected to be assessed at between £3,333 and £6,666 in valued rent. Only 9 towns, ranging from Stirling to Kirkcudbright, fall into this category and 3 of them lay within 20 miles of Edinburgh. Only a further 9 towns outside greater Edinburgh, ranging from Aberdeen to Ayr, were assessed at over £7,000 in valued rent and may have exceeded 4,000 in population. Below this there is a steep fall in rental, with a dozen or so towns, ranging from Banff to Dunfermline or Renfrew, with populations likely to have been somewhere between 1,600 and 1,000. It is likely that the remaining 16 royal burghs and 3 burghs of barony for which returns were given, ranging from Lanark to Dornoch, all had populations of less than 1,000.

What happened to the small and medium-sized towns in the second half of the seventeenth century? If the 1639 roll is compared with the hearth or poll taxes of the 1690s, the results point to a marked fall of population in many such towns. The complaints made by many burghs in the 1692 reports of abandoned or ruinous properties, falling trade and general urban decay, which are often treated with scepticism by historians, begin to ring true. The total valued rent for Ayr fell by almost a half between 1639 and 1691, and that for Irvine by two-thirds (although the 1691 figure excluded heritors' rents). If the valued rent of 1639 is compared with the number of paid hearths in 1691, it would seem that Inverness (with £8,888 but only 397 paid hearths) and Elgin (£5,066 but only 228 hearths) were significantly larger in 1639 than half a century later. So were Kirkcudbright (£3,353 rent but 150 hearths) and Dumbarton (£3,189 but 282 hearths). The level of fall seems to have been uneven but general in towns rated in 1639 at £3,333 or less, which probably then had populations of less than 2,000. The evidence points to real and possibly substantial drops in the population of inland towns like Renfrew, Rutherglen and Lauder, as well as in ports suffering from the late seventeenth-century drop in parts of the

[52] According to the 1692 Reports, rents in small burghs, like Lauder or Rothesay, ranged from £4–£20 p.a. In some, like Rutherglen, the range was much narrower, from £4–£8. SBRS Misc. (1881): 139, 141, 145. For Dunfermline, see Flinn (1977): 119.

export trade. The fall was as steep in west-coast ports like Kirkcudbright, Irvine and Rothesay as in Fife ports like Burntisland.

The most striking entry in the 1639 roll is that for Glasgow, which had caught up with Perth in the 1635 burgh tax rolls, sharing fourth place. Here it is placed a clear third, above Dundee, and with double the rental figure for Perth. This suggests that the rise of Glasgow was earlier and more dramatic than has previously been thought, at least in terms of its population. Although calculations based on annual baptismal entries which produced guesses that Glasgow's population was about 7,600 in 1609 deserve sceptical treatment, it is worth remembering that an English visitor of 1636 estimated that it had 6,000 to 7,000 adult communicants, in contrast to Edinburgh's 16,000.[53] This would produce a total population of between 10,000 and 12,000, which is not out of line with a rental of £23,643. By c.1650 the platform had been created for Glasgow's subsequent growth, on the new basis of its trans-Atlantic trade.

Scotland's urban experience seems to match closely that of other European countries, as described by de Vries. Most towns had gained in population, though unevenly, between 1500 and 1650. But in the century after 1650 significant population increase was confined to the two largest cities, Edinburgh and Glasgow, which grew on the the basis of government and new trade routes respectively.[54] Most other established towns, whether inland trading centres, east- or west-coast ports, stagnated or decayed.

SOCIAL AND OCCUPATIONAL STRUCTURE

The rise of Glasgow has been described as the most interesting phenomenon of seventeenth-century Scottish urban history, partly because, according to some historians, Glasgow was different in organisation and ethos from other towns. Yet there were marked differences, as in many parts of Europe, in the occupational structure of the main provincial centres in Scotland.[55] The chronology and pace of its growth also seem to need reconsideration. In 1639 Glasgow had a higher valued rental than Perth or Dundee. But, in contrast to them it was assessed at a *lower* rate in conventional taxation. This suggests that it was, despite its growth in population, economically under-developed for its size in terms of the usual criteria used for burgh taxation, which gave heavy weighting to overseas trade. The interesting question is not so much why it rose in the seventeenth century as why it took so long to do so. Glasgow's story can be told too much or too early in terms of the growth of its mercantile

53 See Smout (1960): 195; P.H. Brown (ed.), *Early travellers in Scotland* (1891): 141, 150.
54 de Vries (1984): 255–8.
55 Lynch (forthcoming).

community. It is worth bearing in mind the striking difference between the rise of Edinburgh and that of Glasgow: Edinburgh managed to accumulate a very large slice of a number of sectors of the export trade between 1370 and 1500, *before* it rose markedly in population.[56] Glasgow's story was largely the converse of this. There is little to suggest that it was throughout the sixteenth century anything other than a regional centre, relying largely on inland trade. Although probably already larger than Ayr by 1587, it was assessed at the same rate for overseas trade. Its occupational structure, which is partly revealed in a membership list of 1605 of the merchant guildry which included merchants and various crafts,[57] suggests a town with a modest mercantile community and an unusually broad manufacturing base, with its strengths in textiles and clothing and food processing: Glasgow had more maltsters, cordiners and weavers than Edinburgh, but less than half the capital's merchants, who comprised a surprisingly modest number.[58] There was no significant shift in the proportions of merchant and craft apprentices in Glasgow beyond a ratio of 1:2 before the 1670s.[59] The evidence of Glasgow merchants spreading their wings in overseas trade is minimal and anecdotal before the 1650s. Even then Glasgow's share of overseas trade is often exaggerated, either by claiming all the returns quantified by the Cromwellian customs official, Thomas Tucker, in 1655–6 as belonging to Glasgow, whereas they summarised all west-coast trade north of Irvine, or by claiming for Glasgow the bulk of Bo'ness's returns, which also aggregated those of all the Upper Forth towns, including Linlithgow and Stirling, as well as some Perth trade.[60]

If the burgh tax returns are used as an index of Glasgow's rise, they reflect a pattern shared by other medium-sized towns in the century after 1535 of a certain amount of fluctuation, both upward and downward. The indications are that it benefited from revival in the herring industry in the second quarter of the sixteenth century and early in the seventeenth.[61] It also probably shared in the general tendency of the larger regional centres to accumulate a greater slice of inland, as distinct from overseas, trade by the 1590s.

Three special factors other than the growth of its trans-Atlantic trade

[56] Lynch *et al.* (forthcoming).

[57] D. Murray, *Early burgh organisation in Scotland* (1924): i. 484.

[58] The numbers are tabulated in Lynch (forthcoming). Glasgow had 213 merchants in 1605, Edinburgh had 414 in 1583, but 44 were widows.

[59] See graph in T.M. Devine, 'The Cromwellian Union and the Scottish burghs: the case of Aberdeen and Glasgow, 1652–60' (1976): 9.

[60] SBRS Misc.: 35–46. See Smout (1963): 139 for Perth trade. There is a serious arithmetical error in the Tucker figures as tabulated in A. Gibb, *Glasgow: The making of a city* (1983): 38–9. The actual percentage share of custom and excise were: Leith 39.4 and 51.6 respectively; Bo'ness 24.7 and 11.2; Glasgow 9.3 and 12.9; Dundee 8.4 and 6.8; Aberdeen 7.9 and 5.2; Burntisland 6.9 and 3.7; Ayr 1.2 and 5.3; Inverness 2.0 and 3.3.

[61] Guy (1982): 125, 132; Smout (1960): 197, 199; Smout (1963): 220.

assisted Glasgow's later dramatic rise. The first, which can be overstated, was its relative immunity from the disasters of the late 1640s. The most significant effect of mid-century crisis was not the rise of Glasgow but the marked slackening of the grip held in Edinburgh on overseas trade. The capital still figured largely in Scotland's overseas trade but did not dominate it to the extent it had earlier in the century.[62] Tucker's figures show that Leith's share of customs fell from 72 per cent in 1600 to 39 per cent in 1655–6. This was more than a temporary setback: in 1670 Edinburgh's tax assessment was grudgingly lowered from 36 per cent to 33 per cent.[63] Added to this was the shift in the last two decades of the seventeenth century away from some of the commodities which Edinburgh had come to monopolise, such as skins and hides, as the focus of Scotland's markets turned towards England rather than the Netherlands.[64] The third factor is simply that the most spectacular rise in Glasgow's tax assessment, from 7 per cent in 1649 to 12 per cent in 1670, came within a year of the confirmation of the grant to the burgh of the barony of Provan; assessments took account of the size of burgh's common good and Glasgow's was, after 1669, twice as valuable as that of Perth and five times the size of Dundee's.[65] The tax rolls are, at best, a general statement of the economic health of towns: rises or falls in assessment do not always indicate a growth in the mercantile sector of an urban economy.

The history of pre-industrial Scottish towns needs to be considered more widely than the mercantile communities with which much of their fortunes are often supposed to have been bound up.[66] Both sixteenth-century Edinburgh and seventeenth-century Glasgow were only in a narrow sense merchants' towns. In both there were fewer merchants, of all kinds, than craft masters – they comprised 43 per cent of the burgesses in Edinburgh in 1583 and 37 per cent in Glasgow in 1605, whereas in Aberdeen the figure was 74 per cent.[67] But was Glasgow different in that there were fewer barriers within it between merchants and craftsmen? This may be so, if it is contrasted with smaller towns, where the emergence of merchant and craft guilds often was delayed until the seventeenth century.[68] It was the smaller burghs which tended to be most firmly wedded to the traditional divisions in burgh life, partly because many had adopted them so recently. Yet much of the experience of larger towns since 1400 had gone towards blurring the distinction between these sectors as they had competed against each other for a greater share of diminishing export markets. The notion that Glasgow was more open in its pattern of entry to apprenticeship or burgess-ship, or less strait-jacketed by traditional divisions between merchandising and

[62] SBRS Misc.: 35–46; Brown (1987): 141. [63] See table 5. [64] Smout (1963): 237–8.
[65] APS, VI: 647; SBRS Misc.: 58, 61, 74.
[66] Eg. see Gordon and Dicks (1983): 7. [67] Lynch (forthcoming): table 2.
[68] Less than half the royal burghs had a merchant guild by 1560; a corrected list, with dates, is given in *Scottish Review*, 32 (1898): 61–81.

handicrafts, carries with it a view of medieval burgh society which had not fully operated for decades, if not centuries.

By the sixteenth century each of the major towns showed differences in basic elements of their social structure and merchandising practices.[69] The two key sectors in Scotland's later medieval towns were wool and leather. Both depended on a certain amount of putting-out, from town to rural hinterland; both also were largely geared to exports; in both the town acted as a reception or finishing centre, before shipping partly-treated wool, rough (but rarely fine), dyed woollen cloth, or partly-finished hides and skins to the Netherlands or the Baltic. The merchants controlled the wool trade, but it was craft masters who by 1500 had gained control of much of the industrial processes involved in the leather trade and were also gaining access to the export trade. Such was the volume of the trade generated by Edinburgh's growing monopoly of the overseas shipment of hides and skins – 66 per cent of exports in hides in 1500, 88 per cent by 1562 – that exporting could no longer be practicably reserved to merchants alone. Only 31 per cent of the hides exported from Edinburgh in 1562 were handled by members of the merchant guild, and no individual held more than a 4 per cent share of the trade.[70]

The skinners were amongst the earliest of the crafts to be given incorporated status in the larger Scottish towns during the period 1475–1525. They, along with the metal workers, were recognised as a craft aristocracy, not least by their favoured position in the new Corpus Christi procession. This development closely parallels the consolidation in other European towns, such as Leiden and Lille, of small commodity production, which was organised around small industrial masters, whose products involved a limited amount of putting out to rural industry and were also geared toward export markets.[71] Typically, these small producers had a limited number of assistants – Edinburgh's 66 metal workers had 85 employees in 1558[72] – and varied sources of income. Their wives often brewed – there were over 280 female brewsters in Edinburgh in 1530 and over 150 in Aberdeen in 1509[73] – and their children were put to carding and spinning. Different sources of income were a hedge against price inflation and the severe fluctuations in demand which continued to mark the export trade in staple commodities. The natural conservatism of urban rulers generally persuaded them to protect the position of the small craft master, although he was hedged about, especially in the food-processing trades, with price and quality controls. Brewing and spinning were officially

[69] The following passage summarises an argument set out more fully in Lynch (forthcoming). Only additional references have been cited.

[70] This is based on an analysis of an Edinburgh customs book for 1561–3 (SRO E71/30/12).

[71] R.S. DuPlessis & M.C. Howell, 'Reconsidering the early modern economy: the cases of Leiden and Lille' (1982):49–84, esp. 50–7, 61–3, 80–4.

[72] Edin. Recs., iii:25. [73] *Ibid.*, ii:44; Lynch (forthcoming).

restricted to burgess households; town councils had a particular dislike of the habit of female domestic servants setting up in their own households and supporting themselves by brewing or selling foodstuffs.[74] Their aim was the preservation of traditional urban society, organised around the privileges of the community of burgesses. They feared masterless men and women, and any proletarianisation of the workforce.

Yet by the end of the sixteenth century there were some signs of change, although it was gradual and uneven, usually the result of changing circumstances rather than policy. The position of some in the craft aristocracy was slipping. A drop in the Baltic trade in hides and skins resulted in a 50 per cent drop in the income of Edinburgh's fleshers and skinners between 1565 and 1583; and the number of skinners in the capital fell by a quarter between then and the 1630s, despite a marked increase in the overall population. By 1600 most of the capital's textile workforce which had always been the smallest and least prosperous craft activity, had migrated to the suburbs.[75] The formation in Edinburgh of the Society of Brewers in 1596, backed by merchant capital, seriously undermined a traditional domestic industry.[76] It was the first explicit change of policy made by urban authorities towards small commodity production; it also probably did more than any single other act to undermine the economic status of women, whether as wives or widows. Protected monopolies like brewing had been an important safety net in a society where as many as 20 per cent of households were made up of single women yet where there was no compulsory poor rate.[77]

The late fifteenth and early sixteenth centuries had seen the explicit recognition by burgh authorities of a middling sort in urban society, against a background of a temporary shift in the economic climate in favour of urban craftsmen.[78] Metal and leather workers were usually among the first to be granted guild status. By 1600 the climate had changed considerably and the urban craft aristocracy was refashioning itself as a direct result. The new factor was the growing home market in seventeenth-century Scotland, as in England, for manufactured goods.[79] The new craft aristocracy, like the old, varied somewhat from town to town. In the larger towns it was generally crafts producing luxury goods, like glovers, tailors and goldsmiths, which prospered, as did the providers of services. The numbers of stablers and horse hirers in Edinburgh increased by 50 per cent between 1650 and 1680 and the number of

[74] Edin. Recs., ii: 27, 40. [75] Lynch (forthcoming).
[76] Edin. Recs., 1589–1603: pp. xix–xx, 158.
[77] Lynch (forthcoming).
[78] A. Grant, *Independence and nationhood: Scotland, 1306–1469* (1984): 85–6; Stevenson (1982): pp. iv, 262–3.
[79] Clark (1981): 17.

apothecaries doubled.[80] The capital was evolving from being largely a finishing centre for exported commodities into a centre of increasingly conspicuous consumption. The position of its traditional guilds varied from one craft to another, and even within the same craft; there was a slippage for those skinners who were not able to cater for the shift of demand away from tanning and treating for the overseas market towards the finer end of the domestic market, in the form of gloves and fancy leather work. In Perth it was glovers and dyers who prospered, and metal workers and bakers who declined.[81]

This shift in demand had important consequences for the balance between urban and rural industry as well as for the structure of the old, amalgamated craft guilds. Parallel to the development of urban specialist occupations – such as the 65 wigmakers Edinburgh had in 1691[82] – went a shift of gravity, from the town to its suburbs or its rural hinterland, of parts of the leather and textile trades, in order to reduce costs of production. The new specialisms, which extended the occupational structure of the larger towns more in the course of the seventeenth century than in any other previous century, took place mostly outwith the traditional guilds. But the rise of other groups entailed their escape from the control of the established incorporated crafts: in Perth, for example, maltsters broke free of the baxter guild, and glovers and dyers (who would by the 1690s be better housed than even Perth's merchants) shook off the skinner guild.[83] In one sense, the key to the shifting structure of early modern urban society lies in the emergence of a merchant elite. As towns grew in size a hierarchy developed, usually largely, if not wholly, dominated by merchants. But in another sense, it also lies in tracing the more complicated story of a shifting middling sort.[84] Its core, the traditional craft master, still existed in 1700, but in lesser numbers, in both absolute and relative terms, than in 1600.

CONCLUSION

There was no sudden transformation of the structure of urban society, even in the hothouse atmosphere of Scotland's two great seventeenth-century towns, Edinburgh and Glasgow. There was no general, sudden injection of merchant capital into urban-based industry. The seventeenth-century Scottish economy had a dual nature – a basic agricultural sector, which

[80] J. McMillan, 'A study of the Edinburgh burgess community and its economic activities, 1600–1680' (Unpublished Ph.D. thesis, University of Edinburgh, 1984): 98.

[81] Lynch (1987): 10, 27. By the 1690s Perth's metal workers accounted for only 3.9 per cent of the workforce; Whyte (1987): 230.

[82] Whyte (1987): 237.

[83] M. Verschuur, 'Perth and the Reformation: society and reform, 1540–1560' (Unpublished Ph.D. thesis, University of Glasgow, 1985): 276, 486; Flinn (1977): 194.

[84] Cf. DuPlessis & Howell (1982).

still produced a narrow range of staple commodities, and a largely new, more sophisticated sector of consumption, for which most materials were still imported but some, such as soap, glass and woollen cloth, were increasingly manufactured at home.[85] Urban society worked in both of these sectors: Edinburgh merchants still in the 1620s exported skins and hides to a staple port in the Netherlands as they had done for centuries. The same merchants were involved in new joint stock ventures but these were largely confined to the import trade, and it was only in that sector that they had by then broken away from the monopoly of the staple port, importing luxury goods and grain from a variety of ports stretching from the Baltic to northern France.[86] Most of the new manufactories were in the suburbs or rural hinterlands of towns, and the earliest investors in them were largely merchants, who continued to rely on their traditional activities in trade; the 'proto-capitalists' who first established the Newmills cloth manufactory at Haddington were also 'traditionalists'.[87] But the rationalisation of a putting-out system on more capitalist lines by urban merchants was as yet modest and not widely spread. Such patterns of mercantile investment, however nascent, had the same general effect as the other major influences on seventeenth-century urban development – the flight of some crafts to the suburbs of towns; the growth of satellite towns, often with a specialised workforce; and the spread of burghs of barony. The century after 1650 saw the consolidation of a rural proletariat rather than the creation of an urban one.

Newmills was a failure but it was, in another sense, no new departure. Edinburgh had always had a very modest-sized textile sector; it had fewer weavers than either Aberdeen or Glasgow, and their numbers were falling still further during its period of sharpest population growth – in 1634 there were only nine weavers paying tax, half what there had been in 1583.[88] So the Edinburgh merchants investing in the Newmills manufactory were doing no more than extending and formalising a long-established practice of putting-out textile work to rural industry. This is only one example of a much misunderstood topic – the marked integration, over the centuries, of town and country in Scotland. Towns were, of course, set apart from rural society everywhere in Europe by the specialised and concentrated nature of their workforces. Yet, as we have seen, Scottish towns had, until well into the seventeenth century, a rather narrow range of occupations, most of which were geared to the finishing or part-finishing of the commodities of a pastoral, rural economy for the export market. The chartered status of the royal burghs gave them clearly defined privileges in their rural hinterlands;

[85] R. Mitchison, *Lordship to patronage* (1983): 101–2. [86] Brown (1987): 128–31.
[87] The phraseology is that used in G. Marshall, *Presbyteries and profits: Calvinism and the development of capitalism in Scotland, 1560–1707* (1980), which sees in this a fundamental distinction in business practice and moral ethic.
[88] Lynch (forthcoming), table 2.

it bound such towns to their surrounding countryside rather than set them apart from it. The relationship between the two tended to be the major factor in urban politics throughout the sixteenth century. Town and country fed on each other – for materials, labour and capital.[89] The relationship was all the closer because few even of Scotland's largest towns had suburbs before the sixteenth century. Perth was an exception, with one suburban area emerging by the fifteenth century. Yet, by the end of the sixteenth century, it had three, and all were formally represented on the kirk session.[90] Edinburgh invested considerable sums in the early seventeenth century to buy up the various suburbs which lay around it.[91] The likelihood is not that there was a new, closer integration between town and country – in any of the aspects – in the seventeenth century, but that there was, partly because of the appearance of suburbs around larger towns in the period of population growth between 1500 and 1650, a shift in the balance between town and rural hinterland.

The link between urban and rural industry had, until the seventeenth century, operated particularly in the textile and leather trades. There was, however, a fundamental difference between the two. Merchants had tended to control much of the textile trade – both by putting-out systems and a special arrangement in their relationship with their staple port in the Netherlands, whereby fine woven cloth was prohibited from entry into Bruges, whose own weavers were given a virtual monopoly of work on Scottish raw wool, which Scottish merchants then re-exported back to Scotland.[92] The effects of this restricted practice probably left a legacy of a shortage of labour skills long after the transfer of the staple from Bruges in the late-fifteenth century. It helps to explain the highly distinctive feature of the Scottish town until the seventeenth century – the smallness of its textile sector, which is often taken as the touchstone of urban wealth and industry.[93] It was craftsmen entrepreneurs who, by contrast, had by 1500 come to organise and control the leather trade, both inside and outside town precincts.

It was not textile workers but skinners who, along with metal workers, were the small commodity producers *par excellence* in most late medieval Scottish towns.[94] They were allowed to join the merchant guild in numbers. That, for many, was equally important as a passport allowing the bulk purchase of raw materials, whether skins, malt or grain, as it was

[89] Lynch *et al.* forthcoming; Lynch (1987): 25–6.
[90] M. Spearman, 'The medieval townscape of Perth' (1987): forthcoming; Lynch (1987a): forthcoming.
[91] Makey (1987): 195–6. [92] Stevenson (1982): 223.
[93] Dundee, a centre for rough woollen cloth, is a partial exception, although it may have concentrated on the finishing trades; its dyers paid a remarkable 7 per cent of burgh taxation; Lynch (forthcoming).
[94] As in Leiden and Lille: DuPlessis and Howell (1982): 51–9, 63–5.

as a licence to engage in overseas trade. 15 per cent of the Edinburgh merchant guild was made up of craftsmen by 1500 and 27 per cent by 1640; in the 'craft town' of Perth the proportion was higher still.[95] Yet both groups – leather and metal workers – were vulnerable, for different reasons, to the shifts in demand which materialised over at least a century and a half before 1700. The overseas market for skins was volatile, as was that for cheap woollen cloth (on which Dundee's prosperity was partly based). Much of the product of urban metal workers was destined for rural farming; the customers of Perth's hammermen were spread far beyond the shire in the early sixteenth century. They, it is likely, were the heaviest losers in the competition offered by new burghs of barony, located closer to local demand; their numbers dropped, both in Perth and Edinburgh.[96] Leather workers, like textile workers, often drifted to the suburbs or were re-located in satellite towns like Musselburgh.[97] Yet the same craft guilds persisted, enforcing the same regulations, and often raising their own entry fees more sharply than those to either burgess-ship or the merchant guild. The question of the openness of Scottish urban society is often misplaced: the real monopolists were usually not the urban authorities, who controlled the rate of entry to freedom of the town, but the craft guilds which felt under greatest pressure from shifting economic circumstances.

There is a basic paradox to be grasped in the study of the seventeenth-century Scottish town. Most of the traditional institutions of the medieval burgh community remained – and did so well into the eighteenth century. But both institutions and working practices were also being stretched, almost beyond recognition. Although the size of the Edinburgh burgess community remained fairly constant, at about 30 per cent of all householders, the proportion of burgesses who gained entry to the guildry increased from a third to a half by the second half of the seventeenth century.[98] This reflected not so much the increasing openness of urban society but the increasingly honorary nature of burgess-ship and guild membership as well as the fundamental shift which was taking place in Edinburgh towards the distributive, service and professional sectors, all of which expected recognition of their rising status.

These were fundamental changes, even if they were partly camouflaged by the apparent continuance of the old corporate institutions. But they had taken place, for the most part, over a period of centuries rather than decades. The pace of change varied from town to town, and from one sector of urban society to another, even in Edinburgh. The smaller the town, however, the greater was likely to be its attachment to the past. Many, if

95 McMillan (1984): 38; Lynch (1987): 31n.

96 Verschuur (1985): 158–9; Whyte (1987): 230.

97 Whyte (1987): 230–1.

98 McMillan (1984): 37–9. Cf. Devine (1983a): 95, which dates the breakdown of the burgess system in Aberdeen and Glasgow in the 1720s.

not most, Scottish towns decayed in the second half of the seventeenth century, but there was nothing new about that. The underlying pattern, which had persisted since the late-fourteenth century, of a general economic instability exacerbated by temporary crises continued, if for different reasons. The larger, provincial towns had generally survived these economic squalls better, on the basis of their greater ability to diversify from one function to another – as the market place of their regions, as well as its port and natural finishing centre. It seems likely that the rise of Glasgow, like the fall of Aberdeen, Perth and Dundee, which both became marked after 1670, also stemmed from their varying ability to sustain this same balance. The result was a new and growing imbalance in the Scottish urban economy, not between east and west, but between north and south.[99]

The key to any general analysis of the economic or social history of Scottish towns in the two centuries before the Union of 1707 lies not so much in pinpointing the timing of change as in detecting what parts of urban society were in process of transformation and what parts were still being consolidated. It has been argued that it is unrealistic to suppose that towns experienced a watershed in the second half of the seventeenth century which suddenly exposed them to competition and market forces. If there were particularly sharp points of impact in the general collision of continuity and change which marked the whole of this period they lay in three things: the burgh's perception of itself as a community, its revised notion of its standing in the community of the realm and a certain shift of gravity between town and country. In other respects continuity, which should not be mistaken for immobility, was usually the abiding hallmark of Scottish urban society.

[99] The burgh tax rolls were conventionally divided into burghs north and south of Forth until 1563, with each equally assessed overall. Although there was a slight slippage of the northern burghs, it was not serious until after 1650: in 1635 they paid 47 per cent and in 1649 42 per cent. But by 1670 this fell to 37 per cent and by 1705 to 26 per cent. See table. 5.

Table 5 *Tax rolls of the royal burghs: percentage paid*[100]

	1535	1550	1556	1563	1579	1583	1591	1594	1601	1606	1612	1635	1645	Feb. 1649	July 1649	1670	1683	1692	1697	1705
Edinburgh	25.0	25.0	25.0	25.0	28.0*	30.0*	28.8	28.8	28.8	28.8	28.8	28.8	28.8	28.6	36.0	33.3	33.3	32.3	40.0	35.0
Haddington	3.0	3.0	3.0	2.4	2.0	2.0	2.0	2.0	1.9	1.9	1.9	1.8	1.8	1.8	1.8	1.8	1.6	1.6	1.1	1.3
Dunbar	0.7	0.7	0.7	0.7	0.4	0.5	0.5	0.5	0.5	0.5	0.5	0.6	0.6	1.0	1.1	0.6	0.6	0.5	0.4	0.4
North Berwick	0.3	0.3	0.3	0.4	0.3	0.3	0.3	0.3	0.2	0.2	0.2	0.2	0.2	0.2	0.2	0.1	0.1	0.1	0.1	0.1
E. LOTHIAN	4.0	4.0	4.0	3.5	2.7	2.8	2.8	2.8	2.6	2.6	2.6	2.6	2.6	3.0	3.1	2.5	2.3	2.2	1.6	1.8
Crail	0.7	0.7	0.6	0.6	1.5	1.0	0.8	0.8	0.8	0.8	0.8	1.2	1.2	1.2	1.1	0.9	0.4	0.3	0.2	0.2
Kilrenny	—	—	—	—	—	—	—	0.3	0.2	0.2	0.2	0.2	0.2	0.2	0.2	0.1	0.1	0.1	0.1	0.1
Anstruther E.	—	—	—	—	—	—	1.8	2.0	1.7	1.7	1.7	1.6	1.6	1.0	0.8	0.2	0.2	0.2	0.1	0.1
Anstruther W.	—	—	—	—	—	—	0.5	0.6	0.5	0.5	0.5	0.3	0.3	0.3	0.3	0.3	0.3	0.1	0.1	0.1
Pittenweem	—	—	—	—	0.7	1.0	1.0	1.0	0.9	0.9	0.9	0.8	0.8	0.7	0.7	0.7	0.4	0.3	0.2	0.2
Dysart	1.2	1.1	1.2	1.8	1.5	2.0	2.3	2.4	2.0	2.0	2.0	1.5	1.5	1.5	1.4	0.8	0.5	0.3	0.2	0.2
Kirkcaldy	0.7	1.1	0.7	0.7	1.0	1.2	1.8	1.7	1.5	1.5	1.0	2.3	2.3	3.3	2.4	2.3	3.2	2.4	1.6	1.5
Kinghorn	—	—	—	—	*	*	0.7	1.0	0.9	0.7	0.7	0.7	0.7	0.6	0.5	0.5	0.5	0.4	0.4	0.4
Burntisland	—	—	—	—	—	—	0.8	1.3	0.8	0.8	0.8	0.8	0.8	1.2	1.1	1.2	1.2	0.6	0.3	0.3
S.E. FIFE	2.6	2.9	2.5	3.1	4.7	5.2	9.7	11.1	9.3	9.1	8.6	9.4	9.4	10.0	8.5	7.0	6.8	4.7	3.2	3.1
Dunfermline	1.2	0.8	1.0	1.0	0.8	0.8	0.8	0.9	0.9	0.9	0.9	0.6	0.6	0.9	0.9	0.8	0.8	0.8	0.7	0.7
Linlithgow	1.5	1.5	1.5	1.5	1.2	1.2	0.9	1.1	0.9	0.9	0.9	1.5	1.5	1.8	1.8	1.7	1.5	1.3	1.5	1.4
Stirling	2.5	2.5	2.5	2.5	2.3	2.3	2.0	2.0	2.3	2.3	2.3	1.8	1.8	1.3	1.1	1.8	1.8	1.4	1.1	1.3
S. Queensferry	—	—	—	—	—	—	—	—	—	—	—	—	0.4	0.6	0.5	0.5	0.5	0.5	0.4	0.4
Inverkeithing	—	—	—	—	*	*	0.3	0.5	0.5	0.5	0.5	0.5	0.5	0.5	0.5	0.4	0.4	0.3	0.3	0.3
Culross	—	—	—	—	—	—	0.5	0.7	0.5	0.5	0.5	0.6	0.6	0.5	0.5	0.4	0.4	0.2	0.2	0.2
UPPER FORTH	5.2	4.8	5.0	5.0	4.3	4.3	4.5	5.2	5.1	5.1	5.1	5.0	5.4	5.6	5.3	5.6	5.4	4.5	4.2	4.3
Dundee	9.7	12.7	12.7	12.7	11.8	11.0	10.8	10.8	10.8	10.8	10.8	9.3	9.3	6.6	7.0	6.1	5.0	4.7	4.0	4.0
Perth	7.4	7.5	7.4	7.4	6.8	6.0	6.7	6.3	6.2	6.2	6.2	5.5	5.5	4.5	4.0	3.9	3.9	3.0	2.4	4.0
Cupar	2.7	2.6	2.7	2.7	1.8	1.8	1.6	1.6	1.5	1.5	1.5	1.2	1.2	1.2	1.1	1.0	1.0	0.9	0.8	0.8
St Andrews	3.0	3.0	3.0	3.0	3.5	4.0	3.2	3.0	2.8	2.7	2.7	3.0	3.0	4.3	3.3	2.3	1.2	0.6	0.4	0.4
Brechin	1.8	1.7	1.7	1.8	1.5	1.4	1.4	1.3	1.2	1.2	1.2	1.0	1.0	1.2	0.6	0.6	0.6	0.5	0.4	0.5
Arbroath	1.4	1.3	1.4	1.4	1.0	1.0	0.9	0.8	0.7	0.7	0.7	0.5	0.5	0.5	0.5	0.5	0.5	0.5	0.4	0.5
Montrose	2.7	2.7	2.7	1.9	2.2	2.2	1.6	1.7	1.6	1.6	1.6	2.7	2.7	1.8	2.0	1.9	2.9	2.0	1.3	1.7
Forfar	0.5	0.5	0.5	0.5	0.5	0.5	0.5	0.3	0.3	0.3	0.3	0.3	0.3	0.2	0.2	0.2	0.2	0.2	0.2	0.3
Inverbervie	—	—	—	—	—	—	—	—	—	—	—	—	—	—	—	0.1	0.1	0.1	0.1	0.1
TAY	29.2	32.0	32.1	31.4	29.1	27.9	26.7	25.8	25.1	25.0	25.0	23.5	23.5	20.3	18.7	16.6	15.4	12.5	10.0	12.3

100 Burgh Convention Records: i. 73–4, 173–5, 253–4, 365–6, 451–2, 514–15, 519–20, 522, 530–1; ii. 562–4; Smout (1963): 282–3; the 1635 roll is in *Aberdeen Council Recs., 1625–42* (1871): 78–80, and the Maintenance of Feb. 1649 in *APS* VI, ii: 154. Other taxation of both the Covenanting and Cromwellian periods conformed to the formulae set down in the tax rolls. Rolls in which only minor changes were made, such as that of 1557, have been omitted; Edinburgh's assessment in 1579 and 1583 included that for Inverkeitling and Kinghorn.

Table 5 (*cont.*)

	1535	1550	1556	1563	1579	1583	1591	1594	1601	1606	1612	1635	1645	Feb. 1649	July 1649	1670	1683	1692	1697	1705
Aberdeen	9.45	9.42	9.45	9.45	9.45	9.45	8.33	8.00	8.00	8.00	8.00	8.00	8.01	6.96	6.67	7.00	6.00	6.05	4.50	4.90
Elgin	1.19	1.00	1.01	1.00	1.33	1.50	1.25	1.10	1.00	1.00	1.00	1.00	1.00	0.75	0.67	1.00	1.15	1.15	0.90	1.40
Inverness	1.69	1.67	1.69	1.75	1.50	1.33	1.60	1.50	1.67	1.67	1.67	2.00	2.00	2.48	2.50	1.80	1.80	1.50	1.10	1.43
Inverurie	—	—	—	—	—	—	—	—	—	—	—	—	—	—	0.20	0.15	0.15	0.20	0.05	0.05
Kintore	—	—	—	—	—	—	—	—	—	—	—	—	—	—	—	0.10	0.10	0.06	0.05	0.05
Banff	0.68	0.67	0.68	0.70	0.68	0.68	0.50	0.45	0.40	0.40	0.40	0.40	0.40	0.40	0.33	0.40	0.40	0.35	0.30	0.20
Cullen	0.34	0.33	0.34	0.35	0.34	0.34	0.25	0.20	0.20	0.20	0.20	0.20	0.20	0.15	0.15	0.10	0.10	0.06	0.05	0.05
Forres	0.84	0.83	0.84	0.70	0.84	0.50	0.33	0.33	0.30	0.30	0.30	0.30	0.30	0.30	0.30	0.25	0.25	0.20	0.15	0.20
Nairn	0.34	0.33	0.34	0.35	0.34	0.25	0.25	0.25	0.20	0.20	0.20	0.20	0.20	0.20	0.20	0.15	0.15	0.07	0.05	0.15
Fortrose	—	—	—	—	—	—	—	—	—	—	—	—	—	—	—	0.25	0.25	0.15	0.10	0.15
Cromarty	—	—	—	—	—	—	—	—	—	—	—	—	—	—	—	0.25	0.25	—	—	—
Dingwall	—	—	—	—	—	—	—	—	—	—	—	—	—	0.10	0.10	0.10	0.10	0.06	0.05	0.10
Tain	0.51	0.50	0.51	0.45	0.50	0.50	0.60	0.50	0.50	0.50	0.50	0.60	0.60	0.50	0.50	0.35	0.35	0.25	0.20	0.20
Dornoch	—	—	—	—	—	—	—	—	—	—	—	—	—	0.10	0.15	0.15	0.15	0.16	0.05	0.15
Wick	—	—	—	—	—	—	—	—	—	—	—	—	—	—	—	0.16	0.16	0.16	0.15	0.20
Kirkwall	—	—	—	—	—	—	—	—	—	—	—	—	—	—	—	0.50	0.50	0.60	0.60	0.60
NORTH EAST	15.04	14.75	14.86	14.75	14.98	14.55	13.11	12.33	12.27	12.27	12.27	12.70	12.71	11.94	11.77	12.71	11.86	11.02	8.30	9.83
Glasgow	2.01	2.67	2.03	2.03	2.23	3.50	3.50	4.50	4.50	4.50	4.00	5.50	5.51	8.45	6.50	12.00	15.00	15.00	15.00	20.00
Dunbarton	0.84	0.83	0.84	0.83	0.89	0.77	0.90	0.90	1.10	0.93	0.93	0.60	0.60	0.89	0.60	0.50	0.50	0.25	0.25	0.30
Renfrew	1.19	1.00	1.01	1.00	1.01	1.01	0.90	0.80	0.60	0.60	0.60	0.50	0.50	0.50	0.40	0.40	0.40	0.30	0.20	0.20
Rutherglen	0.68	0.67	0.68	0.70	0.40	0.40	0.25	0.20	0.20	0.20	0.20	0.25	0.25	0.25	0.20	0.15	0.15	0.10	0.10	0.20
Lanark	0.84	0.83	0.84	0.70	0.84	0.84	0.90	0.90	0.80	1.03	0.80	0.80	0.80	0.89	0.60	0.60	0.60	0.50	0.45	0.60
UPPER CLYDE	5.56	6.00	5.40	5.26	5.37	6.52	6.45	7.30	7.20	7.26	6.53	7.65	7.66	10.93	8.30	13.65	16.65	16.15	16.00	21.30
Ayr	2.36	2.33	2.36	2.35	3.36	2.37	2.00	2.00	2.17	2.17	2.17	2.07	2.05	1.89	1.40	1.73	1.73	1.07	1.07	1.06
Irvine	1.35	1.33	1.35	1.38	1.40	1.35	1.33	1.20	1.20	1.20	1.20	1.15	1.15	1.39	1.00	0.90	0.90	0.50	0.50	0.52
Rothesay	0.68	0.67	0.68	0.70	0.50	0.33	0.40	0.33	0.20	0.20	0.20	0.25	0.25	0.33	0.30	0.30	0.30	0.25	0.25	0.20
Campbeltown	—	—	—	—	—	—	—	—	—	—	—	—	—	—	—	—	—	—	—	0.07
Inveraray	—	—	—	—	—	—	—	—	—	—	—	—	—	—	—	—	—	—	0.05	0.10
Stranraer	—	—	—	—	—	—	—	—	—	—	—	—	—	—	—	—	0.10	0.10	0.10	0.10
LOWER CLYDE	4.39	4.33	4.39	4.43	5.26	4.05	3.73	3.53	3.57	3.57	3.57	3.47	3.45	3.61	2.70	2.93	3.03	1.92	1.97	2.05

Whithorn	1.19	1.00	1.01	1.01	0.80	0.40	0.50	0.33	0.25	0.25	0.25	0.25	0.25	0.25	0.20	0.10	0.10	0.06	0.05	0.05
Wigtown	1.19	1.00	1.01	1.01	0.80	1.20	1.00	1.40	0.75	0.75	0.75	0.75	0.75	0.75	0.70	0.70	0.40	0.30	0.30	0.30
Kirkcudbright	1.19	1.00	1.01	1.01	0.80	0.80	1.00	1.40	0.90	0.90	0.90	1.00	1.00	1.00	0.80	0.80	0.80	0.30	0.30	0.30
New Galloway	—	—	—	—	—	—	—	—	—	—	—	0.05	0.05	0.10	0.05	0.05	0.05	0.05	0.05	0.05
Dumfries	1.69	1.00	1.73	1.75	1.88	2.00	1.75	1.60	1.83	1.83	1.83	2.20	2.20	1.49	1.67	1.67	1.67	1.91	1.91	1.91
Annan	—	—	—	—	—	—	—	—	—	0.17	0.17	0.17	0.15	0.17	0.10	0.10	0.10	0.10	0.10	0.10
Lochmaben	—	—	—	—	—	—	—	—	—	0.17	0.17	0.17	0.15	0.10	0.10	0.10	0.10	0.15	0.05	0.05
Sanquhar	—	—	—	—	—	—	—	—	—	0.17	0.17	0.17	0.15	0.15	0.10	0.10	0.05	0.05	0.05	0.05
SOLWAY	5.26	4.00	4.76	4.78	4.28	4.40	4.25	4.73	3.73	4.24	4.24	4.76	4.70	4.01	3.72	3.62	3.27	2.92	2.81	2.81
Peebles	0.68	1.00	0.68	0.70	0.75	0.80	0.80	0.75	0.67	0.67	0.67	0.50	0.50	0.60	0.50	0.60	0.60	0.55	0.50	0.45
Lauder	0.68	0.67	0.68	0.70	0.40	0.33	0.33	0.33	0.24	0.25	0.25	0.25	0.25	0.25	0.35	0.30	0.30	0.25	0.25	0.25
Jedburgh	1.19	1.50	1.01	1.00	1.15	1.32	1.20	1.10	1.10	1.10	1.10	0.90	0.90	0.70	0.90	0.90	0.90	0.85	1.30	0.95
Selkirk	0.68	1.00	0.68	0.70	0.68	0.68	0.60	0.50	0.50	0.50	0.50	0.50	0.50	0.70	0.67	0.67	0.67	0.60	0.50	0.51
BORDERS	3.23	4.17	3.05	3.10	2.98	3.13	2.93	2.68	2.51	2.52	2.52	2.15	2.15	2.25	2.42	2.47	2.47	2.25	2.55	2.16

4

WOMEN IN THE ECONOMY AND SOCIETY OF SCOTLAND, 1500–1800

R.A. HOUSTON

INTRODUCTION

More than half the population of early modern Scotland was female. Nevertheless, the status of women in sixteenth-, seventeenth- and eighteenth-century society remains obscure. Often omitted entirely from accounts of the period, women are commonly treated as peripheral and unimportant. Even recent research offers only brief asides about their place in social and economic life.[1] Attempts to render women more visible have concentrated on prominent but atypical members of the upper classes or have simply described women's subordination.[2] This chapter examines the economic, legal, political and cultural status of women in Scottish society between c.1500 and c.1800, concentrating on the middling and lower ranks. The analysis rests on three premises. First, we must understand the common experiences of men and women, more clearly to appreciate those which are distinctive to one gender.[3] This essay seeks to add women to Scottish history, to look at their experience in a predominantly masculine rendering of historical discourse. Despite the presence of certain shared understandings, there is no uniform 'women's experience' except at the most reductionist level.[4]

Second, the neglect of women in historiography is partly attributable to the lack of documentation on their lives. Women's experiences are subsumed in those of men. Most analyses try, perhaps inevitably, to fit women

I should like to thank Cathy Davies, Jane Dawson, Tom Devine, Rowy Mitchison, Christopher Smout, Keith Wrightson, Betty Sanderson and David Sellar for comments on earlier drafts.

[1] R. Mitchison, *Lordship to patronage* (1983): 86–9 offers some useful general comments. O. Hufton, 'Women without men: widows and spinsters in Britain and France in the eighteenth century' (1984) contains only one mention of Scotland.

[2] R.K. Marshall, *Virgins and viragos* (1983).

[3] G. Lerner, 'Placing women in history' (1975).

[4] E. Fox-Genovese, 'Placing women's history in history' (1982); C.N. Degler, *Is there a history of women?* (1975); S. Rowbotham, *Hidden from history* (1977); R.J. Evans, 'Women's history: the limits of reclamation' (1980); O. Hufton, 'Women in history' (1983); L.A. Tilly & J.W. Scott, *Women, work, and family* (1978).

into the categories and value systems of a society defined by men.[5] The areas in which women functioned and their status appear principally to have been determined by men. Some of the problems of lack of evidence are insuperable. There are, for example, no surviving diaries or autobiographies written by lower-class females and precious few by working men.[6] Indeed, almost all the available sources were written by adult males and tend consciously or unconsciously to trivialise, marginalise or even ignore women's concerns. Only sensitive questioning of the available records can open up the lives of women in the past to closer scrutiny.

Third, Scottish society is compared with contemporary England and Europe. Early modern England has been portrayed by Alan Macfarlane as a veritable 'paradise for women'.[7] Women's legal rights were strong, giving them an unusually independent standing in society. By contrast, the societies of southern and eastern Europe placed significant constraints on some areas of female life, including freedom of movement and choice of spouse. Despite these contrasts, the experience of European women was in many other respects uniform.[8] At the same time, concepts drawn from social sciences such as anthropology and sociology have been employed to add greater conceptual clarity to the analysis. The areas of female experience which are discussed can be used as grids for comparing the status of women in a range of different societies. These are: economic roles, roles in marriage and the family, legal status, education and cultural life, political voice, social relationships, and witchcraft.[9]

5 M. Chaytor, 'Household and kinship in Ryton' (1980) draws attention to this problem, which is exacerbated by the nearly universal practice in early modern documents of referring to women as adjuncts of men: wife, widow, daughter. Lerner (1975): 7–9 discusses the same issue. This bias disguises the importance of women as household heads and as labour force participants. In central Edinburgh, poll tax records of 1694 show that some 20 per cent of households were headed by women. T.C. Smout, *A history of the Scottish people* (1972): 164; R. Mitchison, *Life in Scotland* (1978): 69. For the town of Armagh in northern Ireland, a listing of 1770 attributes an occupation to only 3 per cent of married women, 32 per cent of widows and 73 per cent of single women whereas 95 per cent of adult males had identifiable occupations. L.A. Clarkson, 'Anatomy of an Irish town' (1978): 31–2.

6 J.G. Fyfe, *Scottish diaries and memoirs* (1928); J. MacDonald, *Travels in various parts of Europe* (1790): the memoirs of an Edinburgh footman, 1746–79; for nineteenth-century Britain see D. Vincent, *Bread, knowledge and freedom* (1981) and for England, S.H. Mendelson, 'Stuart women's diaries' (1985).

7 A. Macfarlane, *Origins of English individualism* (1978): 80–5, 91–2, 115–18, 131–5, 156–60; C. Hill, *The world turned upside down* (1975): 308; A. Fraser, *The weaker vessel* (1984): 464–70 offers a less optimistic view of women's changing status during the seventeenth century.

8 R. Wall (ed.), *Family forms in historic Europe* (1983): chaps. 2–6; C. Poni, 'Family and *podere*' (1978); R.M. Smith, 'The people of Tuscany' (1981); J.K. Campbell, *Honour, family, and patronage* (1974) deals with twentieth-century Greek rural society but the values and constraints he depicts apply to the Mediterranean world in earlier centuries. J. Black, *Citizens for the fatherland* (1979): 152, affirms that 'To be a woman in Muscovy and in the opening years of Peter I's Imperial Russia was to be illiterate and a virtual slave to father and husband'.

9 S. Ardener, 'The nature of women in society' (1978); R. Hirschon, 'Property, power and gender relations' (1984).

ECONOMIC ROLES

The economy of early modern Scotland was overwhelmingly agrarian. Women were vitally important to that economy, and their participation in the labour force was extensive.[10] The division of labour and the extent of specialisation in farming were limited before the nineteenth century and women were deeply involved in the multiple tasks which had to be performed on the farm and in the household. Single servants in husbandry, unmarried workers who lived in their employer's household and worked for their keep and a small cash wage, were employed in a range of tasks from milking and feeding livestock to spinning. Nor were they exempted from all but the hardest physical labour. An example from the Lothians in 1656 illustrates the sorts of work which wives of hinds were expected to do in the mixed farming economy.

> The Wives of Hinds, whether whole or half Hinds, are to Shear dayly in Harvest, while their Masters Corn be cut down. They are also to be assisting with their Husbands in winning their Masters Hay and Peats, setting of his Lime-kills, Gathering, Filling, Carting, and spreading their Masters Muck, and all other sorts of Fuilzie [manure] fit for Gooding and Improving the Land. They are in like manner, to carry th[e stac]ks from the Barn-yards to the Barns for Threshing, carry meat to the Goods [livestock], from the Barnes to the Byres, Muck, Cleange, and Dight [clean out] the Byres and Stables, and to help winnow and dight the Cornes.[11]

Women participated in a variety of ways in the agricultural labour force. Some worked for day wages, some on a yearly contract, some for no cash remuneration for themselves but as half of a partnership where the husband contracted to provide his and his wife's labour.[12] A fit and able wife was useful to any adult male agricultural worker, and essential if he was to be hired as a hind on the farms of the east–central Lowlands. This is made explicit in the case of Andrew Corsbie, a hind who was under church censure for fornication in the Midlothian parish of Lasswade. Just before the main hiring date of the year, Whitsunday (1661) he petitioned the kirk

[10] In 1871, 26 per cent of the total permanent agricultural workforce in Scotland was female, compared with only 6 per cent in England; their participation was particularly marked in south-east Scotland. T.M. Devine, 'Women workers' (1984c):98, 100. This widespread involvement of women in Scottish agriculture almost certainly had a long lineage but is impossible to quantify for earlier centuries.

[11] Quoted in C.H. Firth (ed.), *Scotland and the protectorate* (1899):406; A. Fenton, *The northern isles* (1978):58–9, 219, 279, 282, 413; St Andrews presbytery decided to relax penalties imposed on John Cairnes for 'loose carriage' in order to permit his remarriage, 'he being a widow, and having diverse small and young children'. *Ecclesiastical records* (1837):68. The assumption was that a man with children could not manage a home without a wife.

[12] M. Gray, 'Farm workers in north-east Scotland' (1984); Devine (1984c):119; W. Howatson, 'Grain harvesting and harvesters' (1984).

session for permission to marry in church since 'he could not be in service without marriage'.[13]

Until 1815 overall opportunities for women to engage in agricultural work did increase: improved rotations created new work peaks, augmented labour demand and helped to reduce the seasonal unemployment which had characterised the traditional agricultural world. Specialist dairy production in the west–central Lowlands in the later eighteenth century increased employment opportunities for women. However, changes in agricultural technology from the end of the eighteenth century did alter the nature of female participation in the agricultural labour force. The adoption in some parts of Scotland of the scythe in place of the sickle for reaping corn meant that women reapers were increasingly replaced by men who were physically better equipped to wield the heavier implement. When the two-horse plough came into use, the specialist horsemen who operated it assumed a higher status in a job from which women were excluded. Women still had jobs in agriculture but with developing specialisation during the nineteenth century, they were either reduced to menial tasks such as weeding and hoeing (in company with children), gathering and stacking or were required to leave the agricultural labour force for rural domestic industry, factory work or urban domestic service.[14]

Female participation in the labour force was not confined to farming. In much of the east–central Lowlands women were an important component of the workforce in seventeenth- and eighteenth-century coal mining.[15] Colliers in that area had to provide bearers to carry the coal which they had cut from the face to the surface. Normally they used members of their own family, generally wives and daughters. In pits such as Loanhead in Midlothian in the 1680s or Bo'ness in West Lothian during the 1760s women outnumbered men 2 to 1. Bearers carried loads of up to 75 kilograms along low passages and up step ladders to the pit head some 20 times a day.[16] Female bearing was less common in the western Lowlands where men and boys were used for this arduous job. In England the phenomenon was almost unknown.[17]

All the above employments are classified in conventional economics as 'work': labour for exchange value. It hardly needs to be stated that women were involved in a wide range of tasks in the household which were for use value and which, though vitally important, are not classified as productive work. These included cooking, cleaning, mending, child-minding and, in

[13] SRO CH2/471/3: 5 May 1661.
[14] W. Howatson, 'Scottish hairst' (1982): 26–7; I am grateful to Tom Devine for these points.
[15] R.A. Houston, 'Coal, class and culture' (1983a); B.F. Duckham, *History of the Scottish coal industry* (1970): 94–100; M. Flinn, *History of the British coal industry* (1984): 334–6.
[16] Smout (1972): 408; Duckham (1970): 99–100.
[17] A.G. Campbell, *Lanarkshire miners* (1979): chap. 1; Flinn, (1984): 333–4; T.S. Ashton & A. Sykes, *The coal industry of the eighteenth century* (1964).

the earlier part of the period, making clothes for the family. Indeed, many employments for women were simply an extension of their domestic tasks. Among the bulk of the population the concept of a 'housewife' – a married woman who simply looked after her house and family – cannot have existed, though for the growing urban middle and upper classes of the eighteenth century it was gaining currency. For these sections of society, female leisure was increasingly an indication of a man's social status. For the lower orders it was an unthinkable luxury.

The foregoing discussion has concentrated on basic manual employments. Yet, especially in the towns, women followed a variety of other occupations including teacher, brewer, midwife, trader, bonnetmaker, postmistress, shopkeeper, alehouse keeper, bookseller, printer and lodging-house keeper. The range of jobs open to women was expanding in the eighteenth century with urban growth and the development of the division of labour. However, in those occupations which would have given them economic independence, such as brewing for retail sale, they do not appear in numbers which are commensurate with their proportion of the total population. Only 77 (14 per cent) of 538 named brewers prosecuted for excise offences in Fife during 1697 and 1698 were females. Among 42 brewers in and around Edinburgh recorded in 1725, 7 (17 per cent) were women. The figure for Aberdeen in 1693–5 is 10 (7 per cent) of 144. In the sixteenth century, female participation in brewing had been more extensive: there were more than 230 women brewers in Edinburgh in 1530 and more than 150 in Aberdeen in 1509. The trade came increasingly to be dominated by men, a step marked by the 1596 foundation of the Society of Brewers of Edinburgh.[18]

Women's participation in trade was generally confined to shopkeeping, but they can be found among the ranks of international merchants. Port books of the late seventeenth century contain a sprinkling of women who signed for goods received. Some may simply have subscribed for one or two items in lieu of their husbands; some might have been buying in bulk for household consumption; others must have traded on their own account. A Fife woman, Isobel Anderson, received lintseed from Middleburg and Veere in the Low Countries; pepper, sugar, candy, soap, starch and hemp in addition to a ton of tea from Bruges. Throughout Scotland, women were a small proportion of the tax-paying craft and trade occupations.[19] There

[18] Brewing at this time was a small-scale operation carried out mainly by individual craftsmen and women. I. Donnachie, *History of the brewing industry in Scotland* (1979):6; SRO CS236/A1/19; SRO GD110/1147; SRO CS96/1/113. See Lynch (forthcoming). Towns contained a majority of adult females: Edinburgh, St Cuthberts in 1790 had a sex ratio of 74 males per 100 females compared with a national average of about 90. M.W. Flinn (ed.), *Scottish population history* (1977):283. See below pp. 108–9.

[19] SRO E7/9/12; I am grateful to Christopher Smout for this reference.

were certainly variations over the life-cycle, some widows enjoying greater economic status, and women were not entirely excluded from most crafts and trades. Some earned piece-wages for domestic spinning or weaving, and these were crucial to the textile industry. Yet, opportunities for economic independence without the help of a father or husband were few.[20]

True of the middling ranks of crafts- and trades-people, this was also the case for the wage-dependent workforce. The wages which were paid to women for their labour were much inferior to those paid to men. The median cash wage for female agricultural workers over Scotland as a whole was 48 per cent of the male wage in 1791 and 33 per cent in 1797.[21] A differential of 50–60 per cent seems to have been the norm over long periods. Lower female wage rates had become 'customary', but the decision had been made by (male) authorities and was perpetuated by them. Differentials may well have been endorsed by male workers. Women's wages were designed to be adequate only when pooled with those of a man. The same was true of industrial work. Ann Debnam, who worked at Newmills cloth works in East Lothian, received a pay rise from 3 Scots shillings to 4 shillings a day in 1687, 'to continue during the Companie's pleasour and her non mariage'.[22]

To some extent at least, women were paid less than men because they were physically less able or because they were doing different jobs. At Newmills women were paid the same as boys for 'picking', (making wool flexible and free of foreign bodies), which was at a level of 46 per cent of the male weaver's wages.[23] All the weavers were men, a restriction which may have been designed to keep male wages and job status high. At some eighteenth-century paper works, women were employed in collecting rags, a menial task not felt to merit full wages.[24] Lanarkshire JPs set maximum

20 C. Gulvin, *The tweedmakers* (1973): 103–6, 168–83; Marshall (1983): 155–7. There are certainly examples of women working in the same jobs as men and on the same terms: renting houses and business premises in sixteenth-century Edinburgh; prosecuted for retailing offences; acting as moneylenders and pawnbrokers. *Maitland club* 2,2 (1840): 84–91; *Maitland club* 1,1 (1840): 106–7, 112. However, the proportion of women in a given occupational group was almost always small except in some of the distributive trades and in service. Marshall (1983): 153. A similar picture can be found across Europe. Clarkson (1978): 31–2 for northern Ireland in the eighteenth century; N.Z. Davis, 'Women in the crafts in sixteenth-century Lyon' (1982); K. Stadin, 'Den gömda och glömda arbetskraften' (1980) shows that more than four-fifths of workers in the Swedish cloth industry were female but that in 1750 70 per cent of 'self-supporting' women worked as domestics; for late medieval Danish towns the status of women as providers of supplementary income or as a reserve labour force is discussed by G. Jacobsen, 'Women's work and women's role' (1983).

21 V. Morgan, 'Agricultural wage rates' (1971): 197.

22 W. Scott (ed.), *Records of a Scottish cloth manufactory* (1905): 163; changes in spinning technology in the late eighteenth century made it possible for women to earn 30 per cent more in this occupation than they could in agricultural day labouring. Smout (1972): 377.

23 Scott (1905): xxiii.

24 I am grateful to Professor Rowy Mitchison for this information.

female wages for farm work at roughly 60 per cent of the male earnings in 1708 and this level was also established by the Dumfries authorities in 1751.[25] Figures as low as these are unlikely to give a true indication of the variations in output between men and women. Differentials were less for seasonal, harvest labour where workers were paid on a daily basis. Strong, adult women received 5 shillings per day for shearing in early eighteenth-century Lanarkshire, 83 per cent of the rate for able-bodied men. For younger women the wage was 3 shillings as opposed to 4 shillings for men: 75 per cent.[26] These latter differences probably reflect more accurately the slight gap between the physical abilities of men and women than do the half wages commonly paid to women who worked as farm servants. However, physique does not explain the whole differential. Women's wages were meant to be supplementary, as they were across early modern Europe.

Rural wages were less variable across Scotland for women than for men. They were highest during the 1790s in the Borders and in west central Scotland, lowest in the Highlands and Islands. Proximity to large towns where alternative, non-agricultural employments were important in raising male remuneration did not have as much impact on female cash wages. Interestingly, however, nineteenth-century observers felt that a choice between industrial and agricultural work made female farm servants more independent.[27]

Rural domestic industry was important as an income supplement for the peasantry in some regions. Because 3 or 4 spinners were needed to keep a weaver going there must have been a predominance of women and children in the textile industry.[28] In the mid eighteenth century roughly 80 per cent of adult women were involved in spinning, many producing yarn for sale and thus generating valuable cash income for a family. The women of parishes such as Arbuthnott in Angus at the end of the eighteenth century could make 3 or 4 shillings a week spinning flax, which was then taken for manufacture into cloth at nearby Montrose. Stocking knitting was a significant employer of women in eighteenth-century Aberdeenshire.[29] The division of labour between industry and agriculture and between male and female employments is illustrated in the Highlands and north-east Lowlands where the men farmed and fished while the women and children spun yarn which was sold to entrepreneurs for making into linen or woollen cloth. Rural domestic industry reinforced rather than reduced the sexual division of labour in the pre-industrial period.[30]

[25] Malcolm, *Lanarkshire JPs* (1931): 17–18; T. Johnston, *History of the working classes in Scotland* (1920): 59.

[26] Malcolm (1931): 18.

[27] NSA XI (1845): 389; Morgan (1971): 194–5.

[28] M. Berg, *The age of manufactures* (1985): 139.

[29] G.A. Henderson, *Kirk of St Ternan, Arbuthnott* (1962): 184, 308.

[30] R.A. Dodgshon, *Land and society in early Scotland* (1981): 268, 313; Berg (1985): 154 notes the existence in north-west Ireland of separate households composed of women and children

Lower-class females found other ways of contributing to their own wages or to the family budget. Women who lived around large towns such as Edinburgh had the opportunity to market vegetables, fruit and dairy products there. Fishwives from Fisherrow and Prestonpans walked the few miles to Edinburgh to sell the seafood caught by their husbands or fathers.[31] Women participated in buying and selling, and they were important cash earners in an economy where specie was of growing importance. Commercial spinning in the Highlands and north-east Lowlands could bring in cash to pay rents and buy consumer products. For poor rural families in the Lothians there was an active market in wetnursing children who were farmed out by their middle-class Edinburgh parents for reasons of personal preference, fashion or physical inability to breast feed.[32]

It was assumed by Engels that the division of labour within the family regulated the division of property between husband and wife, and that women's status depended on participation in the public sphere, the labour force, whereas the management of the household under the prevailing conjugal family household was essentially private.[33] Women were tied to the household and the family was 'founded on the open or concealed domestic slavery of the wife'. The view that paid work was good for women's status in society was shared by the early twentieth-century middle-class feminists of whom Alice Clark is a well known example.[34] Women's position was felt to be closely linked to domestic work plus,

which subsisted by selling linen yarn on the open market. This clustering of spinsters may have helped to overcome the problems of low female wages and to allow poorly paid women to exist more easily without husbands.

[31] A. Fenton, *Scottish country life* (1976): 176. In addition, women were part of the 'black economy' of the early modern period. Women coal bearers stole coal from the owner's stocks or secreted pieces from the burdens they carried and sold it as a supplement to their husbands' or fathers' wages. Duckham (1970): 200. Servant girls in sixteenth-century Edinburgh made a little money on the side by washing other people's clothes along with those of their master or mistress on washdays. *Maitland club* 2,1 (1840): 104. And women fleeced Dutch fishermen in Lerwick while pretending to sell them goods. *Maitland club* 2,1 (1840): 200. These additions to the family budget were part of an 'accumulation of innumerable forms of subsidiary income' which comprised the economy of makeshifts of the lower orders. O. Hufton, *The poor of eighteenth-century France* (1974): 16. Women participated with men in the black economy. Conceivably, this enhanced the status of women so involved, though it is not at all clear whether work was important in determining their status in the community or their standing in the eyes of spouse or peers. There is little information available on prostitution in pre-nineteenth-century Scotland, but it seems unlikely that it could have provided more than an income supplement.

[32] This is based on my own work in progress on Edinburgh in the social and economic development of Scotland, 1660–1760. For wetnursing in England see R.A.P. Finlay, *Population and metropolis* (1981); A. Roberts, 'Mothers and babies' (1976); D. Maclaren, 'Marital fertility and lactation' (1985). Except in London and the biggest provincial towns, it was unusual to send children far from home to be nursed. In France commercial wetnursing was a major and deadly industry practised on a much larger scale than in early modern Scotland or England. R.K. Marshall, 'Wetnursing' (1984).

[33] F. Engels, *The origins of the family* (1972): 137–8, 221.

[34] *Ibid.*, 137; A. Clark, *The working life of women in the seventeenth century* (1919).

crucially, their contribution to the family budget by work beyond the immediate domestic sphere. Production for use and exchange had to be balanced. We have, unfortunately, no evidence on who controlled family earnings or about attitudes towards work which would help to resolve the question of whether women valued their participation as a way of enhancing their standing in family and community. Personal relationships rather than occupation may, alternatively, have been the main criterion by which they judged their status. We need a fuller understanding of the social and cultural context of employment.[35]

MARRIAGE

Part of that context was created by the demographic realities of the age. Expectation of life at birth was low, perhaps 30 to 35 years, though women lived on average some 2 years longer than men.[36] For those who survived their childhood, expectation of life was much improved. Yet, the likelihood of dying was a constant and largely autonomous fact of life for both sexes, and it exercised a powerful constraint on their lives. Unlike some eastern European societies, however, freedom of personal movement was only slightly restricted.[37] Population turnover among hired labour was common at this time. Women were particularly mobile. Among domestic and agricultural servants employed on the Leven and Melville estates in Fife between 1754 and 1793, 83 per cent of women stayed less than a year and 97 per cent had moved on within four years. The figures for males are 68 per cent and 90 per cent respectively. As in north-west Europe as a whole, women were more migratory than men.[38]

In addition to this normal and frequent turnover of labour in rural areas, there existed a considerable stream of temporary seasonal migrants from the Highlands to the Lowlands, especially after the mid eighteenth century. Some Highland women had worked as reapers and stackers in Lowland harvests during the seventeenth and eighteenth centuries, but from the later eighteenth century girls and young women formed the majority of seasonal migrants. It was estimated that half the eligible females in the southern Highlands participated in this movement at the

[35] Hirschon (1984); B.J. Todd, 'The remarrying widow' (1985):55–6; S. Collini, 'J.S. Mill and the subjection of women' (1984):36. Mill argued that women's task in life is 'accomplished rather by being than by doing', providing not the means which supported life but those which enhanced its quality.

[36] Flinn (1977):266–70.

[37] Wall (1982): *passim*; R.M. Smith, 'Some reflections on the origins of the "European marriage pattern"' (1979):87–8, 92, 96.

[38] SRO GD26/6/187. That women were more migratory than men is confirmed by the evidence of testimonials, certificates issued to mobile elements of the Scottish population, from a sample of central Lowland parishes between 1652 and 1811. R.A. Houston, 'Geographical mobility in Scotland' (1985b).

time of the Napoleonic Wars.[39] For men, military service was a unique form of temporary migration. New job opportunities in industry and as domestics in the growing towns of the Central Lowlands were emerging at this date, making more permanent movement possible. Women involved in this mobility would have been able to expand their geographical horizons while earning some money to remit to their families.[40]

Much movement was for economic purposes: learning and earning. Mobility could also help in locating a suitable marriage partner: the vast majority of domestic and agricultural servants were single.[41] Most women were likely to have married at some stage in their lives and there were strong economic incentives to do so. Low wages made permanent spinsterhood a risky proposition for the lower classes. However, marriage was not an economic necessity for all women. During the eighteenth century just over 20 per cent of women in a sample of Lowland parishes had never been married by the time they reached the end of their childbearing span.[42] Those who married did so on average in their mid-20s, like most women in north-western Europe before the nineteenth century. There is some impressionistic evidence that in the Highlands and Islands a marriage pattern closer to eastern or Mediterranean Europe prevailed with women marrying for the first time in their late teens. These estimates, based on literary sources, are not entirely reliable, though they are lent credence by the high birth rate in the region during the eighteenth century.[43]

Demography both reflected underlying socio-economic realities and exerted its own independent influence. One of the principal functions of marriage in the eyes of contemporary observers was the procreation of legitimate children and, once married, women had little opportunity to avoid the uniquely female experience of pregnancy. Contraceptive techniques – abstinence, abortion, coitus interruptus and prolonged breastfeeding – were certainly unreliable, though not wholly ineffective.[44] Indeed, women were not constantly pregnant. Work by demographers on populations with fertility much higher than prevailed in early modern Scotland has shown that only five years, or perhaps a quarter of the time

[39] Howatson (1982): 19–22; T.M. Devine, 'Temporary migration and the Scottish Highlands' (1979c): 344.

[40] *Ibid.*, 352

[41] I. Whyte, *Agriculture and society* (1979); Houston (1985b); for England see A.S. Kussmaul, *Servants in husbandry* (1981).

[42] Flinn (1977): 280. This figure is extremely high in the context of other pre-industrial European societies and may be based on suspect evidence.

[43] *Ibid.*, 274, 276, 279; M. Martin, *Description of the western isles of Scotland* (1703): 287; Smith (1979): 76–83; J. Casey, *Kingdom of Valencia in the seventeenth century* (1979): 17.

[44] Marshall (1983): 42, 109–14; Records of the central criminal court in Edinburgh, the High Court of Justiciary, contain very few cases of infanticide, even after the law was tightened up in 1690. Childlessness was not regarded as grounds for divorce but could attract adverse comment. Isobel Edmonstone was driven to stealing a baby to pass off as her own in 1686 by her husband's 'base discourse calling her a baren bitch'. SRO CH2/471/9 f.75.

during which a woman was married and capable of conceiving, would be spent in a state of pregnancy. The intergenesic interval in early modern Scotland averaged 25–30 months.[45]

Not surprisingly childbirth was viewed with some trepidation in a world where medical knowledge was rudimentary and medical intervention often counter-productive.[46] The Aberdeenshire minister James Gordon wrote of his wife's fifth delivery in 1697 that she 'was safely brought to bed of another son which we had reason to reckon a more than ordinary mercy in that she was so surpryzed that she brought forth the child under God with such small help as some few women could give her without the assistance of a midwyfe'.[47] Burial registers from mid eighteenth-century Newbattle in Midlothian give instances where women died in or after childbirth: a common cause of death among *recorded* burials in this parish.[48] Dangers there certainly were, but we should not exaggerate the frequency of maternal mortality. Of 15,306 burials in Edinburgh Greyfriars and St Cuthberts churchyards between 1739 and 1769, only 4 per cent of women had died in childbirth.[49]

LEGAL STATUS

Limited medical care and rudimentary contraceptive techniques certainly constrained women's lives, not least because they had to stay at home to feed and bring up children. An equally pervasive intrusion was made by the law. Legal frameworks structured people's aspirations and the ways in which they sought to achieve these. In particular, they created differential access to forms of property – land, money and goods – control over which

[45] J. Bongaarts, 'High birth rates' (1975): 294–5; Flinn (1977): 287, though these figures are based on a single parish. Marshall (1983): 42, claims that married women were likely to spend most of their married lives pregnant, though Fraser (1984): 59 is more careful in restricting her generalisations to the elite who did not normally breastfeed their children in person.

[46] S.H. Mendelson, 'Stuart women's diaries' (1985): 196–7 for England; Marshall (1983): 109–14; E. Shorter, *A history of women's bodies* (1982); A. Eccles, *Obstetrics and gynaecology in Tudor and Stuart England* (1982).

[47] G.D. Henderson & H.H. Porter (eds.), *James Gordon's diary* (1949): 78.

[48] GRO OPR 695/4.

[49] Marshall (1983): 227. Shorter (1982): 98–9 shows that maternal mortality levels for Edinburgh were similar to other European towns in the mid and late eighteenth century. At Tranent, a small town to the east of Edinburgh, the maternal mortality rate was 6 per 1,000 between 1754 and 1782, a rate close to that obtaining in the late nineteenth and early twentieth century. Flinn (1977)): 296–7. Martin Martin (1703): 233 was told that no woman had died in childbearing on the Isle of Jura in the previous 34 years. Figures for deaths in childbirth do not include later deaths which resulted from complications at the delivery, or the effects of comparatively frequent childbearing on life expectancy. Shorter (1982): 72 also opines that while 95 per cent of births are without complication in late twentieth-century developed countries, poor medical care before 1800 means that we cannot assume the same about the early modern period.

was central to freedom.[50] Individual rights in property were highly developed in Scots law, but how did women fare in terms of autonomy or dependence in its use or transmission?

The property rights of married women were strong in some respects and weak in others. A wife's moveable property was under her husband's control and she was unable to dispose of personal property without his consent. With the exception of her paraphernalia (personal clothes and jewels), he was able to sell it, give it away, use it to pay creditors or enter into contracts which involved it.[51] There must have been many examples like that of the woman prosecuted before the High Court of Justiciary in 1661 who had called down the devil on her husband for selling her cow.[52] The wife could bequeath her separate goods by means of a will, though she required her husband's permission to make a testament until the seventeenth century. Property acquired during marriage was entirely controlled by the husband. Ante-nuptial marriage contracts could be used to enlarge or restrict the wife's rights. After initial doubt, the competence of such contracts was finally established in the mid-eighteenth century. Marriage contracts entered into by substantial Glasgow merchants between 1740 and 1815 generally include a liferent provision and sometimes oblige the husband to buy land in order to provide an annuity.[53]

In the case of heritable or immoveable property the married woman had stronger rights. She could not dispose of this without consent, but neither could the husband sell her land without his wife's permission.[54] This would only affect those with land to alienate, but it does show that the husband had defined obligations to his wife. He was, for example, liable for any debts she had accumulated before their marriage, and he could not arbitrarily deny his wife permission to dispose of her separate estate without good cause. This was part of a wider obligation for the husband to act in his spouse's best interests. Of domestic matters, which the law held to be a married woman's 'natural and proper province', the wife was deemed to be in control, meaning that she could enter into contracts for food and furnishings necessary to the dwelling.[55]

Unmarried women enjoyed superior legal rights. Widows were effectively on a par with men. The dowry, if there was a formal transfer of resources in this form, was not legally recoverable by the husband during the marriage, though he controlled the usufruct. This arrangement provided security in the event of dissolution of the marriage through death or

50 Hirschon (1984). 51 G.C.H. Paton, 'Husband and wife' (1958): 99–100.

52 W.G. Scott-Moncrieff (ed.), *Records of the justiciary court*, vol. 1 (1905): 6.

53 Paton (1958): 101–2, 114; A.D.M. Forte, 'Some aspects of the law of marriage in Scotland' (1984): 110. I am grateful to Tom Devine for the Glasgow reference. Similar constraints on female freedom to dispose of property existed in late medieval Denmark. Jacobsen (1983): 4–5.

54 Paton (1958): 104. 55 *Ibid.*, 104–6.

divorce, but it also denied the woman full rights to dispose of the property involved. Resources could also be transmitted from one generation to the next. Inheritance through the female line was possible, but male primogeniture was preferred for heritable property (land) and daughters only inherited in the event of a father dying without living sons. Women could therefore inherit and transfer both freehold property and certain forms of tenancy.[56] Access to property for women depended on class, kin-ties and life-cycle stage.

Parental control over daughters was not extensive. Unlike some societies, fathers in Scotland had no interest at law in the property acquired by their children: there was no lifelong legal subjugation of females in this respect.[57] Until recently, historians assumed that arranged marriages for material reasons were all that young men and women could expect. They believed that freedom of choice was limited by the interference of parents or wider kin groups until the concept of romantic love gained currency in the eighteenth century. In the societies of eastern and southern Europe, and indeed of parts of northern France and Germany, control of courtship and marriage by the older generation was indeed strict.[58] For English men and women this was not the case. The work of Wrightson, Houlbrooke and others has shown that for the ordinary person in sixteenth- and seventeenth-century England the choice of partner was largely a matter of individual preference.[59] Relations within marriage could therefore be warm and companionate, not simply cold and instrumental.

Marriage in Scots law depended wholly on the mutual consent of the parties entering into the bond. In this respect, Scots law was identical to English until Hardwicke's marriage act of 1753 which established marriage by a clergyman as the only binding form.[60] Parents were unable to force a child to marry against his or her wishes, and could not prevent a son or daughter marrying someone whom they felt to be unsuitable. The only parental sanctions were moral and economic. Arranged marriages were rare and apparently confined to aristocracy and royalty where political

[56] J.I. Smith, 'Succession' (1958): 209–10; M. Sanderson, *Scottish rural society* (1982): 59; Forte, (1984): 106. The dowry was returnable in the event of divorce on the grounds of the husband's adultery or desertion.

[57] A.E. Anton, 'Parent and child' (1958): 119.

[58] Marshall (1983): 18–26; L. Roper, 'Weddings in Reformation Augsburg' (1985); L. Stone, *The family, sex and marriage in England* (1977); Smith (1979): 92–3, 96; W. Kula, 'La Seigneurie et la famille paysanne en Pologne' (1972); C. Klapisch & M. Demonet, 'La famille rurale toscane' (1972); J-M. Govesse, 'Parenté, famille et mariage en Normandie' (1972); R. Muchembled, 'La femme au village' (1981): 589. Charivari were almost unknown in Scotland, suggesting that community control over the sexual and marital behaviour of individuals was more limited than (or perhaps different in form from?) many other parts of Europe. M. Ingram, 'Ridings, rough music' (1984); J. Le Goff and J-C. Schmitt (eds.), *Le charivari* (1981).

[59] K. Wrighton, *English society* (1982); R. Houlbrooke, *The English family* (1984).

[60] T.C. Smout, 'Scottish marriage' (1981).

considerations and the economic interests of a much wider kin group had to be taken into account in the formation of personal union.[61]

The law created the potential for individualistic action and prevented direct compulsion.[62] However, this did not preclude indirect pressures being exerted by parents or kin. We know little of the social norms surrounding such intervention or their likelihood of success. Parental consent was held by the kirk to be highly desirable but this was in no way used to interfere with the legal and religious rights of the couple to do as they wished. Parents seem to have taken a sympathetic back-seat in some cases. A sixteenth-century laird, Robert Colville of Cleish, ordered his son in his will to provide a tocher or dowry for his daughter though 'gif it sal happin my said dochter to leid ane simpill [single] lyf and nocht to be movit in hir hairt to tak ane husband' the son was to keep her in an appropriate style of life.[63] Another father, this time from Stirlingshire, went to the trouble of setting up a marriage contract with his daugher's intended husband and had given his consent to the bond when the girl changed her mind. He was nevertheless prepared to support her in her change of heart.[64] Fathers did not invariably insist on union with a particular partner, nor even that their daughters should marry.

For the gentry and the aristocracy, the option not to marry was more economically realistic. Girls who inherited goods or property could remain single, and could live off money lent out at interest, as could widows: Edinburgh's New Town was full of them. Nearly a third of the girls from laird families never married in the mid eighteenth century since their parents concentrated on preserving the patrimony intact by marrying off any sons to rich bourgeois girls.[65] For women from the lower ranks in society, spinsterhood offered the near certainty of a bleak existence.

In some respects the legal status of women improved in the seventeenth and eighteenth centuries. However, this went along with a growth in their personal responsibility which removed certain protections they had enjoyed in the medieval period. Until the end of the sixteenth century, women were the responsibility of their fathers and husbands as far as the

61 Arranged *re*marriages by the clan chief, MacNeill of Barra, for both sexes on his estate during the seventeenth century were remarked upon by Martin Martin in the 1690s. The power of kin ties and of the lords was much stronger in this area than in most of the rest of Scotland (Martin (1703):97). Inter-clan marriages in the Highlands during the sixteenth and seventeenth centuries were arranged by families rather than by the individuals concerned, and there is some evidence that women were used as a form of 'currency' between groups. I owe this information to Bob Dodgshon.

62 Smout(1981):206, 210, 213–16; D.H. Fleming (ed.), *Register of St Andrews*, vol. 1 (1889):367; *Ibid.*, vol. 2 (1890):.

63 Quoted in Sanderson (1982):181.

64 J. Kirk (ed.), *Stirling presbytery records* (1981):125.

65 Based on the 1974 Stanford doctoral dissertation of P.C. Otto, quoted in Hufton (1983):129. As with the earlier figure for lifetime celibacy, this is extremely high and may be based on questionable data.

law was concerned. Yet, even in the eighteenth century, attitudes to women's personal liability on the part of judges and lawyers remained ambivalent, notably in the case of regulations governing evidence. An act of 1591 allowed women to give evidence in witchcraft trials for the first time.[66] Cases such as witchcraft or infanticide where, because of the nature of the crime and the circumstances surrounding it, women were often the only people present, illustrate that they were only called upon when their testimony was absolutely essential. As late as 1674, women were rejected out of hand as witnesses at the High Court of Justiciary in a case involving adultery. And in his influential legal textbook of 1678 Sir George Mackenzie speculated that women were by nature either too passionate or too compassionate and that this would render their judgement imperfect.[67]

The position of Scottish women before the law was not substantially different from that of their English contemporaries, though divorce was much easier for the Scots. Yet, as Engels remarked, the equalities created by the law between the genders or between social classes may be overcome by economic and social realities – fear, mistrust or ignorance – which structured actual differences in power and status.[68] Social norms, and the force of fear, ignorance or mistrust might prevent women and members of the lower orders generally from enforcing a notionally equal legal position.

Women were important both in the family economy and as agents of socialisation. Many, presumably, married out of choice, but the economic disadvantages of being single were also buttressed by legal and institutional constraints. Women who had never been married were not supposed to live alone or to work on their own account. In 1530 Edinburgh burgh council was persuaded that it had become too common for servant women, who had saved up enough money, to leave their master or mistress and set up in business on their own, usually in the victualling trade. As a result, the town council ordered that only married women should be allowed to rent premises and to conduct business unless specifically licensed by the council.[69] The problem recurred. In the early eighteenth century, Edinburgh burgesses complained that women and male unfreemen were setting up shops illegally.[70] Competition from anyone who did not have official

[66] C. Larner, *Enemies of God* (1981): 51.

[67] G. Mackenzie, *Institutions of the laws of Scotland* (1678): 530–1; Scott-Moncrieff, vol. 2 (1905): 196; D.M. Walker, 'Evidence' (1958): 306. The sex ratio among deponents at the High Court of Justiciary between 1640 and 1770 was 396 males for every 100 females. Women were allowed to pursue crimes against their close kin or against themselves: rape for instance. Until the seventeenth century, women had had to display the injuries incurred in a rape publicly and alert the authorities to the violation within 24 hours. After this date, it was only necessary to raise a criminal charge before magistrates. Rape of a man was held to be impossible without his consent. Mackenzie (1678): 160–1; 165–6. Sodomy or bestiality was punishable by death but there is no mention of lesbianism in legal texts.

[68] Engels (1972): 136; Hirschon (1984): 17.

[69] *Maitland Club* 2,1 (1840): 100.

[70] A. Heron, *The rise and progress of the company of merchants of Edinburgh* (1903): 44.

burgess privileges to trade within the town was the issue, rather than an attempt to control women's aspirations for economic independence. The reiteration of these regulations suggests that they were limited in their effectiveness and that some women were able to live alone and run their own businesses. Marion Alexander, prosecuted at Stirling burgh court in 1621, 'confessis she brew[s] eall in ane house be hir self and sellis it; quhilk tread she is commanded to leave off seeing she is ane singill woman be hir self, and commanded to entir in honest serveice'. Opportunities for women to work on their own account were more limited than for men.[71]

One reason for this discrimination was to prevent any immorality and scandal which might arise from women living alone. A 1699 act of Edinburgh burgh council was designed to stop women convicted of fornication from working in pubs as a way of limiting prostitution.[72] Moral considerations help to explain why there was no comparable ban on men living alone. However, the principal aim seems to have been to maintain labour supplies of a kind favourable to the established members of local communities. Moral prejudices went hand in hand with the economic interests of the dominant groups. For not only were females forced to work as servants, but also adolescent and young adult males. Where prevailing employment conditions meant that individuals could earn more as day labourers than as live-in servants, laws were instituted by those with economic and political power in the society which compelled them to do otherwise. In the Northern Isles, a labour shortage evoked regulations in 1615 which forbade boat skippers to transport male servants to the main-

[71] Dunfermline burgh council passed regulations that single women who had not been retained as servants for a term of months were not to live and work in the town. The aim was to ensure that all unmarried women worked as servants in households, and there are similar examples in Stirling during 1597 and 1621, at St Andrews in 1595 and 1597 and at Kirkintilloch in 1680. In the burgh of Kirkintilloch, landowners could only rent plots of ground to householders, not to 'idle servant women'. Lint was not to be given to such people to be spun, but only to indigent householders. A. Shearer (ed.), *Extracts from the burgh records of Dunfermline* (1951):87, 266–7; *Maitland Club* 1,2 (1834):459 for Marion Alexander; G.S. Pryde (ed.), *Court book of the burgh of Kirkintilloch* (1963):51, 128–9; Fleming vol. 2 (1890):806, 836. Similar restrictions are found in England. A. Dyer, *The city of Worcester in the sixteenth century* (1973):155; J. Harland (ed.), *Court leet of Manchester* (1864):157–8; a restrictive order by Bradford court leet (1687) is quoted in Berg (1985):155. M. Prior, 'Women and the urban economy' (1985b):111–12 demonstrates how in the early eighteenth century, hard-pressed Oxford tailors strove to exclude competition from (mainly single) female milliners and mantua-makers in an effort to maintain their own employment levels.

[72] SRO GD50/198/1. Notorious prostitutes were, by the orders of Edinburgh burgh council, to be ducked 'in the deepest and foulest pool of the town'. Smout (1972):75. Laws were passed concerning women which nobody would have dreamed of passing against men. During the sixteenth century, Edinburgh burgh council had the power to adjudicate on the virginity of a burgess's daughter since her right to pass on burgess status to a husband depended on this. M. Lynch, *Edinburgh and the Reformation* (1981):14–15.

land without a licence or testimonial.[73] Discrimination there certainly was, but it was against the economically and politically weak rather than against women as a gender. Efforts to limit a free market in wage-labour hit all members of subordinate socio-economic groups. Wedded to an hierarchical concept of society in which the family was the basic unit, authorities displayed their disapproval of 'masterless men' as well as independent women.

EDUCATION AND CULTURAL LIFE

Women's freedom to own and transfer property or to sell their labour were restricted by the law. These explicit limitations were reinforced by forms of cultural confinement. Poor educational standards and low literacy for females were a salient feature of this. Discrimination against females is visible both in the curriculum which girls were taught, in their access to educational resources and in their attainment of reading and writing skills.[74] In the official parish schools, boys and girls were segregated, and in all but the most elementary establishments boys outnumbered girls. The same was true of the charity schools run by the Society in Scotland for Propagating Christian Knowledge in the eighteenth century. The ratio of boys to girls in these averaged 5 to 1.[75] SSPCK schools were created mainly to teach English to the Gaelic-speaking Highlanders, and the predominance of boys in them helped to widen the existing cultural split between males and females by giving males the opportunity to speak English and Gaelic while leaving females as monoglots. If men used English and literate forms more commonly over time, women's status as transmitters of traditional oral culture may have been enhanced. Yet the standing of the whole cultural form was being eroded.[76]

Women were employed as teachers, though usually only of girls, and generally only of the most basic skills. Faced with the problem of providing rudimentary education for children in outlying parts of a large parish, Arbuthnott kirk session hired Anne Henderson in 1724: 'a woman sufficiently capable to teach reading and several things that properly

[73] *Maitland Club* 2,1 (1840): 176; Pryde (1963): 16, laws were passed at a local and national level to ensure that servants of either sex should not leave masters before the end of their 6- or 12-month contract. The Justices of the Peace of Lanarkshire in 1708 and of Dumfries in 1751 specified that servants were not to work for unregulated day wages, but must hire themselves for at least 6 months. Employers were entitled to insist that servants stayed for 12 months and could even compel 'idle' men and women to enter their service. Johnston (1920): 59–60.

[74] R.A. Houston, *Scottish literacy* (1985a) chap. 2 and *passim*.

[75] C.W.J. Withers, *Gaelic in Scotland* (1984): 123–33; J.M. Beale, 'History of the burgh and parochial schools of Fife' (1953): 44–5, 224; J. Scotland, *A history of Scottish education* (1969): 68, 81.

[76] Houston (1985a); V. Durkacz, *The decline of the Celtic languages* (1983).

belong to women, such as working stockings'. The tradition, particularly common in the Highlands, where women taught girls, helped to perpetuate low educational standards among females.[77]

Even where boys and girls sat in the same class, female children generally did not recieve the same education. The Church wished that both sexes receive a basic education in reading and writing and religious knowledge, but cultural values among the Scottish population dictated that girls' learning be limited to practical skills which would prepare them for their approved role in society. The baron court of Stichill in Roxburghshire ordered that nobody was to send their daughter to the sewing school until she had received at least two years of basic literacy teaching.[78] This late seventeenth-century regulation suggests that parents had different ideas. Their preconceptions were neatly summed up by Adam Smith, who wrote of girls:

> They are taught what their parents or guardians judge it as necessary or useful for them to learn; and they are taught nothing else. Every part of their education tends evidently to some useful purpose; either to improve the natural attractions of their person, or to form their mind to reserve, to modesty, to chastity, and to economy: to render them both likely to become the mistresses of a family, and to behave properly when they have become such.[79]

For the middle-class women of whom Smith was speaking, socialisation in education was a preparation for dependence. Education was only useful if it helped make a good marriage, while for the lower classes the practical skills taught to girls would enable them to be productive partners in marriage.[80]

If anything, the educational position in the Highlands was worse. In his 1764 report on the Hebrides, John Walker observed: 'Wherever there is access to a School, the boys are carefully put to it; but the Parents consider Learning of any kind as of little Moment to the Girls, on which Account, great Numbers of them never go to any School'.[81] In the eighteenth-century Lowlands, a broader range of education was available for middle- and upper-class girls and a more sympathetic attitude to female learning is evident. Yet the subjects they were taught, notably French, were ornamental rather than practical in nature. Designed not to enhance personal

[77] Henderson (1962): 286–7.

[78] G. Gunn (ed.), *Records of the baron court of Stitchill* (1905): 103–4.

[79] A. Smith, *Wealth of nations*, eds. R.H. Campbell and A.S. Skinner, vol. 2 (1976): 781.

[80] Alexander Munro's 'Essay on female conduct contain'd in letters from a father to his daughter' contains a thoughtful and sympathetic section 'On the education of girls' in which he argues that education should be designed not purely to make women decorative. He advocates teaching them practical skills and allowing them vicarious experience in order to mitigate 'the Extravagancies . . . of your Sex' and to fit girls to become companions for thinking husbands (NLS MS 6658).

[81] Quoted in Withers (1984): 123. For a similar observation by a traveller in the 1690s see Martin (1703): 115.

adequacy or employment opportunities, developments in female education in the eighteenth century reinforced rather than relaxed male preconceptions of women's social role. The new curricula aimed to make the middle-class girl more of a status symbol when she became a wife.

Given the restricted access which females had to education, it is scarcely surprising that their literacy was much lower than that of men. Women lagged far behind men in ability to sign their names until the end of the nineteenth century. In the mid-eighteenth century when Lowland men were only 35 per cent illiterate, their wives, widows and daughters were 70 per cent;[82] 9 out of every 10 Highland women were illiterate. Improvements in female literacy came later and more slowly than male: men's illiteracy was halved between 1640 and 1770 but that of women was only reduced by a third. There was a distinctive gender experience of literacy but, like their male counterparts, women's literacy was influenced by the place in which they lived and the social class from which they came.[83] Scottish women, like their European contemporaries, were much less literate than men. Their achievements were close to those of the women of north-east France though slightly inferior to those in northern England. All were far more literate than comparable social groups in southern and eastern Europe.[84]

The social hierarchy of illiteracy reminds us that women are divided by social class and economic status. Yet, gender itself was an important determinant of literacy. Restricted access to education and low literacy were used to explain, justify and perpetuate women's lower status in Scottish society. The Enlightenment's identification of men with reason (culture) and of women with instinct, emotion and frivolity (nature) built on a long-established intellectual tradition.[85] Conceivably, many more women were able to read than could write their name. It may be that in terms of access to literature and ideas in print women were not seriously disadvantaged. Yet only 9 of the 131 individuals who borrowed books from the library at Innerpeffray near Crieff between 1747 and 1757 were women.[86]

[82] Houston (1985a): 56–7, 67–9.

[83] *Ibid.*, chap. 2 based on depositions before the High Court of Justiciary.

[84] *Ibid.*, 67–9. In mid nineteenth-century Spain, women were still 86 per cent illiterate. R. Kagan, *Students and society in early modern Spain* (1974): 27. Around 1800 girls made up only 9 per cent of the pupils in the minor school network of Russia: a much more extreme imbalance than in eighteenth-century Scotland. P.L. Alston, *Education and the state* (1969): 19.

[85] Degler (1975): 10.

[86] M. Spufford, *Small books and pleasant histories* (1981): 25, 34–6, 45; NLS Mf. 19 and Houston (1985a): 174–9 for analysis.

POLITICAL VOICE

In other respects the standing of women in Scottish society remained low throughout this period. Females were formally excluded from high politics and were largely prevented from taking part in church government, though when heads of household voted on the appointment of a new minister, some parishes allowed women to vote, and in all cases female landowners were entitled to subscribe the call to the successful candidate.[87] Women's participation in riots was their most potent and direct form of mass political activity.[88] In 1655 a group of around 70 people, mostly women, gathered at Ferry in Fife to protest vocally about the transfer of their minister to the parish of Strathmiglo by the Kirk authorities. Condemning field conventicles in 1684, the Privy Council of Scotland recorded that 'women were the chief fomenters of these disorders'.[89] These protests took place within the mainstream of church life and organisation. Women certainly took an active role in religion. Membership of groups such as the Quakers, who were outside the established church, may have given women greater freedom of expression and more influence on their spiritual destiny than was conventionally allowed them.

Joint actions with men allowed expression of distinctively female viewpoints. During the 1797 Tranent militia riot, for instance, the women of this East Lothian community complained that 'it was a hard thing for them to have the trouble of bringing up children . . . and then to have them taken away from them' to do military service.[90] When the hated press-gang descended on a seashore village in late-eighteenth-century Argyllshire, the men hid in the hills while the women and children drove the sailors away by throwing clods of earth at them.[91] The wives who tried to shield their

[87] I am grateful to Rowy Mitchison for this point which is based on her research into the papers of the General Assembly of the Church of Scotland.

[88] One does not have to go far into early modern records before discovering that reticence was not a failing common to women. They can be found defying authority in a variety of contexts. Agnes Lamb fought off the sheriff's officer who came to seize her husband's goods to settle a debt in late seventeenth-century Roxburghshire. In 1673, Isobel Lindsay railed against the mighty archbishop of St Andrews during a church servce, and 30 years later the spokesperson in a serious labour dispute at the Loanhead coal mine near Edinburgh was one Margaret Girdwood. Gunn (1905): 126–7; *Ecclesiastical records* (1837): 89; Houston (1983a): 9.

[89] Lamont (1830): 88; Marshall (1983): 160; Mitchison (1983): 87; Smout (1972): 209. During the English Civil War political and social disruption allowed women more latitude in religious matters. In particular, prophesying gave them unusual freedom of political and religious expression: it was felt that their irrational and ecstatic natures made it possible for them to speak with the voice of God. P. Mack, 'Women as prophets' (1982); Hill (1975): 310–11. Conceivably the English occupation of the 1650s may have loosened some of the traditional constraints. K. Thomas, 'Women and the civil war sects' (1965): 323, points out that women had more involvement in church government and preaching in the Low Countries than they did in England.

[90] Quoted in K. Logue, *Popular disturbances in Scotland* (1979): 106.

[91] K.W. Grant, 'Peasant life in Argyllshire' (1918): 146–7.

husbands from the beatings inflicted on them by drunken soldiers at Ravenshaugh Toll in October 1760 were pistol-whipped for their trouble.[92]

Women played a part in food, militia and church patronage riots, forming 28, 6 and 46 per cent of identified rioters in these categories of disturbance between 1780 and 1815. Females were less likely to be prosecuted before the secular courts than men, and only 15 per cent of 453 rioters were women. Their concerns were, however, similar to those of men, and were not solely related to their role as mothers or 'housewives'.[93] Women were closely involved in one of the few early modern rural protest movements in Scotland, the Levellers of Dumfries and Galloway in the 1720s. The aim of the Levellers was to pull down the hated dykes erected by the landowners to create pastures for commercial cattle and sheep farming. One indignant official wrote of how women threw stones at local landowners who tried to arrest a group of fellow rioters. And in a group of 2,000 men and women who set about breaking down the walls in May 1724, 'there were a great many lusty young women among them who yet performed greater wonders than the men'.[94] Class conflict could be more powerful than gender divisions, or at least class experience was more openly questioned than gender.

SOCIAL RELATIONSHIPS: MEN AND WOMEN, WOMEN AND WOMEN

The fact that men and women were engaged in both conflict and co-operation suggests that there was no absolute segregation by space or function in early modern Scottish communities. There was little exclusive male or female space, but there were occasions on which women dominated a particular situation or space. The area of the market, the household and the well, or the event of childbirth were all mainly female preserves. In the Highlands, the association of females with life and fertility was evidenced in their special role as mourners, wailing at the funeral procession. And at the end of the seventeenth century, Martin Martin reported that on some of the Outer Hebrides the mistress of the family and her servants would dress up a sheaf of oats in women's clothes as part of a ritual to predict the harvest.[95] Groups of women worked, talked and sang together while fulling cloth at the waulk-mills of the seventeenth and eighteenth centuries. Their songs were about love, matchmaking, eulogies for clan leaders, laments for menfolk lost at sea, complaints about loneliness, ill-treatment and pregnancy. In the Lowlands, the division of space was less developed. Sir William Brereton remarked, while travelling

[92] A. Murdoch, 'Beating the lieges' (1982):40. [93] Logue (1979):199.

[94] W.A.J. Prevost, 'Letters reporting the rising of the Levellers' (1967):200, 203.

[95] Martin (1703):119; I.F. Grant, *Highland folk ways* (1961):369; D.C. Mactavish (ed.), *Minutes of the synod of Argyll* (1943):61.

in Scotland in 1636, on the groups of women washing clothes in large tubs by treading them with their feet.[96] Eighteenth-century Edinburgh saw the development of a social season, Princes Street acting as the fashionable promenade for young ladies, and other towns such as Perth followed suit on a lesser scale.[97]

Women were significant in other fields. Until well into the seventeenth century, healing was a predominantly female area. Women's control over informal medicine was substantial and those who had a superior knowledge of healing and childbirth may have enjoyed a high standing among their peers.[98] Between the seventeenth and the eighteenth century a professionalisation and masculinsation of medicine took place, one stage of which was marked by the petition of Edinburgh surgeons in 1641 to stop women practising surgery. In the eighteenth century, men were even beginning to encroach on medical care at childbirth, though this was still mainly a female preserve.[99] Edinburgh University ran classes for midwives from the late eighteenth century, and some kirk sessions in north-east Scotland were prepared to pay for a parish midwife to attend the courses offered by Dr Chalmers at Aberdeen University in the 1770s. Women enrolled in numbers at the 'scientific' classes at the Andersonian Institution in Glasgow from 1796 to 1820.[100]

Medical and magical knowledge was normally passed on by word of mouth in local communities. Women enjoyed a prominent role as the purveyors of oral culture. The ability to read and write was growing among the people of Scotland between 1500 and 1800 but, as we noted above,

[96] Grant (1918): 148–9; Smout (1972): plate opposite page 145; T.J. Byres, 'Scottish peasants and their song' (1976)): 240; Martin (1703): 57; P.H. Brown (ed.), *Early travellers* in Scotland (1891): 135, 143.

[97] Some historians see this as part of a greater freedom which was allowed to females in the eighteenth century; Marshall (1983): 169–79. We can, of course, safely assume that men walked where they pleased and had always done so. L. Davidoff & C. Hall, 'The architecture of public and private life' (1983): 328, 332, 343 argue that social conventions about where it was acceptable to be seen were tightened up during the eighteenth century. As upper-middle-class women became increasingly confined to domestic and ornamental roles, their social space became the churches, some shops, certain streets and specific leisure areas. See also J. Topham, *Letters from Edinburgh, 1774–5* (1776); Mitchison (1978): 119. Another index of this trend in polite society in eighteenth-century Edinburgh was the change in fashion regarding women's surnames after marriage. In traditional Scottish society, the married woman retained her father's surname. Among the Edinburgh middle classes, however, the convention of adopting the husband's surname began in the late seventeenth century and became the norm by the later eighteenth. The late seventeenth-century observer, Thomas Morer, believed that retention of the maiden name implied that Scottish women were more independent of their husbands than was the case in England (Brown (1891): 276). J. Wormald, 'Bloodfeud and kindred' (1980): 67 echoes this suggestion and argues that the wife and her relatives were not fully joined to her husband and his family since descent in Scotland was reckoned agnatically rather than cognatically as in England.

[98] Muchembled (1981): 586.

[99] Larner (1981): 101; Grant (1961): 309–12.

[100] Marshall (1983): 226; Henderson (1962): 309; I am grateful to Tom Devine for the Glasgow reference.

women were always less literate as a group than men. For this reason, females may have placed greater importance on oral forms as a means of communication. This was true in the Highlands, and there is evidence that women were more significant as informal teachers of reading. Conversation and song were a central part of the cultural experience of women and girls, Martin Martin observing that the people of the Western Isles had extremely retentive memories and were good at composing verse. On St Kilda, widows composed lamentations for their menfolk killed climbing the cliffs in search of gulls and their eggs. These obituaries described their courage, their love of their families and their nimbleness at climbing [sic].[101] Sir Walter Scott collected a number of his famous Border ballads from women. In the seventeenth century, women came for the first time to occupy a place as poets in the Gaelic bardic tradition, helping to shape the subject matter of the verses. As late as 1824 three Kilbarchan women were still producing ballads on traditional lines.[102]

In the north-east Lowlands during the eighteenth century, there are tantalising indications of a separate women's tradition of ballad-singing: one in which the subject matter of the songs was the marvellous rather than the martial topics favoured in men's ballads, and one in which women occupied a more central place in the story line. The ballads from this area analysed by David Buchan were collected by one Anna Gordon, who learned them from her aunt, mother and maid-servant who in turn had learned them from other women.[103] These individuals were purveyors of what was quickly becoming a 'minority' culture.

There were many situations in which women could meet to exchange ballads, information or gossip: waiting to buy or sell produce at the market for example. Defamation cases show that concern for reputation in this society, especially sexual reputation, was strong. One defamation suit before Arbuthnot kirk session at the start of the eighteenth century lasted for 20 months.[104] In so far as gossip was a way of creating public opinion and a sanction against unconventional behaviour, women policed themselves through its medium. Gossip reaffirmed conformist behaviour and identified the boundaries of deviance. It could also provoke bitter discord. St Andrews kirk session ordered that all the women's seats should be removed from the parish church, 'for eschewing of trubill amongis wemen in the kirk'. Men's gossip was not, one assumes, defined as divisive. In late

[101] Martin (1703): 200, 294; Grant (1961): 135–7; F.G. Thompson, 'Technical education in the Highlands' (1972–4): 248.
[102] Based on material provided by Rowy Mitchison.
[103] D. Buchan, *The ballad and the folk* (1972): 62–3, 76.
[104] Henderson (1962): 122–5.

seventeenth-century Aberdeen, seating was segregated by gender and by social class.[105]

Women needed men for a variety of reasons and vice versa. Yet, mutual dependence can exist within an unequal set of power relations, and its implications for the quality of social interactions between individuals or groups is determined by wider economic and cultural characteristics. Examples of gratuitous misogyny certainly exist. Famous as an advocate of equality among mankind, Robert Burns had a patronising and deeply sexist attitude towards women. John Knox's polemic against his queen, the *First Blast of the Trumpet*, spoke of women as 'weak, frail, impatient, feeble and foolish ... inconstant, variable, cruel and lacking in spirit of counsel and regiment'.[106]

Against such comments we can use evidence of shared recreations by males and females. Working together in fields or shops or mines, married and unmarried alike frequented drinking establishments. Many of the misdemeanours and altercations which arose between neighbours and which found their way into the kirk session minutes started or took place in alehouses. This does not necessarily indicate equality since mixing may take place between dominant and subordinate groups. Strictly speaking, unaccompanied women were not allowed to drink in a brewer's house on pain of a fine and twenty four hours in the stocks: or so the baron court of Taymouth ordered in 1621.[107] Nevertheless, drink formed a ubiquitous part of social life and drunken men and women appear regularly in the documents: women such as the three wives who were found drinking in Stirling during the whole of Sunday afternoon and until 4am the next morning. Or the dipsomaniac Lady Wemyss who in 1652 had a door made between her chamber and the wine cellar because of 'a great desire after strong drink'.[108]

Men and women must have met most commonly in informal situations

[105] Fleming, vol. 2 (1890): 864. I am grateful to Gordon Desbrisay for this detail which is based on his research on Aberdeen society in the seventeenth century.

[106] Quoted in Marshall (1983): 46. Men certainly wrote about women, and many more of their thoughts survive in this form than do those of women about men. Male views might be descriptive or prescriptive, or they might try to examine the nature of women to explain, for example, why they were the weaker sex. However, their analyses of symbolic states, mainly based on Lapsarian theology, are difficult for the historian to translate into concrete terms. The typicality of their views is questionable, and writing about women only tells us what men thought they should do rather than what they thought about themselves. On the last point, there was no conscious feminism in the twentieth-century sense. The brave individuals who spoke out against patriarchy were labelled as misfits. There was no Scottish equivalent of the feminist writing of Mary Astell and others in late seventeenth-century England (J.K. Kinnaird, 'Mary Astell' (1979)). Some writers like Defoe and individuals such as Alexander Munro did adopt a more sympathetic stance towards women's condition yet retained the idea of separate roles and the broader social framework of degree, order and authority. Rowbotham (1977): 14.

[107] C. Innes (ed.), *The black book of Taymouth* (1855): 359.

[108] *Maitland Club* 1,1 (1840): 135; Lamont (1830): 40; Kirk (1977): 299.

such as at the pub, market or church. In the Highlands, on the other hand, there were semi-formal institutions such as 'rockings' which resembled in certain respects the *veillée* or *mattinata* found in some contemporary southern European cultures.[109] Young women brought their rocks and reels (distaffs and spindles) to a house where they would engage communally in song and conversation with the young men of the area. When factory spinning came to the county of Angus c.1790 the older women warned their daughters not to work in them or they would never find a husband.[110]

Most women married at some stage in their lives. There were emotional as well as material reasons for marrying, though the balance between both these far from incompatible goals is difficult to measure and the quality of relations after the spousals is hard to characterise. Of relationships between men and women in marriage we know comparatively little, especially among the lower classes. Moralist prescriptions stressed that servitude, submission and respect were to be expected from a wife. In return, the husband had a duty to protect and support his spouse. What exactly people made of their marriages is unclear. Relations within marriage were notionally based on an interaction between dominance and subjection, activity and passivity, with the women chaste, silent and obedient. Some men presumably wished more active wives and companionate marriages. Among the atypical minority of society who wrote diaries, the relationship of James Gordon, an Aberdeenshire minister of the late-seventeenth and early-eighteenth century, with his wife seems to have been a close and companionate one as far as we can tell from his oblique references to her. They commonly travelled to Aberdeen together and in his absences she looked after important financial matters on his behalf.[111] Women brought dowries or skills to a marriage in order to create the basic unit of production, consumption, reproduction, socialisation and welfare. Presumably they expected more out of it than being chattels. Some sort of *modus vivendi* must have been worked out by each couple to suit their own feelings, material circumstances and the prevailing social norms.

Relationships could contain coolness as well as warmth. In 1699 Livingston kirk session uncovered a marital dispute while investigating an irregular baptism. A child had been presented by its grandfather rather than by its father. The mother of the infant, Agnes Ralton, explained that her husband had deserted her. According to her account, he 'had taken on much debt before she was married, and since those to whom he was owing hes come and taken away anything she had, at which she grudged . . . then

[109] Graham, vol. 1 (1889): 186; C. Klapisch-Zuber, 'The medieval Italian *mattinata*' (1980); N.Z. Davis, *Society and culture in early modern France* (1975): 201; O. Hufton, 'Women, work and marriage' (1981): 199–200.

[110] Reference to Angus mothers from Christopher Smout.

[111] Henderson & Porter (1949): 56–7, 83; Marshall (1983): 88–94.

he said he could not have life with me & that he would leave me'. Agnes assured him that if he stayed, 'she would be content to beg her bread with him ... but he said that he did not love her & would not stay with her'.[112] The texture of relationships is hard to reconstruct because emotions are not often expressed directly in this way.

Marital discord leaves more trace in the records than does love and affection. Examples of relationships breaking down suggest indirectly that people had individual expectations and were prepared to act in order to realise them. Isobel Gow told Dingwall presbytery in 1679 that since she had married her husband, 'shee could not obtaine of herselfe to love him or live with him' despite attempts at reconciliation by her neighbours. Another woman was banished from the town of Stirling in 1598 for verbally and physically abusing her husband.[113] A notion of individual fulfilment clearly existed for women as for men.

As a way of terminating an unsatisfactory marriage, divorce was more easily obtained than in England, but proceedings were still lengthy and cumbersome, and it is scarcely surprising that only a tiny number of parties resorted to them. A study of Edinburgh Consistory Court records shows that the few divorces which were pursued between 1658 and 1707 involved the middling and upper classes.[114] By the last 3 decades of the eighteenth century, divorce had become more common and covered a slightly wider social spectrum. It was still a rare event. Divorce was only possible on the grounds of adultery, non-consummation or desertion. Cruelty was regarded at law as an abuse of the legitimate right of a man to correct his wife (or children or servants) by the moderate application of force: judicial separation *a mensa et thoro* was the best a battered wife could hope for.[115]

Rather than through divorce or desertion, most marriages ended through the death of one or other partner. Economically, widows were often in a parlous position, and church records are full of their petitions. Tulliallan kirk session considered a petition in the spring of 1688 showing 'the deplorable condition of Margaret Littlejohn by reason of the death of her husband & of her own distraction and poverty for present scarce able to defray the charges of her husband's burial, much less to maintain herself

[112] SRO CH2/467/3: 60.

[113] W. Mackay (ed.), *Records of the presbyteries of Inverness and Dingwall* (1896): 342.

[114] Marshall (1983): 96–7, 196; Forte (1984): 112–14 shows that full divorce was only possible after the Reformation in Scotland.

[115] *Ibid.*, 105; R.D. Ireland, 'Husband and wife' (1958): 97. There are only a handful of recorded instances of wife sales in pre-industrial Scotland. One, at Humbie in 1646, seems more like a joke or a misunderstanding which resulted while a man, his wife and another man were drinking. Another which took place at Stirling in 1638, resembles more closely the wife sales described by Edward Thompson for eighteenth-century England. Here, William Williamson, a stranger, paid Robert Baird £8 for his wife, and gave her £6. *Maitland club* 1,2 (1834): 434–5, 474; Scott-Moncrieff, vol. 1 (1905): 90–2; S.P. Menefee, *Wives for sale* (1981) suggests, rather weakly, that Calvinism explains the rarity of Scottish wife sale.

and children, being under a weighty burden of debt'.[116] Many cottars who appear in the poll tax records of the 1690s were single women, probably widows, and their economic marginality is plain. In towns poor widows could eke out a meagre living. Margaret Gardiner, a stabler's widow, described herself in 1694 as 'ane old widow womane and only lives be vertew of keepeing ane small chainge [pub]'. Other Edinburgh dwellers like Janet Weir, whose husband had been a skinner, was constrained 'to live upon the Lord's providence'. The great bulk of poor relief was given to lone women.[117]

For other women, widowhood was the only stage of the life cycle in which they could be truly economically and legally independent. Servants had some freedom, but were of course working for somebody else.[118] Some widows may have had substantial wealth and were entitled by law to at least a third of their husband's moveable estate (*ius relictae*) or to take over his burgess-ship. A seventeenth-century woman's hospital was endowed by several wealthy Aberdeen widows and was designed to cater for widows and aged spinsters from craft and trade families.[119]

116 SRO CH2/710/1.

117 Smout (1972):135; M. Wood (ed.), *Poll tax records of Edinburgh* (1951):22, 28, 46, 62. Petitions of widows who had lost husbands in the Irish rebellion of the 1640s testify to the potential marginality of this group: e.g. Kirk (1977):148–51; R. Mitchison, 'The making of the old Scottish poor law' (1974); R. Mitchison, 'A parish and its poor: Yester' (1975); Rowy Mitchison has discovered a sex ratio of about 50 males per 100 females in the poor rolls of 30 parishes during the 1690s.

118 Later stages of the life-cycle may have created opportunities for independence, stages which were sometimes signalled by dress. One contemporary commentator remarked that different forms of dress were used to signify marital status, whether single, married or widowed. However, this was by no means an infallible indicator since he allowed that some women were obviously 'apparelled according to their own humour and phantasy'. Sartorial regulations were not rigidly enforced, but the kirk session of Edinburgh took a dim view of a servant girl who in 1574 was prosecuted for dressing up in men's clothes and dancing in public. Two girls were prosecuted at Ceres kirk session in 1650 for the same offence. The visible distinction between men and women was strongly enforced. William Brereton quoted in Brown (1891):140–1; *Maitland Club* 1,1 (1840):104–5; J.A. Di Folco, 'Discipline and welfare' (1977):174. Men who dressed as women might also be prosecuted, as in the case of William Hutchison, servant, delated to Arbuthnott kirk session in 1723 for sartorial irregularities and over-zealous celebration of Halloween. Henderson (1962):158.

119 I am grateful to Gordon Desbrisay for this material. We must not argue too strongly for the independence of the widow. Women who ran their late husband's business might have to rely on a male employee, a provision explicitly set out in the apprentice indenture of James Cheape in 1726. He was bound to William Bell, cooper in Leith, for 6 years and in the event of Bell's death to his widow, 'she always keeping a sufficient journeyman for his instruction in the art and trade of Couper Craft'. St Andrews University Library, Cheape of Rossie papers 5/72. Women who leased farms on their own account, usually after being widowed, can certainly be found in estate records but this was often only a temporary expedient. Sanderson (1982):179; I. Whyte & K. Whyte, 'Structure of rural society' (1983):38. For England see S. Wright, 'Employment of women in Tudor and Stuart Salisbury' (1985).

WITCHCRAFT

Lone women were particularly vulnerable to witchcraft accusations. Popular beliefs coupled with official attempts to delineate the boundaries of acceptable behaviour and to enforce conformity to certain religious and secular norms produced one of the most appalling yet intriguing aspects of early modern life: the great witchcraze which swept through Europe in the sixteenth and seventeenth centuries.[120] The witch-hunt in Scotland was fiercer than in England, the execution rate per head of population being 10 times higher. Women made up 80 per cent of those prosecuted as witches over the period 1560 and 1709. This proportion was less than in sixteenth- and seventeenth-century England, but in other respects the social profile of the witch was similar: a mature female well-known to the accuser, poor, quarrelsome and with a reputation for healing or harming.[121]

The preponderance of females has made the apparent connection between witch-hunting and women-hunting an important area of debate.[122] There are a variety of reasons why women should have formed the bulk of witches, not only in Scotland but across much of Europe. First, the benign manipulation of occult forces, white witchcraft, had long been a mainly female province. In the Western Isles, women were believed to have the ability to influence milk production among humans and animals. The weakness of the Calvinist church and continued popular acceptance of pagan, magical practices in the Highlands and Islands meant that witchcraft prosecutions were much rarer there. Women commonly learned their charming from other women and used it either for healing or harming. This lent them power and identity in a world otherwise dominated by men and by the wealthy.

Women seem also to have clung longer to what were defined by the post-Reformation church as 'superstitious' practices, both as patients and as healers. In sixteenth-century Stirlingshire, groups of women went on pilgrimages to 'Christ's Hole' a medieval holy place, to try to cure their illnesses.[123] Proscription of occult manipulation or of religious practices associated with the collective Christianity of the medieval church must have reduced the status of women and have opened them up to attack by ecclesiastical authorities.

There are, however, a number of reasons why the craze cannot be seen as an extreme example of direct misogyny.[124] First, the hunt for witches was part of a search for moral conformity, an attempt to root out 'enemies of God' and 'enemies of humanity'. Women were perceived to be intrinsically

[120] Larner (1981). [121] *Ibid.*, 91, 97; C. Larner, *Witchcraft and religion* (1984): 72–3, 84.
[122] *Ibid.*, 84–8.
[123] Kirk (1981): 134–40; *Maitland Club* 1,2 (1834): 416, Mackay (1896): 196; Martin (1703): 120–2, 249.
[124] Larner (1984): 84–8, 152; Larner (1981): 10, 92–3.

more evil than men and innately weaker. They were thus more open to the Devil's threats and promises. Women were persecuted as witches more often than men because it was held that the evil was more likely to reside in them rather than because men wished to discipline women. In itself, of course, this was a sexist view.

It is also clear that the witch-hunt was effectively over by the time that medical care was beginning to become a mainly male preserve. Witchcraft accusations were not part of a cynical conspiracy to masculinise medicine. Second, the number of women directly accused of witchcraft by their neighbours was relatively small when compared with those pursued because they were implicated in the demonic pact, which Roman law stressed as the central issue of witchcraft. Third, women were prepared to accuse other females of being witches. They did so because witchcraft stereotypes set a negative standard for female behaviour. Witches did not conform to the male view that women should be meek, passive and concerned with nurture. By establishing negative standards, the notion of witchcraft reinforced positive ones for those women who wished to conform. Attacking deviants strengthened the status of the conformers. The fact that women were accused of being witches gives us indirect insights into their place in Scottish society, but it does nor provide evidence of a concerted attempt to control women as women.

We can reach the same conclusion about the kirk's pursuit of sexual irregularities. The parish minister and his lay officials, elders, searched diligently for moral lapses in their community and sought to punish them by fines and public humiliation. The church's punitive attitude towards sexual misdemeanours covered men and women alike. Females were apparently hounded more than men, but mainly because their lapses were more obvious rather than because of a clerically reinforced double standard. Religious and financial considerations made it essential to identify the father.

The attitude of male authorities towards women was often ambivalent. This was especially true of the kirk and is neatly illustrated in that body's approach to women who had been unreasonably beaten by their husbands. Husbands were reproved for their cruelty, but the session also assumed that the woman must in some way have provoked the beating. It therefore reproved her for slander. The session tried hard to be even-handed in all cases, including the punishment of sexual offences. However, the minister and elders often criticised the woman in fornication or adultery cases in words which were never used towards the man. In eighteenth-century Caithness some sessions ordered that female sexual offenders be beaten, but never men.[125] The men who ran the kirk sessions clearly experienced

[125] This paragraph is mostly based on material provided by Rowy Mitchison. Mackenzie (1678):127 argued against a double standard before the law, but as we have seen, the

difficulty in reconciling the idea that in terms of human souls and salvation the two sexes were equal before God, with their own prejudices that women were inferior to men in all ways.

CONCLUSION

Throughout this chapter the importance of understanding the interaction between economic, legal, political and cultural factors in determining the status of women has been stressed. It is clear that subordination was not the sum total of female existence in this society, but at the same time there is no significant sense in which women enjoyed equality with men. Some improvements did take place in women's status. Growing literacy created new possibilities for communicating, but women's literacy was very basic and if anything they became more culturally marginalised by the developments which were taking place. There were new opportunities too in some areas of the economy, notably industrial work. To some extent, these closed up in the nineteenth century as the progress of mechanisation of spinning cut back opportunities. Female participation in agriculture was probably steady throughout the period, but by its end women were doing more menial tasks and were working for wages more than they had done in the sixteenth or seventeenth century. Men had always had the more skilled jobs in agriculture, but some were now given the high status tasks such as ploughmen in the new labour hierarchy. Women began to be squeezed out of occupations like brewing and the medical 'profession' from the end of the sixteenth century. Legal status improved marginally over the period, especially during the seventeenth and eighteenth centuries. That this occasioned or reflected an amelioration in women's social status is unproven. Indeed there were significant elements of continuity in the three centuries we have discussed. Women retained their central position in the family. They were still denied a full voice in government, being subjects of the forces of authority rather than wielders of its power. The divide between Highland and Lowland culture had, if anything, widened, though we cannot be certain that female status in the Lowlands was necessarily superior to that of their Highland sisters. The reverse is more likely. Throughout, it is hard to escape the impression that women were denied a central part in society. Instead they used its margins to create their own lives.

assumptions of his class and age were deeply sexist. For England see K. Thomas, 'The double standard' (1959); Hill (1975):308–19, 410.

5

SOCIAL RESPONSES TO AGRARIAN 'IMPROVEMENT': THE HIGHLAND AND LOWLAND CLEARANCES IN SCOTLAND

T. M. DEVINE

I

Enclosure and consolidation altered the organisation, function and purposes of land from one in which several members of a community had rights of use to a new condition in which single occupants had complete control. Jerome Blum, in his analysis of the decline of the old rural order in Europe, has characterised it as 'the single most important departure from the traditional agriculture, heralding as it did the switch from communalism with its collective controls to individualism with its private rights of property and its individual freedom of action'.[1] Consolidated holdings were not new in Europe before the seventeenth century. Proprietors sometimes enclosed lands for their own use, while in mountainous and forested regions peasants had long lived in consolidated holdings and they were common also in the maritime provinces of the continent.[2] Enclosures in England were far advanced in the south east and in pockets of the south west and north in the early modern period, mainly, though not exclusively, due to the impact of an expanding market for wool. However, in the eighteenth century the forces making for consolidation accelerated rapidly. Two influences in combination operated throughout western Europe. First, an ideological attack on communalism was mounted by agronomists and political economists. Second, a massive increase in the markets for foods and raw materials as a result of the rise in population and the expansion in towns, cities and industry created both pressures and incentives for improvements in agricultural productivity.[3]

[1] J. Blum, *The end of the old order in rural Europe* (1978): 263.
[2] J. de Vries, *Economy of Europe in an age of crisis, 1600–1750* (1976): 43.
[3] F. Dovring, 'The transformation of European agriculture' (1965): 627–8; A.J. Bourde, *The influence of England on the French Agronomes, 1750–1789* (1953); Blum (1978): 246–64; M. Confino, *Systèmes agraires et progrès agricole* (1969): 286; B.H. Slicher Van Bath, *The agrarian history of western Europe, 500–1850* (1963): 226–8.

It is clear that these stimuli, to a greater or lesser extent, were touching virtually all countries in western Europe. Equally, however, while the trend towards consolidation of land, the enclosure of commons and the rise of big farmers at the expense of small peasants was manifest throughout most regions, in only a few exceptional parts of Europe was there a full-scale adoption of the principles of the new order. By the middle decades of the nineteenth century it was plain that only in England, Scotland, Denmark, the Low Countries, Catalonia, some German states, such as Pomerania and Brandenburg, parts of Sweden and one or two localities elsewhere had the revolution run its full course.[4] This was despite the fact that the campaign to achieve consolidation and agrarian rationalisation had almost become a pan-European movement on the part of the 'enlightened' monarchies of the eighteenth century. In the main, however, even their missionary zeal proved insufficient against the obstacles of poor planning, the vested interests of lords and peasants and, perhaps above all, the threat to social order that such a revolution in traditional patterns of landholding might provoke.

Scotland, therefore, belonged to a select group of regions in Europe where the theories of the agronomists were applied vigorously and wholly successfully. Over a period from the middle decades of the seventeenth century to the nineteenth century in the Lowlands, the old communal or joint tenancies were removed; the average size of farm increased; the numbers with direct access to land declined.[5] In the Highlands and in the Border region, over a much longer period dating back to the sixteenth century and before, large sheep and cattle farms expanded on land which had earlier supported clusters of small farming communities. The peasant society of the sixteenth century, in which the majority had access to land and cultivated it mainly for their own immediate needs, was replaced in many areas, over a relatively limited time-scale, by a new capitalist order. Within it the functions of the consolidated lands were subordinated to the market, the majority of the inhabitants, at least in the rural areas of the Lowlands, became wage labourers, and 'peasants', in the sense applicable in Europe, only survived in any numbers around the fringes of the Highlands and Islands. A thorough-going revolution had been achieved and the scale of transformation can only be truly appreciated when seen within the context of a European world where, in the nineteenth century, the peasant farmer remained dominant in most countries.

The Scottish example stands out even when compared with England and those parts of Scandinavia where consolidation of land was equally

[4] Blum (1978): 263–71; M. Bloch, 'La Lutte pour l'individualisme agraire dans la France du XVIIIe siècle' (1930; B.J. Hovde, *The Scandinavian countries, 1750–1865*: I, 278; R. Herr, *The eighteenth-century revolution in Spain* (1958): 86–120.

[5] The process is summarised in M. Gray, 'Scottish emigration: the social impact of agrarian change in the rural Lowlands, 1775–1875' (1973): 95–131.

extensive. The chronology of revolution differentiates Scotland and England. Although enclosures were still occurring in England on a considerable scale as late as the Napoleonic Wars, it is now generally agreed that they were well under way in the sixteenth and seventeenth centuries.[6] The English case was one of long-run evolutionary change with phases of accelerated development; current knowledge suggests that the time-scale in Scotland was both shorter and later. There were apparently fewer attempts at major rationalisation of tenancies in the early seventeenth century, and before, though the older rural social order was far from static. However, only from the 1660s can a clear trend towards widespread consolidation be detected with the growth of enlarged tenancies in arable areas and large pastoral farms in the southern counties of Peebles, Selkirk, Roxburgh and Kirkcudbright.[7] A note of caution is, however, necessary here. The documentation from c.1660 onwards is so much better than for the sixteenth and early seventeenth centuries that it may give a false impression of change. It would be surprising, for instance, if the spread of feu tenure in the fifteenth and sixteenth centuries was not accompanied by some alteration in farm organisation and lease systems. Equally while the basic organisational changes extended over a much longer time-scale than previously assumed, structural adjustment seems to have accelerated in the last quarter of the eighteenth century. Over two to three generations into the nineteenth century, status, income and employment were irrevocably altered for the majority of the population of Lowland society.[8]

Scotland also differed profoundly from Denmark, the other country where consolidation produced entirely new patterns of land-holding and population distribution.[9] There enclosing and engrossing of land was accomplished to a significant extent by state fiat. In 1757 a special Royal Commission, at the behest of improving proprietors, addressed itself to the issue of how the perceived weaknesses in open fields and common rights might be corrected. Subsequently the recommendations of this body were incorporated in a series of decrees which provided for consolidation, rated its costs among the village land holders and established a fund to help defray the expenses of reform. In Scotland, the state was not entirely irrelevant to the development of agrarian reforms. Legislation of the

[6] J.R. Wordie, 'The chronology of English enclosure, 1500–1914' (1983):483–505; M. E. Turner, *English parliamentary enclosure: its historical geography and economic history* (1980).

[7] R.A. Dodgshon, *Land and society in early Scotland* (1981):206–53; I. Whyte, *Agriculture and society in seventeenth century Scotland* (1979):137–72; J. di Folco, 'The hopes of Craighall and land investment in the seventeenth century' (1979):1–10.

[8] G. Whittington, 'Was there a Scottish agricultural revolution?' (1975):204–6.

[9] H. Thorpe, 'The influence of enclosure on the farm and pattern of rural settlement in Denmark' (1951):123–7; A.E. Christensen, 'The development of large-scale farming in Denmark, 1525–1744' (1960); K. Skovgaard, 'Consolidation of agrarian land in Denmark' (1952).

Scottish parliament in the later seventeenth century facilitated improvement. In 1661, 1669, 1685 and 1695 statutes provided for the division of most commonties, (rough pasture possessed jointly by different proprietors), lands held in proprietary runrig (the system by which separate areas of fragmented land were owned by different proprietors) and for the erection of fences at the boundaries of estates. An Act of Parliament in 1772 assisted landlords of entailed estates to obtain credit for purposes of improvement more readily. Yet such measures (unlike those in Denmark) were permissive rather than compulsory. The revolution in Scotland was essentially carried through by private landlords and tenant farmers responding to the desire for profit, the stimulus of expanding markets and the constraints of cost.

There was another deeply significant distinction between Scotland and Denmark. All European monarchies recognised the enormous social costs of wholesale land consolidation and the obvious threat that general loss of land could pose to social order. Only in theory might land be transformed from its primary function as the basis of a way of life to a source of marketable commodities without causing unacceptable levels of damage to the social fabric. Undoubtedly this recognition was a major barrier to agrarian rationalisation in most regions of Europe.[10] The Danish state tried to reduce these potential social costs by benevolent legislation.[11] Those who suffered loss from the reforms were to be compensated by a leasehold of 4–6 acres. A decree of 1769 went further and forbade the engrossment of peasant holdings. Legislation also banned division of lands into areas too small to support a family. Close scrutiny of the Danish case suggests, therefore, that private landlords were not allowed complete freedom of action; they had to act within a coherent structure of regulation. Further, the aim in Denmark does not appear to have been to impose through state policy the English structure of large farms and a landless labour force. The legislation was rather designed to fashion a moderate consolidation and limit the possibilities of land fragmentation in a period of rising population. Again the Scottish case differs markedly. The law was more concerned to protect the property rights of the landlord than the traditional privileges of the peasant.[12] The state did not try to limit the rate of consolidation or the evictions associated with it. No restraints were placed upon the Improvers. In Scotland the great drama of the agrarian transition was played out by landowners, farmers, peasants and labourers.

The Scottish experience therefore offers a special opportunity to analyse

[10] See, for example, the position in France described in G. Lefebvre, 'La Place de la révolution dans l'histoire agraire de la France' (1921).

[11] Thorpe (1951); Christensen (1960); Skovgaard (1952).

[12] R.H. Campbell, 'The Scottish improvers and the course of agrarian change in the eighteenth century' (1977): 204–5; L. Timperley, 'The pattern of landholding in eighteenth century Scotland' (1980): 137–154.

the social responses to dislocation caused by agrarian rationalisation. Did the loss of land cause unrest and opposition? If not, what influences defused discontent and enabled the revolution to be accomplished successfully and peacefully? The peculiar interest of these questions in a Scottish context is that they provoke a different answer when different regional experiences are considered. Broadly, a distinction can be drawn between the Lowland zone, including the Border country and the marches of the Highlands in southern Argyllshire and eastern Inverness-shire on the one hand and, on the other, the rest of the Highlands north of Ardnamurchan together with the Inner and Outer Hebrides. In the former area, the transformation was completed peacefully by and large; it was with only some exceptions a silent revolution. In the latter region while the success of land consolidation was rarely threatened seriously, it more often evoked bitter, if sporadic, protest and deep hostility. Consideration of the reasons for these contrasting reactions will form the major part of this essay. Initially, however, the responses need to be probed in more detail.

II

The drama of the Highland clearances when entire communities were evicted to make way for large sheep or cattle farms or simply because a destitute population had become an unacceptable burden to landlords, is well known. Less familiar are the 'Lowland clearances'; the phrase itself is an historian's invention to denote the scale of population displacement which took place in the wake of the agrarian revolution in the central and eastern counties of Scotland. It lacks the emotive appeal and the tragic associations of 'the Highland clearances'. The different response to the language is itself revealing. In the north west, uniquely in Scotland, there lingered a folk memory of dispossession, a sense of lost rights.[13] Yet there was also very considerable loss of land in the Lowland countryside which the absence of dissent and alienation has partially concealed. Indeed the revolution was in one sense more fundamental and thorough in the south and east. In the sixteenth and early seventeenth centuries tenant society in the Lowlands was already very markedly stratified. By the early nineteenth century social distinctions had been extended even further and a super

[14] R. Mitchison, 'The Highland clearances' (1981): 16–17. It is important to stress that this attitude was specific not to the Highlands as a whole but to the north-west 'crofting' region and to the Outer and Inner Hebrides. The social formations of the southern and eastern Highlands were more akin to those of the Lowlands: medium-sized farms, small towns and villages, a smallholding population but also a landless labour force and employments in textile industry and specialist fishing. The differences between this area and that of the north west and Islands and their social implications are analysed in M. Gray, *The Highland Economy, 1750–1850*, (1957): 223–38 and T.M. Devine, 'Highland migration to Lowland Scotland', (1983b): 137–49.

ficially simple division of landlords, occupying farmers and wage servants and labourers had emerged in most areas.[14] The size of farms and the status, function and type of the work force varied considerably between regions but in most parts a small elite now held possession of land either as owners or tenants. Only in the north-eastern counties of Banff and Aberdeen was there a substantial small holding or 'crofting' population.[15] But this was no anachronistic survival of the peasant past. The crofts of these areas were created after c.1790 and were specifically designed to form an integral part of the prevailing structure of emerging big and medium-sized capitalist farms in the neighbourhood. From the families of the smallholders were recruited the seasonal workers for the larger units and croft culture was also regarded as an economical method of absorbing waste land – of which the north east had a considerable amount – into regular cultivation. This regional eccentricity apart, most Lowland Scots were landless by the early nineteenth century. It was a different story in the Highlands. There, despite the trauma of the clearances, peasant families lived on, eking out a subsistence whether on the coasts or on the fringes of the big pastoral farms. The western Highlands retained many of the characteristics of the peasant society which had almost entirely disappeared from the Lowlands.

The term, the 'Lowland clearances', is therefore not based on poetic licence but on historical reality. In particular, population displacement in southern society can be classified in three types. First, from about 1660 to the middle decades of the eighteenth century, the Border region evolved as a specialist source of wool, meat, skins and mutton in response to urban growth in northern England and central Scotland.[16] The development was also conditioned by the stagnation in grain prices between c.1680 and c.1740 which affected most areas of western Europe and encouraged a definite continental trend towards large-scale pastoralism.[17] The new peace between England and Scotland after the Union of the Crowns in 1603 brought the necessary stability to the formerly troubled Border country which enabled the transformation to take place. In the later seventeenth century, farms of 1,000 acres and above were being established, with cattle predominating in the western districts and sheep in the central and eastern counties. All over the region, however, the large farms steadily absorbed the arable lands of many small communities and led to depopulation and migration. The social process, in general if not in

[14] T.M. Devine (ed.), *Farm servants and labour in lowland Scotland, 1770–1914* (1984b): 10–96; I.F. Grant, 'Social effects of agricultural reforms in Aberdeenshire' (1926).

[15] I. Carter, *Farm life in north-east Scotland* (1979); M. Gray, 'Farm workers in north-east Scotland' (1984): 10–28.

[16] R.A. Dodgshon, 'Agricultural change and its social consequences in the southern uplands of Scotland, 1600–1780' (1983): 46–59.

[17] De Vries (1976): 80–1.

particular terms, was analogous to the impact of the big sheep farms on the Highlands a century later.[18]

Second, throughout all the Lowland counties, first observed in dim outline in the middle decades of the seventeenth century, there was a trend towards the expansion of single tenancies at the expense of multiple holdings, of extensions to farm size and concentration of land in fewer hands. The process was complex, probably had a longer time-scale than current interpretation suggests, and is still under-researched, but it was already under way by the later seventeenth century, if not before. It varied significantly from area to area and even estate to estate (with the south-eastern counties clearly in the vanguard), and apparently accelerated in response to the stimulus of population increase, urbanisation and industrialistion after c.1780.[19] The nature of change was complicated and diverse but the net result in virtually every area was the same to a greater or lesser extent: a thinning of the ranks of the tenantry, consolidation of multiple tenancies and a sharp increase in the proportion of rural dwellers either entirely landless or with only the most tenuous connection to the soil. The results of such processes evoked from William Cobbett in 1832 a response reminiscent of those who observed the Clearances in the Highlands. 'Everything', he wrote of the Lothians, 'is abundant here but people, who have been studiously swept from the land'.[20]

Third, in the old world, sub-tenants and cottars had formed an important component of the small communities or *ferm touns* which formed the basic work and social centres of the Lowland countryside. Many were craftsmen who held a piece of land for subsistence purposes; others were granted land by larger tenants in return for providing seasonal labour at the grain harvest in the autumn and peat cutting in spring and summer. They rarely appear in estate rentals and so are among the most shadowy groups in seventeenth- and eighteenth-century Scottish social history.[21] They were certainly very numerous and may well have formed the largest single social group in the pre-improved countryside, though there was considerable local and regional variation in the ratios of tenants to

[18] Dodgshon (1981): 255–65.

[19] B.M.W. Third, 'Changing landscape and social structure in the Scottish Lowlands as revealed in eighteenth-century estate plans' (1955): 83–93; J.H.G. Lebon, 'The process of enclosure in the western Lowlands' (1946): 105–10; R.A. Dodgshon, 'The removal of Runrig in Roxburghshire and Berwickshire, 1680–1766' (1972): 121–7; Whyte (1979): 137–72; I.D. Whyte & K.A. Whyte, 'Continuity and change in a seventeenth century Scottish farming community' (1984a): 156–69; di Folco (1979): 1–10.

[20] W. Cobbett, *Rural rides in the southern, western and eastern counties; with tours in Scotland and in the northern and midland counties of England* (1930 edn): 755–6.

[21] They can be most easily studied in the surviving poll tax lists of the 1690s. See J. Stuart (ed.), *List of pollable persons within the shire of Aberdeen, 1696* (1844), 2 vols.; D. Semple (ed.), *Renfrewshire poll tax returns* (1864).

cottars.[22] However, sub-tenancy came under widespread assault in the second half of the eighteenth century. The small plots of land which sub-tenants and cottars held in return for labour services on adjacent farms were absorbed within larger formations. They were now more valuable as sources of marketable grain and cattle, as prices rose in the later eighteenth century, than as subsistence plots for an underemployed labour force. In addition, farmers increasingly gearing their production to market sought higher levels of labour productivity and so came to prefer regular, full-time workers over whom they could exert more discipline and control. There is, therefore, abundant evidence that sub-tenancy was being steadily crushed as the pace of consolidation quickened. By 1815 it was but a minor part of the Lowland agrarian system.[23]

In these three main aspects, the magnitude though not the precise scale of social displacement in the Lowlands can be perceived. On the face of it there does not appear to have been a fundamental distinction between the western Highlands and the Lowland counties in the extent of loss of land. What is certainly clear, however, is the sharp difference in the response of the two communities to social dislocation. For a start, protest in the Lowlands was muted and rare. There is the oft-quoted example of the Levellers Revolt in Galloway in the 1720s.[24] This would appear to be the only instance of large-scale collective opposition to agrarian change in Lowland Scotland. It took place in an area experiencing conversion to big pastoral farms and engrossing threatened the livelihood of many small tenants who could not hope to gain employment within the new structure. The historian, however, is hard put to it to find any similar reaction in the mixed farming or dairying districts which formed the major part of the agricultural territory of the Lowlands. Even the division of the commonties produced only two known episodes of resistance at Smailholm, West Roxburghshire in the 1730s and Aberlady in East Lothian in 1786.[25] Students of the landed class suggest, in addition, that there was sometimes passive resistance which could at least temporarily thwart improvement plans.[26] Given the scale of the transformation, however, it is the silence which is the most remarkable aspect of agrarian reorganisation in the south and east. The process could not have occurred painlessly but in the long-run, whatever the initial shocks, the majority of the population accepted it and worked within it; the labour teams of the new farms became vital factors in their success.[27] In this respect the Scottish experience seemed to run

22 I.D. Whyte & K.A. Whyte, 'Some aspects of the structure of rural society in seventeenth century Lowland Scotland' (1983): 32–45.

23 T.M. Devine, 'Scotland farm service in the Agricultural Revolution' (1984a): 1–8; Gray (1973): 232–8.

24 J. Leopold, 'The levellers revolt in Galloway in 1724' (1980): 4–29.

25 Mitchison (1981): 8–9.

26 Campbell (1977): 207–9.

27 Devine (1984a): 2–5.

counter to the concerns of those European statesmen who feared the impact that land consolidation might have on social order.

It was different in several parts of the Highlands and Islands. At least 20 major incidents have been recorded of significant collective resistance to eviction between 1760 and 1855.[28] These sporadic and ephemeral episodes were, however, only the dramatic manifestations of a deeper opposition. Historians of the Highlands speak of sullen discontent, of simmering hostility and of a widespread refusal to co-operate with landlord plans.[29] Thus the improving initiatives of the 5th Duke of Argyll in the 1770s and 1780s and the more draconian attempts at estate rationalisation of the Sutherland family at a later date foundered partly on the rock of peasant opposition.[30] As the pace of land consolidation quickened, so throughout the western Highlands and Islands it brought to the surface all the classic symptoms of peasant alienation: despairing emigration, the compelling dominance of a rigid and messianic religiosity and a deep sense of betrayal which was to endure in the collective psychology of the society.[31] The urban Scot in the Lowlands did not entirely sever his links with the rustic past but his reactions were of a different order to those of his Highland counterpart and quickly became deflected into the mawkish sentimentality of the Kailyard and Burns nights.[32] The differing cultural traditions of the dispossessed reflect the contrasting responses of the two regions to agrarian capitalism. Only a comprehensive review, evaluating all the major variables involved in the process of land consolidation, can provide an adequate explanation of why this should be so.

III

A key factor in determining whether the transition to the new order was smooth or traumatic was the condition of the 'old' society in both the western Highlands and Lowlands. The major period of dislocation came after c.1760 but, to a significant extent, response to it depended on previous social evolution. In particular, it is important to discover how far earlier developments had produced elements within each region able to accommodate themselves to or even to exploit the opportunities which flowed from the expansion of markets for foods and raw materials in the later eighteenth

[28] E. Richards, 'Patterns of Highland discontent, 1790–1860' (1974): 75–114. An equally interesting question is why the scale of social disruption in the Highlands did not cause more widespread collective resistance. This issue is discussed in T.M. Devine, 'Stability and unrest in rural Scotland and Ireland, 1760–1840' (1987).

[29] E. Richards, *A history of the Highland clearances: agrarian transformation and the evictions, 1746–1886* (1982): 262.

[30] E. Cregeen (ed.), *Argyll Estate instructions, 1771–1805* (1964): xxiii.

[31] J. Hunter, *The making of the crofting community* (1976): 89–106.

[32] C. Harvie, 'Behind the Bonnie Brier Bush: the "Kailyard" revisited' (1978): 55–69.

century.[33] It is also essential to assess changes in landlord attitudes to their subordinates which are not wholly attributable to economic forces alone but result from a radical reappraisal of social priorities.

From the early and middle decades of the seventeenth century both societies were likely to be influenced by moderately rising demand for grain, cattle, wool and meat. Burghal expansion in Scotland, and the fact that the Lowlands already were quite heavily urbanised by European standards, were key factors in this trend. Another powerful influence was the growth of vigorous links with English markets even before 1707.[34] It is important to stress that the western Highlands were not insulated from these stimuli. Indeed, that region, because of its precarious grain supply, had a vital need to enter into commercial relationships with more favoured areas to the south. Not surprisingly, therefore, it did respond in the final few decades of the century when, partly as a result of the stagnation in Scottish grain prices (with the exception of the lean years of 1674 and the 1690s), the market boomed for Highland black cattle.[35] By 1700 the main foundations of the well-known cattle trade of the eighteenth century were all in place: the marketing centres (or trysts) at Crieff and Falkirk; the droving trails; the business connections between Highland lairds and Lowland buyers. This development can be seen as the Highland parallel to the large-scale expansion of cattle and sheep farms in the Border country. In both the rural Lowlands and the western Highlands the new commercial pressures manifested themselves in conversion of rentals in kind to money rents (or as they were known in the north west 'silver rents'), in the new consumer tastes of the landed elite and in a more business-like attitude on some properties to estate management.[36]

There, however, the similarities end and the contrasts begin. The crucial point is that while both societies were exposed to market influence they reacted in quite different ways. By c.1600 the Lowlands were already more stratified and so were better geared towards the production of commercial surpluses. Then, over the later seventeenth and early eighteenth centuries, the region experienced further development of particular social formations and social attitudes which enabled a relatively smooth transition in the later eighteenth century. Two aspects, in particular, require comment.

33 See P. Kriedte, H. Medick & J. Schlumbohm (eds.), *Industrialisation before industrialisation* (1977): 12–33.

34 T.M. Devine, 'The union of 1707 and Scottish development' (1985): 23–40; T.M. Devine, 'The merchant class of the larger Scottish towns in the seventeenth and early eighteenth centuries' (1983a): 92–111; Whyte (1979): 173–97, 222–45; T.C. Smout, *Scottish trade on the eve of Union, 1660–1707* (1963): 206–37. For the European urban comparison see J. De Vries, *European urbanisation*, (1984): 29, 39.

35 D. Woodward, 'A comparative study of the Irish and Scottish livestock trades in the seventeenth century' (1977): 147–64.

36 F. Shaw, *The northern and western islands of Scotland: their economy and society in the seventeenth century* (1980): 155.

First, by the later seventeenth century, the Lowlands were pacified: '... it would have seemed ludicrous by 1688 should a landlord ... have proposed to call out his dependents either to pursue a feud or to challenge the crown'.[37] The combination of peace and developing market influence ensured that land exploitation would be governed more emphatically than ever before by economic criteria. The formerly turbulent Border country became an area of extensive commercial pastoralism. Tenancies on the more progressive estates came to be allocated on the basis of farming competence and ability to pay rather than by kin connection or traditional affiliation. The rapid spread of written leases and their increasing duration after c.1670 reflected the new perception of land as 'property', as an asset to be exploited. The tendency therefore in many parts of the Lowlands was for the economic uses of land gradually to take precedence over its social function of supporting a population at traditional levels of welfare.[38] Not so in the western Highlands. As is well known that region was not fully stabilised for almost a century after the south and east. Lingering lawlessness meant that the clan ethic retained a rationale; the role of land as a source of military power and large followings did not entirely disappear. This happened despite the fact that by the later seventeenth century the Highland landowner was just as conscious of the need to raise increased revenue from his property as any Lowland laird. But martial attitudes and structures endured, albeit less strongly than before, alongside the new commercial forces. As late as the 1770s, on one of the largest and most progressive estates in the West Highlands, that of the 5th Duke of Argyll, tenancies continued to be partly granted on the basis of family connection and political loyalty.[39] The social purposes of land were maintained longer and its primacy as an economic asset continued to be subordinated to other purposes until the second half of the eighteenth century.

Second, there were important changes within the tenant structure of Lowland society. Research covering a wide sample of different properties in the north east, Lothians, the Borders and Ayrshire has indicated the expansion of enlarged tenancies leased by one individual.[40] On current evidence multiple tenancies in many areas of the Lowlands were in slow retreat from at least the middle decades of the seventeenth century. This development was tied in with the expansion of demand for agricultural products. By c.1740, according to a recent estimate, between one quarter to one third of all Lowland farms '... were engaged wholeheartedly in

[37] G. Donaldson, *Scotland: James V to James VII* (1965):401.
[38] Whyte, (1979); Dodgshon (1981).
[39] Cregeen (19964):xxi, xxiv.
[40] Third (1955):83–93; Lebon (1946):105–10; Dodgshon (1972):121–7; Whyte (1979): 137–72; di Folco (1979):1–10.

production for the market'.[41] It was a momentous change within the old social fabric of the region and had a variety of implications for the later smooth adjustment to agrarian capitalism. It implied the early emergence of a tenant elite gradually amassing the skills, capital and experience which would allow greater response to market opportunities after c.1760. The gradual and piecemeal concentration of tenancies meant that, in some areas at least, the majority of the rural population was falling into a dependent position as sub-tenants, cottars or servants who had a weak connection with land but had to sell their labour power to the bigger farmers in order to gain a full subsistence.[42] Here can be seen in outline the kind of social order which was to emerge more clearly and coherently at a later date. Finally, and most crucially of all, the influence of the market had penetrated down to tenant level. In the later seventeenth century it had been common for landlords to be heavily involved in the marketing of their rentals of grain, cattle, sheep and other produce. However, the conversion of rentals in kind to money rents and the rise of a more substantial tenant class ensured that by the early eighteenth century many farmers were facing the market directly. This was of vital importance to the evolution of more commercial values and attitudes within the traditional rural structure of the Lowlands.

This growth in social stratification below landlord level was not duplicated in the western Highlands. There is little evidence there of the widespread emergence of a richer peasant class. Below the level of the greater tacksmen, or clan gentry, few had written leases. The gains from the cattle trade seem not to have filtered down and promoted a significant process of capital accumulation.[43] Partly this was because the region was rarely self-sufficient in grain, and the earnings from pastoral husbandry were often paid out on essential supplies of meal. Also the landlord class, and to some extent also the greater tacksmen, monopolised much of the trade in cattle. The most common way of doing business was for the proprietor or his chamberlain to agree with the drover to take an agreed number of cows belonging to the landowner or his tenants at a fixed price. The tenant's role, however, in these transactions was invariably a passive one. In theory he had to raise a money rent; in practice he supplied his landlord with at least one cow at an agreed rate. This sum was then deducted from the money rent and payment simply became a book transfer.[44] In this way, despite the massive expansion of the cattle trade, the vast majority of the Highland population were still locked within a subsistence system. The fertilising influence of the market rarely penetra-

[41] Dodgshon (1981): 265. [42] Whyte & Whyte (1983): 32–45.

[43] M. Gray, *The Highland economy, 1750–1850* (1957): 11–30; I.F. Grant, *Everyday life on an old Highland farm* (1924); E.R. Cregeen, 'The changing role of the House of Argyll in the Scottish Highlands' (1970): 5–19; Richards (1982): 41–73.

[44] Shaw (1980): 155–6.

ted below gentry level; there was therefore little incentive to practise habits of efficiency and the virtues of 'possessive individualism'. Above all, there was a continued attachment to land as the vital source of all the necessities of life. The notion of a right to land for every family continued to be bolstered by sub-division among kinfolk, shared techniques of fuel gathering and crop cultivation and the use of the common lands as a resource for cattle, sheep and goats. In the Lowlands, the transformation in the purpose of land was already taking place before 1760; in the north west this did not occur as easily or as rapidly. These early divergencies go some way to explaining the contrasting responses to dispossession in the later eighteenth century and thereafter.

The acute feelings of outrage which some clearances in the Highlands caused at that time were related also to the persistence of the martial ethos. There was no neat sundering of the bonds of clanship and lordship after the debacle of the 1745 rebellion and the ruthless imposition of order by the state. Land in several parts of the western Highlands did not suddenly and unambiguously become a unit of resource. The claim to land, for reasons other than the simple ability to pay for it, was perpetuated by the new landlord custom of raising regiments for the British army through the simple expedient of promising tenancies in return for service.[45] This neo-feudalism had a clear economic purpose; it was as effective a means of adding to revenue as such 'economic' developments as the encouragement of fishing or the manufacture of kelp. However, the overtly commercial intent was partially masked by the fact that military entrepreneurship led to land being distributed in return for the most fundamental rent payment of all, the life of a son or a husband. Even after 1800, therefore, the assumption persisted on several estates in the north west that the right to the secure possession of land had been acquired in return for service, not in the distant past, but in very recent times. As one writer has put it '... by invoking this latter-day feudal obligation the landlord class implicitly and sometimes explicitly conceded the right of the people to their lands; they re-asserted the priority of service over rent'.[46]

Two particular points need to be further stressed. First, it is essential to remember the sheer scale of military recruitment, especially during the French Wars, in the Highlands. Few communities could have remained untouched. Rough estimates of the total numbers involved range from 30,000 to 75,000 men from a total regional population of 350,000 in 1801.[47] In Sutherland, about 13 per cent of the county's inhabitants were said to have joined the colours, while in Skye the estimated figure was

[45] S.D.M. Carpenter, 'Patterns of recruitment of the Highland regiments of the British Army, 1756–1815' (1977); A.E.J. Cavendish, *An Reisimeid Chataich* (1928).
[46] Richards (1982): 154. [47] *Ibid.*

closer to 23 per cent of the island's male population.[48] Second, clear evidence exists in estate papers of land being promised in return for service. Such bargains were not a figment of the peasant imagination. Specific lots in Lord Macdonald's properties in Skye and North Uist were allocated in exchange 'for a son' and lists of tenants were prepared in 1802 'who have been promised lands and an exchange of lands for their sons'.[49] One reason given for the extent of sub-division of crofts on the Duke of Argyll's estate in Tiree in the 1820s was that 'four fencible regiments of men' had been raised during the Napoleonic Wars and holdings were carved out of existing tenancies to accommodate those who had seen service in them.[50] The legal status of such arrangements is probably suspect. What is beyond doubt, on the other hand, is that they inevitably perpetuated an emotional attachment to the occupation of land in many areas of the western Highlands. At the same time, the continuation of lordship (and the social reciprocities associated with it) often incited feelings of betrayal and a sense of gross breach of trust when these obligations, for whatever good cause, were dishonoured. Not surprisingly by 1800 the land issue stirred deeper passions in Gaeldom than anywhere else in Scotland.

IV

It is tempting at first glance to argue that one reason for the different regional reaction to land consolidation was that in the Lowlands the whole process took place over a much longer period of time and that in this way adjustment was facilitated. Closer examination, however, reveals that this is not an entirely convincing explanation. The major structural changes in the Lowlands developed over a span of 150 years from the seventeenth to the early nineteenth century; the Highland clearances extended over about 100 years from the 1760s to the 1850s, though there were evictions both before and beyond these dates. In the panorama of history one process seems little more elongated than the other, especially when it is remembered that social dislocation in the Lowlands, as in the north west, was concentrated in particular periods, such as the rise of the big sheep and cattle farms in the Borders between 1670 and 1740 and the rapid increase in farm consolidation together with the associated destruction of sub-tenancy between 1780 and 1815. It may be more pertinent to consider the *different* periods over which consolidation occurred in the two regions and, at the same time, to assess the contrasting manner in which the process of tenant reduction was actually accomplished.

48 Cavendish (1928):5; Carpenter (1977).

49 SRO, Lord Macdonald Papers, GD221/38/1. See also GD221/77, Minutes of the Commissioner for Lord Macdonald, 13 November–13 December, 1802.

50 PP, *First and second reports from Select Committee on Emigration (Scotland)*, vi, 1841, Evidence of Rev. Norman Macleod: 68.

It seems reasonably clear that most loss of land took place in the Lowlands in the last quarter of the eighteenth century. The stresses of this social disruption were likely to be eased, however, by the buoyancy of the agricultural and industrial labour markets at this time. Local employment opportunities were offered by planned estate villages, small burghs and large towns in contrast to the more distant possibilities, in an alien culture, available to Highlanders. Again, the late Henry Hamilton observed that between 1750 and 1790 the price of oatmeal rose by little more than 50 per cent while the wages of labour rose by 2.5 to 3 times.[51] A variety of factors helped to explain this pattern which differentiated late-eighteenth-century Lowland Scotland from most parts of Europe where real income mainly fell at this time due to sharp increases in grain prices.[52] Scottish population rise in the period 1755 to 1801 was relatively modest at about 0.6 per cent per annum compared with 1.0 per cent for England and Wales and 1.4 to 1.9 per cent for Ireland.[53] This reduced the possibility of any major glutting of the labour market. The agricultural sector proved to be responsive and capable of producing more food at lower cost per unit of output. Lowland farmers were adopting labour-intensive rotation systems precisely at the time of the first major acceleration in industrial development and town growth. It was above all the precocious expansion in the Scottish urban population, at a rate recently estimated as much the fastest in Europe, which forced Lowland farmers to bid up wages to retain men.[54]

However, the series of major evictions of peasant communities in the north west carried out to make way for extended sheep farms mainly occurred after c.1810 when the Highland economy was in recession as a result of the collapse in kelp and illicit whisky manufacture, the misfortunes of fishing and the stagnation in cattle prices. Indeed the increasing dominance of commercial pastoralism was partly caused by the manifest failure of the labour-intensive peasant by-employments which had grown in the Highlands in the later eighteenth century. While, therefore, the Lowland small tenant and sub-tenant was set adrift in an expanding job market, most Highlanders lost land after 1815 when regional alternative employments had been drastically curtailed and pressure on land was intensified as numbers rose rapidly. The differing economic contexts

[51] H. Hamilton, *An economic history of Scotland in the eighteenth century* (1963):377. See also V. Morgan, 'Agricultural wage rates in late eighteenth century Scotland' (1971):181–201.

[52] Slicher van Bath (1963):226. In Spain, 1750–1800, cereal prices doubled while money wages increased by about 20 per cent. For France, C.E. Labrousse calculated that between 1771–89 and 1785–9 the cost of living index rose from 154 (with 1726–41 = 100) to 162 while wages over the same period increased from 117 to 122. P. Vilar, 'Histoire des prix, histoire générale' (1949):29–45; C.E. Labrouisse, *Esquisse du mouvement des prix et des revenus en France au XVIIIe siècle* (1932):598–603.

[53] N. Tranter, *Population and society, 1750–1940* (1985):36.

[54] Morgan (1971):181–201; De Vries (1984):29, 39.

within which the consolidation of land took place were thus critically important to the responses of dispossessed communities.

The timing of consolidation in the two societies had another vital effect. By and large, most loss of land had come to an end in the Lowlands by 1815. It had taken place within the structure of a deeply hierarchical society in which the authority of the landlord was rarely questioned. It should not be forgotten that it was only in the Scotland of the 1750s that the heritable jurisdictions, the private courts of the landowner and the legislative symbols of lordship, were finally dissolved. There is some criticism of dispossession in the *Old Statistical Account*, the parish descriptions of life in the 1790s, but the vast majority of those who compiled it accepted it as a necessary and inevitable consequence of material progress in agriculture.[55] On the other hand, clearances in the Highlands were still occurring as late as the 1850s; indeed, some of the most notorious evictions took place in that very decade in the wake of the potato famine of the 1840s. Several involved 'compulsory' emigration; others were carried out with great brutality. They were reported in considerable detail in the contemporary press to a readership which had a more developed social conscience and a more critical attitude to landlordism than that of the eighteenth century.[56] Partly, then, the removals in the Highlands are remembered when those in the Lowlands are forgotten because they endured for so long and offended the sensibilities of a new age which found their social consequences unacceptable.

Consideration of the means employed to thin the ranks of the tenantry and sub-tenantry reveals crucial differences between the two societies. Throughout the mixed farming and dairy farming districts of central and eastern Scotland consolidation of tenancies occurred in a piecemeal fashion through a steady reduction in the numbers of tenants per farm, normally through leases not being renewed at the end of their term. Where the process has been studied in most detail it normally took place over two or three generations.[57] If not entirely painless, it was not a course of action which was likely to incite sustained collective resistance. Only in the pastoral lands of the Borders did consolidation apparently come more abruptly and on a greater scale and significantly it was the western part of that region which witnessed the Levellers Revolt in the 1720s. However, for the most part even the shock of the more radical processes occurring in these areas in the later seventeenth and early eighteenth centuries was partly cushioned by the contemporaneous growth in industrial employments in the woollen

[55] T.M. Devine, 'Social stability in the eastern Lowlands of Scotland during the agricultural revolution, 1780–1840' (1979a): 59.
[56] Hunter (1976): 73–88; Richards (1982): 393–471.
[57] Dodgshon (1972): 121–7; Whyte (1979): 137–72; Lebon (1946): 7–15; Third (1955): 83–93; Gray (1973): 132–3.

manufactures of the eastern and central Border towns.[58] This example apart, the contrast with the north west Highlands and Islands remains valid. In the latter region, consolidation of land, especially for sheep farming, caused the uprooting and dispersal of entire communities over short periods of time. Here was the obvious potential for both opposition and alienation. In addition, examination of the history of agrarian reform in the Lowlands reveals an extended but uninterrupted drive towards consolidation of tenancies over the period c.1660 to c.1815. In the western Highlands, on the other hand, the first phase of reorganisation, namely the creation after 1760 of the croft or smallholding system from the older joint tenancies, tended in the short term actually to increase the number of land units.[59] This strategy was partly designed to provide subsistence plots for the army of peasant workers employed in kelp manufacture and fishing. Thereafter, in the nineteenth century, estate policy swung to the opposite extreme, to the wholesale clearance of these dense communities of smallholders to make way for large pastoral farms. This meant that the scale and intensity of dispossession was always greater in this region than anywhere else in Scotland.

It is important to consider the reasons for these contrasting processes of consolidation. To some extent they reflected differing agrarian specialisations. The Highlands both climatically and topographically were best suited to commercial pastoralism which is most efficiently practised on units of considerable size. The Lowlands, outside the hill areas of the southern Uplands, has a complex mix of physical features and a climatic diversity which enabled arable, dairy and beef farming to be combined. There was a considerable regional and local variation but in most areas an effective integration of grain and stock farming was possible. Such a regime is best suited to medium-sized holdings of 100 to 500 acres with farms of lesser extent common in the dairying districts of the central and western counties of Lanarkshire, Renfrewshire and Ayrshire.[60] As a result of this moderate level of consolidation the scale of disturbance for the Lowland population was likely to be contained especially since the labour-intensive operations of improved mixed husbandry actually demanded more workers per acre, especially of dependent women and children, than the old system.[61] It was tragically ironic, however, for Highland society, which had a surplus of labour but only sparse arable resources, that commercial pastoralism was both land and capital intensive and had little need for many hands.

Further, the reality of rapid transformation in the western Highlands

58 Dodgshon (1983): 46–59.
59 Gray (1957): 124–54.
60 Devine (1984b): 10–70.
61 A. Orr, 'Farm servants and farm labour in the Forth Valley and south-east Lowlands' (1984): 29–54.

and the more paced development elsewhere is indicative of the greater bargaining power possessed by the Lowlands tenantry in relation to their landlords. The early spread throughout the southern countryside of the system of leases for 9, 12 years and even longer ensured that wholesale clearance was very difficult and that tenant reduction was more likely to occur sporadically as leases lapsed. In the western Highlands few small tenants (paying rental of £10 per annum or less) had leases. They held land on an annual basis and were entirely vulnerable to eviction at either the Whitsun or Martinmas terms. In an even more precarious position were the cottars who did not pay rental at all but were often among the majority of the inhabitants of some Hebridean estates. In a sense, however, these formal differences in tenure merely reflected deeper contrasts in the relative economic value placed on the small tenant class by the landowners of the two regions. Improved arable farming was a complicated art which required both capital, technical expertise and commercial acumen. The new Lowland farmers could not therefore evolve overnight. They had to be encouraged and nursed by favourable rentals and long leases. One scholar has even suggested that in the Lowlands by the end of the seventeenth century it was the tenants who were calling the tune in some areas.[62] In the pastoral districts of the north, however, there was less incentive to select able and energetic tenants because they were cattle-rearing rather than fattening areas and in the early eighteenth century at least it was normally the landowner rather than the ordinary peasant farmer who faced the market directly. The boom in sheep farming further diminished the utility of the small tenants because they could not compete against the inflated rentals offered by incoming big farmers from the south. The absolute and arbitrary authority of the landlord and the fact that after 1815 most of the population on his property could be regarded as 'redundant' and of no economic value were key factors in the excesses of the Highland clearances. His Lowland counterpart had to work with restraint within a more disciplined environment whose parameters were set by the different scale and technical requirements of mixed farming.

There is no doubt also that loss of land in the north west caused much more social suffering. The case of the sub-tenants who were removed on most Lowland estates between 1770 and 1815 is superficially analogous to the evictions of peasant farmers in the western Highlands. But the shifts in status were more subtle and less drastic for the former than for the latter. In a subsistence-based society, as many parts of the western Highlands remained until the middle decades of the nineteenth century, land was clearly of critical importance to survival.[63] It was the source of food, fuel,

[62] Whyte (1979): 161.

[63] T.M. Devine, 'Temporary migration and the Scottish Highlands in the nineteenth century' (1979c): 344–59.

shelter, drink and status. Little wonder that both crofters and cottars clung to it with such singular tenacity. The relation of the Lowland sub-tenantry to land by the later eighteenth century was probably somewhat different. By c.1750 the sub-tenant class had evolved to an intermediate position between peasant and proletarian. As early as the seventeenth century cottars were considered as part of the servant group attached to the larger farms. The records of the Justices of the Peace for Midlothian in 1656 list 'servants' as hinds, half hinds, herds, shepherds, taskers and domestic or 'in-servants'. All, except the last group, were normally married with their own accommodation and most received some arable land. They were cottars who received a portion of sub-letted land in return for labour.[64] Any major distinctions between the full-time servant class and the sub-tenants were further blurred by the close family ties between the groups. Since most servants outside the south-eastern counties were unmarried, farmers had to depend on the sub-tenants for their supply of new hands and at marriage it must have been common for former servants to become cottars. Both elements were bound together through the life-cycle of the traditional family and shared work experiences.[65]

The dissolution of the sub-tenancies could not have taken place entirely smoothly but the stresses of the transition to a wholly 'landless' wage earning class were at least alleviated. First, sub-tenant households were an important source in the old society of domestic industrial workers in linen-spinning, woollen manufacture and stocking knitting. The poll tax lists of the 1690s, for instance, habitually refer in several areas to 'cottar and tradesmen'.[66] Industrial earnings were a growing and important source of cash income for the womenfolk of cottar families which did not always contain specialist craftsmen. This brought close intimacy with the market and with the cash nexus and provided the skills and experience which eventually enabled many to gain from the boom in the rural textile industries which began in the last quarter of the eighteenth century.[67] The rapid expansion of the planned villages throughout the rural Lowlands at the same time partly reflected the determination of many landowners to provide accommodation for dispossessed cottars with industrial experience.[68] The assumption that those who lost their small portions of land as consolidation gathered pace had no option but to move to the larger towns is, at least for the eighteenth century, a myth. What the scarce figures and scattered literary comments rather suggest is a complex redistribution of

[64] C.H. Firth (ed.), *Scotland and the protectorate, 1654–9* (1899): 405–8.

[65] Carter (1979): 109; Devine (1984a): 10–13.

[66] Stuart (1844); Semple (1864).

[67] A. Durie, *The Scottish linen industry in the eighteenth century* (1979): 95–114; N. Murray, *The Scottish handloom weavers, 1790–1850* (1978): 13–39.

[68] D.G. Lockhart, 'Planned village development in Scotland and Ireland 1700–1850' (1983): 132–45.

population within a basically rural setting of farms, villages and small towns.[69]

Second, the movement from a structure in which small areas of land were given in return for labour to a system where landless employees were engaged in return for payment was facilitated in the Lowlands by the maintenance of farm service which had been inherited from the old society.[70] Only a minority of the new breed of Scottish farm workers were day labourers paid in cash. The majority consisted of either married servants, paid almost entirely in kind, hired for a year and receiving accommodation as part of their labour contract, or single male and female servants, paid partly in cash and partly in kind and boarded in the farm steading. The reasons for the survival of this apparently archaic system have been explored elsewhere; what needs to be stressed here is that the maintenance of service provided a vital bridge between the old world and the new.[71] Sub-tenants may have seemed superficially to have a greater degree of independence and security because of their access to land whereas the 'landless' servant had to rely entirely on selling his labour power at market and hence was more vulnerable to unemployment. In the final decades of the eighteenth century at least such a distinction was unreal. The vigour of the labour market and the steep rise in money wages already noted in this essay suggest a relative scarcity rather than a surplus of hands. The servant class, when employed, had an impregnable material security. The payments made to them in kind insulated them from the market price for foods and helped to ensure that their material standards rose in broad correspondence with the increasing demand for country labour. Much of this new demand boosted family income as wives and daughters gained because of the burgeoning market for linen and woollen spinners and the labour needs of the 'improved' farms for hoers, pickers and sowers as the advanced rotation systems spread in popularity.[72]

Third, the elite of the new labour force, the horsemen or ploughmen, did not simply become an impersonal cog in a more efficient system of production. They were responsible for the horses, the chief motive power of the new agriculture. Farmers, therefore, put a high premium on recruiting the best horsemen because on their skills, as much as on the more familiar technical innovations, depended the productivity of the new system. The ploughman became the aristocrat of farm labour. His status was boosted by the developing career hierarchy of first, second and third ploughman and boy apprentice or 'haflin', by his key role in the production routine – all work was arranged round the horses – and by his master's requirements not simply for cheap labour but for experienced and skilled men. The structure which linked the lad to the mature horseman offered opportuni-

[69] Gray (1973): 102–6. [70] Devine (1984a): 1–8. [71] *Ibid.*
[72] M. Goldie, 'The standard of living of Scottish farm labourers' (1970).

ties to the ambitious. The new fashion for ploughing competitions which became part of the way of life of country districts accorded respect for experience and expertise within the rural system of values. The fact that in the course of agrarian re-organisation the ploughman became a specialist concerned solely with horsework emphasised his distinctive role in the labour structure.[73] In return, it is very possible that the ploughman and his kin would accept the legitimacy of the unequal distribution of rewards integral to capitalist agriculture. These social processes facilitated adjustment to the new order just as effectively as the favourable economic environment which developed between 1770 and 1815 in the Lowlands but which, in the long run, was notably absent from the western Highlands.

The population of the north west and the Hebrides was confronted with a dramatic collapse in job opportunities and a rapid shrinkage in non-agricultural employment by the second decade of the nineteenth century. Despite this and a significant rate of transatlantic emigration, numbers continued to rise inexorably until the census of 1841. On many estates, landlords had to provide famine relief in subsistence crises in 1816–17, 1836–7 and, above all, during the great potato blight of the 1840s. Properties were burdened with a destitute population which eked out a precarious existence based on potato cultivation, subsistence fishing and temporary migration. In spite of this, many of the inhabitants of the region, while enduring a life of great insecurity which could often sink to one of severe privation, retained the tenacious attachment to land characteristic of all classic peasant societies. As Pierre Goubert has remarked 'No peasant will voluntarily leave his land, be it only half a furrow'.[74] Increasingly, however, proprietors were unwilling to support such a population and sought to devote their territory to the more profitable uses of commercial pastoralism. Large-scale displacement of entire communities became widespread. Brutal methods were sometimes employed and evictions tended to concentrate in years of crop failure and economic distress. The nature and context of land consolidation in the nineteenth-century Highlands, therefore, differed fundamentally from the processes of tenant and cottar removal in the eighteenth-century Lowlands and of necessity produced a radically different series of social responses both at the time and in the eyes of posterity.

[73] G. Robertson, *Rural recollections* (1829): 162–3; Gray (1973): 139–41; Devine (1984a): 1–9.
[74] P. Goubert, *The ancien régime: French society, 1600–1750* (1973): 44.

6

'PRETENSE OF BLUDE' AND 'PLACE OF THAIR DUELLING': THE NATURE OF SCOTTISH CLANS, 1500–1745

R.A. DODGSHON

A Scottish history without the Highland clans would be a greatly impoverished subject, one lacking a considerable part of its *élan vital*. Yet this said, recent surveys of the character of the clans have stressed the incompleteness of our understanding.[1] We still lack, for instance, a sufficient appreciation of the means by which they were integrated as clans. The extent to which they established networks of alliance beyond the bounds of kinship through bonds of manrent and friendship is now clearly understood,[2] but, surprisingly, the central role of kinship remains elusive. Just how elusive is surely underlined by the lack of a Highland dimension to recent reviews of past European kinship structures, despite the region's popular association with such structures.[3] That the kin ties of a clan could be based as much on putative or assumed links as on genuine ties of consanguity has long been accepted. An Act of Parliament passed in 1587 expressed official perceptions when it spoke of them as integrated by 'both pretense of blude' and 'place of thair duelling'.[4] Though there is an element of ambiguity about precisely what is meant by these phrases – whether, that is, they qualify or supplement each other – they leave no doubt over the essentially synthetic character of clans as kinship groups. Yet though this is widely acknowledged, its implications have yet to be explored in full.

It has, for instance, a direct bearing on the question of whether we treat clans as an anachronistic institution, one whose character between 1500 and 1745 posed problems more of survival than formation, or whether we see them as an evolving institution, continually adjusting to historically

[1] D. Stevenson, *Alasdair MacColla* (1980):8.

[2] J. Wormald, *Lords and men* (1985). Bonds of manrent were agreements between lord and man 'binding themselves mutually to protect and serve', *ibid.*, 24, whilst bonds of friendship were simply agreements over mutual support or common cause.

[3] See, for example, D. Sabean, 'Aspects of kinship behaviour' (1976); A. Plakans, *Kinship in the past* (1984). For a recent discussion that does touch on Highland kinship structures, see J. Goody, *Development of the family* (1983).

[4] *Acts of Parliament of Scotland*, III:463.

specific circumstances. Arguably, to emphasise their unity as groups of extended kin fosters the view that they embodied archaic values, since by the very act of defining them as descent groups one is stressing their continuity through time, thereby detaching the conditions under which they were formed from those under which we see them surviving. Seen as such, clans become characterised in ascriptive terms, organised around a network of affinal and determinate links, or the rights and obligations into which an individual is born and over which, in consequence, he had no direct individual control. To emphasise their composite or hybrid character though, is effectively to recover and to restate the problem of how they were constituted. Clans become changing, responsive institutions, in touch with rather than disconnected from the needs of historically specific circumstances. How they were integrated now becomes a problem to be explained rather than taken for granted, a matter of prevailing opportunities and adjustments as much as enduring principles. The nature of the parts and how they responded to needs becomes the essence of any interpretative analysis. But in addition, it must follow that a hybrid system of kinship and alliance must lean more heavily on a ritual of ideology, on self-conscious displays of unity and self-justification, than one reducible to a given set of relations organised mechanically around a given set of rules. It is important to stress here the extent to which clans need to be defined as a complex, interlocking system of activity that had vital economic and cultural inputs as well as the socio-political inputs normally attributed to them. Binding the system together was a belief in a particular order of things, an ideology of relationships. By clarifying this ideology, we will be better able to understand how it conflicted with the pressures for a more centralised, bureaucratic and market-oriented society that were being slowly admitted from the Lowlands by the seventeenth century.

In seeking to explore these problems further, this chapter will concentrate on three aspects. First, it will consider the precise contribution of kinship to clan formation between 1500 and 1745. The unifying role of such ties is reaffirmed but their uniformity, the idea that they expressed the working out of a single coherent system of kin reckoning, is not. Instead, stress is given to the different ways in which a sense of kinship was constituted within the clans, and to how 'place of thair duelling' could be transformed into a 'pretense of blude'. Secondly, it will argue that once we concede the structural and constitutive diversity of Highland clans as kin groups, then the burden of explaining how they were integrated has to be broadened so as to embrace the wider system of behaviour, and associated ideology, from which they drew their meaning. Thirdly, it will explore how this ideology conflicted with the pressures acting on Highland society by the seventeenth century and the social pathologies that resulted from this conflict, particularly the emergence of social banditry as a mutation of traditional feuding.

THE KINSHIP BASIS OF SCOTTISH CLANS?

As a basis for societal integration, kinship structures can be interpreted in two ways. Either they can be seen as something given, a projection of early society's moral order, or they can be seen as a response to functional needs. Without denying the importance attached to deep-rooted sentiments – such as those based around incest and the consequent need to define who was within or without the family group – the view upheld here is that they served to control access to the resources of subsistence.[5] As cultivable land became scarce and its social value inflated, we can expect rights of access to have been progressively tightened around the direct and immediate descendants of those who had claims to its prior occupation. Put simply, individuals acquired land because it had been occupied by their forbears. In other words, rights in land become ancestor-focused.[6] Once established as the basis for rights in land, the role of the descent group broadened so as to embrace other socio-political processes, notably the blood-feud and the different forms of exchange including marriage.

Accepting the functional basis of descent groups is important because it means that a change in their context can produce a change in their character. This is important for any appreciation of kinship structures in the Highlands and Islands. Implicitly or explicitly, it is frequently assumed that whilst clans may not have emerged as large, loosely-bonded kin-groups until the fourteenth century and whilst the fortunes of individual clans may have waxed and waned, the basic values around which they were fashioned represent archaic features that took shape at a much earlier date and which, protected by the physical isolation of the region and the high costs/low rewards of imposing a strong centralised administration, were able to survive. The view maintained here is that we need to see clans as sustained not by inertia or conservatism, but through their adaptation to slowly changing needs and circumstances.

Recent anthropological writing provides a range of possibilities as to how kinship structures might react to changing circumstances. Of particular relevance are those dealing with the conditions under which chiefly-systems of ranking, or chiefdoms, emerge.[7] A recurrent theme of this work is the role ascribed to the growing pressure of population on

[5] E.R. Leach, *Pul Eliya* (1968):11; Sabean (1976):6. For a counter view, M. Fortes, *Kinship and the social order* (1970):289–302.

[6] C. Meillassoux, 'From reproduction to production' (1972).

[7] Throughout the following discussion, I have used the term chief to describe anyone with a significant position of rank and social control over how land was allocated, whether through their position as owner or merely as tacksman.

resources. Writing of Hawaiian chiefdoms, Kirch has suggested that we can see the development of ranking in terms of an evolving adaptation. The initial colonisation of a region involved unfettered growth into new habitats. Social forms adjusted accordingly, with families constantly budding off main stems so as to form new settlements and new groups. With the exhaustion of easy colonisation, social structures adjusted to a more competitive situation, evolving first into descent groups held together across a number of generations and then becoming ranked around the figure of a chief whose managerial control could direct the tribal economy towards more intensive forms.[8] Recent anthropological work has also stressed the tendency for chiefdoms, once formed, to experience cyclical shifts between simple and complex forms. At the start of a cycle, we are faced with a congery of small localised chiefdoms, each petty chief competing for status through feuding and feasting, 'fighting with food' to establish himself as the focal point for a more general eruption of power. Those who succeed use their growing social status and command over basic resources to contract favourable marriage alliances and to strengthen their control over the flow of prestige goods, or goods whose possession helped to confer social status. To conserve land, the lineages that dominated these expanding chiefdoms tended to keep hold of their daughters. However, their surplus sons were married into the network of lesser chiefdoms that surrounded them, creating a slowly expanding network of alliance. In time, though, complex chiefdoms were prone to collapsing back into a congery of smaller chiefdoms as struggles over land and new items of exchange restructured the geography of opportunity and ranking.[9]

A basic contention of this chapter is that our understanding of Scottish clans between 1500 and 1745 is helped by seeing them in relation to this wider debate on kin-based systems of ranking. It provides us with viewpoints that have yet to be considered in the context of the Highlands. Clans cannot be seen as somehow manifesting the de-contextualised operation of socio-political processes, but are a product of the way these processes work to secure control over specific territories and resources. Given the general fragmentation, limited availability and marginality of arable land in the Highlands and Islands, and the regularity with which society must have been stricken with subsistence crises, we can hardly ignore the case for seeing local kinship groupings as the continually-reinvigorated product of competition for such land.

Equally difficult to ignore is the way kinship structures in the region may have shifted cyclically between simple and complex forms of chiefdom,

8 P.V. Kirch, 'Polynesian prehistory: cultural adaptation in island ecosystems' (1980).

9 M.W. Young, *Fighting with food* (1971); K. Ekholm, 'External exchange' (1977): 115–36; Ekholm, 'Structure and dynamics' (1981): 241–61; J. Friedman, 'Catastrophe and continuity' (1982): 175–96.

with different phases in the cycle or different socio-geographical points within more complex forms providing different conditions for the development of kinship structures. In fact, the early part of the period under review is dominated by the adjustment problems created by the collapse of a large complex chiefdom in the 1490s, the Lordship of the Isles, and its replacement by a congery of petty chiefdoms, each competing, through displays of feuding and feasting, to be at thc centre of the next great eruption of power. So widespread was feuding in the sixteenth century that it stands as one of the most turbulent periods in Highland history. Such shifts transformed the local and regional context in which kinship structures operated. By the early seventeenth century, though, any cyclical trend was being replaced by a more profound linear change brought on by the deeper penetration of crown authority into the region. Once mindful of how kinship structures may have adjusted themselves to these changes in circumstance, we cannot approach clans with bland assumptions about how they were all founded on a single or uniform principle. Developing this point further, it is possible to distinguish between three types of kinship structure.

The first is associated with the larger clans and owes its character to a process which I have called downward genealogical emplacement. As a basic pre-condition, it involved the holding of large blocks of land by a single dominant family or chief. This proprietary dominance of chiefs has its parallel in other kin-based systems of ranking.[10] As in the Highlands, it is generally explained as having come about through an assertion of chiefly rights of ultimate authority at the expense of a lineage's exclusive allodial rights in land.[11] In actual fact, the means by which Highland chiefs acquired large territorial estates involved more than a simple transfer of control from lineage to chief. Once a visible process, chiefs can be seen building up large territorial estates through a mix of strategies including conquest, marriage and crown charter grants. A key feature of these territorial chiefs is that they not only acquired control over large areas, but they did so rapidly, with large blocks being gained overnight. In the process, a positive strategy had to be devised for controlling them. Set within a kin-based society, the solution devised involved leasing or making life-grants to members of their own family. In other words, the chief's kinship ties became mapped over a wide geographical area, new segments budding off in response to the windfalls of each generation. Once emplaced as controllers or tacksmen over a district, these segments would have responded biologically to the opportunities for growth now presented to them. We can expect them to have expanded freely as localised-descent groups, slowly infilling the landholding hierarchy of the district by a

[10] P.M. Shipton, 'Strips and patches' (1984): 616–20.

[11] See, for instance, Meillassoux (1972): 101.

process of downward genealogical emplacement, substituting kin for non-kin. In other words, what we are presented with is a kin-group whose constitutive ties, in the first instance, are defined through the role which its members play as controllers or managers of a district. A loose comparison might be drawn between this sort of family growth and that discussed by Duby in the context of tenth-, eleventh- and twelfth-century Maĉon. Acquiring the freedom to bestow their land, the larger territorial landowners secured their control by endowing kinsmen with land. The sum-effect was that descent, or vertical links, became more pronounced than horizontal ties of alliance.[12]

An obvious example of this sort of canopy structure – canopy because it is set over a territory and then extends downwards in a genealogical and tenurial sense – is the clan Donald. When Somerled died in 1164, his land south of Ardnamurchan was divided between his three sons. Islay, Kintyre and part of Arran were given to Reginald. Later, he also acquired Bute and the remainder of Arran following the death of one of his brothers, Angus. With his own death, his territory was divided between his two sons: Angus, who acquired Islay and Kintyre and who was the founder of the clan Donald, and Ruairidh who acquired Arran and Bute and who founded the clan MacRuairidh. Subsequently, Arran was given to the Stewarts by the Scottish King and Ruairidh was given Gormoran in lieu. Following the Wars of Independence, the then Lord of Islay lost possession of his territories for his part in the rebellion against the Scottish Crown. They were given to his younger brother, Angus Og, who subsequently acquired Mull, Lorne and part of Lochaber. Through marriage, his son, John, added still further to the family holding, securing Sleat (Skye) and the whole of Gormoran. As this expansion took place, senior members of the clan were implanted into the different districts. Altogether, 17 different branches or *sliochden* developed. Each was associated with a separate district (e.g. Ardnamurchan, Glencoe, Sleat, Knoydart), their point of segmentation from the main stem being determined not in any normative way but by the chance acquisition of new areas and the need to bind them into a kin-based perception of socio-political control using the social resources available at that moment. Through their command over landholding, each was able to grow freely as a localised descent group, infiltrating down through the landholding hierarchy. In fact, so extensive was the Lordship that we really need to see it at three levels. The major segments into which it was divided, like the Clanranalds, could themselves control extensive estates whose exploitation involved the emergence of numerous branches controlling local districts (i.e. Glengarry, Benbecula, Morar, Kinlochmoidart).[13] On the mainland, we can see similar processes

[12] G. Duby, *Chivalrous society* (1977): 147.
[13] R.G. Fox, 'Lineage cells and regional definition' (1976): 102–7.

at work as regards the clan Donachy or Robertsons. In origin, the clan Donachy was founded by Robert, the eldest son of Duncan de Atholia. From his grandson onwards, the name Robertson was used as an alternative form of designation, becoming the prime form after c.1600. A crown charter of 1451 confirmed their possession of a continuous estate based around the barony of Strowan (Perthshire).[14] If we examine their genealogy, we find each of the 24 branches of the clan became divided and was based on control over a distinct sub-district, with the entire area becoming, in effect, a genealogical map. When we look at their relative seniority or point of segmentation, it is clear that the clan grew down into the resources available to it.[15]

Though lesser clans likewise sought to enhance their socio-political status, the circumstances under which they did so were different from those just outlined for canopy clans in a way that fostered a different circuitry of kinship ties. Whereas the growth of the canopy clans was released by the acquisition of land far beyond their immediate needs, lesser clans were constrained by their limited supply of land. This lack of opportunity must have fostered a restrained definition of clan membership and limited clan behaviour in competition with other kinship groups, channelling activity into competitive bouts of feuding and feasting and into a constant search for favourable alliances at a local level. Given the likelihood that lesser clans probably crowded those townships over which they had control as a means of making maximum socio-political capital out of them, it follows that the food used to sustain fighting men or bouts of feasting would have been less easily afforded. We can put this another way by saying that, because of their relatively higher cost as a proportion of the clan's available resources, feuding and feasting would have had greater ideological value for such clans. These different dimensions of activity were, of course, interconnected. The booty of feuding helped to offset the indulgences of feasting, just as its sagas helped to provide the basis of the latter's entertainment. In turn, feasting promoted goodwill and alliances with other groups. The cattle secured through feuding supplemented those raised by the estate in payment of *tocher-gude* (dowry). Yet precisely because of their limited resource base, these lesser, more localised clans would have struggled hard to turn these various forms of behaviour into still greater resources of land, to convert their socio-political use of land into an inflationary system. For most, territorial growth would have been piecemeal, an accumulation of land on a holding-by-holding or township-by-township basis. Moreover, most would have expanded as tacksmen or tenants on the land of other, more powerful clans, a form of expansion that may have involved the acceptance of client or tributary status.

[14] J.B. Paul (ed.), *Register of the great seal*, 11, 1424–1513 (1882):157.

[15] J.A. Robertson, *Comitatus de Atholia* (1860):39–79.

Whereas canopy clans tended to grow divergently as a kin group, unrestrained by the territorial resources available to them, the same can hardly be said of lesser clans. If we assume that linkages only became meaningful, part of the clan's calculation of itself, once families secured possession of a particular holding or township, then the growth of lesser clans as loosely-coupled descent-groups clearly depended on the advantage gained from a wide range of socio-political dealings. Apart from its narrower, more selective form, its constitution as a kin-group can hardly have been lineal or neatly divergent. So long as the growth of the clan was advanced by the acquisition of individual holdings or townships by diverse members of the clan – rather than through the central acquisition of a large territorial block by a chief or founder-ancestor – then the direction in which it grew as a kin-group would have been determined by the interplay of purely local factors. The development of the clan Macpherson, 1400–1700, provides a well-researched illustration of this sort of growth. Though leading families became wadsetters and feuars by the seventeenth century, the initial growth of the clan was as tenants of major landlords like the earls of Huntly and Moray or the laird of Mackintosh.[16] Though its chief, Macpherson of Cluny, acquired the tack to a fairly large estate, much of the clan's growth involved individual families making their own opportunities, gaining new tacks through marriage into other well-established families and successful cattle dealings.[17] Crucial to the clan's overall expansion was the significant number of endogamous marriages, both in the sense of marriage within the clan and within the lineage, especially the *Sliochd Iain*. Equally revealing is the fact that amongst senior families in each *sliochdan*, there was a tendency for men to marry out into other landed families but for women to marry within, a strategy that raised the chances of securing new land whilst conserving that which was already held.[18]

A third type or kinship structure was that based on hereditary service. Throughout the Highlands and Islands, there existed families who acted as pipers, harpists, *seanchaidhean* (genealogists and story-tellers), brieves (judges), doctors, metalsmiths and so on to the major chiefs. In return, they were given land either rent free or on special terms. Given status and stability through this combination of hereditary land and service, such families inevitably acquired the solidarity of a kin group. The list of these families bound together by hereditary service includes notable examples like the Macfees, who held Colonsay in return for being the hereditary *seanchaidhean* for the Lordship of the Isles, or the MacCrimmons, who acted as pipers to the MacLeods of Macleods.[19] Available rentals suggest that a

[16] A.G. Macpherson, 'An old highland genealogy' (1966): 8 and 11–13. [17] *Ibid.*, 6–23.
[18] *Ibid.*, 17–21. See also, A.G. Macpherson, 'Migration fields in a traditional highland community' (1984): 1–14.
[19] J. Bannerman, 'Lordship of the Isles' (1977): 233–5.

wide range of other, less publicised service roles also existed, with individuals holding land on a privileged basis because they were masons, boatwrights and so on.[20] How such hereditary roles affected kinship ties varied according to their nature. Some ensured continuity from one generation to the next but only in the sense of a son taking over from his father. Others offered more expansive possibilities and could spawn kin structures of greater breadth and depth. Services that involved a long training or some degree of mystery fall into this category. The Beatons provide a good illustration of this sort of growth. Established as physicians to the Lordship of the Isles, members of the family can be found established in a number of localities by the seventeenth century, though we have no way of knowing whether their scattered members maintained a fraternity of craft or kinship.[21] In the case of the Clan Gowan, hereditary smiths in the Morvern area, the sodality provided by their craft is manifest through their clan name.[22]

The smaller clans excepted, genealogies tend to deal with the ties between and within the clan's leading families, those that formed its main stem as well as those of its leading branch or cadet families. What may be the majority of kinsmen find no mention, so that their place in the kinship structure of the clan is elusive. Lifting the veil of assumption which the clan system itself placed over such individuals and deciding whether they were bound into the clan system through genuine or putative ties of kin poses some of the most searching questions that we can ask of the system's integrity. At the crux of the problem is the fact that the ordinary Highland peasant could build up his identity using different co-ordinates. First, there was that acquired through his patronymic or *sloinneadh*, an identity gained through the link with his father and grandfather, as with, say, Calum mac[son of] Iean vic[grandson of] Coile. Occasionally, a person might see himself in relation to his great-grandfather. Thus, a tack issued by Campbell of Glenorchy in 1516 granted land to Alane mcEan vcConoquhy roy vcCoule[23] whilst another Glenorchy tack of 1675 granted land to Lauchlane mcAllane vcConoquhay vcCordquidill.[24] These four-generational patronymics though, appear the exception in the sixteenth and seventeenth

[20] In addition to recording the possession of Sterigerly (S. Uist) by the MacMhuirichs for 'Registring the deeds & Genealogie of the family & making panegyricks' (SRO GD201/1257/5), Clanranald rentals for 1718 can be found giving part of Smearsary on the mainland to a Donald McGillichadam for his services as 'Boatwright or Carpenter to Clanranald' and part of Scardoish to David Cakston for his services as 'Officer & mason' (SRO GD201/1257/1).

[21] Examples occur, for instance, in rentals for Arisaig, 1699 (SRO GD201/1/362/3) and 1718 (SRO GD201/1257/5/2). In the latter, a Malcolm Beaton was allowed part of Keanloid 'gratis', presumably for services.

[22] K.A. Steer & J. Bannerman, *Late medieval sculpture* (1977): 144–5.

[23] SRO GD50/29/20.

[24] SRO GD50/29/18.

centuries. As a rule, it was sufficient to be identified in relation to one's father or grandfather. Being defined through one's lateral relations provided a second but less frequently-used source of identity, with lists and rentals noting individuals by their Christian name and then filling out their identity by describing them as brothers or cousins to someone.[25] In most cases, this appears simply as a shorthand style of making out a list, but in a few cases it suggests that the social identity of the person in question was in some sense contingent on that of their brother or cousin. Adding a third source of identity at this level was the use of epithets. These were widely used. Some are purely descriptive, but many have a classificatory function. In this latter category, I would place such widely-used ephitets as *mór/ogg*(elder/younger), *mór/beg*(great/little), *dubh*, *duie*(black, dark) and *ruaidh*, *roy*(red).[26] By a classificatory function, I mean that they helped to identify a person not in a descriptive or depictive sense – so that someone who is *mor* or *ruaidh* is not big or red in an actual sense – but through categorical contrast or opposition. There is even a case to argue that the branches of a clan were identified in this way.[27] At a broader level, a fourth and major source of identity was that conferred by the use of a clan name i.e. MacDonald, MacGregor, through which individuals signalled their membership of a still wider group or collectivity.

Past treatment of this problem has taken the view that personal and group forms of identity were consistent with each other, the inner and outer forms of a single social consciousness to be employed where appropriate. If we take the two main sources of identity, patronymics and clan names, we might logically expect the former to be used within the social framework of the local community or clan and for the latter to be used in dealings beyond these frames of reference. In fact, surveying when they were used suggests that no simple rules were involved. If we take rentals, a source based around the familiar relationships of the individual community, we might expect a predominance of patronymics. In fact, rentals for the period between 1500 and 1745 display no such overall preference. Some can be found dealing wholly or largely in clan names. This is the case with the fine series of sixteenth-century crown rentals available for the southern Hebrides and adjacent mainland areas. Arguably, their general use of clan names was not simply because being crown rentals they offer an official, extra-local view of identity, one that wanted to attach individuals to their political groupings, but equally, because they dealt largely with tacksmen. One of the few secure generalisations that we can make about prevailing forms of identity is that tacksmen were generally identified by their clan name, a usage which serves to highlight their political role within a clan

[25] Good examples occur in A. Macrae, *Clan Macrae* (1899): 423–5.
[26] R.A. Dodgshon, 'Symbolic classification' (1985): 74–5.
[27] *Ibid.*, 74 and footnote 14.

system of administration. Since they deal only with tacksmen, these sixteenth-century crown rentals give the impression that clan names were widely used in early rentals: this appears to hold true in areas like Ardnamurchan, where individuals like Donald McAlister McKane[28] held a group of townships, as well as on Tiree, where a more complicated political structure seems to prevail, with quite a number of townships seemingly held by more than one tacksmen.[29] Other types of rental can be found manifesting a similar concentration on tacksmen and clan names. Early seventeenth-century rentals for the Marquis of Huntly's lands show the more distant areas as being held in fairly large blocks by territorial tacksmen who invariably identified themselves through their clan affiliations, like Allan Camerone McOuildowy who held the 40 merkland of Mamoir comprising 20 townships.[30] Yet once we are dealing with rentals that list a township's occupiers in detail, we find a tendency for patronymics to be used with greater frequency but not in an evidently consistent way. Thus, a 1678 rental for the Reay estate in Caithness identifies just under 25 per cent of its 220 recorded tenants by a patronymic that extends across three generations and a further 33 per cent by a patronymic that relates individuals to their father. Yet there is little discernible pattern to their use, with most being listed side by side with individuals identified by a clan or craft name.[31] A rental of 1718 for the Seaforth estate hints at order on a larger scale, with tenants in the large townships along Lewis' north-west coast tending to see themselves – the more substantial tenants excepted – through patronymics whereas those in Lochalsh and Kintail were almost uniformly depicted as Murchisons and Macraes.[32]

We again find no overall style when dealing with lists compiled in relation to court actions. If we sample a purely local court list, like that compiled for a session of the Barrisdale barony court in 1739, tenants are listed either by their clan name or their patronymic neither being dominant.[33] When we look at legal actions involving a more distant relationship between individuals and those exercising authority, we might expect a more general use of clan names. In fact, this is far from being the case. When the Earl of Argyll and his brother, Lord Campbell, acted to evict tenants from Shuna, Luing, Torosay and Seil Island in 1669, most were entered under their clan names (i.e. MacDougalls and M^{c}onleas) with only a small proportion identified by a patronymic.[34] Yet, in sharp contrast, we find kinsmen of the Macrae clan using patronymics almost to a man to identify themselves before an Inverness court enquiring into an ambush at

[28] G.P. McNeill (ed.), *Exchequer rolls* (1897): 622–4. [29] *Ibid.*, 647–8.
[30] *Miscellany of Spalding club*, 4 (1849): 261–319; SRO GD44/51/747.
[31] A. Mackay, *Book of the Mackay* (1896): 471–5.
[32] J.R.N. Macphail (ed.), *Highland papers*, II (1916): 312–43.
[33] SRO GD20/1/227A. [34] J.R.N. Macphail (ed.), *Highland papers*, IV (1934): 221–4.

Ath Nam Muileach in 1721.[35] They were surely making their ideological differences with central authority plain by doing so. The cat and mouse game which such a group played – many being related as fathers, sons, brothers and cousins – is underlined by the way this same group were those recorded as Murchisons and Macraes in the 1718 rental for the Earl of Seaforth's estate.[36] The conclusion to be reached is that to establish the context in which a person was identified is not sufficient in itself to explain why clan as opposed to patronymic forms of identity were employed, we must also acknowledge the attitudes brought to bear on specific situations.

A more serious problem standing in the way of any easy generalisation about how the great mass of Highlanders identified themselves concerns the connection between patronymics and clan names. There has always been a tacit assumption that these two forms are related in so far as one captures the linkages of a person's immediate forbears whilst the other expresses the linkages derived from more distant ancestors. Yet, there is a case for arguing that they were forms of identity that were not only different in principle but could actually stand in conflict to each other. The use of patronymics denotes a society in which a person's position was defined through descent. As a way of identifying or positioning individuals, we can trace it back to the organisation of society around lineages or descent groups, with vital social processes like the inheritance of property, the blood feud and marriage alliances being mediated through such groups. However, by the sixteenth century, the basis for these processes had been narrowed and weakened to the extent that we cannot speak of multi-generational kinship groups being constituted in any fixed or normative sense. Admittedly, genealogies still spoke of clans being arranged into lineages and these have sustained a behavioural function but they no longer drew meaning from their allodial possession of land in the same way as the Welsh *gwely*[37] or Irish *fine*[38] maintained their corporate identity down to the fifteenth and sixteenth centuries respectively. This erosion of the descent group as a focus of customary rights, and the corresponding rise of feudal and contractual rights attached to individuals, does not mean that kinship ceased to have meaning. What we are faced with is more a change in structure than values, a shift of rights and social control from the lineage as a corporate group to individuals or chiefs. Socio-political order was still fashioned around kinship but the structures that now emerged were more loosely defined and potentially much larger than the closed, normatively-defined lineages thought to have prevailed back in the medieval period, more capable of negotiation and response to circumstances.

A consequence of the shift away from the lineage as a corporate

[35] Macrae (1899): 376–8. [36] Macphail (1916): 324–30.
[37] R.R. Davies, *Lordship and society* (1978): 354–91.
[38] P.J. Duffy, 'Territorial organisation of Gaelic landownership' (1981): 1–26.

landowning group is that when we begin to see them in rentals from the sixteenth century onwards, most Highlanders were tenants or under-tenants, holding land at will or by agreement.

However, we miss the point if we represent this as a purely contractual, landlord–tenant relationship. Although unquestionably a dilution of earlier allodial rights, tenants believed that their status as kinsmen gave them prior claim to clan holdings. This was no empty claim as a note in a Clanranald rental of 1718 for the Isle of Eigg bears out, with the Captain of Clanranald reserving to himself 'the power of keeping in his own Kinsmen and tenents on this Isle'.[39] In fact, so strong were the assumptions underpinning this favour towards kinsmen that many Highlanders saw themselves as having a customary right to the hereditary possession of their holding, or what was known as right to the *dùthchas* or kindness.[40] These are irritatingly obscure terms. At times, they appear a right so tangible and explicit that tenants could actually bargain over them, as when a John Mcpherson renounced, temporarily, his 'douchtous' and 'kindness' in a third part of Blarogie Beg (Inverness-shire) in 1683.[41] At still other times, they appear an emasculated concept, one that carried little force of meaning. This uncertainty over whether kinsmen had tangible rights to a share of clan territory raises questions about how the chief's superiority was based and makes an interesting comparison with East African chiefdoms where, as in some Scottish sources, chiefs were seen as being the guardian rather than absolute owner of the clan's territory, a qualification that could produce the kind of counter-claim on his superiority that occurs in the Highlands.[42]

In practice, the idea that families had the *dùthchas* of a particular holding, even if it was little more than a claim on the favour that chiefs were expected to show to their kinsmen, fostered a descent-oriented notion of entitlement. If perfectly developed, sons inherited their father's tenure. Consistent with this sort of devolution, a number of contemporary commentators attributed the rapid growth in the region's population over the eighteenth century to the sub-division of holdings between children.[43] If we examine those rentals which detail more than just the tacksman of a toun, there is ample proof of close male kin living within the same township or

39 SRO GD201/1257/3. In 1618, a certain Andrw. Mcferson appears to have received favour from the Earl of Murray when being awarded the tack of Dulcrombie because he was 'of the maill kynd of the name of Clanchattan', SRO GD80/3.

40 Macpherson (1966): 12; *Collectanea de Rebus Albanicis* (1847): 161, reprints a petition in which Islay tenants, in 1613, complain about exactions which, if continued, will force them to 'leave thair kyndlie habitatiounis rowmes and possessionis', a phrase suggestive of continuity in occupation.

41 SRO GD80/162.

42 Shipton (1984): 616–17; L. Mair, *Primitive government* (1970): 173–4. Cf. R. Jamieson (ed.), *Burt's letters* 11 (1876 edn): 177.

43 E.g. NSA XIV (1845): 235–6 and 308.

close by. In the Reay estate rental of 1678, for instance, we find an Alex. McAngus vic Allan, John mcAngus vic Allan, Neal mcAngus vic Allan and Hugh mcAngus vic Allan in the adjacent townships of Lettermoir, Torrandarrow, Achowlogart and Rheanleadain respectively.[44] Likewise, the John mcCoil vic Coil vic Ewn who occupied Booness in Arisaig, 1699, along with John mcEan vic Innis, and is recorded in a rental of 1718 as John mcCoull, along with John mcEan, is the 'old mcCoulle their father' noted after Angus McEachine, John McEachine, Donald McEachine, Ewine McEachine and Dugald 'his [=Ewine] brother' in a court listing of inhabitants drawn up in 1739. The 2 remaining occupiers, another John McEachine and another Donald McEachine, could well be John mcEan and his son.[45] In such circumstances, it is easy to see how patronymics would serve to orientate a person within the local community and establish his right of access to share in its resources. To a degree, we are faced with conditions similar to those which Fox documented for Tory Island, just across the North Channel from Kintyre. There, individuals traced their descent from the person who first established their family occupation of a holding. In some cases, it could produce awareness of a descent chain that spread across five or six generations[46] (the Highland *clann*)[47] even though only one or two were used to identify people in everyday affairs. In effect, they constituted loosely-coupled descent groups that drew their primary meaning from the land which they occupied.

Yet whilst there is a comparison to be drawn, it is doubtful whether the typical Highland family could boast such a continuous occupation of particular holdings over the period between 1500 and 1745. A feature of contemporary rentals is the frequency with which we find townships recorded as lying waste. Such desertions were largely a result of inter-clan feuding, tenant numbers being reduced either through mass slaughter or by simple abandonment in the face of rival or official threats. The townships described as waste or unoccupied in a mid seventeenth-century rental drawn up for Mull fall into this category, a consequence of the pressures being exerted on the clan Maclean.[48] The confiscation and re-allocation of land by the crown was another source of discontinuity, with the new owners securing their grip by inserting loyal kinsmen of their own into the apex if not the base of the landholding hierarchy. The expansion of the Campbells into Glenorchy at the expense of the Macgregors was one of many illustrations of this sort of process, with the adventitious acquisition of a crown charter by a clan chief signalling his clan's

[44] Mackay (1896): 474.
[45] SRO GD201/1/362/3; GD201/1257/5; GD201/1/227A. See also, SRO GD50/156.
[46] R. Fox, *Tory islanders* (1978): 122. [47] Macpherson (1966): 1–2.
[48] J.R.N. Macphail (ed.), *Highland papers*, 1 (1914): 273–83. See also, J.R.N. Macphail (ed.), *Highland papers*, 111 (1920): 73–84.

invasion of the area.[49] The wholesale eviction of tenants from Shuna, Luing, Torosay and Seil in 1669 shows how effective an instrument this could be in the right hands.[50] A measure of the flux we can expect from such processes is illustrated by a fine sequence of 4 crown rentals for South Kintyre between 1502 and 1605. No family appears to hold the tack of a township across all four rentals.[51] A sequence of late seventeenth- and early eighteenth-century lists detailing all males over the age of 14 years in Rannoch provides us with fuller information, covering tacksmen, tenants, sub-tenants and cottars. Admittedly, Rannoch was a notoriously unstable area but it was hardly unique in this respect. The impression conveyed by the lists is that whilst groups like the MacGregors maintained a continuous presence in the area as whole, there was a constant turnover in the occupants of particular townships, with both their number and identity changing from one census to the next.[52] Indeed, to judge from references to the area in the local barony court, there was no guarantee that those attached to a township resided there all year. Its inhabitants were regularly accused of *sorning* – that is, forcing food and hospitality out of other tenants – down to the early eighteenth century.[53]

Given the importance which the sustained occupation of land had for any sort of descent system, it is difficult to see how areas like Rannoch could have supported a local society in which really deep kin structures (i.e. lineages, *clann*) had an exact meaning comparable to those identified for the Clan Chattan in Badenoch.[54] In a sense, we are faced with a paradox. The very processes that enabled local kin-groups to deepen into large, territorial clans also introduced – through the constant rivalry between clans – a potential source of discontinuity, a means for severing the link between kin-groups and their patrimony. Once we appreciate the extent of this discontinuity, then it follows that the relationship between the sort of shallow descent group embodied in patronymics and the wider concept of the clan cannot be taken for granted.

Much can be learnt from establishing a firmer grasp of how clan names were used in relation to patronymics. Put simply, most individuals identified themselves through clan names as well as a patronymic. Where

49 SRO GD112/75/1–10 chart the territorial growth of Campbell of Glenorchy in Perthshire generally.

50 Macphail (1934): 221–4.

51 G. Burnett (ed.), *Exchequer rolls*, XII (1889): 698–701; McNeill (1897): 629–33; Macphail (1920): 75–85.

52 For instance, taking the townships of Kilchonan, Creganon, Ardlarich, Aulich, Kinnach-lachter, Dunan. Annat, Crasanour, we find that of the 42 tenants who were present in 1735, only 24 were still resident in 1739 and 16 in 1743; SRO GD50/156.

53 SRO GD50/136/1/15 December 1686; GD50/136/11/August 29, 1700.

54 There is the possibility that the Invereshie Book Genealogy gives a more organised view of clan structure than actually prevailed. The lineage or branch structure of the MacGregors is discussed in SRO GD50/93 and 103 and detailed in P.H. Brown (ed.), *Register of the privy council of Scotland* VII (1915): 82.

this was done simultaneously, the clan name was either affixed to (e.g. Donald mcAllester McKane[55]) or set beside the patronymic as an alias (e.g. John MacDonald alias mcEan vic Inish[56] or James mcCullum alias Macpherson).[57] The question we need to answer is whether these forms of identity were linked agnatically in the sense that one is merely a specific form of the other, tied through a relationship that was inclusive and immutable, or whether their link had an ideological component so that what determined how one was bound into the other was not the biological fact of kinship *sensu stricto*, but a nexus of shared interests and behaviour which, at the margins or in the right circumstances, could cut across kinship ties, acknowledging putative as well as real ties of kinship. We can find contemporary sources describing clans as composed of kinsmen, as with a 1587 reference to 'the whole kin of Clan Donald and the Kin of Clanchattane',[58] but others qualify the point by talking about those bearing the same name, as in a bond of 1672 between the Marquis of Huntly and Duncan McPherson of Cluny which talked of the latter as 'cheife of the name of Mcpherson' and responsible for 'those of his name wherever they dwelt'.[59] In fact, given the way in which the local geography of many clans was in a state of constant flux, there are good reasons for doubting whether any but the smallest and most localised could boast an absolute unity of kinship.

Writing in 1930, Grant pointed out how the inhabitants of Duthil parish (Strathspey) appear in a list of 1537 as comprised of different kin-groups but in one drawn up in 1569 as being mostly Grants.[60] Her added point about Fraser of Lovat offering a boll of meal to anyone taking his name squares neatly with a society in which food is seen as having socio-political value.[61] The most publicised example of this sort of change concerns the MacGregors. In 1603, after decades of feuding with other clans, use of their name was proscribed. Though restored in 1661, this proved to be only a temporary reprieve, with proscription being re-imposed in 1693. We can assess the impact of this legislation on the clan by tracing the recorded identity of particular individuals through successive township lists for Rannoch. Mid seventeenth-century court lists combined with the late seventeenth- and early eighteenth-century lists of all males provide us with a long-run sequence. Clan affiliation, it seems, was a matter of prevailing political ideologies. Thus, in 1660, we find reference to a Johne Dow McGillespik in the township of Ardlarich. In 1664, he is re-listed along with his son, Archibald. In 1672, after proscription had been lifted, his son now titled himself Archibald Roy McGregor. The son maintained this

[55] McNeill (1897):622–4. [56] SRO GD201/257/5. [57] SRO GD128/11/1.
[58] SRO RH4/90/19/2.
[59] SRO GD80/89. See also GD80/3.
[60] I.F. Grant, *Social and economic development* (1930):501.
[61] I.F. Grant, *Highland folk ways* (1961):24.

identity in the listing of 1683 but, by 1695, had re-oriented himself to being Archibald Menzeis. Finally, in 1698, he is still referred to as Archb. Menzeis but his son appears as 'Duncan Menzeis leat McGrigor'.[62] A number of such name shifts can be pieced together using the Rannoch listings. Their potential complexity is drawn together for us by a reference to 'Dod. Menzeis alias McWilliam leat McGrigor' in the 1698 list for Ardlarich and by the reference to 'Alexr. Menzeis leatlie called Grigor McGregor' in the list for Kinchlacher.[63]

Given its official sponsorship, it is easy to argue that the MacGregors were a special case. Yet whilst we can grasp the obvious impact which the restrictions placed on even small gatherings must have had on the clan's behaviour, it is difficult to see how a change in name could alter the fact of kinship unless clans were seen as generalised kinship structures which, in the right circumstances, could absorb or drop members through the adoption or rejection of a clan name. After all, having abandoned their clan name, the MacGregors did not simply restrict themselves to patronymics alone but adopted new clan names, so that a Duncan MacGrigor became Duncan Menzeis just as his more infamous kinsmen Rob Roy became 'Rob roy Campbell alias MacGregor'.[64] In effect, their patronymic was not sufficient for all purposes: they had to re-assign themselves within the prevailing socio-political order. To be a man 'who haid no syrnam but a patronimick' was worthy of note anywhere in the Highlands.[65] Seen in this way, what was distinct about the MacGregors was not their re-orientation or even the fact that it was forced on them – for many small kinship groups must have been similarly overwhelmed and absorbed by the expansion of a rival – but the fact that it was enacted by crown authority. Just as a growing clan back in the medieval period could underwrite its external alliance with another clan by forging putative links, or through 'the gentle' and seemingly widespread 'art of pedigree faking' as Sellar calls it,[66] so also could a clan contrive to grow internally by absorbing members at its base through a comparable process of clan faking.

The chameleon-like adjustment of clan-names makes it difficult to see them as a straightforward extension of the values embodied in patronymics. Wormald has suggested that 'geographic unity and neighbourhood were of far more relevance to the recognition of kinship than the mere fact of being related by blood'.[67] What she is arguing is that kin-ties tended to be preserved as meaningful only where kin-groups were geographically

62 Based on court listings given in SRO GD50/136/1 and 11, supplemented by reference to lists of inhabitants available in SRO GD50/156.

63 SRO GD50/156.

64 HMC, Third Report, appendix (1872): 381.

65 A. Mackenzie, *Clan Mackenzie* (1879): 61.

66 W.G.H. Sellar, 'Highland family origins' (1981): 103–16. See also, G. Balandier, *Political anthropology* (1972): 69–70.

67 Wormald (1985): 82.

proximate to each other, so that a distantly-related kinsman close by could be valued more than a close kinsman living at a distance. The overriding importance of proximity is indisputable. However, we need to go further and recognise that even non-kin could be absorbed through an apparently looser, more open concept of kinship that prevailed at the clan level. In effect, the two basic co-ordinates of identity – 'pretense of blude' and 'place of thair duelling' – were capable of being confused, so that a person could adopt the identity of a locally-dominant clan.

The suggestion that clans were developed as much around notions of putative kin as of real kin is consistent with anthropological discussions of chiefdoms. Shipton's work on East African chiefdoms has drawn a distinction between *descent-based* and *locality-based* systems. He sees the former as linked to conditions of land scarcity with individuals clinging to their lineage as the most likely source of land and subsistence. The latter, meanwhile, were linked to conditions in which land was abundant. Areas of opportunity attracted men away from their kin so that communities of mixed kin developed. In these circumstances, local chiefs needed to employ more open 'universalistic' concepts of loyalty and power in securing their control.[68] The problem with this argument is that it relies on a mismatch between opportunity and needs so much so that one can plausibly argue its reverse. When land is abundant, men would have less cause to leave their lineage and vice-versa. What is needed is a situation in which resource scarcity for one group is matched by abundance for another, enabling the latter to trade access to its resources for increased socio-political status. This sort of differential endowment could arise through the competitive processes involved in the cyclical shift between simple and complex chiefdoms. Sudden territorial extensions of chiefly control of the kind we see taking place in the Highlands were especially significant for they made it well-nigh impossible for chiefs to exploit closely such land solely through ties of kin, thereby paving the way for the transformation of the clan into a larger, but more hybridised form.

To define the sort of conditions under which individuals broke away from their lineage and took land from a territorial chieftain does not fully answer the question of why they were absorbed into the chief's clan through a 'pretense of blude'. A more complete answer lies in understanding the nature of socio-political order within a kin-based society. As Sahlins put it, we are dealing with a territorialisation of power that is developed through society, an incidental mapping of its major kinship structures and alliances.[69] With the rise of state systems, this relationship was reversed. Socio-political order acquired an abstract, non-affective meaning as land-

[68] Shipton (1984):620.

[69] M. Sahlins, *Tribesmen* (1968):58. How law and order was exercised through kinship in Scotland is well brought out in J. Wormald, 'Bloodfeud, kindred and government' (1980).

scape became organised around a fixed, territorialised framework of administrative jurisdictions, a framework whose administrative functions transcended and, eventually, displaced kinship as the organising force behind socio-political order. The problem for the Highlands and Islands between 1500 and 1745 is that they were still caught between these two systems of social control. The territorialisation of state authority – its detachment from ties of kinship and attachment to state-appointed officials controlling specific areas of jurisdiction – had hardly begun. The districts into which they were divided (e.g. Assynt, Ardnamurchan, and Knapdale) bore a restricted meaning. Most appear in early surveys as the basis for fiscal assessments whilst some appear as a unit of account for local estates.[70] But beyond these limited roles, they appear to have little administrative purpose c.1500. The territorialised functions of a few crown officers hardly made good this deficiency. Social control within the region was still largely exercised through the power structure provided by the dominant clans and not some abstract, transcendental scheme into which society was squeezed. Chiefs themselves, like Campbell of Argyll or Campbell of Glenorchy, may have been co-opted into the state system, but beneath them, control was still exercised through the ties and sentiments of the clan system. In these circumstances, an individual used clan names in addition to his patronymic so as to orientate himself within this wider framework of socio-political order, an orientation that had to be expressed in social terms. More to the point, where the geography of clans became more confused and some chiefs found themselves controlling large territories and tenants who were not of the same kin, we can expect clan names to have been adopted for the very same reason. In fact, when central government began asserting its authority over the Highlands, it reinforced the jurisdictional order built around chiefs by making them responsible for their kinsmen. Yet it knew the distinction between kinsmen and clansmen, making chiefs find caution not simply for their kinsmen but for their 'kyn and frendis'[71] and, more revealingly, for those who carried their name.[72] For those who adopted a clan name, this was not an act of self-deception but an acceptance of the socio-political order that sprang from clanship and the need to have a place in that order. From the chief's point of view, it enabled such individuals to be absorbed without changing the rules that governed the core of the system. This same attitude almost certainly contributed to the character of the many bonds of manrent that Highland chiefs drew up with lesser families over the fifteenth and sixteenth centuries. As Wormald has pointed out, bonds were designed to extend one's 'effective kin' with both sides agreeing to act as if they were

[70] E.g. W. Macfarlane, *Geographical collections*, 1 (1906): 521–2 and 532.
[71] Burnett (1889): 709–10.
[72] SRO GD80/89; Brown (1915): 83–4.

kinsmen.[73] We can better understand this attempt to extend one's 'effective kin' by seeing it in relation to a society in which socio-political order was, first and foremost, a social construct and not a fixed territorialised system of jurisdictions.

THE IDEOLOGICAL BASIS OF THE CLAN SYSTEM 1500–1745

In stressing the different ways in which the kinship ties were constituted within the broad framework of the clan system, we are highlighting lines of cleavage that potentially could divide a clan. Yet what impresses about their character is the gloss of unity that seemingly bound clans together. It is argued here that the conclusion to be drawn from this apparent contradiction is that many clans, especially the larger, more complex examples, were bound together not simply by kinship, or the mere fact of being related, but through an ideology of common interest. To reconstruct this ideology we must not only define its various dimensions – namely, its 'pretense of blude', displays of feasting and feuding, regulation of landholding and so on – but must also establish how these different dimensions were bonded together so as to form a coherent, functioning system.

The saying that a clan without land is a broken clan just as a man without a clan is a broken man captures some of the circuitry through which clans were activated as a social system. Without question, control over land was the key variable. It enabled a clan chief to establish a network of loyal kinsmen and followers. Having a large tenantry gave him access to food rents. In a region of scarce resources, one afflicted by periodic deficits, this was a source of enormous social credit. Martin Martin perceived its significance when he wrote that the Steward of the Southern Isles was considered a great man precisely because he gathered in large quantities of food as rent.[74] Surveys and rentals enable us to calculate the quantities involved. Thus, a government-inspired survey of the Hebrides in 1580 informs us that each year Islay raised 560 cows, 2,240 sheep, 4,480 geese, 8,960 hens, 800 bolls of malt, 960 bolls of meal, 3,200 stones of cheese plus 320 merks of silver mail in rents whilst Mull gave up 680 cows, 1,360 wedders, 4,080 hens, 3,400 stones of cheese, 680 stones of butter, 850 bolls of bear, 1,360 bolls of meal and 340 merks of silver mail.[75] Although food rents were progressively converted into cash rents over the next century or so, they still survived as a payment down to the eighteenth century. A statement of the rent produced by Ardnamurchan, 1727, shows that whilst it paid £244 17*s*. 2d. in cash, it also paid 148 stones of cheese, 148 pints of butter, and 33 sheep as 'meal duty' and 132 stones of cheese, 132 quarts of butter, 62 sheep, 62 kids, and 62 veals as 'presents' plus 82

[73] Wormald (1985): 78. [74] Martin Martin, *Western Isles* (1716 edn): 98.
[75] W.F. Skene (ed.), *Celtic Scotland*, 111 (1880): 432 and 437–8.

bolls of meal as tithe.[76] In addition to the food gathered in as rent, chiefs had rights of hospitality or *cuid-oidhchean*, each tenant being liable to maintain his chief and retinue in meat and drink for one night.

Food – whether grain, livestock, cheese or whisky – played a vital part in sustaining the clan system. First, the large amounts which chiefs gathered into their girnal houses provided a means of insuring tenants against crop failure, thereby increasing their mutual dependence. Second, it enabled chiefs to maintain household men. The possession of pipers, harpists and *seanchaidhean* was part of the means whereby chiefs turned land into status. However, in addition to the hospitality which they regularly received from their chief, families with an hereditary claim to these roles invariably held land in return for their services. Third, it provided for the support of fighting men, securing the clan's ability to sustain feuds. Narrowly defined, a clan's fighting men were traditionally composed of young men from the senior families of its cadet branches. However, a common complaint by the seventeenth century was that they had become a hybrid group, embracing non-kin (or broken men) as much as kin. More serious, they appear as a larger, more burdensome group. When Sir Ranald MacSorlie took control of Islay during the late sixteenth century, he alienated local tenants by having each holder of a merkland maintain a fighting man in meat and cloth in his own household.[77] As an imposition of fighting men from Ulster, the situation on Islay may well have been unique, but the principle of having fighting men maintained by individual townships operated elsewhere. In the Outer Hebrides, for instance, a clear distinction was drawn between those who were charged with fighting and those whose duty was to till the soil, an arrangement which may not have produced the tensions which existed on Islay but as a surcharge on peasant production, the outcome was the same.[78] Nor was the idea alien to attitudes on the mainland. When an English lady challenged an old Highland woman as to why her son-in-law was prepared to sit in full Highland dress watching his wife work in the fields, she retorted that it would undermine his status as a gentleman to do otherwise![79] Fourth, food rents sustained the chief's displays of hospitality and feasting, the means by which he could demonstrate his ability to give as well as to receive. The lavishness of such displays had the effect of centralising goodwill and benevolence around the person of the chief. Fifth and finally, most chiefs collected in cattle as part of their rents. As with other kin-based societies, cattle – a storable form of wealth – played an important role in local exchange schemes. Not only did they feature in fostering agreements, but they also figured as *tocher* in marriage alliances. Logically, those with access to the greatest reserves of

[76] Sir Alexander Murray, *True interest of Great Britain* (1740): appendix.
[77] *Collectanea de Rebus Albanicis* (1847): 160–1.
[78] Skene (ed.), 111 (1880): 429 and 439. [79] Jamieson, 11 (1876 edn): 148.

cattle (i.e. those who controlled areas like Islay and Lorne) were able, over time, to contract the most favourable marriages. In fact, cattle served as *tocher-gude* amongst Hebridean families down to the seventeenth century.[80]

Through the judicious manipulation of these variables, successful clans could create a multiplier effect, gradually raising their socio-political status to a position of territorial dominance. As a competitive system, though, we can hardly regard the rank hierarchies produced under such a system as having a long-term stability. It is on this aspect that recent theoretical work on chiefdoms is instructive, for not only does it stress processes like feasting, feuding and tactical marriage but, more revealingly, it suggests that the power structures built up through such processes tend to be cyclical. As mentioned earlier, a cycle begins with a system of small chiefdoms competing for status via feuding and feasting. The better endowed or the more successful tacticians use their control over resources to expand freely as a kin group, to absorb putative kinsmen and to contract favourable alliances that further enhance their status. However, with their growing status came a strengthening grip not just over the exchange of food and women, but over the exchange of prestige goods. By nature, prestige goods were those whose possession added to a chief's status, with the whole complex network of exchange now taking on a self-reinforcing character. However, in time, these complex systems of chiefdom were fragile affairs. Their control over exchange, especially that of prestige goods, might weaken and the whole edifice of relations would collapse back into a system of smaller, localised chiefdoms again.

Although our perspective is limited by the lack of documentary sources for the period prior to the 1490s, this sort of cyclical swing has a bearing on Highland chiefdoms. Not only did the physical character of the region inhibit its easy integration within the emergent Scottish state, thereby allowing local power structures based on kinship to survive longer, but the broken nature of its resource base fostered a population of localised kin-groups. In form, we can expect these to be comparable to Shipton's *descent-based* systems, with well-defined kin-groups occupying coherent territories. Macpherson's review of how the clan Macpherson consolidated its position in Badenoch, 1400–1700, provides a useful case-study of how lesser clans struggled to break free from the strict limitations of locality. His work says little about feasting and feuding, but it does note their success at cattle dealing and the importance of tactical marriage, with the senior families of the clan tending to marry their men into other clans as a means of accumulating extra land and social credit but keeping hold of their women so as to conserve the land which they already held. Being always subservient to other clans, we can hardly describe the clan MacPherson as

[80] Further comment on Highland exchange systems can be found in R.A. Dodgshon, 'West Highland chiefdoms' (1987).

a complex chiefdom but it was part of such a complex: the clan Chattan. Prior to 1500, the best example of the latter was the web of hierarchical relations and alliance that made up the Lordship of the Isles. The Islay base of the Lordship represented a comparatively rich territory, one which will have fostered the growth of strong localised chiefdoms. The 'external' threat created by the Norse kings over the thirteenth century gave ample opportunity for the transformation of an emergent descent-based chiefdom into a territorial chiefdom under Somerled, though we cannot rule out the possibility of it being a hierarchy whose roots extend back to the first appearance of the Norse in the tenth century. The territorial hierarchy that surrounded Somerled though, was partitioned at his death. We are reminded here of the stress which anthropologists place on the fissiparous tendencies of chiefdoms, with competing interests eventually dividing what others had built up. What distinguished the Lordship over the fourteenth and fifteenth centuries was the fact that it overcame, temporarily, the tendency for elaborate systems of ranking to collapse back into the parts from which they were composed. Yet even at the outset of its foundation, the scale of territory accumulated went far beyond the subsistence needs of its leading families and their immediate kin. Nurtured in this expansive context, the clan Donald developed as a canopy clan, establishing its coherence as a descent group through the kin-based control structure which it established in order to integrate a large, sprawling territory. At the highest level, it formed a carefully calculated set of relations. At the lowest, it must have been an open, continuously expanding clan, trading livelihood for tribute and allegiance. Less clear is the part played by other forms of exchange, particularly the monopolistic control which the Lordship may have exercised over the flow of prestige goods within the region. A hint is provided by the image which local chiefs projected of themselves on late-medieval funerary sculpture within the region. Most appear dressed in the light armour of the region and equipped with the large two-handed claymore.[81] For an area in which iron was scarce, those who controlled the supply of iron and working of such swords would clearly have had a considerable advantage in the competition for socio-political status. Smiths and armourers can be documented for various parts of the Lordship.[82] To judge from their seemingly-official status, their output of armour would have been carefully regulated by chiefs. The relationship which the Lordship maintained with Ulster may have been especially important precisely because it gave the MacDonald chiefs access to a source of prestige goods which their ordinary kinsmen could not hope to share.

With the collapse of the Lordship in the 1490s, power structures in

[81] Steers and Bannerman (1977): 22–8.

[82] *Ibid.*, 144–5; A. Macdonald and A. Macdonald, *Clan Donald*, vol. 3 (1896): 123.

certain parts of the region adjusted to a flatter, more localised form. Significantly, the following century of Highland history was characterised by feuding and extravagant displays of feasting, as localised chiefdoms competed with one another to be at the centre of the next great upwelling of power and status. This is how central government in the form of the Privy Council viewed the prevailing problems of the clan system. As early as the 1500s, when the crown had direct control of Kintyre, it tried to undermine feuding and feasting through the acts which it passed in the local baillie court against the practice of sorning. To judge from contemporary accounts of sorning and feuding, fighting men sorned freely on tenants of both their own clan and those of clans with whom they were at feud with.[83] For the Privy Council, sorning was an unacceptable by-product of having men whose role within the clan system was not to labour the soil but to exercise the status of the clan through feuding and feasting. At a session in 1506, the baillie court of Kintyre set out to rid the area of sorners 'that oppres the cuntrie and the pure commonys or takis mete, drink, or ony uthir thing without payment', condemning those involved to be expelled from the area or, worse still, 'to wirk and labour for thair leving'.[84] When the government came to tackle the Highland problem on a more general scale by enacting the Statutes of Iona in 1609, these same issues were very much to the fore. The Statutes speak of the great burden 'sustenit' by 'tennentis and labourairis of the ground' in the 'furnissing of meit, drink and intertenyment to straingers, passingeris and utheris idill men without ony calling or vocatioun'. As well as trying to control sorning, they restricted the maintenance of 'household men' or 'those chargeable to the cuntrey be haldin in household of ma gentilman ... '. Finally, restrictions were placed on the sale of strong wines and whisky brought in from outside the region, the aim being to control the 'extraordinair drinking' of the region.[85] We cannot make sense of the Statutes or assess their real significance without appreciating the role which feuding and feasting then played in the prevailing ideology of the region.

Once we see the clan system c.1600 in these terms, we can better understand how it declined over the seventeenth and early eighteenth centuries. Its decline can no longer be treated solely as a political process, one symbolised by the eventual failure of the Jacobite Revolutions. Arguably, the ideology which sustained the clan system was in decline for a century or so before it was defeated militarily. The constraints placed on clan behaviour by the Statutes of Iona were one cause of this decline. By curbing the various forms of chiefly consumption, the Statutes forced chiefs to reconsider the food rents which they extracted from the peasant

[83] APS 111:379; Macphail (1916):37–8; MacLeod, *Book of Dunvegan*, 1 (1938):183; Masson (1884):72–3 and 534; C. Innes (ed.), *The black book of Taymouth* (1855):237–9.

[84] Burnett (1889):703–4. [85] D. Masson (ed.), *Register of privy council*, IX (1889):26–30.

economy. The dilemma now facing them was simple. If they were no longer able to 'fight with food', to expend it within the framework of the estate on status-building activities, then how was its latent value to be realised? In the circumstances, their logical response was to market food, converting food rents into cash. In fact, the seventeenth century saw an increasing amount of Highland produce, especially cattle, being marketed. In some cases, it was handled by landowners themselves,[86] but as the century progressed, there was an increasing tendency for them to transfer the burden of marketing on to the tenant by converting food rents to cash. In many cases, though, the switch was gradual rather than being a single, revolutionary change.[87] Even after food rents had been given a specific conversion value, some tenants were still able to pay the equivalent in kind.[88]

Although the Statutes contributed substantially to the changing ideology of the clan system over the seventeenth century, they were not the only source of change. Some Highland chiefs responded to the changing models of landlord behaviour being transmitted from the Lowlands via the ordinary social and economic interactions that were now being forged between the two regions. Their response to these new models of behaviour led to what is best described as a hybridised ideology, one which mixed old and new values in equal measure. Crucial to this hybridised ideology was the growing involvement of Highland chiefs in a cash economy. Even by the seventeenth century, chiefs like Campbell of Glenorchy still paid *tocher-gude* on the marriage of their daughters or sisters, but now it was a payment in cash. In fact, between 1583 and 1631, the seventh chief or laird paid over 130,000 merks in *tocher-gude* for his 2 sisters and 8 daughters, as well as lending substantial sums to one of his 9 sons. His grandson, the ninth laird, 1640–54, paid the more modest sum of 42,000 merks at *tocher-gude* for the 7 of his 9 daughters who married.[89] Adding to this consumption of cash were the developing tastes of Highland chiefs. Visits

86 See, for example, *ibid.*, VI (1884): 184 and 459; SRO GD201/1/54 and 115.

87 In McNeill (1897): 646, mid sixteenth-century crown rentals for areas like Morvern and Kintyre record 'all the martis, cheis and mele ar sauld for silver to the tennantis of the ground', effectively converting them to cash. Presumably, the crown did not relish the transport costs involved. For comparison, 1671 rentals for the MacLean of Duart estate in Macphail (1914): 285–8 show Morvern was the only area which was not still paying meal as part of its rent though it still paid butter, cheese and veal alongside cash rents totalling £2,456 6s. 8d. Elsewhere, we find rents either comprised wholly of cash (see SRO GD14/20; GD64/1/85; GD128/11/1; GD132/541) or showing signs of a shift towards larger cash through the conversion of either grain (GD201/1/362/3 and GD201/1257/1) or stock rents (GD112/9/45). Only a few areas still paid both grain and livestock/cheese/butter as part of the rent by the early eighteenth century (see GD201/1257/5 and GD221/118) though the latter, a 1733 rental for Lord Macdonald's Skye estate shows a few paying extra silver duty 'in lieu of all casualities'.

88 W.C. Mackenzie, *History of the Outer Hebrides* (1903): 535–6.

89 All figures abstracted from SRO GD50/28.

to Edinburgh or to England not only generated requests for large and regular remittances from their estates but also cultivated their taste for more comfortable mansions and finer furnishings. Such consumption generated cash needs which could only be accommodated by converting food rents into cash rents. Given their high level of cash needs, it is hardly surprising that the Glenorchy chiefs shifted towards cash rents over the seventeenth century.[90] Yet not all were so favourably located as Glenorchy. Paradoxically, nothing signals the growing involvement of Highland chiefs in cash-based transactions more clearly than their growing indebtedness, as needs outstripped supply. Successive Macleods of Macleod struggled for much of the seventeenth century to cope with the burden of debts contracted with other Highland families and Glasgow merchants.[91] By the 1640s, the Glenorchy chiefs were also borrowing heavily from Lowland sources.[92] In no way were they alone in their plight. Shaw has painted a remarkable picture of family debt amongst Hebridean clans by the seventeenth century.[93] A common palliative to the problem, one which raised short-term capital at the expense of long-term income, involved the wadsetting of land, whereby a tenant lent money to his landlord who then treated the interest owed as rent. By the late seventeenth and early eighteenth centuries, rentals disclose substantial amounts of property being wadset.[94] Willingly or unwillingly, established Highland lairds were being forced to change the emphasis of their estate economy, to replace strategies that maximised internal consumption and the social credit which it bought with ones designed to raise their financial credit within a wider economic system.

For the ordinary Highland peasant, the shift away from food rents forced them to market part of their produce. Most adopted a policy of selling livestock. There were a number of advantages to this solution. First, taking stock out of the peasant economy was less likely to threaten its viability than taking grain. Second, the quality of Highland stock could be redeemed by feeding them on Lowland pastures in a way that could not apply to Highland grain. Third, in a region of poor communications, livestock had the advantage of taking themselves to market. However, beyond this shift into cash rents, the ordinary peasant was little affected by the ideological change that was taking place amongst landlords. Whereas landowners had previously packed their estates with tenants because it gave them the socio-political status that accrued from a numerous follow-

90 Comparing Breadalbane rentals of 1582–95, SRO GD112/9/6 and 33, and of 1594 in Innes (1855): 268–99 with that for 1733, SRO GD112/9/45, suggests that the increased proportion of cash paid in the latter was partly accounted for by the conversion of cattle, sheep and butter payments into cash.

91 R.C. MacLeod (ed.), *Book of Dunvegan*, 1 (1938): 161–80.

92 The ninth laird borrowed 57,000 merks, see SRO GD50/28.

93 F. Shaw, *Northern and western islands of Scotland* (1980): 43–6.

94 *Ibid.*, 43.

ing and large intake of food rents, they now had a vested interest in doing so because it helped to maximise cash rents. For tenants, such a change did not alter the nature of the clan system as they perceived it, with 'pretense of blude' still being viewed as a means of gaining access to land, at a time when rapidly-increasing numbers were creating a degree of land scarcity, and as a means of mediating one's relationship with the prevailing socio-political order. The point is that by the early eighteenth century, the attitude of landowners may have diverged significantly from those still held by the ordinary peasants. The extent of this divergence is possibly captured for us in the differences highlighted by Cregeen's study of the Argyll estate over the early eighteenth century, with tacksmen and the communities developed around them being seen as having different expectations to those of the Duke and his advisors, with the former not the latter appearing to embody the traditional values of the clan system as an institution concerned as much with the cultivation of men as of land.[95]

These differences in ideology were expressed not only through the tensions within particular clans, but also in the conflict between clans. We can see this clearly by considering the experience of the MacGregors. Emerging as a distinct clan in the fourteenth century, the MacGregors' direct control over land was already being eroded by the fifteenth century.[96] Yet though their capacity to sustain displays of feasting and hospitality and to contract favourable marriages must all have been diminished by this weakened control over land, the MacGregors preserved their self belief as a clan. In 1506, they reportedly entertained the Scottish king besides Loch Tay with a lavish display of feasting that lasted 8 days. Responding to the king's surprise at such lavishness, the MacGregor chief likened Loch Tay to the clan's food bowl and their plaid to their towel. In reality though, their food bowl was being reduced to the more difficult ground of areas like Rannoch and the rough ground around Loch Katrine and the head of Loch Lomond. To maintain their status in a society whose basic values were articulated around those who controlled subsistence, they needed more than could be grown or reared in such areas. Perhaps for this reason alone we find them feuding with Campbells and Colquhouns, raiding the girnal houses of the Buchanans and Dukes of Lennox or acquiring infamy as raiders of cattle droves and organisers of black-mail.[97]

By the mid sixteenth century, the more powerful clans of the district were already using their power to break the MacGregors as an organised clan. Individuals like 'Duncan McGregor McPhadrick and his barnis' were being condemned as 'notorious bandits' and barred from holding

95 Cregeen (1969): 106–7.

96 The retreat of the MacGregors in the face of expansion by the Campbells of Glenorchy is brought out in SRO GD50/93 and the various land grants obtained by the latter, such as SRO GD112/75/110.

97 SRO GD50/93.

land.[98] Following their slaughter of Colquhouns in Glenfruin, 1603, the entire clan was outlawed and their name proscribed. Half-hearted attempts were made to dislodge them from tenancies in core areas like Rannoch.[99] Yet behind the persistent 'outlawry' of the MacGregors and the expressions of outrage at their behaviour, there is a sense in which we are dealing not with spontaneous or ingrained lawlessness but with conflicting concepts of society. This comes over strongly from the events of the late seventeenth and early eighteenth centuries. On the one hand, official perceptions tried to marginalise the MacGregors, stigmatising their behaviour as barbaric. Instead of a clan bidding for status by time-honoured methods, they were now to be seen as 'a desperate wicked crew of bandits ... pillageing and plundering the country people'[100] and – by the early eighteenth century – led by 'a notorious robber', 'an Arch-Rogue', Rob Roy MacGregor.[101] Yet these same sources conceded that Rob Roy appeared 'as one acting from principle'.[102] Furthermore, although those who followed him were described as broken men, without real affinity of kin, they did outwardly function as a clan, gathering regularly in groups of 200–300 men for bouts of feuding and feasting.[103] Put simply, the MacGregors' difficulty was that they tried to preserve a sixteenth-century style of life down into the early eighteenth century, fighting with food over food. Back in the sixteenth century, to sustain a feud with other clans was merely to play a game in which both sides acknowledged the same rules. Martin Martin's description of feuding makes this point clear. Led by its chief, each clan would try to rob each other's cattle or die in the attempt, yet the whole 'custom, being reciprocally us'd among them, was not reputed Robbery' each gaining as much as they lost by the feud.[104] The problem for the MacGregors is that they were still imbued with such values c.1700, while their close neighbours were not. Glenorchy may, back in 1588, have set the two merkland of Glenevern in Lorn to Donald and Dougall McTarlich on the condition that they 'enter deidlie feid with the Clan gregoure ... making slaughter upone thame'[105] and the same Duncan may, for this sort of reason, have had ample cause for describing himself as 'the blakest hand in all the land',[106] but by the end of the seventeenth century, attitudes were different. Those ranged against the MacGregors now sought to exercise crown jurisdiction and to see their feuding behaviour as a threat to law and order not as a means by which law and order was itself maintained. Seen in this way, the MacGregors fit recent definitions of social banditry which underline how such behaviour emerged out of the

[98] D.P. Menzies, *Book of Menzies* (1894): 177.
[99] A. Cunningham, *Loyal clans* (1932): 144–5; HMC, Sixth report (1877), appendix: 692–3.
[100] HMC, Third report (1872: appendix, 382. [101] *Ibid.*, 383. [102] *Ibid.*, 382.
[103] *Ibid.*, 382; OSA 2 (1792): 457. [104] Martin (1716): 101–2.
[105] Innes (1855): 416–17.
[106] Written on fly-leaf of furniture inventory (1599–1610), SRO GD112/22/2.

conflict between traditional kin-based societies, in which pastoralism was important and the feud still active, and the forces of modernisation.[107] By imposing a contractual view of property and an economic evaluation of resources, one which capitalised their meaning, modernisation challenged the basic value system behind these traditional ways of life. Some of those who lost or were marginalised by this process turned to social banditry – in effect, a re-direction of the energies and values of the feud – as a form of protest.

CLANS: A MATERIALIST VIEW

Scottish clans can hardly be described as a neglected theme. Some aspects have the drained appearance of a thrice-squeezed lemon. Yet for all the effort expended, reviews of the problem are greatly restricted by the basic insufficiency of data. The more serious gaps are unlikely to be filled by the opening of some new Pandora's box of historical sources, though new insights may be gained through techniques of record linkage, tracing descent lines and clan affiliation via rentals, lists of inhabitants, kirk session papers and parish registers. These fresh insights may modify but they are unlikely to alter the basic conclusion that Highland kinship structures were founded on the need to regulate access to the resources of subsistence. Such a conclusion must not be seen as pleading for the special character of Highland kinship structures, at least not in this respect, since not only have recent studies documented the survival of kinship structures into the post-medieval period in other parts of Europe but, significantly, they have stressed the extent to which they were founded on the regulation of property rights and the resources of subsistence.

What distinguished Highland kinship structures is the way in which they still served c.1500 as the building blocks of socio-political order, with large, loosely-coupled kinship groups, or clans, competing – under the leadership of chiefs – to expand their territory, numerical strength and status. We can explain why clans still had a socio-political role by stressing the physical character of the region and how this inhibited its easy integration into the political framework of the Scottish state. Yet to explain why they still had a political role does not explain how that socio-political role operated. Recent anthropological work on the cyclical nature of chiefdoms may be helpful here. In particular, it cautions us against seeing clan behaviour as an inter-clan struggle over socio-political status that went on around the economy, treating land as a source of fighting men but not production. In short, we need to link the socio-political dimensions of the clan system to the constitutive or formative role played in clan

[107] D. Moss, 'Bandits and boundaries' (1979): 477–96; C.G. Rossetti, 'The ideology of banditry' (1982): 158–60; E. Hobsbawm, *Bandits* (1969b).

formation by the control exercised over resources. As an environment in which resource opportunities were limited and in which food deficits must have been endemic, control over food and the resources of subsistence would have been the first and most enduring source of chiefly status in the Highlands.

Petty chiefs struggled for status through feuding and feasting, a form of competition which has been described as 'fighting with food' and one which has certainly characterised phases of Highland history. Although the rise of complex chiefdoms involved other strategies – favourable marriages, political alliances, control over prestige goods – these have to be seen as complementing rather than replacing chiefly control over subsistence. The flux between simple and complex forms which some writers now see as of the very essence of the competitive functioning of chiefdoms has considerable relevance for Highland history. What it suggests about the processes underpinning such forms in a Highland context is not diminished by the way clans increasingly sought to secure their position through crown charters over the late medieval period. Such flux also has implications for the composition of Scottish clans. Put simply, it repeatedly relaxed or stressed the balance between the clan as body of kinsmen and its resources of subsistence. Where sudden and dramatic gains in territory occurred – through conquest, marriage or crown charter – we can expect clans to have responded politically and biologically to the extra opportunities now available but we can hardly expect them to have populated whole districts overnight even conceding that some chiefly families had impressive rates of both reproduction and remarriage. It is partly through their need to find interim solutions to the full exploitation of such areas that clans will have contracted alliances with local kin-groups and, in the right circumstances, absorbed some as putative kinsmen so that 'place of thair duelling' became transformed into a 'pretense of blude'. Other factors worked towards the idea of an open clan. Once control over resources passed from lineages to chiefs, then kinship altered from being a bounded framework of genealogical ties within which the legal and resource rights of the individual were defined to being a projection of chiefly interests. These chiefly interests were more pragmatically defined, involving a complex pattern of behaviour designed to enhance the socio-political status of the clan in the personage of the chief. It was a goal that could become more important than the means, so that instead of a situation in which kinsmen contributed to this goal because they were kinsmen, one had a secondary situation in which individuals became kinsmen because they contributed to this goal. The role of clans as a source of socio-political order will have had a similar effect, opening the social margins of the clan to expansion by absorption as well as alliance.

7

NORTH AND SOUTH: THE DEVELOPMENT OF THE GULF IN POOR LAW PRACTICE

R. MITCHISON

INTRODUCTION

Western Europe saw a widespread move in the later sixteenth and seventeenth centuries to replace the basis of charity and support of the poor, hitherto carried by religious bodies and charitable individuals, with a wider and better-organised system of support and control, whether by a city or by a state.[1] In Protestant countries this was an evident need, since the secularisation of monastic property had removed an important if erratic source of alms, and the doctrinal devaluation of good works discouraged private almsgiving. Attempts to provide civic or national structures of relief involved a clearer definition of the poor: the word 'poor' had always meant the less favoured part of society, and continued to, but it also came to mean more specifically people whose need of help was recognised and categorised, whom a later age would label 'objects of charity' and a still later one 'paupers'. In England by the mid sixteenth century a distinction was used between those recognised as suitable for charity and 'sturdy beggars', but those who begged were not clearly marked off in most people's minds from poor householders. In the 1570s, unemployment was recognised as a reason for destitution, and by the time of the dearth of the 1590s it was clearly seen in England that there was a class of poor householders who needed help in times of scarcity.[2]

THE ORIGINS OF THE OLD SCOTTISH POOR LAW

In Scotland there had, from the twelfth century, been statutes which encouraged the gift of alms and the provision of justice to the poor. In the

[1] E.M. Leonard, *The early history of English poor relief* (1900): 13; P. Slack, 'Poverty and politics in Salisbury 1598–1666' (1972); A.L. Beier, *Masterless men: the vagrancy problem in England, 1560–1640* (1985); C. Lis & H. Soly, *Poverty and capitalism in pre-industrial Europe* (1982); O. Hufton, *The poor of eighteenth-century France* (1974); P. Berger, 'Rural charity in late seventeenth-century France (1978).

[2] Leonard (1900): 32–4, 139; J.B. Black, *The reign of Elizabeth 1558–1603* (1959): 265–6.

fifteenth century there were added to this attempts to prevent importunate begging: in 1424 begging was forbidden to those aged between 14 and 70 unless they had no other means of support: in 1503 to all except the blind and impotent: and in 1535 it was permitted only in the parish to which the beggar belonged.[3] Even if these statutes were made operative, and there is no reason to believe that this was the case anywhere, they were not what we should call a Poor Law, for they made no order for the supply of those in need other than by private or haphazard alms. They did not imply a civic duty of almsgiving. This may be because historically it had always been the function of the Church to protect the interests and education of the poor. The first statute which can be seen as creating a Poor Law, holding together the two necessary aspects of provision for those in need and control of vagrants, was the temporary Act of 1574 made permanent with little change in 1579.[4] This Act was an almost exact copy of the English Statute of 1572 which can be seen as the crucial initiation of the Elizabethan Poor Law. The English Act was amplified by the further statute of 1575 which added to orders about relief instructions to towns to provide a stock of materials so that the unemployed could be put to work.[5] This element, important not because the creation of work was a successful policy but because it explicitly recognised the needs of the unemployed, was not added to the Scottish Act: it is not clear whether the omission was accidental or deliberate.

There can be several good reasons for legislating on poverty, need and vagrancy. An obvious one is a concern, sustained by Christian ethic, for the experience of others. Another is fear of loss of life, particularly of young life, in times of food shortage (and hence loss of manpower for labour or for war). Another may be a desire to make all participate in the support of the needy. There may be a fear for public order if vagrants should turn from simple begging to extortion, and are free to gather and move as they choose. But it is difficult to classify as a good reason the desire to copy the legislation of a neighbouring state in a very different stage of economic, social and political development. It has been shown that Edinburgh, on two occasions, attempted to carry out the Acts.[6] Otherwise there is no sign of any local action undertaken to fulfil the legislation of the 1570s in Scotland for over 70 years, and given the apparent motivation for the Acts, this should not surprise.

The failure of these Acts may, at least partly, relate to the inadequacy of

[3] APS II 8, 255, 347, 486: 1424 chap. 24, 1503 chap. 14, 1535 chap. 29, 1551 chap. 16.

[4] APS III 87, 139: 1579 chap. 12 'For punishment of the strong and ydle beggaris and releif of the pure and impotent'.

[5] *Statutes of the Realm* IV pt 1, 14 Elizabeth chap. 5 'For punishment of vagabondes and for releif of the poore and impotent', 18 Elizabeth chap. 3 'For the setting of the poore on work and for the avoyding of ydleness'.

[6] M. Lynch, *Edinburgh and the Reformation* (1981): 19–20.

their language. That of 1572 placed responsibility on 'elders and deacons' in the towns and 'headsmen' in landward parishes: there were no such officials in the lay government of Scotland, though by 1572 numerous Lowland parishes had set up a kirk session with lay elders, drawn usually from the local oligarchy. The Act of 1579 changed the authorities to provosts and bailies in the towns and 'Justices' appointed by the King in landward areas: it was not for another 30 years that Justices of the Peace were appointed. The Acts ordered these largely non-existent officials to 'tax' and 'stent' the inhabitants according to their substance. A 'stent' or rate was not yet laid on land, and Scotland did not yet have a systematic valuation of land. The country had not assumed the habit of paying taxes save under exceptional circumstances, and so had not worked out appropriate mechanisms. Most serious among the weaknesses of the Acts was that they assumed that power for major change lay in Parliament and the central government.

To appreciate the problems which would have been involved in the creation of a nation-wide system of relief we have to understand the limitations of late sixteenth-century Scottish government. Scotland was, like other less developed parts of Europe such as Scandinavia, and even more developed countries like France, a country where the authority of the ruler was limited by geography, by the control of local resources by the aristocracy, by lack of funds and by lack of a civil service. In the Highlands the king had no sources of revenue and no power: he could persuade, influence, offer inducements for action, and impose penalties on local clan leaders if they strayed beyond their own areas, but he could not command or tax. The only effective authority in this area lay in the clan chiefs, modified by the views of the more prestigious vassals of the clans. Even in the Lowlands there were areas where, for the most part, royal instructions had no effect. Great nobles not only had a monopoly of local military force, but also owned 'heritable jurisdictions', or great judicial franchises. Resistance to the wishes of the Crown, even by force, was a venial offence. In Aberdeenshire, for instance, and in the Borders, the monarch might make an occasional military sortie to bring to heel some over-independent magnate or to reduce an unacceptable level of local feuding and disorder, but normally his authority in these areas was exercised by influence or persuasion. In modern states legislative innovations are submitted to the views of the major interests affected by them before they pass into statute form. For the sixteenth century it is simplest to see the views of these interests as expressed once legislation has been formulated, by whether it was acted on or not. Eventually Scots lawyers were to embody this fact in the principle of 'desuetude': the principle that if a statute could be shown to have been ignored it lost all legal force. This principle has, at times, made for considerable doubt as to what parts of a statute should be considered as valid.

The old Scottish Poor Law which was not superseded until 1845 was thus enacted at a time when statutes could be ignored with impunity and rendered invalid. But the central government in the early seventeenth century did not treat the Poor Law as invalid. Parliament issued additional or amending statutes, the wording of which implied that the Act of 1579 was being worked. Gradually through the seventeenth century the Crown created and developed a structure of shire government which, even though kept weak in court authority by the continued existence of franchises in private hands, was of some significance. Sheriffs extended the activity of their courts: an example of this is the system of annual fiars prices for grain settled for each shire in the sheriff court after Candlemas, which appears to have started in the early seventeenth century. In 1609, perhaps a few years earlier, the institution of the Justice of the Peace, that is of unpaid local gentry given duties of an administrative and minor judicial nature, was borrowed from England and set up.[7] The nominal powers of these Justices were markedly more restricted than in England and in practice impeded also by franchises, so that they had only a limited effect: no lesser landowner could at that time have afforded to act against the wishes of his nearby great noble. But the institution was to survive and expand its role. The nobility was politically defeated during the later stages of the mid-century Great Rebellion, and the lesser landowners then could begin to exercise some of the authority which they nominally held. Their power was further increased in 1667 by the creation among them of the office of Commissioner of Supply, with the duty of raising, and distributing the burden of, the 'cess' or land tax. This meant the creation of a system of valued rents, which could be used later for assessment of landowners. It also gave to lesser landowners control of two other minor levies of great local use, the so-called 'Rogue Money', for arresting and incarcerating offenders, and 'Road Money' levied for the repair of roads and bridges. 90 years after the nominal creation of the Poor Law the Crown had, in the Lowlands, a shire government on which it could call for service with some hope of this being delivered, even though the judicial franchises were to persist till the 1740s, and even though the Crown had not the resources in troops and money to exercise any steady authority within the Highlands.

THE DEVELOPMENT OF POOR RELIEF IN THE SEVENTEENTH CENTURY

We have no direct information about the climate of opinion on poverty at the time of the initiating statute of the Scottish Poor Law, except that the Church after the Reformation took over the content of morality taken for granted by the pre-Reformation Church, and the obligation to be generous

[7] APS IV 434: 1609 chap. 14. 'Anent the commissioners and justices of the peace'.

to the poor was part of that morality. It is possible that the concept of poverty was restricted. People were poor, that is unable to support themselves, if their age or physique made hard work impossible. In this category came the very old, the blind, the lame, the insane and young children. In many cases such people received support from their families, but there were always some who had no immediate kin with the resources to carry extra people. In times of harvest failure and famine 'the poor' would include a large number of people whose crops had failed, or who, lacking direct access to land were deprived of their living by the lack of resources of others. Finally, there were people whom we would now call the unemployed: those who had the physical capacity to work but no opportunity of exercising it so as to gain a living. These might be textile workers at a time when there was no demand for their products, failed tenants who had been evicted from their holding through inability to pay the rent, or men whose main skill was in fighting for which there was no opening.

It is possible that this category, the unemployed, was not recognised in sixteenth-century Scotland. This would explain the absence from the Poor Law of orders about the provision of work for such people. Since the usual practice of those without employment was to take to the roads in the hope of finding employment or booty elsewhere, it was only as vagrants that the unemployed were officially acknowledged. But it is clear from the difficulty experienced by seventeenth-century landowners in curtailing almsgiving to incoming beggars, that the ordinary people saw vagrants as in genuine need. 'The preposterous pitie of the countrey people' as the Privy Council in 1623 called unwise almsgiving, meant that the peasantry would respond to begging appeals even when they had not enough for themselves. It is entirely understandable that, for instance, the baron of Stichill should have made his baron court forbid the giving of alms or shelter to strangers during the famine of the 1690s, under penalty of a fine of £10 Scots, and order his tenantry to combine to force out such beggars:[8] he could see that the people of the barony needed all their own resources. Vagrants, often alleged to be a population choosing to live outside the law, were merely the destitute using the last resource of travel. But the burden they put on the parishes through which they passed meant that the only effective way of coping with famine crisis was to order all parishes to support their own poor, and to compel all people to remain in or return to whatever could be called their own parish. This was the policy of the central government in seventeenth-century crises, inevitably ineffective for, until the last third of the century, local government had not developed far enough for obedience to be a normal response to its orders. In time of famine a parish's capacity to support its own depended not only on this control of vagrancy but on

[8] RPC XIII:288. C.B. Gunn (ed.), (1905), *Records of the baron court of Stichill*: 135–6; R.A. Houston, 'Vagrants and society in early modern England' (1980).

whether it could persuade or force its landowners to participate and share the burden of relief. The marked polarisation of Lowland rural society, the absence of a significant group of owner-occupiers, the high levels of rents and the consequent poverty of the tenantry all combined to make landowners the only group which could make a more than marginal contribution towards relief.

The story of Poor Law development in Scotland was therefore from the start very different from its model in England, as was the other copy of the English legislation, the French.[9] In England the statutes of the 1570s were made more precise in definitions and expanded in scope in 1597 and 1601.[10] The need for definition is an indicator that practical problems had been found in the working of the earlier Acts. In Scotland there were also further statutes, but these do not give any reason for belief that the law was being used. There was a search for an effective local agency. In 1592 Parliament picked on the kirk session, the lowest in the hierarchy of church courts which made up the presbyterian system of church government, supervised by the presbytery.[11] At this date and for much of the seventeenth century the church system contained bishops and a presbyterian structure. Kirk sessions, committees of the minister and elected elders, existed in those Lowland parishes which had a fully-qualified Protestant minister, but many parishes in the north east, and the great majority in the Highlands had not yet reached that stage of development. The total absence of sixteenth-century records for synods, presbyteries and kirk sessions in the Highlands, combined with the survival of other types of church record, suggests strongly that the church courts came to be established in that area only in the seventeenth century or later, and indeed clan disputes in the seventeenth century would have made it very difficult to hold any church courts.[12] In an Act of 1617 the Justices of the Peace were instructed to discipline and control vagrants and to arrange the apprenticeships of pauper children. The list of the nominal duties of these Justices suggests an ordered system of local government which did not yet exist.[13] Justices had limited powers of coercion and no power to raise money for apprenticeship premiums. During this period, kirk sessions, where they existed, seem to have accepted the Christian duty of aid to the poor.[14] But this, it seems from their records, meant small occasional payments from collections or fines to cases of outstanding need. The existence of these

[9] Leonard (1900): chap. 13.

[10] *Statutes of the Realm* IV pt 2, 39 Elizabeth chap. 3 and 43 Elizabeth chap. 2 'For the releife of the poore'.

[11] APS III, 576: 1592 chap. 69 'For pvneisment of masterful beggaris and releif of the puir'.

[12] James Kirk, 'The kirk and the Highlands at the Reformation' (1986): 1.

[13] APS IV, 535–40: 1617 chap. 8.

[14] D.H. Fleming (ed.), *Register of the minister, elders and deacons of the Christian congregation of St Andrews*, 1 (1889): 232.

payments in the records is not to be taken as evidence that the sessions were working a statute-based Poor Law, merely that they were fulfilling Christian duty.

The absence of a functioning Poor Law was shown up sharply in the famine crisis of 1623. Awakening belatedly to the approaching failure of a second harvest in the summer of that year the Privy Council went into action with two proclamations. The first of these, dated 14 June 1623, ordered every shire and burgh to raise money, by taxing all of wealth and substance, to buy in grain to carry their poorer householders until the beginning of September when harvest work should give an income. It also provided a ratio between wealth in goods and rents as a basis for assessment. On 11 July the Council turned its attention to beggars and vagabonds: these were to be imprisoned and supported by a further tax on every inhabitant of between 1 and 5 shillings a week, according to means.[15] The replies of 10 shires to these orders survive, some prompt but in 3 cases, Aberdeenshire, Dumfriesshire and East Lothian, not made until November, show the gap between what the Council hoped would be done and the resources and powers of the local authorities.[16] As examples of the replies we have East Lothian stating that the stent of 1 to 5 shillings was totally inequitable, complaining of the 'toylsome and trublesome' service required of the gentry on inadequate expense allowances, and pointing out that the Justices simply did not have the statutory authority to act in the ways ordered: Selkirkshire pointed out that many householders had no money to pay taxation and that what was needed was the provision of work: Midlothian complained that the number of beggars far exceeded the capacity of gaols within the county, and that many families of vagrants knew of no parish to which they could be said to belong, and suggested that those who could get a testimonial from two Justices, containing a full description of the whole vagrant family, should be allowed to beg within the shire.

These answers to instructions which should more realistically be regarded as appeals, show the limited authority of the Council and the lack of a coherent framework of local government. In the case of East Lothian they also show that a county could effectively refuse co-operation. That no answers survive from the far North or the Highlands is an indicator of the absence in these regions of the Crown's authority. In his plans for his first Convention of Estates in 1625 the new King Charles I placed the subject of the Poor Law, which this recent famine had shown to be not functioning,[17] on his agenda but the King's intention of legislation was submerged in the political stress produced by his famous Revocation, requiring all former

[15] RPC XIII: 257–60, 287–90. [16] RPC XIII: 789–840.
[17] APS V: 184, appendix.

church lands belonging to lay proprietors to be surrendered to the Crown, and the consequent hostility of the aristocracy.

The Great Rebellion of the 1640s and 1650s, though it involved periods of civil war and disorder, led to a more effective government in both Church and State, and also revealed the tendency of the Reformed Church to take over functions of the civil government. It was in this period that the Scottish aristocracy was defeated and disciplined, first by the Church and later by the Cromwellian invasion and dictatorship. It was also in this period that the burdens of war and occupation led to the development of regular and heavy taxation.[18] At the start of the open opposition to the Crown, the church courts had been strengthened in political terms, but reduced in independence, by the creation of 'ruling elders', that is representatives of the parish eldership in the higher courts. Initially this change was to enable the aristocracy to dominate the General Assembly of the Church in 1638, but in the long run it did not appear part of the aristocratic way of life to sit in committees with ministers; ruling elders, unpaid but having to afford the cost of travel, would be men of means, but soon ceased to be noblemen. Very often they were lesser landowners, a change which opened to this group a place in a new level of authority. Political decision-making passed to the aristocracy for much of the 1640s, but the events of the second Civil War brought the Church into opposition over the Engagement: this was the political bargain between the King and the Scottish aristocracy that led to a military invasion of England, the defeat of the Scottish army at Preston in 1648, and a vacuum of power in Scotland. In this vacuum the so-called 'Whig' takeover occurred: the lesser landowners of the south-west with the support of the Church formed a government and excluded from power all the traditional political groups. It was in the reduced Parliament held by this government that the Act of 1649 was passed which, for the first time, made the Poor Law effective.[19]

Under this Act, relief was, as before, the duty of the kirk sessions, supervised by the presbyteries: the difference was not in the wording of the law but in the practical situation.[20] By this time the Church courts were also functioning in the far north, though not yet in the Highlands. The power of the aristocracy was in abeyance, many of the great men were being forced to do penance for their recent actions, and the lesser landowners were under the influence locally of the Church. The new Act left the issue of whether landowners were to be assessed to the presbyteries. War taxation had familiarised landowners with the idea of payment, though a full valuation system came somewhat later.

A glance at a few kirk session registers from southern Scotland for 1649

[18] D. Stevenson, 'The king's Scottish revenues and the covenanters, 1625–51' (1974): 17–41.
[19] D. Stevenson, *Revolution and counter-Revolution in Scotland, 1644–51* (1977): chap. 4.
[20] APS VI, ii, 220: 1649 chap. 161 'Anent the poor'.

and the year immediately after shows that some of them attempted to work systems by which the burden of relief, in a country suffering from recent war and plundering, was laid on the landowners. A simple way of doing this, used in Yester (East Lothian), was to break up the list of the poor and assign to each landowner the duty of supporting those living on their estate. In the handful of registers which survive from the North for this period this burdening of landowners is not so frequent. For instance, in Forgue (Aberdeenshire) there was talk of a stent but it does not seem to have been imposed. The same is true of Slains (Aberdeenshire).[21] Elsewhere all that can be found in obedience to the new Act was the compiling of a full list of the poor. But the victory of the Whigs over the aristocracy was also a victory of southern Scotland over the north, and it is likely that there was considerable confusion, disorder and demoralisation in parish life in Aberdeenshire, Mearns and Moray, the stronghold of resistance to the revolutionary party.

In the ensuing 40 years or so, parishes in both the southern and the northern Lowlands enlarged their resources for the support of the poor, and took more regular steps towards this support. Church collections, whether at the church door or by the elders going round 'their bounds', the areas of their personal responsibility, became regular, and many parishes received substantial legacies which gave them capital reserves. Some parishes put on a high level of financial organisation. Gordon (Berwickshire) laid an assessment on the tenantry and cottars, who had to contribute according to the size of their holdings, while it does not appear that any such payment was demanded from the heritors.[22] Assessing heritors, in a period when the power of the aristocracy was reviving, appears to have been seen as a mechanism only for times of stress. Though the poor survival rate of Church records from the North has probably some significance, there is no positive evidence of any basic difference in the interpretation and working of the Poor Law at this time between northern and southern Scotland.

In 1663 and 1672 Parliament produced Acts about the poor which show that vagrancy was still considered a problem. They also show the continuation of the sixteenth-century practice of passing Acts which were totally ignored. This fact is of long-term significance since it was at this time that the English Parliament passed the far-reaching Act of Settlement. This Act, initially a means of ensuring that parishes carried out their duties under the Poor Law and did not leave their poor to be sustained by others, became the basis of an enormous body of further legislation and of case law, and this subsequent development made the English and Scottish relief

[21] SRO CH2/377/2, March 1650, Yester KSR; CH2/539/1, January 1650, Forgue KSR; CH2/480/1, September 1649, Slains KSR.

[22] SRO CH2/451/1, 1687, Gordon KSR.

systems totally different in their application and in their effect on the rights and strategies of the working population. The Scottish Acts of the Restoration period ordered the arrest of vagrants, the assigning of them to Correction Houses which the burghs were to build, and the use of them as slave labour for eleven years in manufactories. The industrialists who were expected to set up these manufactories were to receive payment from the parishes for four years on behalf of their vagrants, presumably because it was expected to take some time to turn vagrants into useful labour.[23] These attempts to promote industry and reduce pauperism at a single stroke do not appear to have got off the ground. There is no evidence that Houses of Correction were built in response to the Acts. Edinburgh had set up such a house in 1632 in response to pressure by Charles I. Glasgow had had one since 1531, Stirling took the decision to set one up in 1725. It is suggested that by the 1720s, Ayr had one, because rural parishes in South Ayrshire were dispatching beggars to the town for incarceration, and one has been alleged for Aberdeen, though the published extracts from the burgh records do not mention it. There is also no mention in the similar extracts of Peebles or Lanark or the more restricted collection for Dundee. Vagrants in the south-west were often imprisoned in the Dumfries tolbooth.[24] Altogether it seems that decisions to build a Correction House, when they were taken, were not related to these statutes.

POOR RELIEF AND THE CRISIS OF THE 1690S

The relative economic tranquillity of the Restoration period came to an end in the after-effects of the Revolution of 1689. The changes in the monarchy and in the system of Church government seriously damaged the machinery of local government and the wars which followed were a heavy burden on local communities. When the English Parliament deposed James II and offered the Crown to William III, with restrictions on his authority, the Scottish parliament followed the same line. The change of king meant at first a civil war in Scotland and later the burdens of war abroad, in Ireland and on the continent. In some parts of Scotland many of the men who made up the functioning part of shire government refused to act under the new regime, and the refusal of the leaders of the episcopal church also meant the

[23] APS VII, 485: 1663 chap. 52 and APS VIII 89: 1672 chap. 42: *Concerning beggars and vagabonds* and *For establishing correction-houses for idle beggars and vagabonds.*

[24] SBRS *Charters and documents . . . of Peebles, 1165–1710* (1872); *Council Register . . . of Aberdeen, 1643–1747* (1872); *Extracts from the Records . . . of Edinburgh, 1626–41* (1936): 107; *Charters . . . and public documents . . . of Dundee, 1292–1800* (1880); *Extracts from the Records . . . of Glasgow, 1630–62* (1881): 33, 34, 43; *Extracts from the Records . . . of Lanark, 1150–1722* (1893); *Extracts from the Records . . . of Stirling, 1667–1752* (1881): 186, 223.
T. Hamilton, *Poor relief in south Ayrshire, 1700–1845* (1942): 72; A.A. Cormack, *Poor relief in Scotland* (1923): 56; SRO JP 1/2/1, March 1732, Quarter session minutes of the Justices of the Peace for the Stewartry of Kirkcudbright.

setting up of a new, revolutionary, purely Presbyterian system in 1690. The small clique of ministers who held power in this because they were untainted by any acceptance of episcopacy ejected from their parishes over two-thirds of the existing parish ministry during the next few years. Some ministers had already been coerced by threats into leaving. Many of those forced out did not go without protest or resistance. Parishes and presbyteries might experience litigation or physical disturbance. In some places the ejected ministers took with them important elements of parish activity; the kirk session register, the church utensils or the poor box. In some the minister could not be ejected because his flock resisted by force, but the existence of two rival church systems claiming such parishes made life difficult: there could be fights or riots. In some northern parishes where episcopacy had been valued, a state of war existed. An example of this was Newtyle, (Angus) where, in an effort to get rid of the episcopal minister, the presbytery broke down the church door and stole the kirk session register.[25] Yet most parishes did their best to carry on the normal church life, even if they had only the elders to provide kirk session continuity, and the system of church courts, where it was already established, remained functioning.

War, as always, proved expensive. The taxes which sustained the war fell hard on the poorer people: the hearth and poll taxes expecially helped to drive households into debt or poverty. The markets for Scottish trade were disturbed and the towns experienced unemployment. More than the usual number of vagrants roamed the roads, and these included injured soldiers and seamen, ejected ministers with their families and the unemployed. The Privy Council has left evidence of social stress in its register. In 1695 it postponed the taking of the poll tax by a month because of the lateness of the harvest, and the broken and uncertain weather. This was the first of the bad harvests which caused the great famine of the 1690s. The harvest was late and inadequate in 1695, failed badly in 1696 and 1698, and was inadequate in 1699. Even in 1694 the Council had complained of difficulty in getting forage for the army. In May 1696 the sheriff of Mearns reported that because of the failure of the white fisheries the fishermen were begging through the county. It was clear by September of that year that a major famine would strike.[26]

Even before the harvests had failed, in August 1692, the Council had begun issuing what became a steady stream of proclamations about controlling vagabonds and supporting the poor of the parishes, a sure indication that many had taken to the roads in desperation. In that of August 1693 it was assumed that heritors were working the Poor Law, and

[25] SRO CH2/284/1, Newtyle KSR.

[26] This and other information for the 1690s comes from the typescript of the unpublished Acts of the Privy Council of Scotland, which I have been allowed to use by the courtesy of the staff of the SRO.

half of the church collections was assigned to them to help in this. The proclamations stressed the need to force beggars to stay in their own parishes or to return to them. In August 1694 sheriffs were empowered to fine parishes not carrying out the Law. In March 1698 the Council was assuming that many burghs had set up Correction Houses to which vagrants could be sent. Finally in September 1699 a proclamation specifically called on sheriffs, Commissioners of Supply and heritors to meet on the second Thursday of October to make arrangements for the poor and to dispatch all vagrants to wherever they had a residence of three years. A few months later the Lord Advocate was 'recommended' to pursue the sheriffs of Fife and Lothian to find out what they had done.

This outbreak of concern and activity by the Council was to equip the Poor Law both with an important feature, the right of assessed heritors to pass half the financial burden to their tenantry, and a long-standing confusion as to whether the residence period which made for settlement was three or seven years. But it also did something to change the response of parishes from the recording of dismay and the inaugurating of hand-to-mouth support, with which they had faced their problems in 1695–7, to a more organised attempt to raise funds and work out who was and who was not a 'proper object' for relief.

Recent work on the administrative problems raised by famine has suggested that these disasters should be seen not simply as the result of a total inadequacy of food supply. Much of twentieth-century famine has been government based, in the sense that it has afflicted areas affected by revolutions and wars, and has been caused or exacerbated by the economic disruptions that these create: if governments were not bent on establishing a particular regime or winning a particular campaign, the people might go short but would not starve.[27] The famines which were a direct consequence of the Thirty Years War in Europe are a good historical example of this. The revolution of 1689, the war that followed and various government efforts to restrict the import of grain from Ireland, form an important contribution to the transformation of bad harvests into a general famine. But in an undeveloped economy with poor transport and with trade only a small part of economic activity, harvest failure was always likely to have such results. The uncertain element is what difference local organisation and effort could make to prevent the worst. In practice it does not take very much food, provided it can be directed to the right people, to make the difference between a period of general hardship and one of famine. But that food, or the purchasing power to obtain it, has to be correctly directed, and this means the shifting of purchasing power away from those with most control over resources.

There are instances of local charitable activity in the 1690s famine,

[27] A. Sen, *Poverty and famines* (1981).

which probably saved lives. But the main interest must lie in the institutional response. How successful were parishes in raising funds from the main surplus generated by farming, in other words from the rents received by landowners, to meet the needs of the poor? It is reasonable in an economy not by any means fully monetised, to regard any system by which the landowning class was made to support the poor either of the parish at large or on their own estates, as a form of assessment. Parishes might 'assess' by raising a stent, a rate on landowners according to their valuation, by requiring a levy in grain, by ordering landowners and others to board the needy in their homes, or by simply giving a list of names to a landowner and telling him to supply these people. In economic terms all of these bring into action the agricultural surplus, and therefore are 'assessment'.

For this period 229 parishes have left kirk session registers which are full enough to indicate what was or was not being done for the poor. Of these only 7 come from the Highlands and Northern Isles. Given what we know of disorder in the Highlands even after the ending of open war, this is not surprising: many places had to wait for an effective ministry till after the establishment of central government control in the aftermath of the rebellion of 1745–6.

Of the registers of 229 parishes, 42 show a decision to assess landowners for the relief of the poor during the famine period, and another 2 parishes show the same decision in other sources. The list of these assessed parishes forms Appendix 1, below. Of course among the 75 per cent of parishes which either did not keep registers or of which the registers do not survive, there may have been others which assessed, but since record keeping and efficiency are not unrelated aspects of activity, it is probable that this 75 per cent would not supply a high proportion of assessed parishes. Among the apparently assessed parishes there are cases where there is room for doubt about what actually happened. In Kettins (Angus) the minister seems to have ordered assessment without holding the meeting with heritors which the Council demanded. In Cramond (Midlothian) the assessment for relief cannot easily be distinguished from an already existing assessment for the repair of the church roof. In Perth the decision to assess did not mean that the needs of the poor were generously assessed, and in the following year the magistrates decided that at the ripe age of five a foundling could be left to support herself by begging. In Lasswade (Midlothian), assessment, introduced late in 1699, was maintained for only three months. It is by no means clear that the statement in the Kennoway (Fife) register, that the heritors and tenants would be liable to the officer, really means assent to assessment. In Glassford (Lanarkshire) a statement about quotas for the poor has been taken as not meaning assessment. In Spott (East Lothian) an agreement by the heritors to support lists of the poor on their land has been taken as a decision to assess even though some of the names on the lists can later be seen receiving parish aid, so that there is a strong likelihood either that assessment ended early or that some of the heritors did not carry out their part of the agreement.[28]

The parishes which can be shown to have implemented assessment lie predominantly in the south. So, of course, do the bulk of parishes leaving records. To evaluate the relative levels of response the percentage of assessment among the parishes with record has been calculated by shires. The figures are relatively high for the Lothians: 56 per cent for East Lothian, 31 per cent for Midlothian and 25 per cent for West Lothian; and are also fairly high for some other counties in the central belt: 15 per cent for Fife, 21 per cent for Lanarkshire, 17 per cent for Renfrewshire and 17 per cent for Ayrshire. Perthshire, for which only the southern part of the county has left record, had 37 per cent. Other counties with a reasonable level of record give markedly lower figures, Angus and Aberdeenshire each 8 per cent, Roxburghshire and Moray each 11 per cent, Stirlingshire none. Some counties had too low a level of record for percentages to be significant. In Selkirkshire the only parish with record, Galashiels, set up assessment; in Peebleshire 2 out of 5 with record were assessed. None of the few parishes leaving record for the Stewartry of Kirkcudbright, or the shires of Berwick, Clackmannan, Wigtown, Dunbarton, Banff, Nairn, Inverness, Bute, Argyll or Orkney were assessed.

The methods by which heritors evaded or refused assessment were many. The easiest way was for them not to turn up to meetings ordered by the Privy Council and organised by the minister. Meetings called for poor relief were systematically not attended, while at very near dates meetings called to debate a subject always dear to the heart of the propertied, church seats, had good attendance. Assessment was not always a simple issue of church versus landowner. In spite of efforts, the church in some parishes could not force assessment of landowners, but in Drainie (Moray), it was Gordon of Gordonstoun, owner of two-thirds of the parish, who arrived and compelled the session to meet and impose assessment.[29] The most striking example of continued passive resistance to orders to assess was in South Leith. Here the sheriff made a strong attempt to get the law fulfilled, and even named a particular heritor to hold a meeting on a specific date, to be advertised from the pulpit, to lay on assessment. 'But none of the heritors compeared' except for three, so these heritors and the session 'concluded that they could not proceed'.[30]

28 SRO CH2/518/1, May 1698, Kettins KSR; CH2/425/4, November 1697, Cramond KSR; CH2/521/10, December 1698, Perth KSR; CH2/471/4 and 10, October 1699, Lasswade KSR; CH2/206/2, December 1698, Kennoway KSR; CH2/463/1, accounts for 1697, Glassford KSR; CH2/333/2, May 1698, Spott KSR.

29 SRO CH2/384//1 (now microfilm), October 1699, Drainie KSR.

30 SRO CH2/716/11, October 1699, South Leith KSR.

Still, 44 assessed parishes for a country under-supplied with administrative machinery was an achievement. However inadequate the supply that was made proved to be, the precedent would lie in the register. The figure also forms a healthy antidote to that offered by the Church of Scotland in 1818 for the total of parishes assessed before 1700. In its report to a Select Committee on the English Poor Laws, the General Assembly stated 'it appears that only 3 instances of assessment existed in the whole 700 reported parishes, prior to the year 1700' and adds 'all in the synod of Merse and Teviotdale'. In the report of 1838 which gives detailed information on every parish, 3 are labelled as assessed before 1700, Edinburgh City, Fogo and Ettrick.[31] Edinburgh, of course, is not in Merse and Teviotdale. No kirk session registers survive for these 3 parishes for this period. It would be surprising if in all 3 cases they existed in the early nineteenth century and have disappeared since. It seems much more probable that for these parishes, and for the rest of the 1838 returns, and the earlier ones, ministers did not delve into local records, particularly not into those written in seventeenth-century handwriting, but passed on a hearsay report or made a guess. The statement on assessment may well be true for Edinburgh. For the other 2 cases it is odd that the kirk should have put early assessment into the Border parishes, because the list of assessed parishes of the 1690s shows that the pattern of assessment there was in no way similar to that in the early nineteenth century: only 3 out of the 20 that have left registers show assessment. Altogether the Church's remarks seem to have been based on unverified local folklore and developed in the light of a particular social theory. It is unfortunate that they have been accepted by historians usually careful in their use of evidence. Miss Leonard, in her study of the early English Poor Law, added a possible gloss to the Church's statement, that it referred only to the adoption of permanent or long-term assessment.[32] But as neither she nor the Church appear to have undertaken examination of the records to see whether parishes persisted in assessment after 1699, or after earlier emergencies, there are no grounds for such an interpretation. The statement of the Church should be taken as having no relation to fact.

The distribution of the assessed parishes is comprehensible in the light of the capacities of shire government and the past pattern of central power. The effective proclamation of the Council, after which most of the decision to assess occurred, was that of September 1699 – too late an event to prevent most of the deaths – and this was effective, where it was, because it called on the machinery of shire government for enforcement. Though East Lothian had been noted in the Privy Council as having had difficulty in getting Commissioners of Supply who would take the oath of allegiance to the new monarchy, the problem there was as nothing to the dearth of men

[31] *Reports from commissioners* (PP XX, 1839) 26, 38, 44. [32] Leonard (1900):286.

willing to act in the north-east and the Highlands, where Jacobitism and Episcopacy still held sway among the landowning class. Beside the damage done by the revolution to the effectiveness of county government in these areas, there had been damage to the parish system by the abrupt change from Episcopacy to Presbyterian rule. It is also worth noticing that the districts of Scotland where there was a relatively good response to the Council's demands were the areas where the Council had been closely concerned since the early part of the century. The Privy Council had been trying to bring feuds to an end in the areas where its writ ran since the reign of James VI, and the printed volumes of its register show a pattern of frequent intervention to this end in Fife, the Lothians, Lanarkshire and other parts of the central valley. No attention had normally been paid to disturbances in the Highlands unless they intruded into Lowland areas, and in the north only if a feud had been particularly severe and its effects widespread. Normally the government made little attempt to assert itself in the north because great franchises stood between it and local affairs. We have not got a full map of the franchises, but it is clear that much of the north was covered by them and as a result the instruments of shire government had not been able to develop by the 1690s.

THE DEVELOPMENT OF POOR RELIEF IN THE EIGHTEENTH CENTURY

By the late eighteenth century there had developed a marked difference in the systems of poor relief between the south of Scotland (the central valley, the Borders and southern Perthshire), and the north (Aberdeenshire, Mearns, Banffshire and Moray in their Lowland districts). By this time the north was conspicuously unwilling to raise funds by assessment, and to prevent pressure on resources making for a strong demand for this, kept allowance to the poor as low as possible.[33] Yet the proportion of the population unable to subsist without some help was very similar in the two regions and had been for some time. Table 6 gives the percentage of the population in receipt of relief and the average annual payment made to each, by synods, as reported by the Church of Scotland in 1818.[34]

Table 6 also confirms the statements made in later reports about the absence of adequate support in the Highlands and far north. Five shillings a year in money and licence to beg within the parish was the most that adults could expect in many parts of this area: in some

[33] *Reports from commissioners* (PP XXI, 1844) *Poor Law Enquiry: Report* XVII; *Evidence* 46, 50, 98, 308–9, 363, 372, 427.

[34] *Reports from commissioners* (PP V, 1818) Returns from the General Assembly, 84–5.

Table 6 *Average annual amounts paid in poor relief by synods, 1818*

synod	paid to each pauper per year £	s.	d.	percentage of poor in population
Lothian and Tweeddale	3	4	8	2.8
Merse and Teviotdale	5	15	3	3.1
Dumfries	4	2	7	3.1
Galloway	4	14	5	1.3
Glasgow and Ayr	5	2	10	2.3
Perth and Stirling	3	3	4	2.4
Fife	5	11	6	1.8
Angus and Mearns	4	3	3	2.5
Aberdeen	2	2	2	3.3
Moray	1	3	4	3.3
Ross		16	11	3.4
Argyll	1	10	11	2.3
Glenelg		16	3	2.3
Orkney		19	0	2.8

PP 1818 V 85–5.

provision was even less. Though any systematic work on figures produced by the Church is likely to cause doubt as to the numeracy of many ministers, the statistics are sufficiently different on the financial side, while similar in the proportion of people involved, to give a strong impression of differential development. The report of 1818 also shows that while all parishes in Merse and Teviotdale synod, which covered the main Border area, were assessed, and 67 out of 96 in Lothian and Tweeddale, none were in Aberdeen, Moray and other northern synods. In order to explain the development of this gap in the levels and methods of poor relief between the north and south, it is necessary to examine the development of parish assessments during the eighteenth century.

After 1700 the instruments of shire government became more effective. The Union of Parliaments in 1707 deflected the ambitions of the aristocracy to London, where crown patronage and advantageous careers lay.[35] This liberated the lesser landowners, already with considerable parish responsibilities as 'heritors' (that is, carrying the burden of financial support of the minister, parish church and manse). It was this class which furnished Justices of the Peace and Commissioners of Supply, and which already had the right to hold baron courts, with minor functions of

[35] A.E. Whetstone, *Scottish county government in the eighteenth and nineteenth centuries* (1981); J.S. Shaw, *The management of Scottish society, 1707–1764* (1983): chap. 3.

government, for their tenantry. The raising of revenue by the Commissioners of Supply and the disbursement of it for crime control and road repair, became regular as this class became able to act independently. It was among landowners that the intellectual current we now label 'civic humanism' began to move. Civic humanism stressed the responsibility of the owners of land for the creation of a desirable society. Under its impetus there were outbreaks of enthusiasm for county 'schemes' of social control, which meant the suppression of undesirable features such as vagrancy, and also recognition that this could not be achieved unless parishes effectively supported their own poor. The first such Poor Law scheme which has been identified is that of 1711 in East Lothian. Only one parish decided as a result of it to levy assessment, but compromise agreements were made in two others by which the heritors would raise funds to hire constables to keep out vagrants and the kirk session would support the local poor.[36] Further research may show that East Lothian was not alone in this scheme, and certainly later outbreaks of such schemes covered numerous counties. That of 1725–31 for the Lothians elicited the support and co-operation of the judges of the Court of Session and Edinburgh City Council.[37] That for the early 1770s in Perthshire made its first priority crime control: it was entitled 'An Act for detecting and prosecuting petty thefts and other Crimes, suppressing vagrants and Begging and for the sufficient Maintenance of the Poor within their own Parishes'.[38] There was also an outbreak in the 1750s, in which Aberdeenshire participated. A scheme was put forward by the sheriff and Commissioners of Supply.[39] The outbreak in the 1770s can be seen to have covered not only Perthshire but also Mid and East Lothian, Berwickshire, Stirlingshire, Dumfriesshire, Roxburghshire, Argyll, Ayrshire, the Stewartry of Kirkcudbright and Fife.[40]

The county schemes of the eighteenth century sometimes operated for several years; more often they faded into nothing almost at once. If they made any impact at all this usually meant that a few parishes found themselves unable to guarantee the support of their poor without using assessment, and since the schemes were launched by the elite of the county's landowners, it was difficult for the parish heritors to resist

[36] SRO CH2/296/2, September 1711, Pencaitland KSR; CH2/335/1, October 1711, Stenton KSR: CH2/1157/2, October 1711, Dirleton KSR.

[37] SRP JP 4/2/1, July 1727, Minutes of the Midlothian Justices of the Peace Quarter Sessions.

[38] SRO JP 20/2/2. Minutes of the Perthshire Justices of the Peace Quarter Sessions.

[39] J.M. McPherson, *The kirk's care of the poor* (n.d.): 187–91.

[40] For Perthshire, SRO JP 20/2/2, 207, OSA VI, 485, Kincardine and IX, 498, Caputh: for Midlothian, *Caledonian Mercury*, February 1773: for East Lothian SRO JP 2/2/2, December 1773, Minutes of the East Lothian Justices of the Peace Quarter Sessions: for Berwickshire, OSA III, 156, Bonkle and Preston: for Stirlingshire, National Library of Scotland MS 9823: for Dumfriesshire, OSA 388, Dunoon and IV 571, Strachur and Stralachlan: for Ayrshire, Hamilton (1942): for the Stewartry SRO JP 1/2/1, August 1772, Minutes of the Kirkcudbrightshire Justices of the Peace Quarter Sessions: for Fife, SRO CH2/365/6, March 1772, Wemyss KSR.

assessment, even though the county authorities had no direct control over them in the matter. Except for some of those in the 1770s, the schemes were put out in periods of relative economic tranquillity, free of sharp price fluctuations or heavy war burdens. Where they led to assessment it was unlikely to be dropped soon after. For this reason the effects of some of the schemes of the 1770s can be discerned in reports about assessment in the *Statistical Account of Scotland* of the 1790s.

Probably more counties took part in such schemes than can easily now be ascertained. The Justice of the Peace material surviving for the eighteenth century is very patchy. We have usually two or three surviving sets of Quarter Session minutes at any one date, but for a country with 26 counties this is not much. Some scraps also exist in estate papers. Only one reference to a scheme in newspapers has been found but this source has yet to be systematically studied. The mixed and haphazard nature of the evidence makes it dangerous to place weight of argument on negatives. But it is clear that many southern counties participated in several of the outbreaks, while as yet no such activity is known from Moray, Nairnshire, Angus or Mearns. But these counties are also thin on surviving Justice of the Peace material. Aberdeenshire appears in only one of the outbreaks, that of the 1750s, though the local response to the scheme then from parishes is similar to that of southern counties. Some parishes raised funds by assessment at least for a short while, for instance, Udny, Ellon and Auchterless. Gamrie in Banffshire also briefly took on assessment in 1752, which suggests that that county may have also had a scheme. In some parishes the heritors failed to attend meetings and so prevented assessment, as in Longside (Aberdeenshire). In some, such as Insch, the orders from the Aberdeenshire county authorities were not mentioned in the register. In Lonmay they were considered but assessment was held to be unnecessary. In Kintore it was decided that the level of assessment needed was so low that it would be simpler to make up the deficit by voluntary contributions. Where assessment was levied it appears to have died out, in silence, soon after. In that way the scheme failed to leave a mark, though part of it was revived in an attack on vagrancy in 1765.[41] No mention of these mid-century outbreaks of assessment was made in the Church's nineteenth-century reports: the memory of them seems to have been lost. The north–south difference, thus, seems established but not ineradicable by the mid eighteenth century. It can also be perceived in the different contributions to the activities of the Court of Session. Of the 24 cases concerning the Poor Law reported in Morison's *Dictionary of Decisions*, only 1 relates to the north.[42] These cases were rarely occasions in which paupers were

[41] McPherson (n.d.): 189; SRO CH2/360/1, Udny KSR: CH2/147/6, June 1751, Ellon KSR.

[42] W.M. Morison, *The decisions of the Court of Session . . . digested under proper heads in the form of a dictionary* XXV (1811): 10,551–95 and Appendix part 1.

litigants. They were between parishes over settlement, or between heritors and parishes over assessment or the keeping of proper accounts. In northern Scotland with assessment rare and temporary it was useless to try and force a parish to take on a case which it did not consider appropriate. The slack handling of the Poor Law suggests that relief was not sufficiently routinely administered to make litigation a sensible practice.

This is not to say that the north of Scotland simply neglected the poor and needy, though it probably sustained many of them at a very marginal level. When a case arose where a large sum of money was needed, for instance when a family had lost home and possessions by fire, there would be an appeal through the church organisation of presbytery and synod. It was also a common feature of Aberdeenshire parishes in the later eighteenth century to pay an annual subscription to the infirmary in Aberdeen, so as to be able to send sick parishioners there.[43] In 1782 the harvest failure which afflicted the whole of Scotland was particularly severe in the north. The county gentry of Aberdeenshire held a meeting early on and set out to measure the shortfall in grain and to raise funds and buy in enough to keep the county until the next harvest. In this exercise they stated that the common people would have to tighten their belts but they saw to it that they did not starve.[44]

In normal times the north economised on levels of relief and it may also have taken a harder line on claims and discouraged or refused some which would have been accepted elsewhere. It is difficult to be sure of this, for kirk session records do not usually give information on requests for help, nor do they give a very clear impression of what types of people received relief. It is clear that many of the beneficiaries were old, sometimes married couples, more often individuals, most often old women. Altogether women were twice as numerous as men as recipients of relief. The low level of women's wages in the eighteenth century did not give much opportunity for saving for old age or infirmity. The meagre lists of possessions which parishes would claim on the death of paupers show the bareness of their resources. People not necessarily old but with severe handicaps, particularly the insane, seem to have been treated with generosity. Orphans and occasionally foundlings figure in poor relief, often handed over to some pensioner for care, with an extra allowance, a policy which made for economy. They were usually sent for service or apprenticeship at some age between 10 and 14, but even after that the parish might still offer support in cases of particular need. For instance Eddleston (Peeblesshire) in 1765 was paying for medical care for a foundling who had fallen sick after going into service and Pencaitland (East Lothian) in 1705 was supplying clothes for an apprenticed orphan.[45] Sessions would normally pay for schooling of

[43] McPherson (n.d.): 130–1.
[44] J. Anderson, *General view of the agriculture of the county of Aberdeen . . .*, (1794), appendix.
[45] SRO CH2/120/6, 1765, Eddleston KSR: CH2/296/2 October 1708 and May 1709, Pencaitland KSR.

some children whose parents could support them but who could not manage school fees. Widows with young children would receive support, and so might single women while they were nursing a child, but it was not common for a session to support illegitimate children after this stage. The absence of bastards on poor rolls is one of the major differences between Scotland and England. The Scottish system of church discipline usually elicited the name of the father of a bastard, and called on these men to admit their involvement. In the great majority of cases this demand was met, and the father accepted responsibility for his child. The other area of difference from England lay in the lack of support for those unemployed or in temporary sickness. These were not clearly debarred, but they do not figure frequently. Those needing surgery might get the surgeon's fee paid, and some period of help. A contribution might be made to, for instance, a carter who had lost his horse, but only for a small part of the cost. Simple lack of work does not often seem to have led to relief, unless it was followed by total destitution.

Within these categories there was clearly room for adjustment, because the basic feature resulting from the statutory uncertainties about the Scottish Poor Law was that claimants had no clear right to relief. What was given was given at the discretion of the session. Occasionally a sheriff court might order relief, but this was not frequent enough to establish a concept of right, and the sheriff had no right to inspect the records of the session. The sessions themselves decided what was a justifiable request, and at what level it should be met. Because of this it was possible for northern parishes to set much meaner standards of support than those accepted in the south.

In contrast to the north, the Borders saw the steady expansion of assessment in the mid and late eighteenth century. Nineteenth-century commentators saw this as a spread of the English example. This may be the case, but if so, one must ask which English example was spreading, and who was active in the process. It is most unlikely that Scottish landowners desired to take from England the obligation to pay an extra tax on land: emulation does not work that way. It was sometimes alleged that potential claimants of relief had become accustomed to a higher standard of living, and that this put pressure on parishes to be generous. It seems unlikely that this could operate differentially in the Border area and Aberdeenshire; in any case the decision to assess had to be made by the landowners themselves, and they had as much authority in one area as in the other.

A more convincing explanation is indirectly shown by the evidence handled by the Royal Commission on the Poor Law of 1843–4. In its material there are expressions of the views of doctors in the Border area where practices straddled the national division. Such men were likely to point out to the members of upper-class society that if a pauper in

Northumberland received 3 shillings a week, and still lived fairly barely, it was ridiculous to expect one in Roxburghshire to manage on sixpence.[46] The medical profession supplied a continuous criticism on the achievements of the Scottish Poor Law from people of some social standing. If parishes were to respond to this by a better standard of relief it had to be by assessment, because in all parts of Scotland by the late eighteenth century there was a high level of non-residence among heritors, and so a low contribution by the landed class to church collections.

It is difficult to evaluate the long-term effects of the county schemes. There clearly existed an opinion, in the minds of the county elite who promoted them, that the Poor Law needed to be observed more systematically so that the two aspects of meeting need and controlling vagrancy were fulfilled. But the view of the county elite was likely to be accepted by most of the landowning class, and so it is not only in the schemes that we should note the influence of civic humanism. Up till the 1780s pressure of elite opinion was for expanding welfare. In times of food shortage, as in the harvest failure of 1740, considerable generosity was shown by landowners. Many gifts of money, meal and sometimes coal, were made to sessions for the use of the poor in all parts of Lowland Scotland. In 1757 and 1783 relief was made available to those Highlanders who came south early in the summer, ostensibly seeking work in the harvest, more truthfully to relieve their own settlements of their appetites. The general expansion of relief in one form or another is presumably the explanation of why John McFarlan in his study of the Poor Laws in England and Scotland was able to treat systems which by then were institutionally very different as having much in common. McFarlan's book stresses the similarities of the two systems. His detailed knowledge of the Scottish system was based on southern Perthshire and Edinburgh.[47] Acquaintance with Aberdeenshire and other northern areas might have modified his statements. Already by the time he wrote, works comparing the English and the Scottish system were being produced, and since these usually originated in Scotland, the emphasis was on the advantages of the Scottish system. But towards the end of the eighteenth century the climate of opinion on the merits of generosity to the poor was changing, and this encouraged emphasis on the Scottish system.

CHANGING ATTITUDES TO POOR RELIEF

The north of Scotland supplies the first example of Scottish satisfaction over the limited scale of normal relief expenditure in a letter of 1781 from James Anderson of Monkshill, in the parish of Daviot, Aberdeenshire, to

[46] *Reports from commissioners, Poor Law inquiry, evidence* (PP XXII, 1844) has comments from medical men with experience on both sides of the Border, e.g. 698, 718.
[47] J. McFarlan, *Inquiries concerning the poor* (1782).

Jeremy Bentham.[48] In this report of the working of the Scottish system, Anderson did his best to minimise the level of aid given: what was done under the Poor Law was merely a supplement to the efforts of kin and neighbours. With satisfaction he recorded that 'the Poor are supported by the Poor'. This attitude may have been the product of Anderson's own social philosophy, but equally it may owe something to the new fashion of opinion, which objected to the existence of Poor Laws as involving the shift of resources from hardworking people to the idle and useless. Occasional statements of such views start up in the press of 1780s; for instance in 1786 the *Caledonian Mercury* carried correspondence which produced remarks such as 'The Poor Laws in England are almost equally pernicious to those who pay and those who receive the bounty'. One writer called assessment 'an odious and oppressive tax'. The most extreme of such views was not found in Scotland but was expressed by the Reverend Joseph Townsend, a Church of England rector, who published in 1786, *A Dissertation of the Poor Laws*, a substantial tract attacking the English laws as creating injustice, discouraging industry by restricting the movement of labour and sustaining improvident habits.[49] For the sake of the economy he proposed a more limited and uncertain support which should come from friendly societies, to which workers would be compulsorily attached, from charity and from a tax on alehouses.

A symptom of, and eventually a contribution to, the distaste for Poor Laws in the north is the legacy of a certain Mr Burnett of Denns, in the parish of Old Deer, Aberdeenshire. This gentleman left his estate so that the rent was to go to poor relief in the parish so long as it was not assessed: that at least is the statement of the schoolmaster in the *Statistical Account*.[50] However, by 1815 it had become a fund available for all never-assessed parishes in the synod of Aberdeen except for those in the presbytery of Fordyce.[51] This meant that a parish would, occasionally, receive £30 or £40, enough to make a great difference to the finance of a particular year. Understandably this floating potential bonus encouraged the existing practice of avoiding assessment. The blindness to the past that it encouraged may also account for the nineteenth century's determined ignorance of the fact that various Aberdeenshire parishes had at some time been assessed.

The national surveys of the original and of the *New Statistical Account* provide a useful measure of the attitudes of the clergy to the whole problem

48 I.R. Christie (ed.), *Correspondence of Jeremy Bentham* III (1971): 18–39.

49 *Caledonian Mercury* 14 March and 20 February 1786; J. Townsend, *A dissertation on the Poor Laws by a well-wisher to mankind*, (1786); D.A. Baugh, 'Poverty, protestantism and political economy: English attitudes towards the poor 1600–1811' (1983): 63–107.

50 OSA 16: 477.

51 Letter from John Craigie, minister for Old Deer, 1815, to Thomas Kennedy of Dunure, Tulliebole MSS (see note 54).

of the support of the poor. In the original *Statistical Account* of the 1790s the common complaint is of inadequate resources, with blame sometimes offered to non-resident or uncharitable heritors, and sometimes to seceders for keeping all their own collections for their ministry. Some ministers congratulate the country on the absence of the excessive burden of poor rates found in England, and the resulting dangers of corruption and demoralisation. Instances of this attitude are Selkirk, East Kilbride and Portmoak. Though several reports make strong statements on the sheer inadequacy of relief available in Scotland it is only occasionally that the ministers put forward a simple demand for assessment. More common is the view expressed from Leslie, that unless heritors contributed more regularly and adequately, assessment, seen as an evil, would be unavoidable. There are, as early as this, occasional examples of a parish having returned from long-standing assessment to a voluntary system, as in Kincardine, and a specific mechanism for helping this process had been created in the form of so-called 'voluntary assessment'.[52] In this system the heritors agreed to pay to the poor's fund by valuation as if assessed: the advantage to them was that any individual heritor could break the system on his own at will, so that it did not seem like a regular charge on land. The disadvantages were that it might be so broken, for instance by trustees for an estate during a minority, and that the raising of half the assessment from the tenantry could not be legally sustained, so it relied on consent. In 1838 the General Assembly claimed that 126 parishes sustained their poor by this system, which, if correct, and simple arithmetic was not a strong point in the Church, shows landowner fear of the obligatory nature of real assessment.[53]

An intermediate stage in the development of anti-Poor-Law sentiment among the clergy can be traced in the responses to a questionnaire launched by the future member of Parliament for Ayrshire, Thomas Kennedy of Dunure, in 1815.[54] Kennedy's questions were clearly designed to show that landowners were oppressed by the level of rates and that this burden had been on the increase. Not many of the clergy answered in such a way as to give the full information asked for, in some cases because they had not adequate records, in others perhaps because of aversion to an enquiry presented and to be replied to through the sheriffs, the lay system of local government, rather than the ecclesiastical. But a large number of

[52] OSA 2: 444 (Selkirk, 1792), III 428 (East Kilbride, 1792), V 108 (Portmoak) and 49 (Leslie) (1793), VI 418 (Kincardine, 1793).

[53] *Reports from Commissioners* (PP XX, 1839), *Report of the General Assembly*: 14–15, 19, 20. Doubts about the accuracy of the Church's figures come from the very different picture of the frequency of this feature in the near contemporary NSA: for instance in the latter only 2 Midlothian parishes were said to be voluntarily assessed.

[54] These are in the possession of Lord Moncrieff of Tulliebole, who has kindly allowed me access. The material is roughly summarised by Sir Henry Moncrieff Wellwood in a Church of Scotland Paper, *Reports from Commissioners* (PP IV, 1817).

returns and accompanying letters expatiate on the evil of poor rates in terms which are surprising since the statistics, when given, show that the total expenditure on the Poor Law was marginally less in real terms in 1814 than it had been in 1790. 'Charity . . . as well as habits of Industry will be destroyed should Poor Rates ever be established in this County' wrote the minister of Old Deer. From a few parishes came the claim that assessment had recently been abandoned: (Moncrieff Wellwood, in whose hands the documents finished up claimed that these were 'a great proportion of the country'), but in most of these assessment had been of only recent establishment.

In the heated debate over the English Poor Laws which raged in the years immediately after the Napoleonic wars, the General Assembly took up a stance often to be repeated in the nineteenth century, that of claiming, usually by dubious statistics, success in handling social problems, with the implicit view that this was the result of the superior quality of Scottish religion. By this time the leading figures in the Kirk held the view that assessment was an evil which should be avoided. But the Kirk was not prepared to dismantle the Poor Law system, and under the leadership of Thomas Chalmers the General Assembly opposed the attempt of Kennedy in 1824 to legislate so as to remove all legal basis of assessment for any new claims for relief.[55] The statements of many ministers in the *New Statistical Account* (mostly written in the 1830s) show that dislike of assessment spread beyond the elite of the ministry. The questionnaire to which this was the response has never been set out, but it is clear from the frequent repetition of particular phrases in the reports that on this topic it was heavily loaded. It is exceptional to find a minister who rebuffs the lead offered by this phraseology and states his own view. But Mr James Ingram in Fala and Soutra states

> If the price of labour and provisions must remain as at present, barely sufficient to enable the peasantry to subsist and educate their children, without enabling them to accumulate any considerable savings, or raise themselves in the scale of society, it is highly desirable that they should enjoy a sure prospect of being provided for in their declining years.[56]

Fala and Soutra was a small parish and unlikely to attract the type of cleric who made opinion in the Kirk.

CONCLUSION

Given the climate of educated and influential opinion, with the clergy supplying the theoretical justification for the resistance of landed wealth to

[55] J.R. Poynter, *Society and pauperism* (1969); Mitchison, 'The creation of the disablement rule in the old Scottish poor law' (1979).
[56] NSA 1 (1845): 540.

paying rates, it is easy to see why, until the new Poor Law of 1845 forced on a more realistic assessment of need, parishes in the north could remain unassessed and mean in their standard of allowances. But the pattern of more generous payments in the south, as well as the recognition of new social and political forces weakening the hegemony of the upper class, and the fact that it was difficult to extract an adequate level of charitable contributions in parishes where the tenantry had long been paying on a compulsory basis, meant that the situation there could not be reversed. 'Voluntary assessment' was too uncertain a mechanism, particularly since any form of agreement and payment from non-resident heritors was difficult to establish and unlikely, in the face of falling rent rolls after 1815, to be maintained. However much the ethos of anti-Poor Law rhetoric had become accepted, the parishes of the south could not easily reduce their levels of support. They remained more generous than those in the north until the failure of the whole system in the industrial towns forced on the change to the new Poor Law of 1845.

APPENDIX:

PARISHES DECIDING TO RAISE MONEY FROM THE HERITORS FOR POOR RELIEF DURING THE 1690S.[57]

Parish	*Shire*		
Ashkirk	Roxburghshire	Kingsbarns	Fife
Blackford	Perthshire	Lasswade	Midlothian
Carriden	West Lothian	Lesmahagow	Lanarkshire
Carstairs	Lanarkshire	Logie	Perthshire
Colinton	Midlothian	Longforgan	Perthshire
Corstorphine	Midlothian	Longside	Aberdeenshire
Cramond	Midlothian	Manor	Perthshire
Crichton	Midlothian	Monzie	Perthshire
Currie	Midlothian	North Berwick	East Lothian
Douglas	Lanarkshire	Ormiston	East Lothian
Drainie	Moray	Perth	Perthshire
Eddleston	Peebleshire	Pettinain	Lanarkshire
Forgan	Fife	Prestonkirk	East Lothian
Galashiels	Selkirkshire	Saltoun	East Lothian
Garvald	East Lothian	Spott	East Lothian
Greenock	Renfrewshire	Stow	Midlothian
Haddington	East Lothian	Temple	Midlothian
Kennoway	Fife	Tibbermuir	Perthshire
Kettins	Angus	Tyninghame	East Lothian
Kilconquhar	Fife	Uphall	West Lothian
Kilmaurs	Ayrshire	Whitekirk	East Lothian
Kilwinning	Ayrshire	Yester	East Lothian

57 SRO, the KSRs for the relevant parishes: for Greenock, CH8/178. 'List of the poor on Sir John Schaw's ground, June 1699' (I owe this reference to Dr David Stevenson): for Stow, NSA 1 (1845):248.

8

SCOTLAND AND IRELAND, 1600–1800: THEIR ROLE IN THE EVOLUTION OF BRITISH SOCIETY[1]

L.M. CULLEN

Ireland and Scotland are two of the four countries that make up the British Isles. They represent over time interesting parallels and contrasts. They also both experienced over time a growing degree of integration into the larger political and economic entity that revolved around London and its imperial interests. For both countries, small and lacking in a wide range of opportunity for the ambitious, London and empire provided a stimulus that powerfully affected their development. Centralisation of power and wealth in London and the rapid economic development of both Scotland and Ireland in the eighteenth century are closely related phenomena. Peripheral resources in manpower and capital helped to reinforce the centralised power of London, and at the same time the opportunity and mobility that London and the empire created powerfully influenced Irish and Scottish society in many ways.

Scotland was the more geographically mobile of the two societies and imperial outlets were greatly to enhance that mobility. The contrast in mobility even at the outset meant that Scotland and Ireland were already different societies in 1600. Close links had long existed of course between the north of Ireland and the Highlands. Indeed, as Scotland was seen more by outside visitors who travelled through the Lowlands but did not cross the Highland line, the similarity between much of Irish and Scots society can be overlooked. However, Lowlanders were predominant in contacts with Ireland in the seventeenth century, and contact with the Highlands recedes to a few patchy ties in trade in the eighteenth century. In fact, the imposition by Lowlanders of their mark on Scots contact with Ireland from the outset of the seventeenth century is but a facet of the success of Lowland Scots society in containing and then pushing back Highland society. The process almost seems to begin in Ireland. By 1641 – on the evidence of the

[1] I am indebted to the editors and to Dr Jonathan Clark of All Souls College, Oxford, for comments on an earlier draft.

celebrated depositions by loyalists distressed in the Irish Rebellion of 1641 – Lowland Scots were often to be found surprisingly far afield in the northern half of Ireland. By 1641, Lowland Scotland seems to have acquired a novel assertiveness in its relations with Ireland, and this facet is but part of the vitality that Lowland Scotland displayed both in the sixteenth and seventeenth centuries.

Scotland's location seems vital and beneficial for its history. Scotland not only had easy access to Ireland but shared a common land frontier with England, and had a long coastline on the North Sea. Thus Scotland faced three ways. Its long North Sea coastline gave it the benefit of access to what was in effect Europe's inland sea, at the heart of economic development in northern Europe well into the seventeenth century. The sea journey from Scotland to Scandinavia and the Baltic was shorter than from any of the more developed parts of eastern England. As a consequence, Scots were not only to the fore in the penetration from these islands of this region and its north German, Polish and Russian hinterland, but they assumed a dominant position in the English-speaking colonies there which they continued to hold in the seventeenth century. Even as early as 1546 Scots were second only to the Dutch in trade with Gothenburg.[2] The Baltic region and its powers were precociously important economically and politically: Denmark and Sweden were military powers of some consequence in the first half of the seventeenth century. All this helped to give an impetus to economic changes in the eastern Lowlands of Scotland. The small coastal towns of Fife were already well developed and numerous in the sixteenth century, and Scottish merchants, pedlars and mercenaries, though their numbers appear exaggerated in some contemporary accounts, had created a very real and far flung establishment across the north of Europe.[3]

Scotland's advantageous geographical position was reflected in the ease with which North Sea fortunes, weakening as the centre of gravity shifted south to the Amsterdam–London axis, could be compensated by new prospects on its west coast both in the direction of Ireland and North America. Significantly few or no west of Scotland merchants seem to have joined the Scottish colony in Bordeaux. That colony remained the prerogative of the Scottish Scandinavian families and of 'Scots' families from Ulster, eastern Scotland or from Dublin,[4] leaving to the Glasgow families the new trades across the Atlantic. Ireland's economic fortunes by con-

[2] J. Wormald, *Court, kirk and community: Scotland 1470–1625* (1981): 48.

[3] See T.C. Smout (ed.), *Scotland and Europe 1200–1850* (1986).

[4] L.M. Cullen, 'The Irish merchant communities of Bordeaux, La Rochelle and Cognac in the eighteenth century', in P. Butel & L.M. Cullen (eds.), *Négoce et industrie en France et en Irlande aux XVIIIe et XIXe siècles* (1980); 'The Dublin merchant community in the eighteenth century', in P. Butel & L.M. Cullen (eds.), *Cities and merchants: French and Irish perspectives in urban development, 1500–1900* (1986b).

trast remained fixed on its east coast and on the Irish Sea. One of Ireland's weaknesses was that the hinterland of its western ports was poor and that that of its southern western ports was underdeveloped in the seventeenth century: that helps to explain the otherwise surprising limits to a westward shift of gravity of the economy. Indeed, the absolute weight of the west actually declined. Galway in particular declined from second or third port of the island to a minor position. That, combined with the fact that Galway Catholics preserved their landed background, explains the impressive mobility of its sons in trade and plantation. Scotland's good fortune was that its most advantageous western port locations on the Clyde and its eastern on the Firth of Forth were both drawing on the same rich hinterland. Hence the growth of the Atlantic trades reinforced the existing wealth of the Lowlands rather than shifted its centre of gravity. The Lowlands, together with Edinburgh and Glasgow, constituted an effective and integrated economy in which talent and capital could be put to the best use, and young men from as far afield as Aberdeen or Edinburgh were able to venture in the western world.

Even as late as 1696, at the end of a century of demographic growth, the hinterlands of Dublin and Waterford were, from the evidence of the cash yield of the poll tax, the most densely populated regions of Ireland. They had, however, already been the two most developed regions of the sixteenth century. However, Dublin's control of the economy in no way compared with the position which Edinburgh had already acquired in Scotland's foreign trade by 1600. Dublin seems to have attained a similar position half a century later. In other words as a centre of foreign trade, Dublin in 1667 or 1683 held a position which Edinburgh already enjoyed in 1600. However, the most intriguing contrast of all is that Dublin's growth in the seventeenth century relied mainly on immigration from outside Ireland. The city's hinterland, the most developed region of Ireland, was largely Catholic (and Anglo-Norman); Dublin itself, though its population rose six-fold or more in the seventeenth century, became largely English and Protestant. In other words, in the most extensive region of dense population in Ireland, there must have been less rural immigration to cities than in Scotland: Dublin (like Cork city at a somewhat later date) grew largely because of immigration from England. This suggests a less mobile, more static society. This picture is all the more plausible because the Scottish and Irish populations were probably closer in 1600 than at any time for the next 250 years: a little below a million in Scotland, a million, or perhaps a little above in Ireland.

Sixteenth- or early seventeenth-century stereotypes, like all stereotypes, may contain a germ of truth. As early as 1546 an interesting contrast is implicit in Andrew Borde's account of both societies.[5] Half a century later

[5] Andrew Borde, *The fyrst boke of the introduction of knowledge* (1979): 21, 25.

Fynes Moryson observed the mobility of the Scots and a dramatic contrast in dress between Scotland and Ireland. His account also hinted at Scottish economic development, as the Scots, taking advantage of their neutrality in England's war with Spain, 'grew somewhat richer and more experienced in navigation, and had better and stronger ships than in former times'. In direct relations between Ireland and Scotland, according to Moryson, 'in many places they use Scots for fisher-men and they together with the English, make profit of the inhabitants' sluggishness'.[6]

Scotland was a country pressing hard on its resources by the end of the sixteenth century. The mobility of its people at home and abroad bears this out, as in the following century do the crisis outflows to Ireland. But the quality of the movement was higher than in Ireland. There was more internal movement, and its emigration, at least apart from that to Ireland, was less dictated by crisis than was the case in Ireland, where there were outflows occasioned directly by military defeat at the end of long wars and subsequently de-mobilisation. Movement to Ireland, where Scots were already settled, was almost an extension of inland movement. Migration to Europe began earlier and was, in the sixteenth and seventeenth centuries, more regular than emigration by the Irish; and significantly, in movement to America, hazardous and into the unknown, the Scots featured less and later than the Irish. When they did they went more to the mainland than to the insalubrious islands of the West Indies, and relatively more seemed to venture out in the role of traders and adventurers than of servants. Scotland's Lowland population density was already much higher than Ireland's, including the most favoured regions of eastern Ireland; its town life was more advanced; and it supported four universities compared with only one in Ireland (that from 1592 only), and two in England. Militarily it was capable, despite and ultimately because of the challenge of a land frontier, to match England, and when it was in an aggressive mood it could, as in the 1640s, take advantage of a divided England to maintain an army in Ireland and simultaneously push its military frontier south to Newcastle. Scotland was for its resources and population already a dynamic and expansive society: the Sweden of the British Isles, even if like Sweden it was unable to sustain its military effort.

By 1689 a vigorous Scotland and a more backward but demographically vibrant Ireland already added to the potential wealth and military capacity of the British Isles. England's military achievement in asserting its power first against Holland and then from the 1690s against France had posed a growing challenge to its own economic resources. One response was centralisation of resources in London. This response, which had created by 1689 an economic and demographic dominance by the metropolitan centre of London unequalled in other societies in Europe, was

[6] Fynes Moryson, *An itinerary* (1617), pt 3: 155, 161, 179–81.

supplemented by resources and manpower drawn from Ireland and Scotland. Well before the middle of the eighteenth century these were not inconsiderable. The standing army of Charles II was in effect retained in Ireland, i.e. English soldiers maintained at the Irish taxpayers' expense, and the garrisons overseas consisted in part of men actually recruited in Ireland. In the first half of the eighteenth century roughly half the British peace-time army was carried on the Irish establishment,[7] and from the early 1740s recruitment of rank and file began in Scotland. In a more informal fashion, the colonies had begun to depend even earlier and more heavily on Irish and Scottish manpower. English population had stagnated between the 1630s and 1680s and real wages had risen. This not only reduced England's capacity to sustain colonial settlement, but made it inherently unattractive to natives whose real incomes at home were rising, explaining why dissenters with political or religious motives were so important in the English emigration that did take place both to Ireland and America. Even in Ireland English colonisation would have faltered disastrously after the 1610s but for the Scots. They were numerous in the 1630s at a time when English immigration had virtually dried up,[8] and the Scottish inflow, though fitful, was the mainstay of later immigration from Britain. A pan-Scottish world grew up on both sides of the North Channel with Glasgow as its intellectual centre. The flow of Scots was two-way, and recruitment in Glasgow's hinterland on both sides of the Irish Sea helps to explain the city's (and Scotland's) economic and intellectual vitality in the eighteenth century. It was after all an Irish-Scot, Francis Hutcheson, going from Dublin to Glasgow, who was the father of the Scottish Enlightenment, just as another Ulster Scot, Joseph Black, was one of the giants of Scottish scientific development. The growth in depth of Scotland's Irish empire coincides roughly with the decisive shift from the North Sea to the Atlantic, and Ireland and America must have been approximately equal in reinforcing the trends in the west of Scotland. In 1689–91, apart from European mercenaries hired by William III and refugee Huguenots, Scots living in Ireland were the backbone of the Williamite armies in Ireland.

The Irish were more numerous than the Scots in the West Indies in the seventeenth century:[9] a significant fact since climate and living conditions in the West Indies were so unattractive for settlement that the presence of Irish and relative absence of Scots suggests that the living standards or material expectations of Irishmen were lower than those of the Scots. For Scots, settlement in Ireland or alternatively after 1683 in mainland North

[7] I.M. Cullen, 'Britain under Westminster' in L.W. Smith (ed.), *The making of Britain: the age of expansion* (1986a): 162; 181, fn 16.

[8] Sir William Brereton in P.H. Brown, *Early travellers in Scotland* (1891): 154.

[9] L.M. Cullen, 'Merchant communities overseas, the navigation acts and Irish and Scottish responses', in L.M. Cullen & T.C. Smout (eds.), *Comparative aspects of Scottish and Irish economic and social history* (1977): 166.

America was more attractive. Scots settlement in New Jersey began in 1683[10] and before the Union the Scots had already provided a governor of the State. Further south in Pennsylvania the influx had emerged as well. In 1700 tobacco in Philadelphia was 'engrossed by the Scots (as almost all other trade here is)', and from Philadelphia the Scots had already made contact with Maryland, carrying goods overland to exchange for tobacco.[11] In the eighteenth century, migration from the British Isles to America relied less on English than, rather selectively, Lowland Scots and in larger numbers, at lower social levels, the Scots–Irish or from the 1760s Scots Highlanders as well.

Within England internal migration to London in the eighteenth century was probably not much smaller in scale than Irish and Scottish emigration combined with internal migration to Dublin, Glasgow and Edinburgh. The scale of this movement and the miscellaneous careers it generated help to explain why the army and the learned professions interested Englishmen less than they did both Scots and Irish. The background of officers moreover was often modest[12] and that reduced the disadvantage of Scots and Irishmen. Within Europe the conduct of trade with the British Isles was largely in the hands of expatriate Scots and Irish. In London itself, despite massive immigration from the English provinces, it seems hard to identify a clear-cut provincial business interest from within England. Migrants from the English provinces seem to have been subsumed into the cosmopolitan and self-sufficient business and political world of the capital dedicated to financing London-based activity or the financial needs of the state, and failed to assert any distinctive provincial presence.[13]

The only exception to this pattern seems to have been the Scots and Irish. For them, if London offered opportunities to businessmen, the Empire created outlets further down the social scale for surplus population. Between the mid seventeenth and mid eighteenth centuries, both countries grew more rapidly than did England: in Scotland's case too its social system tended increasingly to make it difficult for Scots to acquire land in the eighteenth century. The costs of Empire could be high of course, and certainly the Scottish Highlands seem to have borne the brunt in the long run: its population fell, the middle interest of tacksmen was removed; and after the mid eighteenth century its manpower began to be absorbed in the Lowlands, army and Empire. But for other regions the benefits outweighed the costs. Significantly, too, cities grew rapidly in Scotland and Ireland: Dublin, Cork, Glasgow, and despite the loss of its parliament, Edinburgh.

[10] N.C. Landsman, *Scotland and its first American colony* (1985).

[11] *Calendar of state papers, America and West Indies, 1708*: 107, 634.

[12] G. Holmes, 'The professions and social change in England 1680–1730', *Proceedings of the British Academy*, 65 (1979).

[13] Professor J.M. Price's studies are the only sustained published attempt to study aspects of the London eighteenth-century merchant community.

Here at least was a real contrast on the periphery with the fortunes of England's older-established cities: there, with few exceptions, only London and the new industrial towns (with Liverpool as their port) grew. Even urban planning was more in evidence in the industrial towns rather than other English centres. Borsay has observed that 'the fashionable square made its first provincial appearance not in the county centres or spas but in the industrial towns of Manchester and Birmingham and ports of Bristol and Liverpool'.[14] From 1750 roughly half the tobacco exported from the British Isles came through Glasgow, and the trade was handled by Scottish intermediaries in alliance for much of the time with the Irish house of Fitzgerald in London.[15] While the trade of many colonies was handled by London commission houses, and the planters, whatever part of England they came from, became indebted to them, Glasgow preserved its independence through the store system; Scots supplied goods through Scottish traders abroad to colonists, and in turn took their tobacco in payment. The establishment of the store trade itself depended on the emigration from Scotland of young 'adventurers' to represent home interests in the trade. But the consequences were large. Not only did Scots exist as a well-defined interest in London, but in contrast to the English ports outside London they were at the centre of an independent circuit of exchanges between Glasgow and the colonies. This helps in turn to explain why Glasgow and not provincial England displayed a precocious development in banking from the middle of the century.

For some purposes Glasgow and Edinburgh, 50 miles apart across a common hinterland, should be aggregated. If their populations are combined, for instance, Dublin's position as second city of the British Isles is reduced in significance. Their joint population in 1800 of 160,000 was close to Dublin's 180,000. More significantly, combined they account for 8 per cent of Scotland's total population compared with Dublin's 4 per cent of Ireland's.

This reflects Scotland's success in retaining control of Scottish resources throughout the century. In contrast much of the trade of English outports was handled or financed in one way or another from London. A well-defined Irish interest existed in London as well as the Scottish one, but it was less closely intertwined with business interests in Ireland. This was in large part because of the size of Irish rent rolls and the remittance of a significant proportion of them to absentees. Some of the largest landowners: Downshire, Donegal and Abercorn, were absentee, just as some of the largest Irish estates were owned by great English landowners such as Fitzwilliam, Petty-Fitzmaurice and Cavendish. Much more Irish rent

[14] P. Borsay, 'The English urban renaissance: the development of provincial urban culture c.1680–c.1760', *Social History* (1977):593.

[15] J.M. Price, *France and the Chesapeake*, 2 vols. (1973), *passim*.

money flowed to London than did Scots money. Scottish finances in London were much more closely tied up with trade. Rents remitted from Ireland roughly equalled the surplus in Irish commodity trade. In the hands of financiers in London this, at about £1 million per annum in the 1760s, was one of the largest out-of-town flows of liquid funds. The year 1772 itself was the high watermark of peripheral money and business interests, Scottish and Irish, in London business life, a peculiar position created by the novel circumstances of the strain of financing the Seven Years War and the liquidity which remained in the ensuing peace years.

The Scots and Irish interest in the Empire was all-consuming. The colonial or economic aspects of the Union have sometimes been understated as economic arguments of convenience in a primarily political debate.[16] But the interest in the outside world was already marked, and the number of Scots in America far from insignificant. Indeed over the eighteenth century the whole logic of the necessity for colonial outlets for men as much as for their products made the Scots and the Irish impatient of restrictions and of vested interests in trade, such as the East India Company whose trade and finances were in the hands of a powerful few in London. It is a measure of the well-defined nature of the Scottish and Irish interest that the challenge to the company came from them rather than from provincial England. Adam Smith's *Wealth of Nations* reflects in intellectual terms a very distinctive Scottish influence and in a practical sense too in its powerful attack on entrenched commercial interests it could have been written only by a Scot (or an Irishman). In London, Edmund Burke, himself already a patron of Irishmen seeking advance in the company, and Henry Dundas were the main parliamentary figures who took an interest in the Company's affairs, and they both had intriguing and arresting links with the Company. Indeed the Irish interest in the Company came relatively early and the complex politics of the Company conceal the reality of a strong but insecure provincial interest within it in the 1760s. With the potential wealth that followed the pen and sword in India, Scots and Irish alike, though prominent in India, were never as dominant there as elsewhere in the Empire. India was also a magnet for Englishmen, and it helped (indeed it was often decisive) to be well-connected. Henry Dundas's tutelary role from 1784 onwards as head of the government board to supervise the company may, despite some recent suggestions to the contrary, have been significant after all for ambitious young Scots and their future in India. Scots were more numerous than Irishmen among the petitioners for positions as writers, that is, for civil appointments, even before the 1780s.[17]

[16] P.W.J. Riley, *The union of England and Scotland* (1978): 7–8. Other historians have put a heavier emphasis on the trade aspects. See T.C. Smout, *Scottish trade on the eve of Union, 1660–1707* (1963): 261–5, and R. Mitchison, *A History of Scotland*, 2nd edn (1982): 310.

[17] India Office Library, writers' petitions, J/I/6, J/I/7, J/I/8.

Irishmen, however, usually outnumbered Scots in the army cadets embarked for India on the Company's vessels in the 1770s and 1780s.[18] They were both, however, exceeded by Englishmen in both civil and military appointments, a contrast with the position in much of the old Empire.

The Scottish pattern of mobility is closely linked to land and farm structures. A contraction both in ownership and in access to lease-held farms from the middle of the eighteenth century put pressure on young men to move out. In fact, Lowland Scotland had initially a pattern of estates which were smaller than in either Ireland or England, though the smaller ones began to disappear in and before the eighteenth century; hence a greater pressure existed on young men to seek outlets beyond land. To stress that Scottish estates were small may seem surprising, because they have often been seen as large, and the greatest Scottish estates were the largest in acres and sometimes in income in the British Isles. Thus, the Duke of Buccleuch in 1873 owned 460,108 acres and enjoyed a rental of £217,162, the largest figures for acreage and rental respectively in the British Isles. The Duke of Breadalbane was not far behind him in acres with 438,308. Other houses like Bute, Dalhousie, Hamilton and Home were likewise on a princely scale in acres and wealth alike.[19] Because there was no land tax in Ireland, we cannot hope to see the pattern of Irish estates with the relative precision possible for Scotland c.1770.[20] However, the land returns for 1873 prepared for parliament, based on current or recent values, make it possible to look at both landed systems a century later.[21] The Scottish system was not greatly different from a century previously. Moreover, changes on both sides would tend to reinforce the arguments of this chapter: at an early stage, Scottish estates were smaller and more numerous, and Irish properties in the flood days of plantation were much larger than later. The larger Scottish estates were also inflated in 1873 in acreage and in rent income by their extraordinary holdings of mountain land. In 1873 the 171 Scottish estates of 20,000 acres and upwards averaged 64,498 acres compared with 37,701 acres for the 110 Irish estates above 20,000 acres.

Scottish estates in 1873 were distributed in a markedly skew fashion with a low gross value per acre for the larger estates, while the gross value per

[18] Embarkation lists of officers and men for India, India Office Library, L/MIL/9/90.

[19] J. Bateman, *The great landowners of Great Britain and Ireland*, 4th edn, 1883 (repr. 1971).

[20] L. Timperley, 'The pattern of landholding in 18th-century Scotland' in M.L. Parry and T.R. Slater (eds.), *The making of the Scottish countryside* (1980).

[21] The Scottish returns relate to 1873. The Irish returns were begun in 1873 but completed only in 1875. For Scottish estates, the returns are of 'gross value' in 1873, for Irish estates of the official rateable values which understate the current value. Unlike the Bateman figures compiled from these returns, the official returns are set out on a county basis, i.e. estates held in several counties are returned as a separate estate for each county. The figures used here are taken from Parliamentary Papers, 1876, LXXX.

Table 7 *Landed property in Scotland and Ireland, 50 acres and upwards, 1873*[22]

	Scotland			Ireland		
Estate size (acres)	No. of estates	'Total gross value'	Gross value per acre	No. of estates	'Total valuation'	Valuation per acre
20,000 & upwards	171	£2,157,750	£0.20	110	£1,512,594	£0.36
5,000 – 20,000	409	2,008,625	0.52	632	2,627,920	0.46
2,000 – 5,000	587	1,946,506	1.10	1,246	1,997,202	0.52
1,000 – 2,000	591	1,179,755	1.41	1,773	1,305,581	0.56
50 to 1,000	4,406	3,318,241	2.71	11,690	2,549,610	0.67
		10,610,877			9,992,907	

acre rose progressively for the smaller estates. For Irish estates on the other hand, the value per acre did not vary widely, the valuations even for the larger estates being not much lower than those for smaller estate. In other words, despite a concentration of large estates in low-rated areas of Donegal, Mayo and Kerry the large estates were spread fairly uniformly across both good and bad land. Indeed, if Donegal, Mayo and Kerry are excluded, the valuation per acre rose from £0.36 to £0.50, which is little different from the value per acre for smaller estates. Many of the largest estates were in eastern Ireland; Down and Antrim had exceptionally marked concentrations of above average-sized properties, and the huge Leinster and Fitzwilliam properties were spread across some of the highest-valued lands of Kildare and Wicklow respectively. In Irish counties estates of 2,000 acres and upwards usually accounted for more than half of the total valuation of land within the county. In the Scottish Lowlands on the other hand, estates of 2,000 acres and above almost invariably accounted for just half and more frequently less than half the gross value of 'estates' above 50 acres. In the Lowlands, Haddingtonshire was the only county which departed markedly from this pattern. Aber-

[22] As in the case of Ireland, the Scottish returns include leaseholds of 99 years and longer. The Irish returns also return leases renewable which were in effect perpetuities. In Scotland fee simple and long leases were very numerous in the towns; in Ireland on the other hand quite in contrast to the countryside such tenures were very few in the cities, towns and villages. As such tenures in towns and their suburbs were very significant in Scotland both in number and aggregate value, the Scottish returns have been adjusted to exclude all landholdings below 50 acres. In the case of Ireland they were so few as to have a negligible effect on the aggregate county and national figures, and on that account they have not been excluded.

deenshire did so superficially also but at every level of estate, the gross value per acre rose progressively as estate size became smaller, emphasising the concentration of the larger estates in the upland districts of the county, and of the smaller properties in the Lowlands. Indeed in the Lowland counties of Stirling, Renfrew, Linlithgow, Edinburgh, Kinross, Fife and Dunbarton, the proportion of land held in estates of 2,000 acres and upwards varied between 11 and 44 per cent of the total gross value of properties of 50 acres and upwards. Forfarshire would fit into the same pattern, if 2 large estates were excluded, and Kincardineshire and Lanarkshire are distorted by 5 and 4 large estates respectively. Including Forfarshire, Lanarkshire and Kincardineshire, 10 Lowland counties accounted for 41 per cent of the total Scottish rental of properties above 50 acres. The absence of town houses in Edinburgh on the scale of Dublin's great houses is a commentary on a very different level of individual gentry incomes in the Lowlands, just as in London the Scottish gentry interest paled in financial terms beside the Irish. What all this meant was that in the Lowlands at large, and in many of the richest Lowland districts in particular, estate sizes measured by rental were comparatively small. Only one Irish county, Dublin, could compare with the Scottish Lowland counties in the relatively small proportion of its total rental in the hands of estate owners of 2,000 acres and above.

However, the 1873 returns embrace both landed 'estates', that is properties of landowners rented out to tenants, and lands directly occupied and farmed by their owners. By and large the properties of 2,000 acres and upwards are estates; those below that level, especially as the acreage falls, are predominantly, though not exclusively, owner-occupied. A contrasting situation existed between the countries; estate size tended to fall in Ireland, and sub-estate units to multiply. In Scotland, estate size grew, and estate and more particularly sub-estate units fell in numbers in the Lowlands. By 1873 the number of the smaller properties, mainly farms, was very large in Ireland, whereas such properties were fewer in Scotland, though commanding in the Lowlands a very high gross value per acre. In one sense their paucity in Scotland was a consequence of the process of reduction of the number of estates and farms noted so frequently in the parish reports in the Old Statistical Account in the 1790s. In the Scottish figures for 1873 of course it should be remembered that the total for the lesser properties appears even smaller when compared with the Irish total because it reflected a very different process over time where *tenancy* was concerned: the large number of small properties in Ireland was mainly the outcome of a process of conversion of what had been tenancies at the outset of the eighteenth century effectively into ownership. The terms of tenancy did not change in Scotland, and tenancies had become larger and fewer. In Ireland on the other hand the larger tenancies in particular not only enjoyed more favourable legal terms than in Scotland but over time many tenancies were turned into what were in effect perpetuities. The fact that unlike the English returns the 1873 returns for Scotland embraced not only owners in fee, but also lessees for 99 or more years failed to inflate the number of properties in the countryside precisely because such tenures, common in the Scottish towns, scarcely survived in the countryside. The tenures included in the Irish returns – perpetuities as well as leases of 99 or more years – arose originally from tenancies whose terms improved – more accurately were metamorphosed – over the eighteenth century (a situation enshrined in the tenantry act of 1780) to the point that they were regarded with the passage of time as the equivalent almost of fee simple.

It was these properties whose easy acquisition in the eighteenth century not only retained many in the countryside but offered to younger sons of gentry and of upwardly mobile farmers an avenue to income and status. There was no equivalent in Scotland where what was virtually a reverse process was underway: the smaller properties were becoming fewer. Beside the established landed class in Ireland, a host of lesser gentlemen multiplied in the eighteenth century. These are the so-called 'middlemen', so often misunderstood in historical analysis, who are quite distinct in nature from the disappearing 'tacksmen' of the Scottish Highlands. Indeed army officers returned regularly to assume tenancy and status in the countryside. In Scotland by contrast the lesser gentry were disappearing. From Duthill in Moray and Inverness it was reported in the Old Statistical Account that 'about twenty years ago there was a considerable number of very creditable gentlemen with families in this parish, most of whom have now become extinct, and the few remaining are soon likely to become so, their sons preferring various pursuits abroad'.[23]

In Scotland, reflecting this social mobility, and indeed despite the alternative outlets that mobility itself created, the numbers in the universities were much larger still. The number rose from around 1,000 in 1700 to 3,000 by 1800; in Trinity College, Dublin, there were a mere 933 in 1792, and the 2 English universities would have had only roughly twice the Dublin figure.[24] Tellingly Adam Smith noted that poor universities were better academically than others,[25] and Samuel Johnson, visiting Scotland, had noted the low costs – only £10 to £15 at St Andrews – of a Scottish university education.[26] Interesting too as a measure of the wider mobility

23 OSA 4: 310.

24 C. Maxwell, *A history of Trinity College Dublin* (1946): 130; B.P. Lenman, *Integration, enlightenment and industrialisation: Scotland 1746–1832* (1981): 96; T.C. Smout, *A history of the Scottish people 1500–1830* (1972): 449.

25 A. Smith, *An enquiry into the wealth of nations*, ed. R.H. Campbell and A.S. Skinner (1976), vol. 2, 772–3.

26 Samuel Johnson, *A journey to the western isles of Scotland* in *The works of Samuel Johnson, LL.D.* (1881): 550.

even the professions engendered (restricted in the case of Irish Catholics in the Empire by religious discrimination), medical doctors and lawyers were very numerous among Scottish plantation owners.[27] In Scotland, the absolute number of army officers was probably about the same as in Ireland, hence significantly larger if expressed on a per capita basis. Moreover, they came from the Lowlands as well as the Highlands (the counties of the Firth of Forth, especially Fife, had been the main source of recruitment for the Scottish Brigade in Holland).[28] What is particularly marked in the case of Scotland is not simply a relatively greater move into the army and the universities (and hence into the professions at large) but a much greater emphasis on trade. While the report from Duthill would seem misleading if its author's assertion about sons becoming adventurers instead of college students were generalised for Scotland, his basic point about the prominence of trade outlets is well-established. In fact, the numbers entering mercantile pursuits in London and, at the level of overseers, apprentices, clerks and merchants, abroad, must have been large. The numbers going abroad also rose with time, and their position in the East India Company may also have increased sharply in the late eighteenth century. Movement to North America and to the West Indies, while small, was qualitatively important: repeatedly the Old Statistical Account draws a distinction between emigration, little known or only recent in the reporter's parish, and a more commonplace movement of 'adventurers' abroad. This movement got an accelerated fillip from the increased exploitation of Jamaica which held out new and exciting prospects for settlers from the 1750s: already one quarter of the landholders in 1754, Scots accounted for 40 per cent of the inventories after death of above £1,000 in 1771–5.[29] With the new-found importance of the West Indies trade with Glasgow after 1782 the trend must have accelerated, and merited fairly frequent attention in the Old Statistical Account.[30] The most telling individual account is for Kells in Kirkcudbrightshire:

> Several young men of spirit go to the West Indies as planters and merchants. Some go to England to push their fortunes, as pedlars, and when sober and industrious, commonly return, after 10 or 12 years, with £800 or £900 or £1,000. Several return from the West Indies, after 16–17 years, with genteel fortunes.[31]

In Ireland by contrast the movement abroad not only seems not to have accelerated but may have reached its peak in the great speculative decade

[27] R.B. Sheridan, 'The rise of a colonial gentry: a case study of Antigua, 1730–1775', *Economic History Review*, 2nd series, 13, no. 3 (1961): 349–50; *Sugar and slavery, an economic history of the British West Indies 1623–1775* (1974): 197–200, 369–73.

[28] James Ferguson, *Papers illustrating the history of the Scots brigade in the service of the United Provinces* (Scottish history Society, 1899), i: xxv.

[29] Sheridan, *Sugar and slavery*: 369–70.

[30] OSA 4: 68, 301, 351; 6: 145; 7: 301; 8: 390.

[31] OSA 4: 264.

of the 1760s whose prospects were not quite repeated in the 1780s. Thus overall there is a sharp contrast between Scotland and Ireland. First, estates and farms alike were growing in scale and contracting in number in Lowland Scotland, whereas in Ireland the numbers of both tended to multiply. The overly large size of Irish estates was already reflected in some break-up: in Cork, Tipperary and Kilkenny some major estates, redistributed for special reasons, had created a much broader land market. At the same time, the tenurial structure created an avenue for younger sons unknown in Lowland Scotland. Secondly, the mobility of sons of laird and farmer alike was massive by Irish standards: this reflected a different land market and very different conditions within landholding itself.

Ireland is a barometer of Scotland's development because comparison affords some measure of the extent to which social conditions diverged in the two countries. For what it is worth as a vehicle of generalisation about the respective economies, the real wages of unskilled labourers seem to have been higher in Edinburgh than in Dublin in the 1560s.[32] Wages in the rather well-defined areas of colonisation in Ireland were higher, however, in the seventeenth century: lower real wages in Scotland and intermittent emigration to Ireland are a reminder that Scotland was densely populated, and pressing against some sort of barrier in that century. Thus Scotland in the seventeenth century is in something of an intermediate position between Ireland with rising population and wages alike, and England where population stagnated or fell and real wages rose from the 1630s to the 1680s. More striking still is the difference in the wage structure in the two countries. In Scotland the relationship of the wages of skilled and unskilled workers was akin to England's: the wages of the unskilled were a half to two-thirds of the wages of the skilled. Indeed Adam Smith was to note this in 1776, as a well-established fact,[33] whereas in Ireland even at the most favourable the differential was double: in other areas the ratio for many was as wide as 4:1.

Ireland, it should be added, had no 'Highlands'; the Highland line so often referred to in modern Scottish accounts had no Irish parallel, and while there were spectacularly barren regions along the west coast, backwardness like a tide lapped around and even into the pockets of economic development. The contrast in wages also reflects the comparative absence of internal migration in Ireland – such movement as an orderly flow probably emerged only in the early eighteenth century. The contrast also reflects the much greater role of cottagers in Ireland, something which in turn reflected the fact that land was at less of a premium in Ireland, and that labourers were less often divorced from easy

32 L.M. Cullen, A. Gibson & T.C. Smout, 'Wages and comparative development in Ireland and Scotland 1565–1780' (1987).

33 Smith, *An inquiry into the nature of causes of the wealth of nations* (1976) vol. 1: 120.

access to land, a factor which tended to hold them at low wages where they were. Farm servants had never been as well-established a category as in Scotland, and cottagers' plots were let readily to a prospective work force. Cottagers were then retained for labour at wages which were as much as one half those of the rates of regularly employed estate or town labourers sometimes even in the same region. In Scotland from the mid eighteenth century the cottagers were decidedly in decline. This combined with the greater mobility of the population at large gave point to the comment from Kinnettles in Forfarshire in the Old Statistical Account that 'perhaps thirty years ago, the boundaries between the ranks were more distinctly marked, the more attentively observed. Inferior ranks begin not to scruple to invade the boundaries of those above them'.[34]

Scotland's emigration, though small in absolute numbers, was real enough to service the Scottish interest in mainland America, the West Indies and the East Indies. The volume of Irish emigration before the 1790s has tended to be exaggerated: Dr Wokecke's estimates of Irish arrivals at Philadelphia reduce the numbers to well below 1,000 in most years.[35] Even the seasonal migration to Newfoundland has to be related to the decline in military service by rank and file from the region from which the migrants came in the south-east. Indeed much evidence suggests that internal demand absorbed labour supply more readily in the 1760s and 1770s than either previously or later: ironically the social unrest about wages and conacre plots in that period may reflect not so much that such employment was under threat as that it had rather abruptly become a more central feature of the economy. Perhaps it is not surprising, given the decline in migration, that study of wage data in the two countries suggests (on an admittedly narrow base of evidence) that real wages of unskilled labourers in Edinburgh rose decisively compared with Dublin in the 1770s.[36] Adam Smith noted that wages varied less in the greater part of the Scottish Lowlands than in England[37] and the Old Statistical Account figures in the 1790s show that wages in the Lothians did not greatly differ from those in the rest of Scotland.

In Scotland not only did Highland emigration rise from the 1760s as the tacksmen and their followers began to go abroad, but army recruitment increased, whereas in Ireland rank and file movement into armies stagnated or actually declined for over three decades. Indeed, it is quite likely that on roughly twice the population, Ireland failed to provide a greater absolute number of emigrants. In Scotland, where eighteenth-century rank and file service outside the country (apart from the Scots Brigade in Dutch

[34] OSA 9: 210.
[35] M. Wokecke's paper read at Brendan Society Conference, Ennis, Co. Clare, September 1986.
[36] Cullen, Gibson & Smout (1988): 7. [37] Smith (1976): 1, 92.

service) only began in 1742, the number of regiments levied in the Highlands rose from 2 in 1757 to 6 in 1777–8[38] and the levies for British service from 1757 were already a reason why the Dutch Brigade could no longer find Scottish recruits.[39] Over time Lowland recruitment was by no means insignificant, despite the greater attention Highland service has attracted in study. In Towie in Aberdeenshire, the Old Statistical Account reported that 'they have no dislike to a military life, especially when any of the heritor's sons gets a commission'.[40] In Hamilton in Lanarkshire 'the young men of this parish have always shown a great ardour for a military life'.[41] Even in Fife, no doubt drawing on the traditions long kept alive by service in Holland, the story is the same: 'a martial spirit seems to pervade the lower ranks, who can scarcely be prevented from entry into the army or navy on the report of a war'.[42]

One of the arresting aspects of Scottish life is its political calm of the second half of the eighteenth century. While the American Revolution had a profound effect on Ireland, its repercussions in Scotland were minimal. As Bruce Lenman has remarked, 'the great English county of Yorkshire showed more critical and independent spirits active in politics in the latter part of the America crisis than all Scotland put together'.[43] The French Revolution too passed over Scotland not quite unnoticed but with little sign of a likelihood of upheaval. At first sight this quietude is surprising, Scotland had a very stormy history in the seventeenth century, its intellectual thought was speculative and critical, and Irish Presbyterians, largely of Scottish background and even education, developed a growing radicalism over the century. In the 1790s Irish landlords and their agents in the north of Ireland feared the radicalism of their Presbyterian tenants far more than that of their Catholic tenants. The Old Statistical Account breathes a smug complacency of staggering proportions. Yet Scotland's political system was conspicuously the most unrepresentative in the British Isles. In 1820 a mere 2,889 voters returned all 30 Scottish county members of parliament, and a great burgh like Edinburgh had only 33 electors.[44] Indeed the questions that agitated France or America or even Ireland largely passed Scotland by. In 1778 Scottish opinion at large favoured recruitment to strengthen the British army, and Scots in America in the main fought on the loyalist side, whereas Ulster Scots were the mainstay of the rebel armies.[45] Even Adam Smith, critical though he was of vested interests, took a highly complacent view of the justice of the imperial cause at large. In this he was in sharp contrast with Edmund Burke, the Irishman who took a much more balanced view of the rights of the parts within the

[38] Lenman (1981):65–6. [39] Ferguson (1899) 2:394. [40] OSA 4: 552.
[41] OSA 2: 201.
[42] OSA 1: 383. [43] Lenman (1981):67. [44] Smout (1972):203.
[45] Lenman (1981):63, 66.

whole, and was, while a supporter of Empire, the most powerful spokesman in London of the rights of the colonists. It is true, of course, that England itself was, at least from the effervescent perspective of Ireland or France, a somewhat somnolent country: electoral contests there too declined over the century. But it is hard not to agree with Bruce Lenman's view that Scotland was 'the most undemanding and subservient of British provinces'.[46] In the 1790 election a mere 9 counties and 7 boroughs were contested.[47] This is in sharp contrast with Ireland where political activity at local level outpaced that in Scotland and England alike.

The Irish system was far more representative than the Scottish. County constituencies ran from 1,000 electors up to 6,000, and in 1793 the electorate for the boroughs and counties was about 60,000.[48] England in 1803 had 160,000 freeholders.[49] This suggests crudely that on a population basis Irish Protestants were almost twice as well-represented in the electorate as the English population. Even if Catholics (without the vote until after 1793) are added to the figures, the Irish system though substantially less representative than the English system was not dramatically less so.[50] Moreover, the intervening middle interest, the so-called 'middleman', unique to Ireland, was often Catholic: though as a Catholic he did not have the vote, the Catholic landowner and in many cases the Catholic middle interest could determine the votes of his Protestant tenants. The great contrast of the Irish system is that its effective representative character actually increased as middle interests grew. Indeed the number of electors and the intervention of middle interests in a situation where contested elections became almost the norm made political management necessary and gave the middle interests a political leverage which made politics increasingly lively and turbulent. Issues were not lacking embracing not only Anglo-Irish relations, but the general relationship between members of parliament and the managing parliamentary group, and the question of radical political reform. In Scotland a much higher proportion of the young men of comfortable background and education were taken off by army, professions, colonies and trade than in Ireland. Even before 1780 Irish politicians were beginning to experience

[46] *Ibid.*, 58. [47] *Ibid.*, 79.

[48] (Irish) *Parliamentary Register*, 13: 113. P.J. Jupp suggests that the electorate in the Irish counties in 1793 was about 50,000. See 'Irish parliamentary elections and the influence of the Catholic vote: 1801–1820', (1967): 184.

[49] P. Colquhoun 1803 quoted in R. Porter, *English society in the eighteenth century* (1982): 388. It was stated in the Irish parliament in 1793 that there were 150,000 voters in England ('A full and accurate report of the debates in the parliament of Ireland in the session 1793 on the bill for relief of his majesty's catholic subjects': 304).

[50] These figures do not provide for the exclusion of borough population in the case of Ireland or England. The data are too uncertain to justify an attempt to do so without more research. It would seem probable that if both borough voters and urban population were excluded, county representation would be somewhat more equitable in England but without the result affecting the basic validity of what is said here in the text.

the need to play to the masses, and they became even more irresponsible from the outset of the 1780s in the pursuit of short-term political advantage. The tenantry act of 1780 itself represented a surrender by many politicians to 'popular' demands. Perhaps more importantly, the numbers going abroad from Ireland actually fell off in the 1780s: the French army was in retrenchment in the 1780s, and trade outlets abroad for young men from Ireland also contracted. Unlike Scotland, the West Indies were no longer a magnet for young Irishmen, as Irish transatlantic trade lost momentum in the face of a decline in the demand for salt provisions. Many who would otherwise have gone abroad were unable to do so, and some even returned. Even in Dundas's East India Company, while peace was good for business and civil administration (in which Scots were well represented), it was bad for the Company's army in which the Irish were better represented. It was indeed the presence of restless spirits in Ireland, Protestants like Thomas Russell who had returned on half-pay from India or Catholic younger sons who either did not go to or actually came back from France, in harness with young men like Wolfe Tone who had dreamed of employment in the empire but failed to find it that provided the driving force of radicalism in the early 1790s. No doubt Ireland was on the verge of a social crisis: the abrupt but massive rise in recruitment for the army after 1800 is a reflection of this as is the upsurge in emigration after 1815. But the crisis in the 1790s was first and foremost, and was perceived as such at the time, a political crisis.

In Scotland, by contrast, the relationship with England was not a problem: it was in the long term even seen as beneficial, and much of the improvement of Scotland was, rather falsely in some respects, represented as a consequence of Union. The Scots system of political management remained unchallenged not only under the Duke of Argyll and his brother but under Henry Dundas, whereas Ireland became progressively more unmanageable. Reform was scarcely an interest at all, partly because politics were not destabilised by the middle interests, which grew in Ireland, and partly because migration took away so many young, educated men who, had they remained in leisure in the countryside, would have had the time their Irish counterparts had for agitation.

To the outsider, especially to the Irish observer, Scotland seems a very different society. In keeping its Church and laws at the Union, Scotland had saved itself from the traumas of legal exclusion and discrimination that in varying degrees Presbyterians and Catholics experienced in Ireland (just as it also effectively excluded the Englishmen who flooded into the rich pickings of legal office and church in Ireland). So radical had feeling become that much of the story of the 1780s and 1790s in Ireland is of a retreat from previous radical stances by landowners, and rich merchants alike. Only Presbyterians around Belfast, a Catholic circle in Dublin and a mixed group of radical Protestant and Catholic gentry in Wexford and Kildare were finally overwhelmed by the force of conspiracy they had promoted. The course of political relationships between Scotland and London was very different from that of Ireland. But it seems that the course of political events in Scotland was influenced both by the rapid economic development and by the quite stifling complacency which it also bred. That in turn was helped by the social structure of the Lowland gentry which hinged on small estates, a sharp decline in small properties and a growth in the size of farms, and a proportionately larger number of emigrants aiming towards careers outside Scotland. These features of themselves do not explain why political issues were absent in Scotland, but they did ensure that Scotland was free from the social forces which augmented the great swell of political questioning in Ireland. The Highland counties had remarkably few gentry apart from a handful of magnates with the largest acreages and some of the largest rent rolls in the British Isles. The relative absence of magnates in the Lowland counties meant that politics was spared the rivalries derived from competing magnate groups in Ireland, a factor which also helped to ensure the apolitical character of the lesser gentry. In Irish counties politics took wing on political contests which had little doctrinal about them. However, cynical though the major participants were, the popular upheaval was deep and far-reaching. Contests provided the vehicle for wider participation by lesser gentry and middle interests and gave currency to new ideas. Thus Scotland contrasted sharply with Ireland: its economic development was greater, its politics devoid of great issues, and its public life marked by an overwhelming, not to say nauseous, complacency.

9

KINDRED ADJOINING KINGDOMS: AN ENGLISH PERSPECTIVE ON THE SOCIAL AND ECONOMIC HISTORY OF EARLY MODERN SCOTLAND*

K. E. WRIGHTSON

If comparisons are odious, it is largely so because of the perennial difficulty of separating the recognition of difference from the ascription of worth. If, among comparisons, international comparisons are commonly more odious than others, this is principally a result of the fact that both the detection of differences and the accompanying evaluation are so frequently coloured by national sentiment. Nowhere is this more apparent than in the historiographies of England and Scotland. If these 'kindred adjoining kingdoms' have experienced a complex social, political and cultural interrelationship throughout most of their recorded histories – an involvement which became closer in the course of the early modern period – it is one which has attracted surprisingly little disciplined historical analysis outside the political and diplomatic spheres. Historians of early modern England, for the most part, have shown a marked tendency to ignore the Scottish dimension of British history. Scottish historians have been far less indifferent to the existence of their closest neighbour. Yet they have demonstrated a certain ambivalence in their attitudes towards the interrelationship of the two nations; on the one hand insisting upon aspects of Scottish uniqueness and autonomy, while on the other hand hitching Scotland's wagon to processes of historical development which the English persist in regarding as essentially their own. Both the insularity (and on occasion blinkered anglocentricity) of the English, and the Scottish oscillation between a truculent exceptionalism and an insistence upon inclusion have many causes. The most immediately obvious of these are the

* This contribution was invited as a means of presenting the response of a specialist in the economic and social history of early modern England to the findings of recent research on Scotland. It will be evident that I have no special expertise in Scottish history. I write as an interested and partially-informed outsider, attempting to bring out what seem to me some of the broader implications of the exciting work now being done on the society and economy of early modern Scotland.

conventional structures of academic curricula and the imperfect overlap between the areas of specialisation which they encourage. Behind these curricular and professional influences, however, may lie habits of mind which have deeper roots in both the English and the Scottish approaches to their national pasts.

Promoting a positive self-image by slighting the manners, morals and institutions of foreigners – and conversely the highlighting of domestic deficiencies by reference to the superior achievements of rivals and neighbours – are ancient and ubiquitous cultural phenomena. In sixteenth- and seventeenth-century England, however, any pre-existing tendency to nationalistic bluster was markedly reinforced and elaborated by the wave of patriotically-inspired writing which W.G. Hoskins termed 'the rediscovery of England'.[1] The period witnessed a flowering of cartography, topography, antiquarian and historical awareness which sought for the first time to describe and to explain the peculiarities and the peculiar virtues of England and the English. William Harrison, whose 'Description of England' was published in 1577 as a preface to Holinshed's influential historical chronicle, described himself as 'one desirous to set foorth the truth absolutelie, or such things in deed as were most likely to be true'. But such scholarly objectivity did not inhibit him from writing enthusiastically of the manifold advantages of Englishness. In Harrison's view the English were 'blessed in everie waie, and there is no temporall commoditie necessarie to be had or craved by any nation at God's hand that he hath not in most aboundant manner bestowed upon us Englishmen'.[2] It was a view shared a generation later by Thomas Wilson, who declared that 'England, for the Commodityes it yields, is knowne to be inferior to no Country, saving that it wanteth wine and spicery, but to answer that defect it aboundeth in more sorts of other things necessary to life than any other Country'.[3] 'Oh England, England, thou knowest not thine own wealth: because thou seest not other countries penury', insisted Bishop John Aylmer in 1559: 'Wee live in paradise ... Oh if thou knewest thou Englishman in what wealth thou livest and in how plentiful a Country: Thou wouldest vii times of the day fall flat on thy face before God, and give him thanks, that thou wert born an English man, and not a French peasant, nor an Italian, nor German'.[4]

The same glowing patriotism which lauded England's wealth, was, of course, equally manifest in accounts of other spheres of national life subjected to scholarly appraisal. The uniqueness of the English common law and the liberties which it guaranteed to the subject were celebrated in a

[1] W.G. Hoskins, 'The rediscovery of England' (1965).
[2] F.J. Furnivall (ed.), *Harrison's description of England* (1877): cx, 66.
[3] F.J. Fisher (ed.), *The state of England Anno Dom. 1600 by Thomas Wilson* (1936): 10.
[4] Quoted in A. Macfarlane, *The origins of English individualism* (1978): 178–9.

burgeoning literature which adopted the lawyers' expository habit of tracing the advance of English freedom from precedent to precedent, underscoring what gradually became a familiar litany of historical reference points: the heritage of the freeborn Englishman.[5] Historical justifications of the legitimacy and peculiar identity of the Church of England, pioneered by John Bale and triumphantly brought off in John Foxe's *Acts and Monuments*, sought to demonstrate that the English were an elect nation, accorded a special place in the unfolding of the divine plan and a central role in the cosmic war of Christ and Antichrist.[6] By the time that Milton, along with not a few of his countrymen, detected God 'decreeing to begin some new and great period in His church, even to the reforming of Reformation itelf', it seemed no more than to be expected that in revealing himself to his servants he should begin 'as His manner is, first to His Englishmen'.[7]

Such early conceptions of a national identity linked to a particular reading of a national past and fuelling projections of national destiny, were not, of course, unique to the English. The Scots, as a covenanted nation could perceive 'a verrie near paralel' betwixt Israel and themselves as 'the only tuo suorne nations to the Lord', proclaiming 'now, O Scotland, God be thanked, thy name is in the Bible'.[8] Yet the peculiarly comprehensive nature of the English vision of national uniqueness – involving as it did notions of economic, social-structural, constitutional, legal, military and spiritual superiority, and extending as it did from the liberty, plenty and social opportunity enjoyed by the sturdy yeoman at home to the manifest destiny explored by English navigators abroad – left a particularly powerful legacy in the manner in which the English were to approach their national history for centuries to come. The sense of frustrated self-doubt occasioned by the relative disappointment of expectations experienced in the earlier seventeenth century, when some Englishmen perceived their liberties threatened, others feared a national apostasy and still others compared their people's achievements unfavourably with those of such rivals as the Dutch, was overcome by the very successes which thereafter seemed to confirm time and again their historical destiny. The English were an exceptional people. In their successful pursuit of wealth, power, liberty and Empire they were a precocious people. The ideological national costume which we have come to disparage as 'the whig interpretation of history' was tailored over the early modern centuries from the broadcloth

[5] For the origins of this tradition, see: J.G.A. Pocock, *The ancient constitution and the feudal law* (1957); C. Hill, 'The Norman yoke' in *Puritanism and revolution* (1958); J.P. Sommerville, *Politics and ideology in England, 1603–1640* (1986).

[6] W. Haller, *Foxe's book of martyrs and the elect-nation* (1963); F.J. Levy, *Tudor historical thought* (1967): chap. 3.

[7] J. Milton, *Areopagitica* (1644), in *Milton's prose writings* (1958): 177.

[8] T.C. Smout, *A history of the Scottish people, 1560–1830* (1972): 63.

of national self-esteem and the brocade of repeated success. And it was worn with sheer swank for more than a century.

The excesses of unreconstructed whiggery have long been discountenanced. The influence of the underlying assumptions and habits of mind from which it developed, however, can still be detected, albeit in transmuted form, in the historiography of early modern England. To be sure, the political and constitutional historians of the sixteenth and above all the seventeenth centuries have suffered an interpretative loss of confidence which in the view of some critics has exchanged teleological certainty for myopic confusion.[9] The old highroad to political liberty and constitutional monarchy has become an accident blackspot, a maze of diversions and contraflows. Yet if the senior branch of the historical profession now stumbles through the early modern period uncertain of whether it is heading towards British Liberty or a stable 'ancient regime', the junior branches of economic and social history seem far more certain of their direction. English political and constitutional history may have been marginalised, even devalued. But England as the best example in Europe of a low-pressure, fertility-dominated demographic regime, the seat of the 'agricultural revolution', the 'First Industrial Nation', the locus of the rule of law, the childbed of the birth of class and the cradle of the modern family still demands attention. In the spheres of economic and social history, England still matters. The conviction remains that there are great processes of universal significance to be explained, and their explanation necessarily involved a consideration of England's uniqueness and England's precocity.

To this extent a hint of the old bias of nationalistic historiography lingers on in the discussion of such deceptively 'neutral' issues as demographic growth, commercialisation, industrialisation, urbanisation and the transformation of social structure. Explanations tend to be narrowly anglocentric. The most familiar international comparisons tend to be introduced rather to sharpen appreciation of English uniqueness than to explore areas of shared experience. Thus, if much of north-western Europe shared Hajnal's 'European Marriage Pattern', England allegedly provides the most pronounced example of this vital demographic regulator.[10] So the English peasantry lost their vulnerability to famine two generations before

[9] For recent reappraisals of the Reformation, the 'Tudor revolution in government', the role of parliament in Elizabethan and early Stuart England and the continuing debate over the origins of the English Civil Wars, see: J.J. Scarisbrick, *The Reformation and the English people* (1984); C. Coleman & D. Starkey (eds.), *Revolution reassessed* (1986); G.R. Elton, 'Parliament' (1984); C. Russell 'Parliamentary history in perspective, 1604–29' (1976), and *Parliaments and English politics, 1621–1629* (1979); T.K. Rabb & D. Hirst, 'Revisionism revised: two perspectives on early Stuart parliamentary history' (1981); C. Hill, 'Parliament and people in seventeenth-century England (1981); M. Fulbrook, 'The English revolution and the revisionist revolt' (1982).

[10] P. Laslett, 'Characteristics of the Western family considered over time' (1977).

their Scottish and a good century or more before their European counterparts, saved by a combination of prudential demographic restraint, agricultural development and efficient social welfare.[11] If the Dutch showed the way to commercial supremacy, the English were close behind and were able to capitalise upon their advantages in the later seventeenth century to move ahead.[12] 'Proto-industrialisation' may have been a pan-European phenomenon, but it was different in England and England initiated the transformation to industrialisation proper.[13] If anything, the recent penchant for cross-cultural comparison, drawing upon social anthropology to place early modern England in a worldwide comparative perspective, has served to accentuate this tendency. Certainly the most prolific exponent of the genre has gone further towards an explicit and comprehensive reassertion of England's uniqueness and the complementary implication that it was England's uniqueness which bred English success. To Alan Macfarlane 'England has been inhabited since at least the thirteenth century by a people whose social, economic and legal system was in essence different not only from that of peoples in Asia and Eastern Europe, but also in all probability from the Celtic and Continental countries of the same period'. Given these alleged realities, 'it begins to become clear why England should have been precocious in its economic and social development in the eighteenth and nineteenth centuries'.[14]

The English historiographical tradition, then, was from its first foundations pervaded by notions of English exceptionalism and English precocity, a combination which both explained and celebrated English success and which implied English superiority. And the echoes of this cultural tradition can still be heard sounding around the economic and social history of early modern England. Muffled by the specialisation and compartmentalisation of academic history, they break upon the ear periodically when English historians attempt broader essays in interpretation. The persisting insularity and anglocentricity of English historiography rests comfortably upon the secure belief that in certain crucial areas of human endeavour England was, after all, first – a dazzling career of historical tape-breasting which most English historians still regard as having begun in earnest in the later sixteenth and seventeenth centuries.

[11] A.B. Appleby, *Famine in Tudor and Stuart England* (1978); P. Laslett, *The world we have lost further explored* (1983): chap. 6.

[12] J. de Vries, *The economy of Europe in an age of crisis 1600–1750* (1976): chap. 4; C.G.A. Clay, *Economic expansion and social change: England 1500–1700* (1984): vol. 2, chap. 9.

[13] For the debate over 'proto-industrialisation' see D.C. Coleman, 'Proto-industrialisation: A concept too many' (1983); R. Houston & K. Snell, 'Proto-industrialisation? Cottage industry, social change and industrial revolution'(1984); L.A. Clarkson, *Proto-industrialisation: the first phase of industrialisation?* (1985).

[14] Macfarlane (1978): 165, 201. For Macfarlane's further elaboration of his view of the unique characteristics of English society, see his *The justice and the mare's ale* (1981), and *Marriage and love in England* (1986).

The case of Scotland, however, appears somewhat different. England can be said to have enjoyed a single dominant historiographical tradition which has been only partially disturbed by historical revisionism. Scottish historiography, in contrast, appears to an outsider of limited knowledge to have at least two distinguishable (if sometimes overlapping) interpretative traditions. On the one hand there is what can be termed the tradition of Scottish exceptionalism – a stress upon the unique features of Scottish institutions, society and culture and the separateness of the Scottish experience. On the other hand there is what might be called the historiography of Scottish participation or incorporation – an emphasis upon the Scottish contribution to the making of modern Britain, the elaboration of a composite national history which involves, at least in part, a 'me too' endorsement of English prejudices, a Britishing of the English national myth.

This ambivalence or tension within Scottish historiography may perhaps have its origins in the ambivalence and internal tensions of the Scottish historical experience – and in particular the formative experiences of the early modern period. The period between the Scottish Reformation and the Union of 1707, was clearly of vital importance in the making of modern Scotland. It witnessed a strengthening of royal authority and the associated development of Scotland's distinctive legal institutions. It saw the establishment and spreading influence of the reformed Kirk, with all the implications which that great watershed had for the creation of the distinctive texture of Scottish culture; the genesis of the national educational system and the Scottish poor laws; the beginnings of the transformation of agriculture and rural society; the nascent phase of Scottish industrial development. And yet on the other hand, the same period witnessed Scotland's political marginalisation, the removal to London of the apex of the political and social order, and Scotland's eventual absorption as a junior partner in the larger political unit of the United Kingdom. Similarly, Scotland was increasingly incorporated into a larger economic and social system in which the centre of gravity lay far to the south. Whatever Scotland's particular achievements, they were increasingly overshadowed by, harnessed to, or subsumed within those of a bigger, richer, more powerful, more self-confident neighbour. Such an experience might well breed a complex and uncertain response in the subsequent contemplation of the national past.

Be that as it may, the distinctive, though not necessarily opposing, traditions of Scottish historiography can be said to have had quite profound consequences for the development of the economic and social history of early modern Scotland. The national feeling embodied in the exceptionalist tradition of Scottish historiography found its happiest expression in the history of the independent Kingdom of the Scots and in the history of those distinctively Scottish institutions – above all the Kirk, but also the legal and educational systems – the integrity which had been guaranteed at the Union of 1707. At the same time, however, this tradition should not be characterised as narrowly introspective, for it also involved the exploration of Scotland's independent relations with France, the Low Countries, Scandinavia and Ireland. In such subjects lay the surest reminder of the separate identity of a nation which, while it had been incorporated into a political, social, economic and cultural constellation dominated by England, had been neither conquered nor effaced. The participatory tradition, in contrast, was drawn naturally enough to the shared political history of the United Kingdom and, as interest in economic history developed, to the Scottish dimension of the emergence of industrial and imperial Britain. It really took off from the eighteenth century, and in particular from the later eighteenth century with the stirrings of the agricultural and industrial revolutions and the dawning of the age of reform. In neither case was the nature of the economy and society of early modern Scotland a matter of particular concern. The agenda of Scottish exceptionalism had been set before the emergence of economic and social history as a valued sub-discipline. If early modern Scotland had any part to play in the pre-conditioning of British commercial, agricultural, and industrial development, it went largely unremarked. For these processes were approached in a British context, and one in which the roots of economic and social change were largely assumed to lie outwith Scotland. Scotland participated in these transformations, to be sure, but Scotland's participation was not taken to be that of an initiator. It required description rather than explanation. Change was not generated within Scotland as such. Rather, Scotland was brought into, and came to make a signal contribution to, a set of historical developments which had their origins in England.

To this extent, the social and economic condition of early modern Scotland long suffered a dual neglect, falling between the two stools of Scottish historical preoccupation. It might engage the interest of the antiquarian and it proved fertile ground for the purveyors of the romantic and sentimental myths of the clan and the kailyard. But it was assumed not to matter greatly in the hierarchy of historical concern. Lack of concern meant lack of sustained investigation, and in the absence of evidence to the contrary the image of Scottish society in the early modern period became dominated by a stereotype which is only now breaking down. Among those few scholars who seriously addressed these issues prior to the late 1970s the dominant interpretative tone established was a distinctly negative variant of Scottish exceptionalism. Early modern Scotland was different all right; and the difference was held to lie in Scotland's poverty and backwardness; in the peripheral, archaic, largely static nature of Scotland's economy and society prior to the eighteenth century.

All these adjectives are relative and implicitly comparative – and the comparison generally held in mind was one with England (though Scotland did not escape denigratory comparison with other 'leading' European nations). Thus early modern Scotland was regarded as having got off to a poor start in that, as compared with England, France and the Netherlands, 'Scotland was distinctly and markedly exceptional in the static nature of her economic development during the fourteenth, fifteenth and sixteenth centuries'.[15] In the sixteenth and early seventeenth centuries Scotland was 'not only essentially a rural nation, but a nation whose rural economy was for the most part primitive', the setting for an agriculture which was 'static in technology and inefficient in organization'.[16] In all respects the Scottish economy was 'at best peripheral', and in 'an exceedingly backward state' as compared with England and other 'core' states of the European economy.[17] This economic backwardness was complemented by an extraordinary social archaism. In early modern Scotland feudalism held sway in a manner and to a degree long absent from England and scarcely paralleled in Europe.[18] It was a polarised rural world of landlords and peasants, there being no Scottish equivalent to the prosperous and relatively independent English yeomanry.[19] The system of land tenure was highly exploitative, insecure and peculiarly archaic (most notably in the institution of multiple tenancy which made each fermtoun a 'small collective farm').[20] Both rents and wages were commonly paid in kind.[21] This was a society in which the place of the individual was still defined by personal bonds of lordship, service and kinship (again in contrast to England).[22] And it needed to be so, for it was a chronically insecure world, weakly controlled from the centre, prone to feud and disorder, impoverished; lacking the peace, personal security and modest prosperity necessary for orderly economic and social development.[23] Moreover, about all this there was a certain quality of timelessness. The principal forces for change in early modern Scotland appear to have been the growing penetration of the authority of the state and the cultural aggression of a reformed kirk which, in the establishment of its dominance, forged an alliance with the lairds which gripped lowland Scottish society

[15] I.F. Grant, *The social and economic development of Scotland before 1603* (1930): 107.
[16] S.G.E. Lythe, 'The economy of Scotland under James VI and I' (1973): 59, 60.
[17] Lythe (1973): 72; C. Larner, *Enemies of God. The witch-hunt in Scotland* (1981): 46.
[18] Larner (1981): 44.
[19] R. Mitchison, *Life in Scotland* (1978): 67–8; I. Whyte, 'The emergence of the new estate structure' (1980): 117.
[20] Smout (1972): 137; Grant (1930): 247; Mitchison (1978): 18; Larner (1981): 48.
[21] Grant (1930): 202; Smout (1972): 125, 129.
[22] J. Wormald, *Court, kirk and community, Scotland, 1470–1625* (1981): 29–30; Mitchison (1978): 13–15.
[23] Grant (1930): 174, 187; S.G.E. Lythe, *The economy of Scotland in its European setting 1550–1625* (1960): 25, 247.

'as a vice', promoting a shift from a society 'in which the bonds on most men took the form of simple disorganized oppression to one of systematic, structured repression'.[24] For the rest, Scotland awaited the 'Age of Transformation' initiated towards the close of the seventeenth century, which within four generations was to bring Lowland Scotland more closely into line with its precocious southern neighbour. And as for the Highlands, they sheltered an 'alternative society' which was socially archaic and economically primitive even by the generous standards of the Lowlands. Not even the Kirk wrought much with the Highlanders.[25]

Such is the traditional stereotype – a characterisation of the economy and society of early modern Scotland which until recently had scarcely been challenged, let alone carefully revised. From the perspective of an English historian weaned in an historiographical tradition which emphasises gradual processes of economic and social development which had their roots deep in the Middle Ages and which gathered pace steadily from the sixteenth century, Scotland would indeed appear to have been different. Yet the picture sketched above remains in the final analysis unconvincing. We are surely dealing here less with a well-researched account of Scottish actualities than with a forceful but thinly supported argument which has long held sway largely because of its conformity to a particular set of historiographical preferences. What we seem to have in the stereotypical account of early modern Scotland's exceptionalism and relative backwardness is a set of assertions; assertions which might have plausibility in the context of certain culturally-conditioned expectations, but which in fact go much further than the available evidence justifies. For embedded within the very works which provide some of the sweeping interpretative judgements quoted above lies evidence of alternative dimensions of the economic and social experience of early modern Scotland. Such evidence, together with the results of more recent research, some of which is surveyed in this volume, suggests that while Scotland certainly had its distinctive social and economic characteristics, it also had features in common with England and other parts of north-western Europe which have been insufficiently considered. Nor was Scotland immune from most of the broader socio-economic trends of the sixteenth and seventeenth centuries.

For the sake of developing this point it is worth setting against the exceptionalist/backward model of early modern Scotland a review of those characteristics which Scotland appears, on the available evidence, to have shared with England. To start with so basic a unit as the household, the

[24] For the growing authority of central government, see Wormald (1981): chap. 9. For the impact of the reformed kirk, Wormald (1981): chap. 8; Mitchison (1978): 29–34 (which includes the passage quoted). Cf. Larner (1981): 53.

[25] Mitchison (1978): 56–60. Smout (1972): 310–21 is careful to avoid the suggestion that Highland society was timeless or unchanging, but argues that any change was sluggish, largely as a result of social and cultural factors.

Scots appear to have lived in small and structurally simple nuclear family households – much as did the English.[26] Their familial values and characteristic domestic relations seem to have had much in common with those prevalent in England – not least in the distinctly similar experiences of Scottish and English women.[27] If the English family system, as has been alleged, was 'advanced', then so was that of Scotland. Demographically, Scottish marital behaviour, like that of England, fell within the 'European Marriage Pattern', with a relatively high age at first marriage for women and a substantial proportion of adult women remaining unwed.[28] The geographical mobility of the Scottish population has a great deal in common with that observable in England.[29] If Scottish population history appears more dominated in aggregate by the restraining power of mortality than that of England, this may be partly an illusion fostered by the relative weakness of the evidence relating to fertility in early modern Scotland. But in any case English historical demographers are far from monolithic in their views of the relative importance of fertility and mortality in English population history prior to the eighteenth century.[30]

Again, there are some clear parallels in the English and the Scottish experience of socio-economic change in the early modern period; more than enough to render absurd the old assertion that Scotland existed in a condition of virtual social and economic stasis. Scotland, like England and much of Europe, experienced significant demographic growth and population pressure in the later sixteenth and early seventeenth centuries.[31] Scotland also shared, with England, the familiar European phenomena of price inflation and falling real wages.[32] As in England, pressure of numbers produced land hunger and efforts to expand the cultivated area.[33] It promoted urban growth and an enlarged market-dependent sector of the population.[34] The growing marketing opportunities of the age fostered an enhanced commercialisation of Scottish agriculture, observable from at least the late sixteenth century.[35] Rising rent demands from landlords

[26] See Introduction above, pp. 4, 21.

[27] Most of the points made by Houston in chapter 4, above, would apply equally well to England.

[28] See chap. 4 above. [29] See chap. 1 and 4 above.

[30] The stress on mortality fluctuations in the interpretation of population trends is very marked in M. Flinn, *Scottish population history* (1977) in contrast to E.A. Wrigley & R.S. Schofield, *The population history of England 1541–1871* (1981) in which the emphasis is placed on changes in nuptuality and fertility. Wrigley & Schofield, however, fully recognise the importance of mortality as an influence on English population trends before 1750, a point highlighted by Flinn in his review of their work, 'The population history of England, 1541–1871' (1982).

[31] Lythe (1960): 29; Mitchison (1978): 35–6; Wormald (1981): 166.

[32] Lythe (1960): 30, 110.

[33] R.A. Dodgshon, 'Medieval settlement and colonisation' (1980): 49, 53.

[34] See above chap. 3.

[35] A. Fenton, 'The traditional pastoral economy' (1980): 103–5; Whyte (1980): 128–30.

forced the primarily subsistence-oriented sector of the peasantry, who might otherwise have been insulated from inflation and indifferent to market trends, to increase production and to modify patterns of husbandry, either to meet their rents or for direct sale.[36] The seventeenth century witnessed the emergence in the most commercially penetrated areas of Scotland of larger, consolidated, single-tenant farms, the granting of securer written leases to tenants, greater direct market involvement by a growing body of substantial farmers and the adoption of improved farming techniques.[37] By the later seventeenth century, Scotland's 'feudal' agrarian society and mainly subsistence-oriented agriculture was firmly set along the road towards the 'highly capitalistic' agriculture of late eighteenth-century Scotland.[38]

Much of this has a familiar ring to historians of early modern England. And there is more. If Scotland, as we are repeatedly told, remained vulnerable to widespread famine for two generations longer than did England, it nonetheless benefited from an increased food supply and improved networks of international trade which meant that vulnerability to dearth was diminishing throughout the later seventeenth century. The famine of the 1690s was both an exceptional misfortune and the last such national disaster in Scottish history. Both France and Scandinavia retained their vulnerability long thereafter.[39] Moreover, the later sixteenth and seventeenth centuries saw growth in Scottish trade.[40] They saw also an expansion of Scottish industrial activity, and not only in the putting-out textile industry but in the precociously large-scale, highly capitalised and technically sophisticated mining industry.[41] By the later seventeenth century Scotland was also a relatively urbanised society by both English and European standards.[42] The towns sheltered the development from the later sixteenth century of a growing body of professional men which paralleled the emergence of the professions in England.[43] They fostered, by the early eighteenth century, an 'expansion of amenity' in living standards which (as in England) was most marked among prosperous townspeople

36 Lythe (1960): 114; Smout and Gibson, above pp. 81–3.

37 Whyte (1980): 125–8.

38 Whyte (1980): 117.

39 I. Whyte, *Agriculture and society in seventeenth-century Scotland* (1979): 12; M.W. Flinn, 'The stabilisation of mortality in pre-industrial western Europe' (1974): 301.

40 Lythe (1960): chaps. 4–8; B. Lenman, *An economic history of modern Scotland, 1660–1976* (1977): 36–42. The growth of Scottish trade was, however, faltering at the turn of the seventeenth and eighteenth centuries, and moved forward again strongly only from the mid-eighteenth century: Smout (1972): 225–7.

41 Lythe (1960): 37–49; J.U. Nef, *The rise of the British coal industry* (1932): vol. 1, 19, 43–51 and *passim*.

42 See above p. 5.

43 Wormald (1981): 153, 165; Mitchison (1978): 63. For two important recent contributions to the history of the professions in England, see C.W. Brooks, *Pettyfoggers and vipers of the commonwealth. The 'lower branch' of the legal profession in early modern England* (1986), and G. Holmes, *Augustan England, professions, state and society, 1680–1730* (1982).

and the class of lairds to which they were closely connected.[44] Meanwhile, a combination of religious and commercial incentives promoted a development of popular literacy in Scotland which was strikingly similar in its nature to the 'literacy process' in England.[45]

All this considered, the case for Scottish exceptionalism, backwardness and stasis seems fatally flawed (and so, incidentally, does any argument suggesting the uniqueness of the English response to the pressures and the opportunities of the sixteenth and seventeenth centuries). Where distinctions can and should be made between the Scottish and the English experience they surely lie not in the stark juxtaposition of backwardness and precocity, stasis and momentum, but in the subtler exploration of differences in the contexts, the pace, the precise chronology and the degree of change. In each of these spheres valid distinctions might indeed be drawn which would further appreciation of the genuinely unique features of the two national experiences of what were in many ways similar socio-economic trends.

Yet here too there are reasons to proceed cautiously, for it is a moot point how far we can speak meaningfully of a characteristic 'English' or 'Scottish' experience in this period. Early modern England was nothing if not diverse, both geographically and socially. One of the principal preoccupations of the last generation of English economic and social historians has been the exploration of the range of regional variation within its economic and social structure. Scotland was clearly no less diverse, to say the least. And yet so often the comparisons made introduce into the argument what are essentially textbook stereotypes; the one based upon the more 'advanced' features of the English situation, the other generalising from the more 'backward' aspects of the Scottish.

Such a procedure has something to recommend it if the object of the exercise is to celebrate national distinctiveness, to underscore the direction of change or to emphasise the extent of subsequent change. But it is not a recipe for more sophisticated historical understanding and balanced judgement, for the stereotypes obliterate time, place and social variation. We are told that sixteenth-century Scotland was an insecure and disorderly society prone to physical violence – a judgement which both undervalues the extent to which the Scottish crown had been able to mitigate the effects of feud and slaughter in the course of the sixteenth century and which fails to recognise the difficulties experienced by the Tudor monarchy in curbing

[44] Mitchison (1978): 76–81. For a discussion of rising consumer demand in England in the seventeenth century, see Clay (1984): vol. 2, 36–43. For a recent attempt to explore the sociology of the new 'consumerism', see L. Weatherill, 'Consumer behaviour and social status in England, 1660–1750' (1986).

[45] R. A. Houston, *Scottish literacy and the Scottish identity* (1985). Hereafter Houston (1985a).

habits of aristocratic violence.[46] We read that Scotland for long lacked a commercially-oriented rural middle class comparable to the English yeomanry. Yet the same was true of substantial areas of England, notably the pastoral uplands, fens and forests. The process of social differentiation in England was markedly uneven. If some areas had a substantial yeomanry and considerable numbers of landless wage labourers already in 1500, other areas saw such polarisation only in the seventeenth century or later.[47] Scotland was allegedly a society still dominated by bonds of lordship and kinship. The former assertion was certainly true of substantial areas of England also in the sixteenth century, and not only in the 'archaic' and 'backward' north.[48] The latter has been commonly applied to England also by historians generalising from the experience of the aristocracy and gentry. More recent research on the realities of kinship bonds among the common people has tended to stress their markedly 'optional' and variable quality – yet comparable work has not yet been undertaken for Scotland.[49] The proposition that Scottish society was less open to social mobility than that of England remains undemonstrated in either case. The advanced nature of English agriculture is yet another judgement based upon a national stereotype which needs heavy qualification by regional and social specificity. It is now argued that the sixteenth century saw surprisingly little enclosure in England, despite the fulminations of the pamphleteers. It was a highly localised phenomenon. For the greater part of open-field England the later seventeenth century was the principal period of change.[50] Again, the extent to which technical improvements in agriculture were taken up before the mid seventeenth century has been seriously questioned and a recent article has re-emphasised the enduring elements of 'backwardness' in the husbandry of many of England's small farmers.[51] Conversely, it has been argued of Scotland that multiple

46 J. Wormald, 'Bloodfeud, kindred and government in early modern Scotland' (1980); L. Stone, *The crisis of the aristocracy, 1558–1641* (1965): chap. 5.

47 The association of social structural variation with England's varied farming regions has become a commonplace of English agrarian history. See J. Thirsk (ed.), *The agrarian history of England and Wales Vol. 4: 1500–1640* (1967): chap. 1, and the same author's, 'Seventeenth-century agriculture and social change' (1970) and *England's agricultural regions and agrarian history, 1500–1750* (1987) for many examples. Particularly useful local studies bringing out the distinctive social structures of fielden, fen and forest areas are M. Spufford, *Contrasting communities* (1974); B. Sharp, *In contempt of all authority* (1982); K. Lindley, *Fenland riots and the English revolution* (1982).

48 R.B. Smith, *Land and politics in the England of Henry VIII* (1970); M.E. James, 'Change and continuity in the Tudor north' (1965); M.E. James, *Family, lineage and civil society* (1974); A. Hassell Smith, *County and court* (1974): chap. 2.

49 For surveys of recent work on English kinship, see K. Wrightson, *English society 1580–1680* (1982): 44–51, and R.A. Houlbrooke, *The English family, 1450–1700* (1984).

50 J.R. Wordie, 'The chronology of English enclosure, 1500–1914' (1983).

51 R.B. Outhwaite, 'Progress and backwardness in English agriculture, 1500–1650' (1986). For the most recent survey of the debate over improvement and 'agricultural revolution', see Thirsk (1987).

tenancy was neither so widespread nor so dominant as was once thought: that the practice of runrig reallocation and its gradual disappearance is probably a myth; that infield/outfield cultivation, far from being an archaic anachronism, was an innovation of the fifteenth and sixteenth centuries, and a form of improvement.[52] In the sixteenth and early seventeenth centuries Scottish agriculture had its advanced areas too: in the Merse, the Lothians and on Tayside.[53] The general picture of the backwardness of Scottish agriculture has been attributed in part at least to the penchant of eighteenth-century observers for noting archaic survivals.[54] And as Dr Whyte points out there was little that a seventeenth-century Scottish traveller would find unfamiliar in the agriculture of northern England.[55]

It would be tedious to continue in this vein. The point is that there were many Englands and many Scotlands in the early modern period. In both kingdoms the processes of economic and social change were singularly uneven in their geographical and social impact and in the chronology of their advance. This being so, we might do well, in comparing the economic and social development of early modern England and Scotland, to place less reliance on the generalities of convenient national stereotypes and to pay more attention to those regional, social, and chronological specifics which might enable us to undertake comparisons which are appropriate, meaningful and mutually illuminating.

The potentialities of such comparisons have been demonstrated more than once in recent years, and it is not without significance that they have been demonstrated primarily by Scottish historians. To take only three examples: T.M. Devine has explored the contrasting responses of the rural populations of southern England, Lowland Scotland and the Highlands to agrarian change in the eighteenth and early nineteenth centuries in a manner which illuminates both the distinctiveness of regional experience and the nature of an overall process of change.[56] Christina Larner's work on witchcraft in Scotland and England has demonstrated similarities which explode the parochialism of current interpretations of the rise of witchcraft prosecutions in England, and differences which underline the real importance of national institutions in the shaping of witchcraft persecution, while at the same time adding new issues to the agenda of historians of this phenomenon in both countries.[57] Rab Houston, by means of disciplined comparison of literacy levels in both Scotland and northern England has laid bare the inadequacies of the celebratory Scottish historiography of popular education, rescued the distinctive experience of northern

[52] R.A. Dodgshon, 'The origins of traditional field systems' (1980): 70–1, 73–5, 84–5, 86ff; Whyte (1980): 121–2.

[53] Lythe (1960): 3–4. [54] Whyte (1979): 3ff. [55] Whyte (1979): 21.

[56] T.M. Devine, 'Social stability and agrarian change in the eastern lowlands of Scotland, 1810–1840' (1978), and chap. 5 above.

[57] Larner (1981) and *Witchcraft and religion* (1984).

England from the condescension of English historians and cogently readdressed the entire problem of the nature of the 'literary process' in early modern Europe.[58]

Such exercises are the more telling and the more imaginatively enriching precisely because Scotland and England, for all their national and regional differentiation were involved in a kinship and a neighbourhood, a tangled historical interrelationship which renders their comparison peculiarly appropriate and revealing. To be sure, that relationship was all too frequently asymmetrical. Its asymmetry is reflected in the historiographical traditions which have been touched upon in this essay. And of course it persists. Historians of early modern England, however agonising their reflections on the current loss of direction within their subject, remain content in the main to ignore the Scottish dimension of the British experience. In his recent eloquent appeal to British historians Dr Cannadine was able to give an account of those 'seminal books on British history which between them established the identity and image of the subject' in the years after 1945 – most of them by early modernists – without apparently recognising that he was describing works almost exclusively concerned with English history and an English historical paradigm.[59] We have much to learn from those of the current generation of Scottish historians who have sought to overcome a marginalisation of their national past too readily conceded by some of their predecessors, by adopting a consciously comparative strategy of historical research and interpretation.

In the reassessment of British history currently facing us all such a strategy has much to recommend it. It can help both to expose and to overcome the shortcomings of the traditional historiographies of the 'kindred adjoining kingdoms'. For if the formerly dominant English historiography is in crisis, that crisis provides a constructive opportunity to develop a British history which has at its very heart the vital critical purchase provided by both awareness of national and provincial diversity and consciousness of the common, albeit varied, experience of shared processes of change. It has been argued, and with some justice, that the current fretful, uncertain and faltering state of British history reflects not only government policy and the outcome of professional shortcomings but also the state of Britain itself. 'This country has a weaker sense of national identity now than at any time this century: its self-esteem is battered and eroded; its belief in its own unique good fortune has disappeared; . . . and there is more real disagreement in public life about great issues than at any time since the First World War.' And yet, ironically, 'we live in a nation with a popular appetite for the past which may, indeed, be distorted, but which is nevertheless, insatiable'. The course recommended to British

58 Houston (1985a) and 'Literacy and society in the west, 1500–1850' (1983).
59 D. Cannadine, 'British history: past, present – and future?' (1987): 171–2.

historians is 'that we should try to put Humpty Dumpty together again ... that we should deliberately set out to regain our position as public teachers who deserve both public attention and public funding, which we have too readily surrendered'.[60] Perhaps so. But there would be little to be gained if that aspiration turned out to mean the patching together of a refurbished English myth. The opportunity exists rather to bring into the mainstream of British culture an awareness of both the pluralism and the shared identity of the British past – a past which, once shorn of the distorting excesses of English national feeling, can be the better appreciated as a complex collective experience of considerable consequence not only in the shaping of the curious cultural constellation of British identity but also in the making of the modern world.

[60] Cannadine (1987): 186, 187, 188.

BIBLIOGRAPHY OF PRINTED SOURCES AND SECONDARY WORKS

Abrams, P. & Wrigley, E.A. (eds.), 1978. *Towns in societies*. Cambridge.

Accounts of the Lord High Treasurer of Scotland.

Acts of the Parliament of Scotland. 12 vols. 1814–75. London.

Adams, I.H., 1967. 'Division of commonty in Scotland'. (Unpublished Ph.D. thesis, Edinburgh University.)

1978. *The making of urban Scotland.* Montreal.

1980. 'The agents of agricultural change'. In: Parry & Slater (eds.), 1980.

Adams, J., 1690. *Index Villaris*. London.

Adamson, D. (ed.), 1981. *West Lothian hearth tax.* 1691. Edinburgh.

Alexander, W., 1859. *The practice of the Commissary Courts in Scotland.* Edinburgh.

Alston, P.L., 1969. *Education and the state in tsarist Russia.* Stanford.

Anderson, J., 1794. *General view of the agriculture of the country of Aberdeen* . . . appendix. Edinburgh.

Anon., 1834–5. 'On the hiring markets in the counties of Northumberland, Berwick, and Roxburgh'. *Quarterly Journal of Agriculture*, 5: 378–86.

Anon., 1898. 'Mr Gross on Scottish guilds'. *Scottish Review*. 32: 61–81.

Anton, A.E., 1958. 'Parent and child'. In: *An introduction to Scottish legal history*, 1958.

Appleby, A.B., 1978. *Famine in Tudor and Stuart England.* Liverpool.

Ardener, S., 1978. 'Introduction: the nature of women in society'. In: Ardener, S. (ed.), *Defining females. The nature of women in society*. London.

Armet, H. (ed.), 1962. *Extracts from the records of the burgh of Edinburgh 1689–1701.* Edinburgh.

Arnot, H., 1779. *The history of Edinburgh.* Edinburgh.

Ashton, T.S., 1977. *The industrial revolution, 1760–1830.* Oxford.

Ashton, T.S. & Sykes, J., 1964. *The coal industry of the eighteenth century.* Manchester.

Bain, A., 1965. *Education in Stirlingshire from the Reformation to 1872.* London.

Bain, E., 1887. *Merchant and craft guilds: a history of the Aberdeen incorporated trades.* Aberdeen.

Balandier, G., 1972. *Political anthropology*. Harmondsworth.

Bannerman, J., 1977. 'The Lordship of the Isles'. In: Brown (ed.), 1977.

1983. 'Literacy in the Highlands'. In: Cowan & Shaw (eds.), 1983.

Barrow, G.W.S., 1974. *The Scottish tradition.* Edinburgh.

1981. *Kingship and unity: Scotland, 1000–1306.* London.

Bateman, J., 1971. *The great landowners of Great Britain and Ireland.* New York reprint of 4th edition of 1883.

Baugh, D.A., 1983. 'Poverty, protestantism and political economy: English attitudes towards the poor'. In: Baxter, S.B. (ed.), *England's rise to greatness*. Berkeley.

Beale, J.M., 1953. 'A history of the burgh and parochial schools of Fife from the Reformation to 1872'. (Unpublished Ph.D. thesis, Edinburgh University.)

Beckett, J.C., 1986. 'Introduction: eighteenth-century Ireland'. In: Moody & Vaughan (eds.), 1986.

Beier, A.L., 1974. 'Vagrants and the social order in Elizabethan England'. *Past and Present*, 64: 3–29.

1985. *Masterless men: the vagrancy problem in England 1560–1640*. London.

Bercé, Y-M, 1979. 'La mobilité sociale, argument de révolte'. *XVIIe Siècle*, 31: 61–72.

Berg, M., 1985. *The age of manufactures, 1700–1820*. London.

Berger, P., 1978. 'Rural charity in late seventeenth-century France: the Pontchartrain case'. *French Historical Studies*, 10: 393–415.

Beveridge, C., 1982. 'Childhood and society in eighteenth-century Scotland'. In: Dwyer, J., Mason, R.A. & Murdoch, A. (eds.), 1982. *New perspectives on the politics and culture of early modern Scotland*. Edinburgh.

Black, J.B., 1959. *The reign of Elizabeth, 1558–1603*. Oxford.

Black, J.L., 1979. *Citizens for the fatherland. Education, educators and pedagogical ideals in eighteenth-century Russia*. New York.

Blanchard, I., 1986. 'The continental European cattle trade, 1400–1600'. *Economic History Review*, 2nd series, 39: 427–60.

Bloch, M., 1930. 'La Lutte pour l'individualisme agraire dans la France du XVIIIe siècle'. *Annales E.S.C.*, 2: 336–49.

Blok, A., 1972. 'The peasant and the brigand: social banditry reconsidered'. *Comparative Studies in Society and History*, 14: 494–503.

Blum, J., 1978. *The end of the old order in rural Europe*. New Jersey.

Bongaarts, J., 1975. 'Why high birth rates are so low'. *Population and Development Review*, 1: 289–96.

Borde, A., 1979. *The fyrst boke of the introduction of knowledge*. Salzburg edition.

Borsay, P., 1977. 'The English urban renaissance: the development of provincial urban culture, c.1680–c.1760'. *Social History*, 5: 581–603.

Bourde, A.J., 1953. *The influence of England on the French agronomes*, 1750–1789. Cambridge.

Brackenridge, R.D., 1969. 'The enforcement of Sunday observance in post-Revolution Scotland, 1689–1733'. *Records of the Scottish Church History Society*, 17: 33–45.

Braudel, F., 1972. *The Mediterranean and the Mediterranean world in the age of Philip II*. London.

1973. *Capitalism and material life, 1400–1800*. London.

Brodsky, V., 1981. 'Single women in the London marriage market: age, status and mobility, 1598–1619'. In: Outhwaite (ed.), 1981.

Brooks, C.W., 1986. *Pettyfoggers and vipers of the commonwealth. The 'lower branch' of the legal profession in early modern England*. Cambridge.

Brown, E.H., Phelps & Hopkins, S.V., 1962. 'Seven centuries of the prices of consumables compared with builders' wage rates'. In: Carus-Wilson (ed.), 1962.

1981. *A perspective of prices and wages*. London.

Brown, J.J., 1985. 'The social, political and economic influences of the Edinburgh merchant elite, 1600–38'. (Unpublished Ph.D. thesis, Edinburgh University.)
1987. 'Merchant princes and mercantile investment in early seventeenth-century Scotland'. In: Lynch (ed.), 1987.

Brown, J.M. (ed.), 1977. *Scottish society in the fifteenth century*. London.

Brown, K.M., 1987. 'Burghs, lords and feuds in Jacobean Scotland'. In: Lynch (ed.), 1987.

Brown, P.H. (ed.), 1891. *Early travellers in Scotland*. Edinburgh.
1893. *Scotland before 1700*. Edinburgh.
1915. *Register of the privy council of Scotland*, VII. Edinburgh.

Buchan, D., 1972. *The ballad and the folk*. London.

Bukdahl, J., 1959. *Scandinavia past and present*. Copenhagen.

Bumsted, J.M., 1982. *The people's clearance: Highland emigration to British North America, 1770–1815*. Edinburgh.

Burke, P., 1978. *Popular culture in early modern Europe*. London.

Burns, T. & Saul, S.B. (eds.), 1967. *Social theory and economic change*. London.

Byres, T.J., 1976. 'Scottish peasants and their song'. *Journal of Peasant Studies*, 3: 236–51.

Cage, R.A., 1981. *The Scottish poor law, 1745–1845*. Edinburgh.

Caledonian Mercury.

Calendar of state papers, colonial series, America and the West Indies, 1661–1738. 38 vols., 1880–1969. London.

Calendar of the state papers relating to Scotland. 1509–1603. 1858–1969. Edinburgh and London.

Callander, R., 1986. 'The pattern of landownership in Aberdeenshire in the seventeenth and eighteenth centuries'. In: Stevenson (ed.), 1986.

Cameron, J. (ed.), 1949. *The justiciary records of Argyll and the Isles, 1664–1705*. vol. 1. Edinburgh.

Cameron, J.K., 1986. 'Some continental visitors to Scotland in the late sixteenth and early seventeenth centuries'. In: Smout (ed.), 1986.

Camic, C., 1985. *Experience and enlightenment. Socialization for cultural change in eighteenth-century Scotland*. Edinburgh.

Campbell, A.B., 1979. *The Lanarkshire miners. A social history of their trade unions, 1775–1974*. Edinburgh.

Campbell, J.K., *Honour, family and patronage*. Oxford.

Campbell, J.L., 1984. *Highland songs of the Forty-Five*. Edinburgh.

Campbell, R.H., 1977. 'The Scottish improvers and the course of agrarian change in the eighteenth century'. In: Cullen & Smout (eds.), 1977.
1983. 'The influence of religion on economic growth in Scotland in the eighteenth century'. In: Devine & Dickson (eds.), 1983.

Cannadine, D., 1987. 'British history: past, present – and future?' *Past and Present*, 116: 169–91.

Carpenter, S.D.M., 1977. 'Patterns of recruitment of the Highland regiments'. (Unpublished M.Litt. thesis, St Andrews University.)

Carter, I., 1973. 'Marriage patterns and social sectors in Scotland before the eighteenth century'. *Scottish Studies*, 17: 51–60.
1979. *Farm life in north-east Scotland, 1840–1914*. Edinburgh.

1981. 'The changing image of the peasant in Scottish history and literature, 1745–1979'. In: Samuel (ed.), 1981.

Carus-Wilson, E.M. (ed.), 1962. *Essays in economic history, vol. 2.* London.

Casey, J., 1979. *The kingdom of Valencia in the seventeenth century.* Cambridge.

Cavendish, A.R.M., 1928. *An Reisimeid Chataich: the 93rd Sutherland Highlanders.* London.

Chambers, W. (ed.), 1872. *Charters and documents . . . of Peebles, 1165–1710.* Edinburgh.

Charters, writs and public documents . . of Dundee, 1292–1800. Scottish Burgh Record Society. Dundee.

Chaytor, M., 1980. 'Household and kinship: Ryton'. *History Workshop Journal,* 10: 5–60.

Chitnis, A.C., 1976. *The Scottish enlightenment: a social history.* London.

Christensen, A.E., 1960. 'The development of large-scale farming in Denmark, 1525–1744'. *Scandinavian Economic History Review,* 8: 180–6.

Christie, I.R.. (ed.), 1971. *Correspondence of Jeremy Bentham.* vol. 3. London.

Clark, A., 1919. *The working life of women in the seventeenth century.* London.

1972. 'The migrant in Kentish towns, 1580–1640'. In: Clark & Slack (eds.), 1972.

Clarke, P., 1976. 'The ownership of books in England, 1560–1640: the example of some Kentish townsfolk'. In: Stone (ed.), 1976.

1979. 'Migration in England during the late seventeenth and early eighteenth centuries'. *Past and Present,* 83: 57–90.

(ed.), 1981. *Country towns in pre-industrial England.* Leicester.

Clark, P. & Slack, P. (eds.), 1972. *Crisis and order in English towns 1500–1700.* London.

1976. *English towns in transition. 1500–1700.* Oxford.

Clarkson, L.A., 1978. 'An anatomy of an Irish town: the economy of Armagh, 1770'. *Irish Economic and Social History,* 5: 27–45.

1980. 'The writing of Irish economic and social history since 1968'. *Economic History Review,* 2nd series, 33: 100–11.

1985. *Proto-industrialisation: the first phase of industrialisation?* London.

Clay, C.G.A., 1984. *Economic expansion and social change: England, 1500–1700,* 2 vols. Cambridge.

Clive, J., 1970. 'The social background of the Scottish Renaissance'. In: Phillipson & Mitchison (eds.), 1970.

Cobbet, W., 1930. *Rural rides in the southern, western and eastern counties . . .* London edition.

Cochran, L.E., 1985. *Scottish trade with Ireland in the eighteenth century.* Edinburgh.

Coleman, C. & Starkey, D., 1986. *Revolution reassessed: revisions in the history of Tudor government and administration.* Oxford.

Coleman, D.C., 1983. 'Proto-industrialisation: a concept too many?'. *Economic History Review,* 2nd series, 36: 435–48.

Collini, S., 1984. 'J.S. Mill on the subjection of women'. *History Today,* 34: 34–9.

Collins, E.J.T., 1976. 'Migrant labour in British agriculture in the nineteenth century'. *Economic History Review,* 2nd series, 39: 38–59.

Confino, M., 1969. *Systèmes agraires et progrès agricole.* Paris.

Constant, J-M., 1979. 'La Mobilité sociale dans une province de gentilshommes et de paysannes: la Beauce'. *XVIIe Siècle*, 31: 7–20.
Cormack, A.A., 1923. *Poor relief in Scotland.* Aberdeen.
Cowan, E.J., 1980. 'Calvinism and the survival of folk'. In: Cowan, E.J. (ed.), 1980. *The people's past.* Edinburgh.
Cowan, I.B., 1978. *Regional aspects of the Scottish Reformation.* London.
Cowan, I.B. & Shaw, D. (eds.), 1983. *The Renaissance and Reformation in Scotland.* Edinburgh.
Craig, D., 1961. *Scottish literature and the Scottish people, 1680–1830.* London.
Craigie, W.A. (ed.), 1923. *The Asloan manuscript.* Edinburgh.
Cregeen, E. (ed.), 1964. *Argyll estate instructions, 1771–1805.* Edinburgh.
1969. 'Tacksmen and their successors. A study of tenurial re-organisation in Mull, Morvern and Tiree in the early eighteenth century'. *Scottish Studies*, 13: 93–144.
1970. 'The changing role of the house of Argyll in the Scottish Highlands'. In: Phillipson & Mitchison (eds.), 1970.
1979. 'Tradition and change in the west Highlands of Scotland: a case study'. In: Dyrvik, Mykland & Oldervoll (eds.), 1979.
Cullen, L.M., 1975. 'Population trends in seventeenth-century Ireland'. *The Economic and Social Review*, 6: 149–65.
1977. 'Merchant communities overseas, the navigation acts and Irish and Scottish responses'. In: Cullen & Smout (eds.), 1977.
1980. 'The Irish merchant communities of Bordeaux, La Rochelle and Cognac in the eighteenth century'. In: Butel, P. & Cullen, L.M. (eds.), 1980. *Négoce et industrie en France et en Irlande aux XVIIIe et XIXe siècles.* Paris.
1981. *The emergence of modern Ireland 1600–1900.* London.
1983. 'Incomes, social classes and economic growth in Ireland and Scotland, 1600–1900'. In: Devine & Dickson (eds.), 1983.
1986a. 'Britain under Westminster'. In: Smith, L.M. (ed.), 1986. *The making of Britain.* London.
1986b. 'The Dublin merchant community in the eighteenth century'. In: Butel, P. & Cullen, L.M., 1986. *Cities and merchants: French and Irish perspectives in urban development, 1500–1900.* Dublin.
Cullen, L.M. & Smout, T.C. (eds.), 1977. *Comparative aspects of Scottish and Irish economic and social history. 1600–1900.* Edinburgh.
Cullen, L.M., Gibson, A. & Smout, T.C., 1987. 'Wages and comparative development in Ireland and Scotland, 1565–1780'. In: Mitchison & Roebuck (eds.), 1987.
Cunningham, A., 1932. *The loyal clans.* Cambridge.
Daiches, D., Jones, P. & Jones, J. (eds.), 1986. *A hotbed of genius. The Scottish enlightenment, 1730–1790.* Edinburgh.
Davidoff, L. & Hall, C., 1983. 'The architecture of public and private life: English middle-class society in a provincial town, 1780–1850'. In: Fraser, D. & Sutcliffe, A. (eds.), 1983. *The pursuit of urban history.* London.
Davies, N.Z., 1975. *Society and culture in early modern France.* London.
1982. 'Women in the crafts in sixteenth-century Lyon'. *Feminist Studies*, 8: 47–80.
Davies, R.R., 1978. *Lordship and society in the march of Wales, 1282–1400.* Oxford.

Davies, S.J., 1980. 'The courts and the Scottish legal system, 1600–1747: the case of Stirlingshire'. In: Gatrell, Lenman & Parker (eds.), 1980.
De Vries, J., 1976. *The economy of Europe in an age of crisis, 1600–1750*. Cambridge.
1984. *European urbanisation, 1500–1800*. London.
Deane, P., 1965. *The first industrial revolution*. London.
Defoe, D., 1978. *A tour through the whole island of Great Britain*, ed. P. Rogers. Harmondsworth.
Degler, C.N., 1975. *Is there a history of women?* Oxford.
Desbrisay, G., 1986. '"Menacing their persons and exacting on their purses": the Aberdeen justice court, 1657–1700'. In: Stevenson (ed.), 1986.
Devine, T.M., 1975. *The tobacco lords*. Edinburgh.
1976. 'The Cromwellian Union and the Scottish burghs: the case of Aberdeen and Glasgow'. In: Butt, J. (ed.), 1976. *Scottish themes*. Edinburgh.
1978. 'Social stability and agrarian change in the eastern Lowlands of Scotland, 1810–1840'. *Social History*. 3: 331–46.
1979a. 'Social stability in the eastern Lowlands of Scotland during the agricultural revolution, 1780–1840'. In: Devine (ed.), 1979b.
(ed.), 1979b. *Lairds and improvement in the Scotland of the Enlightenment*. Glasgow.
1979c. 'Temporary migration and the Scottish Highlands in the nineteenth century'. *Economic History Review*. 32: 344–59.
1979d. 'The demand for agricultural labour in East Lothian'. *Transactions of the East Lothian Antiquarian and Natural History Society*, 16: 119–61.
1981. 'Farm servants and labour in East Lothian after the Napoleonic wars'. *Journal of the Scottish Labour History Society*, 15: 11–23.
1983a. 'The merchant class of the larger Scottish towns in the seventeenth and eighteenth centuries'. In: Gordon & Dicks (eds.), 1983.
1983b. 'Highland migration to Lowland Scotland, 1760–1860'. *Scottish Historical Review*, 72: 137–49.
1983c. 'The social composition of the business class in the larger Scottish towns, 1680–1740'. In: Devine & Dickson (eds.), 1983.
1984a. 'Scottish farm service in the agricultural revolution'. In: Devine (ed.), 1984b.
(ed.), 1984b. *Farm servants and labour in Lowland Scotland, 1770–1914*. Edinburgh.
1984c. 'Women workers, 1850–1914'. In: Devine (ed.), 1984b.
1985. 'The union of 1707 and Scottish development'. *Scottish Economic and Social History*, 5: 23–40.
1987. 'Stability and unrest in rural Scotland and Ireland, 1760–1840'. In: Mitchison & Roebuck (eds.), 1987.
Devine, T.M. & Dickson, D. (eds.), 1983. *Ireland and Scotland, 1600–1850. Parallels and contrasts in economic and social development*. Edinburgh.
Devine, T.M. & Mitchison, R. (eds.), 1988. *Scottish society. 1750–1830*. Edinburgh.
Dickson, A. & Speirs, W., 1980. 'Changes in class structure in Paisley, 1750–1845'. *Scottish Historical Review*, 59: 55–62.
Dickson, W.K. (ed.), 1939. 'Memories of Ayrshire about 1780 by the Reverend John Mitchell'. *Scottish History Society Miscellany*, 3rd series, vol. 6. Edinburgh.
Di Folco, J.A., 1975. 'Aspects of seventeenth-century social life in central and north Fife'. (Unpublished Ph.D. thesis, St Andrews University.)

1977. 'Discipline and welfare in the mid-seventeenth-century Scots parish'. *Records of the Scottish Church History Society*, 14: 169–83.
1979. 'The Hopes of Craighall and land investment in the seventeenth century'. In: Devine (ed.), 1979b.
Dodd, W., 1972. 'Ayr: a study of urban growth'. *Ayrshire Archaeological and Natural History Society Collections*. 10: 302–82.
Dodgshon, R.A., 1972. 'The removal of runrig in Roxburghshire and Berwickshire, 1680–1766'. *Scottish Studies*, 16: 121–7.
1976. 'The economics of sheep farming in the Southern Uplands during the Age of Improvement, 1750–1833'. *Economic History Review*, 2nd series, 29: 551–69.
1980a. 'Medieval settlement and colonisation'. In: Parry & Slater (eds.), 1980.
1980b. 'The origins of traditional field systems'. In: Parry & Slater (eds.), 1980.
1981. *Land and society in early Scotland*. Oxford.
1983. 'Agricultural change and its social consequences in the Southern Uplands of Scotland, 1660–1780'. In: Devine & Dickson (eds.), 1983.
1985. 'Symbolic classification and the development of early Celtic landscape'. *Cosmos*, 1: 61–83.
1987. 'West-Highland chiefdoms, 1500–1745: a study in redistributive exchange'. In: Mitchison & Roebuck (eds.), 1988.
Dodgshon, R.A. & Butlin, R.A. (eds.), 1978. *An historical geography of England and Wales*. London.
Donaldson, G., 1965. *Scotland: James V to James VII*. Edinburgh.
1966. *The Scots overseas*. Edinburgh.
1974. *Scotland: the shaping of a nation*. Newton Abbot.
Donnachie, I., 1979. *A history of the brewing industry in Scotland*. Edinburgh.
1986. 'Economy and society in the seventeenth century in the Highlands'. In: *The seventeenth century in the Highlands*.
Donnelly, T., 1981. 'The economic activities of the Aberdeen merchant guild, 1750–1799'. *Scottish Economic and Social History*, 1: 25–41.
Donovan, R.K., 1979. 'Voices of distrust: the expression of anti-catholic feeling in Scotland, 1778–1781'. *Innes Review*. 30: 62–76.
Douglas, F., 1782. *A general description of the east coast of Scotland from Edinburgh to Cullen*. Paisley.
Dovring, F., 1965. 'The transformation of European agriculture'. In: *Cambridge economic history of Europe*.
Doyle, W., 1978. *The old European order, 1660–1800*. Oxford.
Drummond, J.C. & Wilbraham, A., 1939. *The Englishman's food: a history of five centuries of English diet*. London.
Duby, G., 1977. *The chivalrous society*. London.
Duckham, B.F., 1969. 'Serfdom in eighteenth-century Scotland'. *History*, 54: 178–97.
1970. *A history of the Scottish coal industry. 1700–1815*. Newton Abbot.
Duffy, P.J., 1981. 'The territorial organisation of Gaelic landownership and its transformation in county Monoghan, 1591–1640'. *Irish Geography*, 14: 1–26.
Duncan, A.A.M., 1975. *Scotland. The making of the kingdom*. Edinburgh.
Duncan, J.F., 1919. 'Scottish farm labour'. *Scottish Journal of Agriculture*. 2: 498–507.

Duplessis, R.S. & Howell, M.C., 1982. 'Reconsidering the early modern economy: the cases of Leiden and Lille'. *Past and Present*, 94: 49–84.

Durie, A.J., 1979. *The Scottish linen industry in the eighteenth century*. Edinburgh.

Durkacz, V.E., 1983. *The decline of the Celtic languages*. Edinburgh.

Durkan, J., 1959. 'Education in the century of the Reformation'. *Innes Review*, 10: 67–90.

Dyer, A., 1973. *The city of Worcester in the sixteenth century*. Leicester.

1979. 'Growth and decay in English towns'. *Urban History Yearbook*. 59–70.

Dyrvik, S., *et al.*, 1979a. *Norsk Økonomisk Historie, 1500–1970*. Bergen.

1979b. 'The social structure of Norway and Denmark'. In: Dyrvik, Mykland & Oldervoll (eds.), 1979.

Dyrvik, S., Mykland, K. & Oldervoll, J. (eds.), *The satellite state in the 17th and 18th centuries*. Bergen.

Eccles, A., 1982. *Obstetrics and gynaecology in Tudor and Stuart England*. London.

Ecclesiastical Records. Selections from the minutes of the presbyteries of St Andrews and Cupar, 1641–1698. Edinburgh. 1837.

Ekholm, K., 1977. 'External exchange and the transformation of central African societies'. In: Friedman, J. & Rowlands, M.W. (eds.), *The evolution of social systems*. London.

1981. 'On the structure and dynamics of global systems'. *Dialectical Anthropology*, 5: 155–66.

Elton, G.R., 1984. 'Parliament'. In: Haigh, C. (ed.), 1984. *The reign of Elizabeth I*. London.

Engels, F., 1972. *The origins of the family, private property, and the state*. London.

Evans, R.J., 1980. 'Women's history: the limits of reclamation'. *Social History*, 5: 273–81.

The exchequer rolls of Scotland, 1264–1600, 23 vols. 1878–1908. Edinburgh.

Extracts from the council register of the burgh of Aberdeen. 1398–1570, 1844–8. Aberdeen.

Extracts from the records of the burgh of Edinburgh, AD1403–1528, 1869. Edinburgh.

Family expenditure survey: report for 1984 giving the results for the United Kingdom. 1986. London.

Feenstra, R., 1986. 'Scottish–Dutch legal relations in the seventeenth and eighteenth centuries'. In: Smout (ed.), 1986.

Fenton, A., 1974. 'Scottish agriculture and the Union: an example of indigenous development'. In: Rae (ed.), 1974.

1976. *Scottish country life*. Edinburgh.

(ed.), 1977. *Food in perspective: proceedings of the third international conference on ethnological food research*. Edinburgh.

1978. *The northern isles: Orkney and Shetland*. Edinburgh.

1980. 'The traditional pastoral economy'. In: Parry & Slater (eds.), 1980.

Ferguson, C.M.F., 1981. 'Law and order on the Anglo–Scottish border, 1603–1707'. (Unpublished Ph.D. thesis, St Andrews University.)

Ferguson, J. (ed.), 1899. *Paper illustrating the history of the Scots brigade in the service of the United Provinces*. Edinburgh.

Ferguson, J.A., 1982. 'A comparative study of urban society in Edinburgh, Dublin and London in the late seventeenth century'. (Unpublished Ph.D. thesis, St Andrews University.)

Ferguson, W., 1969. *Scotland, 1689 to the present.* Edinburgh.
1972. 'The problems of the established church in the West Highlands and Islands in the eighteenth century'. *Records of the Scottish Church History Society*, 17: 15–32.
1984. 'The electoral system in the Scottish counties before 1832'. In: Sellar, D. (ed.), 1984. *Stair society miscellany*. vol. 2. Edinburgh.
Fergusson, J., 1951. *Argyll and the Forty-Five.* London.
Finlay, R.A.P., 1981. *Population and metropolis: the demography of London, 1580–1650.* Cambridge.
Firth, C.H., (ed.), 1899. *Scotland and the Protectorate.* Edinburgh.
Fischer, T.A., 1902. *The Scots in Germany.* Edinburgh.
1907. *The Scots in Sweden.* Edinburgh.
Fisher, F.J. (ed.), 1936. *The state of England anno dom. 1600 by Thomas Wilson.* Camden Miscellany. Camden Society vol. 16. London.
Fleming, D.H. (ed.), 1889. *Register of the minister, elders and deacons of the Christian congregation of St Andrews*, vol. 1, 1559–82. Edinburgh.
1890. *Register of the minister, elders and deacons of the Christian congregation of St Andrews*, vol. 2, 1582–1600. Edinburgh.
Flinn, M.W., 1967. 'Social theory and the industrial revolution'. In: Burns & Saul (eds.), 1967.
1974. 'The stabilisation of mortality in pre-industrial western Europe'. *Journal of European Economic History*, 3: 285–318.
(ed.), 1977. *Scottish population history.* Cambridge.
1981. *The European demographic system, 1500–1820.* London.
1982. 'The population history of England, 1541–1871'. *Economic History Review*, 2nd series, 35: 443–57.
1984. *The history of the British coal industry, vol. 2. 1700–1830: the industrial revolution.* Oxford.
Floud, R. & McCloskey, D. (eds.), 1981. *The economic history of Britain since 1700. volume 1, 1700–1860.* London.
Forte, A.D.M., 1984. 'Some aspects of the law of marriage in Scotland, 1500–1700'. In: Craik, E.M. (ed.), 1984. *Marriage and property.* Aberdeen.
Fortes, M., 1970. *Kinship and the social order.* London.
Fox, R., 1978. *The Tory islanders. A people of the Celtic fringe.* Cambridge.
Fox, R.G., 1976. 'Lineage cells and regional definition in complex societies'. In: Smith, C.A. (ed.), *Regional analysis, vol. 11: social systems.* New York.
Fox-Genovese, E., 1982. 'Placing women's history in history'. *New Left Review*, 133: 5–29.
Fraser, A., 1984. *The weaker vessel. Woman's lot in seventeenth-century England.* London.
Friedman, J., 1982. 'Catastrophe and social continuity in social evolution'. In: Renfrew, C., Rowlands, M.W. & Segraves, B.A. (eds.), *Theory and explanation in archaeology.* New York.
Fritz, P. & Morton, R. (eds.), 1976. *Women in the 18th century and other essays.* Toronto.
Fulbrook, M., 1982. 'The English revolution and the revisionist revolt'. *Social History*, 7: 249–64.
Fullarton, W., 1793. *General view of the agriculture of the county of Ayr.* Edinburgh.
Furnivall, F.J. (ed.), 1877. *Harrison's description of England.* London.

Fyfe, J.G., 1928. *Scottish diaries and memoirs, 1550–1746*. Stirling.
Gatrell, V.A.C., Lenman, B. & Parker, G. (eds.), 1980. *Crime and the law. The social history of crime in western Europe since 1500*. London.
Gibb, A., 1982. *Glasgow: the making of a city*. London.
Gibson, J., 1777. *The history of Glasgow*. Glasgow.
Gilbert, A.D., 1976. *Religion and society in industrial England. Church, chapel and social change, 1740–1914*. London.
Gilbert, J.M., 1979. *Hunting and hunting reserves in medieval Scotland*. Edinburgh.
Gillon, S.A. (ed.), 1953. *Selected justiciary cases. 1624–1650*. vol. 1. Edinburgh.
le Goff, J. & Schmitt, J-C. (eds.), 1981. *Le charivari: actes de la table ronde organisée à Paris, 1977*. Paris.
Goldie, M.E., 1970. 'The standard of living of the Scottish farm labourer in selected areas at the time of the first two statistical accounts, 1790–1845. (Unpublished M.Sc. thesis, Edinburgh University.)
Goody, J., 1983. *The development of the family and marriage in Europe*. Cambridge.
Goody, J., Thirsk, J. & Thompson, E.P. (eds.), 1976. *Family and inheritance. Rural society in western Europe, 1200–1800*. Cambridge.
Goose, N., 1982. 'English pre-industrial economies'. *Urban History Yearbook*, 24–30.
Gordon, G. & Dicks, B., (eds.), 1983. *Scottish urban history*. Aberdeen.
Goubert, P., 1973. *The ancien régime. French society. 1600–1750*. London.
Govesse, J-M., 1972. 'Parenté, famille et mariage en Normandie aux XVIIe et XVIIIe siècles'. *Annales E.S.C.*, 27: 1139–54.
Graham, H.G., 1899. *The social life of Scotland in the eighteenth century*. London.
Grant, A., 1811. *Essays on the superstition of the Highlanders of Scotland; to which are added translations from the Gaelic*. 2 vols. London.
Grant, A., 1984. *Independence and nationhood: Scotland. 1306–1469*. London.
Grant, F.J., 1897–9. *The Commissariot records of Edinburgh: register of testaments, 1514–1800*. 3 vols. Edinburgh.
1906. *Register of apprentices of the city of Edinburgh 1583–1666*. Edinburgh.
Grant, I.F., 1924. *Everyday life on an old Highland farm*. London.
1926. 'The social effects of the agricultural reforms and enclosure movement in Aberdeenshire'. *Economic History*. 1: 89–116.
1930. *The social and economic development of Scotland before 1603*. Edinburgh.
1959. *The Macleods: the history of a clan, 1200–1956*. London.
1961. *Highland folk ways*. London.
Grant, K.W., 1918. 'Peasant life in Argyllshire in the end of the eighteenth century'. *Scottish Historical Review*, 16: 144–52.
Gray, M., 1957. *The Highland economy, 1750–1850*. Edinburgh.
1973. 'Scottish emigration: the social impact of agrarian change in the rural lowlands, 1775–1875'. *Perspectives in American History*, 7: 95–174.
1976. 'North-east agriculture and the labour force, 1790–1875'. In: MacLaren (ed.), 1976.
1983. 'Migration in the rural lowlands of Scotland, 1750–1850'. In: Devine & Dickson (eds.), 1983.
1984. 'Farm workers in north-east Scotland'. In: Devine (ed.), 1984b.
Gray, W.F., 1944. *A short history of Haddington*. Edinburgh.

von Greyerz, K., 1980. *The late city Reformation in Germany: the case of Colmar, 1522–1638.* Mainz.
von Greyerz, K. (ed.), 1984. *Religion and society in early modern Europe, 1500–1800.* London.
Grigg, D., 1980. *Population growth and agrarian change: an historical perspective.* London.
Gulvin, C., 1971. 'The Union and the Scottish woollen industry, 1707–1760'. *Scottish Historical Review*, 50: 121–57.
1973. *The tweedmakers. A history of the Scottish fancy woollen industry, 1600–1914.* London.
Gunn, G. (ed.), 1905. *Records of the baron court of Stitchill, 1655–1807.* Edinburgh.
Guy, I., 1982. 'The Scottish export trade, 1460–1599 from the Exchequer rolls'. (Unpublished Ph.D. thesis, St Andrews University.)
1986. 'The Scottish export trade, 1460–1599'. In: Smout (ed.), 1986.
Haldane, A.R.B., 1952. *The drove roads of Scotland.* London.
Haller, W., 1963. *Foxe's book of martyrs and the elect nation.* London.
1961. 'Old Scottish fairs and markets'. *Transactions of the Royal Highland and Agricultural Society of Scotland*, 6th series, 6: 1–12.
Hamilton, D., 1981. *The healers: a history of Scottish medicine.* Edinburgh.
Hamilton, H., 1946. *Life and labour on an Aberdeenshire estate, 1735–50.* Aberdeen.
1947. *History of the homeland.* London.
1963. *An economic history of Scotland in the eighteenth century.* Oxford.
Hamilton, T., 1942. *Poor relief in south Ayrshire. 1700–1845.* Edinburgh.
Hanawalt, B.A. (ed.), 1986. *Women and work in pre-industrial Europe.* Bloomington.
Handley, J.E., (1953). *Scottish farming in the eighteenth century.* Edinburgh.
Hanham, H.J., 1969. *Scottish nationalism.* London.
Hans, N., 1951. *New trends in education in the eighteenth century.* London.
Harding, A. (ed.), 1980. *Law-making and law-makers in British history.* London.
Harland, J. (ed.), 1864. *A volume of the court leet records of the manor of Manchester in the sixteenth century.* Manchester.
Harris, D.F., 1899. *Saint Cecilia's Hall in the Niddry wynd. A chapter in the history of the music of the past in Edinburgh.* Edinburgh and London.
Harrison, J., 1888. *The Scot in Ulster.* Edinburgh.
Harrison, J.F.C., 1985. *The common people of Great Britain.* Bloomington.
Harvie, C., 1978. 'Behind the bonnie brier bush: the kailyard revisited'. *Proteus*, 3: 55–69.
Hay, D., Linebaugh, P. & Thompson, E.P., 1975. *Albion's fatal tree.* Harmondsworth.
Hayes, A.J., 1976. *Edinburgh Methodism, 1761–1975.* Edinburgh.
Hechter, M., 1975. *Internal colonialism: the Celtic fringe in British national development, 1536–1966.* London.
Heckscher, E.F., 1935–49. *Sveriges Ekonomiska Historia från Gustav Vasa.* Stockholm.
Henderson, G.A., 1962. *The Kirk of St Ternan, Arbuthnott.* Edinburgh.
Henderson, G.D. & Porter, H.H. (eds.), 1949. *James Gordon's diary, 1692–1710.* Aberdeen.
Henderson, J.B., 1898. *Borgue: its parish churches, pastors, and people.* Castle Douglas.
Henderson, T.F. (ed.), 1902. *Sir Walter Scott's minstrelsy of the Scottish border*, vol. 1. Edinburgh.

Hendrie, J., 1909. *History of Galston parish church.* Paisley.
Herbert, D. (ed.), 1887. *The works of Tobias Smollet.* Edinburgh.
Heron, A., 1903. *The rise and progress of the company of merchants of the city of Edinburgh, 1681–1902.* Edinburgh.
Herr, R., 1969. *The eighteenth-century revolution in Spain.* New Jersey.
Hill, C., 1958. 'The Norman yoke'. In: *Puritanism and revolution.* London.
1975. *The world turned upside down. Radical ideas during the English Revolution.* Harmondsworth edition.
1981. 'Parliament and people in seventeenth-century England'. *Past and Present,* 92: 100–24.
Hirschon, R., 1984. 'Introduction: property, power and gender relations'. In: Hirschon, R. (ed.), 1984. *Women and property. Woman as property.* London.
Hobsbawm, E., 1964. 'The British standard of living, 1790–1850'. In *Labouring men.* London.
1969a. *Industry and empire.* Harmondsworth.
1969b. *Bandits.* Harmondsworth.
1983. 'Introduction: inventing traditions'. In: Hobsbawm & Ranger (eds.), 1983.
Hobsbawm, E. & Ranger, T. (eds.), 1983. *The invention of tradition.* Cambridge.
Hobsbawm, E. & Rude, G., 1973. *Captain Swing.* Harmondsworth.
Hogg, J., 1831–2. 'On the changes in the habits, amusements, and condition of the Scottish peasantry'. *Quarterly Journal of Agriculture,* 3: 256–63.
Holderness, B.A., 1975. 'Credit in a rural community, 1600–1800'. *Midland History,* 3: 94–116.
1976. *Pre-industrial England: economy and society 1500–1750.* London.
Holmes, G., 1979. 'The professions and social change in England, 1680–1730'. *Proceedings of the British Academy,* 65: 313–54.
1982. *Augustan England. Professions, state and society, 1680–1730.* London.
Hont, I. & Ignatieff, M. (eds.), 1983. *Wealth and virtue: the shaping of political economy in the Scottish Enlightenment.* Cambridge.
Hope, R., 1814. 'On rural economy'. In: Sinclair (ed.), 1814.
Horn, B.L.H., 1977. 'Domestic life of a duke. Cosmo George, 3rd duke of Gordon'. (Unpublished Ph.D. thesis, Edinburgh University.)
Hoskins, W.G., 1965. 'The rediscovery of England'. In: *Provincial England.* London.
Houlbrooke, R.A., 1984. *The English family, 1450–1700.* London.
Houston, R.A., 1980. 'Vagrants and society in early modern England'. *Cambridge Anthropology,* 6: 18–32.
1981. 'Aspects of society in Scotland and north-east England, c.1550–c.1750: social structure, literacy, and geographical mobility'. (Unpublished Ph.D. thesis, Cambridge University.)
1982a. 'The literacy myth? Illiteracy in Scotland, 1630–1760'. *Past and Present,* 96: 81–102.
1982b. 'The development of literacy: northern England, 1640–1750'. *Economic History Review,* 2nd series, 35: 199–216.
1983a. 'Coal, class and culture: labour relations in a Scottish mining community, 1650–1750'. *Social History,* 8: 1–18.

1983b. 'Literacy and society in the west, 1500–1850'. *Social History*, 8: 269–93.
1983c. 'Marriage formation and domestic industry: occupational endogamy in Kilmarnock'. *Journal of Family History*, 8: 215–29.
1985a. *Scottish literacy and the Scottish identity*. Cambridge.
1985b. 'Geographical mobility in Scotland, 1652–1811'. *Journal of Historical Geography*, 11: 379–94.
1986. 'British society in the eighteenth century'. *Journal of British Studies*, 25: 436–66.
1988. 'The demographic regime, c.1750–c.1830'. In: Devine & Mitchinson (eds.), 1988.
Houston, R.A. & Snell, K., 1984. 'Proto-industrialisation? Cottage industry, social change and industrial revolution'. *Historical Journal*, 27: 473–92.
Hovde, B., 1948. *The Scandinavian countries, 1750–1865*. Ithaca.
Howatson, W., 1982. 'The Scottish hairst and seasonal labour, 1600–1870'. *Scottish Studies*, 2: 13–26.
1984. 'Grain harvesting and harvesters'. In: Devine (ed.), 1984b.
Hudson, P., 1981. 'Proto-industrialization: the case of the West Riding wool textile industry in the 18th and early 19th centuries'. *History Workshop Journal*, 12: 34–61.
(ed.), 1988. *Regions and industries*. Cambridge.
Hufton, O.H., 1974. *The poor of eighteenth-century France*. Oxford.
1981. 'Women, work and marriage in eighteenth-century France'. In Outhwaite (ed.), 1981.
1983. 'Women in history. Early modern Europe'. *Past and Present*, 101: 125–41.
1984. 'Women without men: widows and spinsters in Britain and France in the eighteenth century'. *Journal of Family History*, 9: 355–76.
Hunter, J., 1976. *The making of the crofting community*. Edinburgh.
Hutchison, R., 1869. 'Report on the dietaries of Scotch agricultural labourers'. *Transactions of the Highland and Agricultural Society of Scotland*, fourth series, 4: 86–107.
Imrie, J. (ed.), 1969. *The justiciary records of Argyll and the Isles, vol. 2. 1705–1742*. Edinburgh.
Ingram, M., 1984. 'Ridings, rough music and the "reform of popular culture" in early modern England'. *Past and Present*, 105: 79–113.
Innes, C. (ed.), 1855. *The black book of Taymouth*. Edinburgh.
An introduction to Scottish legal history. (Stair Society vol. 20) 1958. Edinburgh.
Ireland, R.D., 1958. 'Husband and wife: divorce, nullity of marriage and separation'. In: *An introduction to Scottish legal history*, 1958.
Jacobsen, G., 1983. 'Women's work and women's role: ideology and reality in Danish urban society, 1300–1500'. *Scandinavian Economic History Review*, 31: 1–20.
James, M., 1983. 'Ritual, drama and the social body in the late medieval English town'. *Past and Present*, 98: 3–29.
James, M.E., 1965. 'Change and continuity in the Tudor north'. *Borthwick Papers*, no. 27. York.
1974. *Family, lineage and civil society*. Oxford.
Jamieson, J.H., 1933. 'Social assemblies of the eighteenth century'. *Book of the Old Edinburgh Club*, 19: 31–91.
Jamieson, R., 1876. *Burt's letters from the north of Scotland*. 2 vols. Edinburgh.

Johnson, D., 1972. *Music and society in Lowland Scotland in the eighteenth century*. London.
1984. *Scottish fiddle music in the eighteenth century*. Edinburgh.
Johnson, S., 1773. *A dictionary of the English language*. London.
1775. *A journey to the western islands of Scotland*. London.
Johnston, T., 1920. *The history of the working classes in Scotland*. Glasgow.
Jones, E.L., 1981. *The European miracle: environments, economies and geopolitics in the history of Europe and Asia*. Cambridge.
Jupp, P.J., 1967. 'Irish parliamentary elections and the influence of the Catholic vote, 1801–1820'. *Historical Journal*, 10: 183–96.
Kagan, R., 1974. *Students and society in early modern Spain*. London.
Kamen, H., 1974. 'Public authority and popular crime: banditry in Valencia, 1660–1714'. *Journal of European Economic History*, 3: 654–87.
1984. *European society, 1500–1700*. London.
Kelsall, H. & K., 1986. *Scottish lifestyle 300 years ago. New light on Edinburgh and Border families*. Edinburgh.
Kemp, D.W. (ed.), 1886. *Bishop Pococke's tours in Scotland, 1747–1760*. Edinburgh.
Kinnaird, J.K., 1979. 'Mary Astell and the conservative contribution to English feminism'. *Journal of British Studies*, 19: 53–75.
Kirk, J. (ed.), 1977. *The records of the synod of Lothian and Tweeddale, 1589–96, 1640–49*. Edinburgh.
(ed.), 1981. *Stirling presbytery records, 1581–1587*. Edinburgh.
1986. 'The kirk and the Highlands at the Reformation'. *Northern Scotland*, 7: 1–22.
Kirsch, P.V., 1980. 'Polynesian prehistory: cultural adaptation in island ecosystems. *American scientist*. 68: 39–48.
Klapisch, C. & Demonet, M., 1972. ' "A uno pane e une vino": la famille rurale toscane au debut du XVe siècle'. *Annales E.S.C.*, 27: 873–901.
Klapisch-Zuber, C., 1980. 'The medieval Italian *mattinata*'. *Journal of Family History*, 5: 2–27.
Knox, J., 1905. *The history of the Reformation in Scotland with which are included Knox's Confession and the Book of Discipline*, ed. C. Lennox. London.
Knox, J., 1784. *A view of the British empire, more especially Scotland; with some proposals for the improvement of that country, the extension of its fisheries, and the relief of the people*. London.
Kriedte, P., Medick, H. & Schlumbohm, J., 1981. *Industrialisation before industrialisation*. Cambridge.
Kula, W., 1972. 'La Seigneurie et la famille paysanne en Pologne au XVIIIe siècle'. *Annales E.S.C.*, 27: 949–58.
Kussmaul, A., 1981. *Servants in husbandry in early modern England*. Cambridge.
Kyd, J.G. (ed.), 1952. *Scottish population statistics including Webster's analysis of population 1755*. Scottish History Society, 3rd series, vol. 44. Edinburgh.
Labrousse, C.E., 1932. *Esquisse du mouvement des prix et des revenus en France au XVIIIe siècle*. Paris.
Lamb, H.H., 1982. *Climate, history and the modern world*. London.
Landsman, N.C., 1985. *Scotland and its first American colony, 1683–1765*. Princeton.
Langbein, J.H., 1974. *Prosecuting crime in the Renaissance*. Cambridge, Mass.
Langton, J., 1975. 'Residential patterns in pre-industrial cities: some case studies

from seventeenth-century Britain'. *Transactions of the Institute of British Geographers.* 65: 1–27.

Larner, C., 1981. *Enemies of God. The witch-hunt in Scotland.* London.

1984. *Witchcraft and religion: the politics of popular belief.* Oxford.

Laslett, P., 1969. 'Scottish weavers, cobblers and miners who bought books in the 1750s'. *Local Population Studies.* 3: 7–15.

1971. *The world we have lost.* London.

1977. 'Characteristics of the western family considered over time'. In: Laslett, P., 1977. *Family life and illicit love.* Cambridge.

1983. *The world we have lost further explored.* London.

Law, A., 1965. *Education in Edinburgh in the eighteenth century.* London.

Leach, E.R., 1968. *Pul Eliya.* Cambridge.

Lebon, J.H.G., 1946. 'The process of enclosure in the western Lowlands'. *Scottish Geographical Magazine,* 62: 103–17.

Lefebvre, G., 1921. 'La place de la révolution dans l'histoire agraire de la France'. *Annales E.S.C.,* 1: 16–36.

Leinster-Mackay, D.P., 1976. 'Dame-schools: a need for review'. *British Journal of Educational Studies,* 24: 33–48.

Leneman, L., 1986. *Living in Atholl: a social history of the estates, 1685–1785.* Edinburgh.

Leneman, L. & Mitchison, R., 1987. 'Scottish illegitimacy ratios in the early modern period'. *Economic History Review.* 2nd series, 40: 41–63.

Lenman, B.P., 1977. *An economic history of modern Scotland. 1660–1976.* London.

1981. *Integration, enlightenment, and industrialization: Scotland, 1746–1832.* London.

1982. 'Reinterpreting Scotland's last two centuries of independence'. *Historical Journal,* 25: 217–28.

1984a. 'The limits of godly discipline in the early modern period with particular reference to England and Scotland'. In: von Greyerz (ed.), 1984.

1984b. *The Jacobite clans of the Great Glen.* London.

Lenman, B.P. & Parker, G., 1980. 'The state, the community and the criminal law in early modern Europe'. In: Gatrell, Lenman & Parker (eds.), 1980.

Leonard, E.M., 1900. *The early history of English poor relief.* Cambridge.

Leopold, J., 1980. 'The Levellers' revolt in Galloway in 1724'. *Journal of the Scottish Labour History Society,* 14: 4–29.

Lerner, G., 1975. 'Placing women in history: definitions and challenges'. *Feminist Studies,* 3: 5–14.

Levine, D., 1977. *Family formation in an age of nascent capitalism.* London.

Levitt, I. & Smout, T.C., 1979. *The state of the Scottish working class in 1843.* Edinburgh.

Levy, F.J., 1967. *Tudor historical thought.* San Marino.

Lewis, G.R., 1834. *Scotland a half-educated nation.* Glasgow.

1838. *An address on the subject of education.* London.

Lindley, K., 1982. *Fenland riots and the English revolution.* London.

Lis, C. & Soly, H., 1982. *Poverty and capitalism in pre-industrial Europe.* Brighton.

Loch, D., 1778. *A tour through most of the trading towns and villages of Scotland.* Edinburgh.

Lockhart, D.G., 1980. 'Sources for studies of migration to estate villages in north east Scotland'. *Local Historian,* 14: 35–43.

1983. 'Planned village development in Scotland and Ireland, 1700–1850'. In: Devine & Dickson (eds.), 1983.

Lockhart, J.G., 1830. *The life of Robert Burns*. Edinburgh.

Logue, K.J., 1979. *Popular disturbances in Scotland. 1780–1815*. Edinburgh.

1980. 'Eighteenth-century popular protest: aspects of the people's past'. In: Cowan, E.J. (ed.), 1980. *The people's past*. Edinburgh.

Lovett, A.A., Whyte, I.D. & Whyte, K.A., 1985. 'Poisson regression analysis and migration fields: the example of the apprenticeship records of Edinburgh in the seventeenth and eighteenth centuries'. *Transactions of the Institute of British Geographers*, new series, 10: 317–32.

Lynch, M., 1981. *Edinburgh and the Reformation*. Edinburgh.

1984. 'Whatever happened to the medieval burgh? Some guidelines for sixteenth and seventeenth century historians'. *Scottish Economic and Social History*, 4: 5–20.

1985. 'Scottish Calvinism, 1559–1648'. In: Prestwich, M. (ed.), 1985. *International Calvinism*. Oxford.

(ed.), 1987. *The early modern town in Scotland*. London.

forthcoming. 'Towns and townspeople in fifteenth-century Scotland'. In: Thomson, J.A.F. (ed.), 1988. *Towns and townspeople in the fifteenth century*. Gloucester.

forthcoming. 'The social and economic structure of the larger towns, 1450–1600'. In: Lynch, Spearman & Stell (eds.), 1987.

Lynch, M., Spearman, M. & Stell, G. (eds.), forthcoming. *The Scottish medieval town*. Edinburgh.

Lythe, S.G.E., 1960. *The economy of Scotland in its European setting, 1550–1625*. Edinburgh.

1973. 'The economy of Scotland under James VI and I'. In: Smith, A.G.R. (ed.), *The reign of James VI and I*. London.

Lythe, S.G.E. & Butt, J., 1975. *An economic history of Scotland, 1100–1939*. Glasgow.

MacDonald, A. & MacDonald, A., 1896–1904. *The clan Donald*. 3 vols. Inverness.

MacDonald, J., 1790. *Travels in various parts of Europe, Asia and Africa*. London. (1927 edition used)

Macdonald, W.R., 1966. 'Scottish seventeenth-century almanacs'. *The Bibliotheck*, 4: 257–322.

McDowell, R.B., 1986. 'Ireland in 1800'. In: Moody & Vaughan (eds.), 1986.

McFarlan, J., 1782. *Inquiries concerning the poor*. Edinburgh.

Macfarlane, A., 1978. *The origins of English individualism*. Oxford.

1981. *The justice and the mare's ale*. Oxford.

1986. *Marriage and love in England*. Oxford.

Macfarlane, W., 1906–8. *Geographical collections relating to Scotland*, 3 vols., ed. A. Mitchell. Edinburgh.

MacGillivray, E., 1953. 'Richard James, 1502–1638: description of Shetland, Orkney and the Highlands of Scotland'. *Orkney Miscellany*, 1: 48–56.

MacInnes, A., 1987. 'Political disruption and social change within Scottish gaeldom'. In: Mitchison & Roebuck (eds.), 1987.

Mack, P., 1982. 'Women as prophets during the English civil war'. *Feminist Studies*, 8: 19–46.

Mackay, W. (ed.), 1896. *Records of the presbyteries of Inverness and Dingwall, 1643–1688.* Edinburgh.

1905. *Chronicles of the Frasers.* Edinburgh.

1915. *The letter book of baillie John Steuart of Inverness, 1715–1752.* Scottish History Society, 2nd series, vol. 9. Edinburgh.

MacKenzie, A., 1879. *History of the clan MacKenzie.* Inverness.

MacKenzie, G., 1678. *The laws and customes of Scotland in matters criminal.* Edinburgh.

MacKenzie, W.C., 1903. *History of the Outer Hebrides.* Paisley.

Mackenzie, W.M., 1949. *The Scottish burghs.* Edinburgh.

McKerral, A., 1948. *Kintyre in the seventeenth century.* Edinburgh.

Mackie, J.D., 1978. *A history of Scotland.* Harmondsworth.

Mackinnon, K.M., 1972. 'Education and social control: the case of Gaelic'. *Scottish Educational Studies*, 4: 125–37.

Mackintosh, J., 1729. *An essay on ways and means of enclosing.* Edinburgh.

MacLaren, A.A. (ed.), 1976. *Social class in Scotland past and present.* Edinburgh.

MacLaren, D., 1985. 'Marital fertility and lactation, 1570–1720'. In: Prior (ed.), 1985a.

Maclean, S., 1986. 'Obscure and anonymous Gaelic poetry'. In: *The seventeenth century in the Highlands.*

MacLeod, R.C. (ed.), 1938. *The book of Dunvegan. vol. 1, 1340–1700.* Aberdeen.

MacMillan, J., 1984. 'A study of the Edinburgh burgess community and its economic activities, 1600–1680'. (Unpublished Ph.D. thesis, Edinburgh University.)

McPhail, J.R.N. (ed.), 1911–34. *Highland papers.* 4 vols. Edinburgh.

Macpherson, A.G., 1966. 'An old Highland genealogy and the evolution of a Scottish clan'. *Scottish Studies*, 10: 1–42.

1984. 'Migration fields in a traditional Highland community 1350–1850'. *Journal of Historical Geography.* 10: 1–14.

McPherson, J.M., n.d. *The kirk's care of the poor.* Aberdeen.

MacRae, A., 1899. *History of clan MacRae.* Dingwall.

McRoberts, D., 1957 *The Fetternear banner.* Glasgow.

MacTavish, D.C. (ed.), 1943. *Minutes of the synod of Argyll, 1639–51.* Edinburgh.

MacWilliam, A.C., 1973. 'A Highland mission: Strathglass, 1671–1777'. *Innes Review*, 24: 75–102.

Mair, L., 1970. *Primitive government.* Harmondsworth.

Maitland Club.

Makey, W.H., 1970. 'The elders of Stow, Liberton, Canongate and St Cuthbert's in the mid-seventeenth century'. *Records of the Scottish Church History Society*, 17: 155–67.

1987. 'Edinburgh in the mid-seventeenth century'. In: Lynch (ed.), 1987.

Malcolm, C.A. (ed.), 1931. *The minutes of the justices of the peace of Lanarkshire, 1707–1723.* Edinburgh.

Marshall, G., 1980. *Presbyteries and profits: Calvinism and the development of capitalism in Scotland, 1560–1707.* Oxford.

Marshall, J.S., 1969. 'A social and economic history of Leith in the eighteenth century'. (Unpublished Ph.D. thesis, Edinburgh University.)

Marshall, R.K., 1983. *Virgins and viragos. A history of women in Scotland from 1080 to 1980.* London.
Marshall, R.K., 1984. 'Wetnursing in Scotland, 1500–1800'. *Review of Scottish Culture*, 1: 43–51.
Marshall, W., 1794. *General view of the agriculture of the central Highlands.* London.
Martin, M., 1703. *A description of the western isles of Scotland.* London.
1716. *A description of the western isles of Scotland*, 2nd edition. London.
Marwick, J.D. (ed.), 1866–90. *Records of the convention of royal burghs of Scotland.* Edinburgh.
1881. *Extracts from the records of the burgh of Glasgow, 1630–1662.* Glasgow.
1909. *The river Clyde and the Clyde burghs.* Glasgow.
Mathew, W.M., 1966. 'The origins and occupations of Glasgow students, 1740–1839'. *Past and Present*, 33: 74–94.
Mathias, P., 1979. *The transformation of England.* London.
Maxwell, C., 1946. *A history of Trinity college, Dublin.* Dublin.
Maxwell, M.P., 1973. *The Scottish migration to Ulster in the reign of James I.* London.
Meillassoux, C., 1972. 'From reproduction to production'. *Economy and Society*, 1: 93–115.
Mendelson, S.H., 1985. 'Stuart women's diaries and occasional memoirs'. In: Prior (1985a).
Menefee, S.P., 1981. *Wives for sale. An ethnographic study of British popular divorce.* Oxford.
Menzies, D.P., 1894. *The 'red and white' book of Menzies.* Glasgow.
Mill, A.J., 1970a. 'The Perth hammermen's play. A Scottish Garden of Eden'. *Scottish Historical Review*, 49: 146–53.
1970b. 'The Edinburgh hammermen's Corpus Christi Herod pageant'. *Innes Review*, 21: 77–80.
Millard, J., 1982. 'A new approach to the study of marriage horizons'. *Local Population Studies*, 28: 10–31.
Miller, K. (ed.), 1970. *Memoirs of modern Scotland.* London.
Milton, J., 1644. *Areopagitica.* In: *Milton's prose writings* (1958 Everyman edition). London.
Mitchell, A. & Cash, C.G., 1917. *A contribution to the bibliography of Scottish topography*, vol. 2 Edinburgh.
Mitchell, J., 1939. *Memories of Ayrshire about 1780.* Edinburgh.
Mitchison, R.M., 1974. 'The making of the old Scottish poor law'. *Past and Present*, 63: 58–93.
1975. 'A parish and its poor: Yester in the second half of the seventeenth century'. *Transactions of the East Lothian Antiquarian and Field Naturalists Society*, 14: 15–28.
1978. *Life in Scotland.* London.
1979. 'The creation of the disablement rule in the Scottish poor law'. In: Smout (ed.), 1979.
1981. 'The Highland clearances'. *Scottish Economic and Social History*, 1: 4–21.
1982. *A history of Scotland.* 2nd edition, London.
1983. *From lordship to patronage. Scotland, 1603–1745.* London.
1987. 'Who were the poor in Scotland, 1690–1820'. In: Mitchison & Roebuck (eds.), 1987.

Mitchison, R. & Roebuck, P. (eds.), 1987. *Scotland and Ireland: a comparative study in development*. Edinburgh.

Moody, T.W. & Vaughan, W.E. (eds.), 1986. *A new history of Ireland, IV. Eighteenth-century Ireland*. Oxford.

Moral Statistics of the Highlands and Islands of Scotland, compiled from returns received by the Inverness society for the education of the poor in the Highlands. 1826. Inverness.

Morell, M., 1987. 'Eli F. Heckscher. The "food budgets" and Swedish food consumption from the 16th to the 19th century'. *Scandinavian Economic History Review*, 35: 67–107.

Morgan, V., 1971. 'Agricultural wage rates in late eighteenth-century Scotland'. *Economic History Review*, 2nd series, 24: 181–201.

Morison, W.M., 1811. *The decisions of the court of Session . . . digested under proper heads in the form of a dictionary*, vol. 25. Edinburgh.

Morris, C. (ed.), 1984. *The illustrated journeys of Celia Fiennes*. London.

Moryson, F., 1617. *An itinerary*. London.

Moss, P., 1979. 'Bandits and boundaries'. *Man*, 17: 477–96.

Mowat, I.R.M., 1979. 'Literacy, libraries and literature in 18th and 19th century Easter Ross'. *Library History*, 5: 1–10.

Muchembled, R., 1981. 'La femme au village dans la region du nord (XVIIe–XVIIIe siècles)'. *Revue du Nord*, 63: 585–93.

Munro, A., 'Essay on female conduct contain'd in letters from a father to his daughter', NLS, MS 6658.

Murdoch, A., 1982. ' "Beating the lieges": the military riot at Ravenshaugh Toll on 5 October 1760'. *Transactions of the East Lothian Antiquarian and Field Naturalists Society*, 17: 39–47.

Murray, Sir A., 1740. *The true interest of Great Britain, Ireland, and our plantations . . .* London.

Murray, D., 1924–32. *Early burgh organisation in Scotland as illustrated in the history of Glasgow and some neighbouring burghs*, 2 vols. Glasgow.

Murray, N., 1978. *The Scottish handloom weavers, 1790–1850: a social history*. Edinburgh.

Nef, J.U., 1932. *The rise of the British coal industry*, 2 vols. London.

New Statistical Account of Scotland. 14 vols. 1845.

Ogden, P., 1980. 'Migration, marriage and the collapse of traditional peasant society in France'. In: White & Woods (eds.), 1980.

Oldervoll, J., 1979. 'The rural society of Norway'. In: Dyrvik, Mykland & Oldervoll (eds.), 1979.

Old Statistical Account of Scotland. 21 vols. Edinburgh 1791–9.

Ommer, R.E., 1986. 'Primitive accumulation and the Scottish *clann* in the Old World and the New'. *Journal of Historical Geography*, 12: 121–41.

Orr, A., 1984. 'Farm servants and farm labour in the Forth valley and south-east lowlands'. In: Devine (ed.), 1984b.

Outhwaite, R.B. (ed.), 1981. *Marriage and society*. London.

1986. 'Progress and backwardness in English agriculture, 1500–1650'. *Economic History Review*, 2nd series, 39: 1–18.

Parry, M.L. & Slater, T.R. (eds.), 1980. *The making of the Scottish countryside*. London.

Paton, G.C.H., 1958. 'Husband and wife: property rights and relationships'. In: *An Introduction to Scottish legal history*, 1958.

Paton, H. (ed.), 1936. *The session book of Dundonald. 1602–1731*. Privately printed.
Patten, J., 1976. 'Patterns of migration and movement of labour to three pre-industrial East Anglian towns'. *Journal of Historical Geography*. 2: 111–30.
1978. *English towns 1500–1700*. Folkestone.
Paul, G.M. (ed.), 1896. *Fragment of the diary of Sir Archibald Johnston, Lord Warriston, May 21–June 25 1639*. Edinburgh.
Payne, P.L. (ed.), 1967. *Studies in Scottish business history*. London.
Pennant, T., 1774. *A tour in Scotland, 1769*. Warrington.
1776a. *A tour in Scotland, 1769*, 4th edition. Edinburgh.
1776b. *A tour of Scotland and a voyage to the Hebrides in 1772*. Edinburgh.
Phillipson, N.T., 1980. 'The social structure of the faculty of advocates in Scotland, 1661–1840'. In: Harding (ed.), 1980.
Phillipson, N.T. & Mitchison, R. (eds.), 1970. *Scotland in the age of improvement*. Edinburgh.
Phythian-Adams, C.V., 1979. 'Dr Dyer's urban undulations'. *Urban History Yearbook*: 73–6.
Plakans, A., 1984. *Kinship in the past*. Oxford.
Plant, M., 1952. *The domestic life of Scotland in the eighteenth century*. Edinburgh.
Pocock, J.G.A., 1957. *The ancient constitution and the feudal law. A study of English historical thought in the seventeenth century*. Cambridge.
1974. 'British history: a plea for a new subject'. *The New Zealand Journal of History*, 8: 3–21.
(ed.), 1977. *The political works of James Harrington*. Cambridge.
Poni, C., 1978. 'Family and *podere* in Emilia Romagna'. *Journal of Italian History*, 1: 201–34.
Porter, R., 1982. *English society in the eighteenth century*. Harmondsworth.
Pound, J., 1971. *Poverty and vagrancy in Tudor England*. London.
Pour une histoire de l'alimentation, recueil de travaux présentés par J.J. Hermardinquier. Cahiers des Annales. 28 (1970).
Poynter, J.R., 1969. *Society and pauperism*. London.
Prevost, W.A.J., 1967. 'Letters reporting the rising of the Levellers in 1724'. *Transactions of the Dumfries and Galloway Natural History and Antiquarian Society*, 3rd series, 44: 196–204.
Price, J.M., 1973. *France and the Chesapeake*, 2 vols., Ann Arbor.
Prior, M. (ed.), 1985a. *Women in English society, 1500–1800*'. London.
1985b. 'Women and the urban economy: Oxford, 1500–1800. In: Prior (ed.) (1985a), above.
Pryde, G.S. (ed.), 1963. *The court book of the burgh of Kirkintilloch, 1658–1694*. Edinburgh.
1965. *The burghs of Scotland*. Oxford.
Quinault, R. & Stevenson, J. (eds.), 1974. *Popular protest and public order: six studies in British history*, 1790–1920. London.
Rabb, T.K. & Hirst, D., 1981. 'Revisionism revised: two perspectives on early Stuart parliamentary history'. *Past and Present*, 92: 55–99.
Rae, T.I., 1966. *The administration of the Scottish frontier, 1513–1603*. Edinburgh.
Rae, T.I. (ed.), 1974. *The union of 1707: its impact on Scotland*. Glasgow.

Register containing the state and condition of every burgh within the kingdom of Scotland, in the year 1692, 1881. Edinburgh.

Register of the great seal of Scotland, 11 vols., 1882–1914. Edinburgh.

Register of the privy council of Scotland. 1st series, 1877–98, 14 vols. 2nd series, 1898–1908, 3 vols. 3rd series, 1908–date, 16 vols. Edinburgh.

Renwick, J. (ed.), 1893. *Extracts from the records of the burgh of Lanark, 1150–1722.* Glasgow.

Renwick, R., 1889. *Extracts from the records of the burgh of Stirling, 1667–1752.* Glasgow.

Report on the manuscripts of the earl of Mar and Kellie preserved at Alloa House. 1904. Historical Manuscripts Commission.

Reports from commissioners; report of the select committee on the Poor Laws (Appendix, report of the committee of the General Assembly). *Parliamentary papers* IV. 1817.

Third report from the select committee on the Poor Laws: (Appendix containing the returns from the General Assembly of the Church of Scotland). *Parliamentary papers* V. 1818.

Report by a committee of the General Assembly on the management of the poor in Scotland. *Parliamentary papers* XX. 1834.

Poor Law inquiry, report, minutes of evidence. *Parliamentary papers* XX, XXI, XXII. 1844.

Reports on the state of certain parishes in Scotland [1627] made to his majesty's commissioners for plantation of kirks. 1835. Edinburgh.

Richards, E., 1974. 'Patterns of Highland discontent, 1790–1860'. In: Quinault & Stevenson (eds.), 1974.

1982. *A history of the Highland clearances.* London.

Richardson, J., 1949. 'Some notes on the early history of the Dean Orphan Hospital'. *Book of the Old Edinburgh Club*, 27: 155–68.

Riley, P.W.J., 1978. *The union of England and Scotland.* Manchester.

Roberts, A.A., 1976. 'Mothers and babies: the wetnurse and her employer in mid-nineteenth-century England'. *Feminist Studies*, 3: 279–93.

Robertson, G., 1793. *General view of the agriculture of the county of Midlothian.* Edinburgh.

1829. *Rural recollections.* Irvine.

Robertson, J.A., 1860. *Commitatus de Atholia. The earldom of Atholl: its boundaries stated.* Privately printed.

Rogers, J.R.T., 1866–1902. *A history of agriculture and prices in England.* Oxford.

Romanes, C.S. (ed.), 1914–17. *Selections from the records of the regality of Melrose, 1605–1706.* 3 vols. Edinburgh.

Roper, L., 1985. '"Going to church and street": wedding in Reformation Augsburg'. *Past and Present*, 106: 62–101.

Ross, I. & Scobie, S., 1974. 'Patriotic publishing as a response to the union'. In: Rae (ed.), 1974.

Rossetti, C.G., 1982. 'The ideology of banditry'. *Man*, 17: 158–60.

Rothberg, R.I. & Rabb, T.K. (eds.), 1983. *Hunger and history: the impact of changing food production and consumption patterns on society.* Cambridge.

Russell, C., 1976. 'Parliamentary history in perspective, 1604–29'. *History*, 61: 1–27.

1979. *Parliaments and English politics, 1621–29.* Oxford.

Saalfeld, D., 1980. 'Die ständische Gliederung der Gesellschaft Deutschlands im Zeitalter der Absolitismus'. *Vierteljahrschrift für Sozial- und Wirtschaftsgeschichte*, 67: 457–83.

Sabean, D., 1976. 'Aspects of kinship behaviour and property in rural western Europe before 1800'. In: Goody, Thirsk & Thompson (eds.), 1976.

Sahlins, M., 1968. *Tribesmen*. Englewood Cliffs.

Salmon, T.J., 1913. *Borrowstouness and district*. Edinburgh.

Samuel, R. (ed.), 1981. *People's history and socialist theory*. London.

Sanderson, M.H.B., 1970. 'Catholic recusancy in Scotland in the sixteenth century'. *Innes Review*, 21: 87–107.

1974. 'The feuing of Strathisla: a study in sixteenth-century social history'. *Northern Scotland*, 2: 1–11.

1982. *Scottish rural society in the sixteenth century*, Edinburgh.

1983. 'The Edinburgh merchants in society, 1570–1603: the evidence of their testaments'. In: Cowan & Shaw (eds.), 1983.

Scarisbrick, J.J., 1984. *The Reformation and the English people*. Oxford.

Scotland, J., 1969. *The history of Scottish education*. vol. 1. London.

Scott, H. (ed.), 1883. *Fasti ecclesiae Scoticanae*. Edinburgh.

Scott, W. (ed.), 1905. *Records of a Scottish cloth manufactory at New Mills, Haddingtonshire, 1681–1703*. Edinburgh.

1916. *The parish lists of Wigtownshire and Minnigaff*. Edinburgh.

Scott-Moncrieff, W.G. (ed.), 1905. *Records of the proceedings of the justiciary court of Edinburgh. vol. 1, 1661–1669. vol. 2, 1669–1678*. Edinburgh.

1911. *The household book of Lady Grisell Baillie, 1692–1733*. Edinburgh.

Scottish burgh record society miscellany. 1881.

Sellar, D.W.H., 1981. 'Highland family origins – pedigree making and pedigree faking'. In: MacLean, L. (ed.), *The middle ages in the Highlands*. Inverness.

Semple, D. (ed.), 1984. *Renfrewshire poll tax returns*. Glasgow.

Sen, A., 1981. *Poverty and famines: an essay on entitlement and deprivation*. Oxford.

The seventeenth century in the Highlands. 1986. (Inverness Field Club) Inverness.

Shammas, C., 1983. 'Food expenditures and economic well-being in early modern England'. *Journal of Economic History*, 43: 89–100.

1984. 'The eighteenth-century English diet and economic change'. *Explorations in Economic History*, 21: 254–69.

Sharp, B., 1980. *In contempt of all authority. Rural artisans and riot in the west of England, 1586–1660*. Berkeley, Los Angeles and London.

Shaw, F.J., 1980. *The northern and western islands of Scotland: their economy and society in the seventeenth century*. Edinburgh.

1986. 'Sources for the history of the seventeenth-century Highlands'. In: *The seventeenth century in the Highlands*.

Shaw, J.S., 1983. *The management of Scottish society, 1707–64*. Edinburgh.

Shearer, A. (ed.), 1951. *Extracts from the burgh records of Dunfermline in the 16th and 17th centuries*. Edinburgh.

Sheridan, R., 1961. 'The rise of a colonial gentry: a case study of Antigua, 1730–1775'. *Economic History Review*. 2nd series, 13: 342–57.

1974. *Sugar and slavery: an economic history of the British West Indies, 1623–1775*. Barbados.

Shipton, P.M., 1984. 'Strips and patches: a demographic dimension in some African land-holding and political systems'. *Man*, 19: 613–34.

Shorter, E., 1982. *A history of women's bodies*. New York.

Sinclair, J. (ed.), 1791–7. *The statistical account of Scotland*. 21 vols. Edinburgh.

1814. *General report of the agricultural state and political circumstances of Scotland*. Edinburgh.

1826. *Analysis of the statistical account of Scotland*. part 2. London.

Skene, A., 1685. *Memorials for the government of royal burghs in Scotland*. Aberdeen.

Skovgaard, K., 1952. 'Consolidation of agrarian land in Denmark'. *International Journal of Agrarian Affairs*, 1: 16–34.

Slack, P., 1972. 'Poverty and politics in Salisbury, 1597–1666'. In: Clark & Slack (eds.), 1972.

Slicher van Bath, B.H., 1963. *Agrarian history of western Europe, 500–1850*. London.

Smart, R.N., 1974. 'Some observations on the provinces of the Scottish universities, 1560–1850'. In: Barrow (ed.), 1974.

Smith, A., 1976. *An inquiry into the nature and causes of the wealth of nations*. Skinner, A. & Campbell, A.H. (eds.), 2 vols. Oxford.

Smith, A.H., 1974. *County and court: government and politics in Norfolk, 1558–1603*. Oxford.

Smith, J.A., 1970. 'Some eighteenth century ideas of Scotland'. In: Phillipson & Mitchison (eds.), 1970.

Smith, J.I., 1958. 'Succession'. In: *An Introduction to Scottish legal history*. 1958.

(ed.), 1972. *Selected justiciary cases*, 1624–50. vol. 2. Edinburgh.

Smith, R.B., 1970. *Land and politics in the England of Henry VIII. The West Riding of Yorkshire, 1530–46*. Oxford.

Smith, R.M., 1979. 'Some reflections on the evidence for the origins of the "European marriage pattern" in England'. In: Harris, C. (ed.), 1979. *Sociological review monograph on the family*, 28.

1981. 'The people of Tuscany and their families in the fifteenth century'. *Journal of Family History*, 6: 107–28.

Smout, T.C., 1958–9. 'The foreign trade of Dumfries and Kirkcudbrightshire, 1672–1696'. *Transactions of the Dumfries and Galloway Natural History and Antiquarian Society*, 3rd series, 37: 36–47.

1960. 'The development and enterprise of Glasgow, 1556–1707'. *Scottish Journal of Political Economy*, 7: 194–212.

1963. *Scottish trade on the eve of the Union, 1660–1707*. Edinburgh.

1967. 'Lead mining in Scotland, 1650–1850'. In: Payne (ed.), 1967.

1968. 'The Glasgow merchant community in the seventeenth century'. *Scottish Historical Review*, 47: 53–71.

1970. 'Problems of modernisation in multi-sectoral economies: the role of non-economic factors in Scottish growth in the eighteenth century'. *V International Congress of Economic History, Leningrad*. Moscow.

1972. *A history of the Scottish people, 1560–1830*. Glasgow.

1977. 'Famine and famine relief in Scotland'. In: Cullen & Smout (eds.), 1977.

(ed.), 1979. *The search for wealth and stability: essays in economic and social history presented to M.W. Flinn*. London.

1980. 'Centre and periphery in history, with some thoughts on Scotland as a case study'. *Journal of Common Market Studies*, 18: 256–71.
1982. 'Born again at Cambuslang: new evidence on popular religion and literacy in eighteenth-century Scotland'. *Past and Present*, 97: 114–27.
1983. 'Where had the Scottish economy got to by the third quarter of the eighteenth century?'. In: Hont & Ignatieff (eds.), 1983.
1986. *Scotland and Europe, 1200–1850*. Edinburgh.
1987. 'Landowners in Scotland, Ireland and Denmark in the age of improvement'. *Scandinavian Journal of History*, 12: 79–97.
Smout, T.C. & Fenton, A., 1965. 'Scottish agriculture before the improvers – an exploration'. *Agricultural History Review*, 13: 73–93.
Sogner, S., 1976. 'Freeholder and cottar. Property relationships and the social structure in the peasant community in Norway during the eighteenth century'. *Scandinavian Journal of History*, 1: 181–99.
Soltow, L., 1979. 'Wealth distribution in Denmark in 1789'. *Scandinavian Economic History Review*, 27: 121–38.
Sommerville, J.P., 1986. *Politics and ideology in England, 1603–40*. London.
Spearman, M., forthcoming. 'The medieval townscape of Perth'. In: Lynch, Spearman & Stell (eds.), 1987.
Spreull, J., 1705. *An accompt current betwixt Scotland and England*. Glasgow.
Spufford, M., 1974. *Contrasting communities*. Cambridge.
1981. *Small books and pleasant histories. Popular fiction and its readership in seventeenth-century England*. London.
Stadin, K., 1980. 'Den gömda och glömda arbetskraften. Stadskvinnor i productionen under 1600 – och 1700 talen'. *Historisk Tidskrift*, 100: 298–319.
Statistical account of Scotland. 21 vols., ed. J. Sinclair. Edinburgh.
Statutes of the realm. vol. 4 pts 1, 2. 1814. London.
Steer, K.A. & Bannerman, J.W.M., 1977. *Late medieval monumental sculpture in the west Highlands*. Edinburgh.
Steven, M., 1985. *The good Scots diet: what happened to it?* Aberdeen.
Stevenson, A.W.K., 1982. 'Trade between Scotland and the Low Countries in the later middle ages'. (Unpublished Ph.D. thesis, Aberdeen University.)
Stevenson, D. 1974. 'The king's Scottish revenues and the covenanters, 1625–51'. *Historical Journal*, 17: 17–41.
1977. *Revolution and counter-revolution in Scotland, 1644–51*. London.
1980. *Alasdair MacColla and the Highland problem in the seventeenth century*. Edinburgh.
(ed.), 1986. *From lairds to louns. Country and burgh life in Aberdeen, 1600–1800*. Aberdeen.
1987. 'The burghs and the Scottish Revolution'. In: Lynch (ed.), 1987.
Stone, L., 1964. 'The educational revolution in England, 1540–1640'. *Past and Present*, 28: 41–80.
1965. *The crisis of the aristocracy, 1558–1641*. Oxford.
1977. *The family, sex and marriage in England, 1500–1800*. London.
Stone, L. & Stone, J.C.F., 1984. *An open elite? England, 1540–1880*. Oxford.
Stuart, J. (ed.), 1844. *List of pollable persons within the shire of Aberdeen, 1696*. Spalding Club, Aberdeen.
1872. *Council registers . . . of Aberdeen, 1643–1747*. Edinburgh.

Terry, C.S., 1909. *Sir Thomas Craig's 'De Unione Regnorum Britanniae Tractatus'.* Edinburgh.

Third, B.M.W., 1955. 'Changing landscape and social structure in the Scottish lowlands as revealed by eighteenth-century estate plans'. *Scottish Geographical Magazine*, 71: 83–93.

Thirsk, J. (ed.), 1967. *The agrarian history of England and Wales, vol. 4: 1500–1640.* Cambridge.

1970. 'Seventeenth-century agriculture and social change'. In: Thirsk, J. (ed.), 1970. *Land, church and people. Agricultural History Review Supplement.* London.

(ed.), 1985. *The agrarian history of England and Wales, vol. 5: 1640–1750.* 2 parts. Cambridge.

Thirsk, J., 1987. *England's agricultural regions and agrarian history, 1500–1750.* London.

Thomas, K., 1959. 'The double standard'. *Journal of the History of Ideas*, 20: 195–216.

1965. 'Women in the civil war sects'. In: Aston, T. (ed.), 1965. *Crisis in Europe, 1560–1660.* London.

1973. *Religion and the decline of magic.* Harmondsworth.

Thompson, F.G., 1972–4. 'Technical education in the Highlands and Islands'. *Transactions of the Gaelic Society of Inverness*, 48: 244–388.

Thorpe, H., 1951. 'The influence of enclosure on the form and pattern of rural settlement in Denmark'. *Transactions of the Institute of British Geographers*, 17: 123–39.

Tilly, L.A. & Scott, J.W., 1978. *Women, work, and family.* New York.

Timperley, L., 1980. 'The pattern of landholding in eighteenth-century Scotland'. In: Parry & Slater (eds.), 1980.

Todd, B.J., 1985. 'The remarrying widow: a stereotype reconsidered'. In: Prior (ed.), 1985a.

Topham, J., 1776. *Letters from Edinburgh written in the years 1774 and 1775.* London.

Towill, E.S., 1956. 'The minutes of the Merchant Maiden Hospital'. *Book of the Old Edinburgh Club*, 29: 1–92.

Townsend, J., 1786. *A dissertation on the Poor Laws by a well-wisher to mankind.* London.

Tranter, N.L., 1981. 'The labour supply, 1780–1860'. In: Floud & McCloskey (eds.), 1981.

1985. *Population and society, 1750–1940.* London.

Turner, M.E., 1980. *English parliamentary enclosure: its historical geography and economic history.* Folkestone.

Tyson, R.E., 1986. 'Famine in Aberdeenshire, 1695–99: anatomy of a crisis'. In: Stevenson (ed.), 1986.

Verschuur, M.B., 1985. 'Perth and the Reformation: society and reform, 1540–1560'. (Unpublished Ph.D. thesis, Glasgow University.)

Vilar, P., 1949. 'Histoire des prix, histoire générale'. *Annales E.S.C.*, 4: 29–45.

Vincent, D., 1980. *Bread, knowledge and freedom. A study of nineteenth-century working-class autobiographers.* London.

Walker, D.M., 1958. 'Evidence'. In: *An introduction to Scottish legal history.*

Wall, R. (ed.), 1983. *Family forms in historic Europe.* Cambridge.

Walter, J. & Wrightson, K., 1976. 'Dearth and the social order in early modern England'. *Past and Present*, 71: 22–42.

Warden, A.J., 1872. *The burgh laws of Dundee.* Dundee.

1880–5. *Angus or Forfarshire. The land and people, descriptive and historical*, 5 vols. Dundee.

Wareing, J., 1980. 'Changes in the geographical distribution of recruitment of apprentices to the London companies, 1486–1750'. *Journal of Historical Geography*, 6: 241–9.

Weatherill, L., 1986. 'Consumer behaviour and social status in England, 1660–1750'. *Continuity and Change*. 1: 191–216.

Whatley, C., 1984. 'A saltwork and the community: the case of Winton, 1716–19. *Transactions of the East Lothian Antiquarian and Field Naturalists' Society*, 18: 45–59.

Whetstone, A.E., 1981. *Scottish county government in the eighteenth and nineteenth centuries*. Edinburgh.

White, A., 1985. 'Religion, politics and society in Aberdeen, 1543–1593'. (Unpublished Ph.D. thesis, Edinburgh University.)

1987. 'The impact of the Reformation on a burgh community: the case of Aberdeen'. In: Lynch (ed.), 1987.

White, P. & Woods, R., 1980. *The geographical impact of migration*. London.

Whittington, G., 1975. 'Was there a Scottish agricultural revolution?' *Area*, 7: 204–6.

1983. 'Agriculture and society in Lowland Scotland 1750–1870'. In: Whittington & Whyte (eds.), 1983.

Whittington, G. & Whyte, I.D. (eds.), 1983. *An historical geography of Scotland*. London.

Whyte, I.D., 1978. 'Scottish historical geography – a review'. *Scottish Geographical Magazine*, 94: 4–23.

1979. *Agriculture and society in seventeenth-century Scotland*. Edinburgh.

1980. 'The emergence of the new estate structure'. In: Parry & Slater (eds.), 1980.

1987. 'The occupational structure of Scottish burghs in the late seventeenth century'. In: Lynch (ed.), 1987.

1988. 'Proto-industrialisation in early modern Scotland'. In: Hudson (ed.), 1988.

Whyte, I.D. & Whyte, K.A., 1981. 'Sources for Scottish historical geography. An introductory guide'. *Historical Geography Research Series*, 6.

1983. 'Some aspects of the social structure of rural society in seventeenth-century Lowland Scotland'. In: Devine & Dickson (eds.), 1983.

1984a. 'Continuity and change in a seventeenth-century Scottish farming community'. *Agricultural History Review*, 32: 159–69.

1984b. 'Geographical mobility in a seventeenth-century Scottish rural community'. *Local Population Studies*, 32: 45–53.

1986. 'Patterns of migration of apprentices to Aberdeen and Inverness during the seventeenth and eighteenth centuries'. *Scottish Geographical Magazine*, 102: 81–91.

1987. 'Poverty and prosperity in a seventeenth-century Scottish farming community'. In: Mitchison & Roebuck, (eds.), 1987.

Withers, C., 1984. *Gaelic in Scotland, 1698–1981: the geographical history of a language*. Edinburgh.

1985. 'Highland migration to Dundee, Perth and Stirling 1753–1891'. *Journal of Historical Geography*, 11: 295–318.

Withrington, D.J., 1971. 'Non-church going, c.1750–c.1850: a preliminary study'. *Records of the Scottish Church History Society*, 17: 99–113.

Withrington, D.J. & Grant, I.R. (eds.), 1975–9. *Statistical account of Scotland.* Wakefield.

Wood, M. (ed.), 1936. *Extracts from the records of the burgh of Edinburgh, 1626–41.* Edinburgh.

1950. *Extracts from the records of the burgh of Edinburgh, 1665–80.* Edinburgh.

1951. *Edinburgh poll tax returns for 1694.* Edinburgh.

Woodward, D., 1977. 'A comparative study of the Irish and Scottish livestock trades in the seventeenth century'. In: Cullen & Smout (eds.), 1977.

Wordie, J.R., 1983. 'The chronology of English enclosure, 1500–1914'. *Economic History Review*, 36: 483–505.

Wormald, J., 1980. 'Bloodfeud, kindred and government in early modern Scotland'. *Past and Present*, 87: 54–97.

1981. *Court, kirk, and community. Scotland, 1470–1625.* London.

1985. *Lords and men in Scotland: bonds of manrent, 1442–1603.* Edinburgh.

Wright, S., 1985. '"Churmaids, huswyfes and hucksters": the employment of women in Tudor and Stuart Salisbury'. In: Charles, L. & Duffin, L. (eds.), 1985. *Women and work in pre-industrial England.* London.

Wrightson, K., 1982. *English society, 1580–1680.* London.

Wrigley, E.A., 1985. 'Urban growth and agricultural change: England and the Continent in the early-modern period'. *Journal of Interdisciplinary History*, 15: 683–728.

Wrigley, E.A. & Schofield, R.S., 1981. *The population history of England, 1541–1871: a reconstruction.* London.

Wyczański, A., 1979. 'La stratification sociale au XVIe siècle vue par les gens de l'époque'. *Academie Polonaise des Sciences, Centre Scientifiques à Paris. Conferences Fascicule, 124.* Warsaw.

1985. *La consommation alimentaire en Pologne aux XVIe et XVIIe siècles.* Paris.

Young, M.W., 1971. *Fighting with food: leadership, values and social control in a Massim society.* Cambridge.

Youngson, A.J., 1966. *The making of classical Edinburgh.* Edinburgh.

1973. *After the Forty-Five.* Edinburgh.

INDEX